Canto is an imprint offering a range of
titles, classic and more recent, across a
broad spectrum of subject areas and interests. History, literature, biography, archae-
ology, politics, religion, psychology,
philosophy and science are all represented
in Canto's specially selected list of titles,
which now offers some of the best and most
accessible of Cambridge publishing to a
wider readership.

The English Stage: A History of Drama and Performance tells the story of the drama through its many changes in style and convention from medieval times to the present day. With a wide sweep of coverage, John Styan analyses the key features of staging, including early street theatre and public performance, the evolution of the playhouse and the private space, and the pairing of theory and stagecraft in the works of modern dramatists. He focuses on the *conventions* by which a playwright, his actors and their audience create the phenomenon of theatre and the way such conventions have changed over time.

Styan is among a small number of influential scholars who have developed performance criticism and theatre history from their origins in literary studies into an independent and respected field. From the vantage point of a lifetime's study he examines and illustrates the multitude of factors which have brought and continue to bring plays to life.

The English Stage

By the same author

The Elements of Drama
The Dark Comedy
The Dramatic Experience
Shakespeare's Stagecraft
Chekhov in Performance
The Challenge of the Theatre
Drama, Stage and Audience
The Shakespeare Revolution
Modern Drama in Theory and Practice
    1. Realism and Naturalism
    2. Symbolism, Surrealism and the Absurd
    3. Expressionism and Epic Theatre
Max Reinhardt
Shakespeare in Performance: All's Well That Ends
  Well
The State of Drama Study
Restoration Comedy in Performance

The English Stage

A history of drama and performance

J.L. Styan

Franklyn Bliss Snyder Professor Emeritus
of English Literature and Theatre
Northwestern University

CAMBRIDGE
UNIVERSITY PRESS

Published by the Press Syndicate of the University of Cambridge
The Pitt Building, Trumpington Street, Cambridge CB2 1RP
40 West 20th Street, New York, NY 10011–4211, USA
10 Stamford Road, Oakleigh, Melbourne 3166, Australia

© Cambridge University Press 1996

First published 1996

Printed in Great Britain at the University Press, Cambridge

A catalogue record for this book is available from the British Library

Library of Congress cataloguing in publication data
Styan, J. L.
The English stage: a history of drama and performance / J. L. Styan.
p.   cm.
Includes index.
ISBN 0 521 55398 9 (hardback)   ISBN 0 521 55636 8 (paperback)
1. Theater – England – History.   2. Theater – England – Production and
direction – History.   I. Title.
PN2581.S89   1996
792'.0941–dc20   95–40921   CIP

ISBN 0 521 55398 9 hardback
ISBN 0 521 55636 8 paperback

Contents

List of illustrations	*page*	xi
Preface		xiii
Acknowledgments		xvi
1	Medieval drama, secular and religious	1
2	The early morality play	40
3	The Tudor interlude	60
4	The Elizabethan theatre	88
5	Marlowe's stagecraft	118
6	Shakespeare's practice	136
7	Ben Jonson's comic stagecraft	168
8	The Court masque	187
9	Jacobean experiment: exploring the form	199
10	The Restoration stage	237
11	The Georgian theatre	274
12	The Victorian theatre	302
13	Bernard Shaw and his stage practice	338
14	Twentieth-century developments and variations	360
Index		415

Illustrations

1   The pageant wagon as a 'processional'
    presentation: a *tableau vivant* of the Nativity
    in the Triumph of Isabella, Brussels, 1615; an
    angel sits on the roof. (Courtesy of the
    Victoria and Albert Museum, London)   *page* 18

2   The plan for *The Castle of Perseverance* (early
    fifteenth century), appended to the manuscript.
    (Courtesy of the Folger Library, Washington)   45

3   *Fulgens and Lucrece, c.* 1497: frontispiece from
    the facsimile in the Huntington Library, California;
    the costumes are not in Roman style, but in that
    contemporary with the printed play (*c.* 1520)   66

4   The well-known de Witt sketch of the Swan
    Theatre, *c.* 1596: the only contemporary picture
    of the interior of an Elizabethan playhouse.
    (Courtesy of the Library of the University of
    Utrecht, Holland)   97

5   Thomas Kyd, *The Spanish Tragedy, c.* 1587: the
    title-page of the 1615 edition. The scene in the
    woodcut is of 2.4, the murder of Horatio in the
    arbour. (Courtesy of the Folger Library,
    Washington)   114

6   Christopher Marlowe, *Doctor Faustus, c.* 1592: the
    title-page of the Quarto of 1624. Faustus draws his
    magic circle to protect himself before conjuring the
    Devil (scene 3). (Courtesy of the British Library)   132

7   Inigo Jones, *Oberon*, 1611. Oberon's palace in the
    rocks. (Courtesy of the Duke of Devonshire at
    Chatsworth)   195

8   *Arden of Faversham*, anon., 1592: the frontispiece
    to the Quarto of 1633. The death of Master Arden

at the 'game of tables' (scene 14). (Courtesy of
the British Library)   212

9   A Restoration playhouse, probably the Theatre
Royal, Drury Lane as designed by Christopher
Wren in 1674. (Model by Edward A. Langhans)   239

10 William Smith as Alexander in Nathaniel Lee,
The Rival Queens, 1677 at Drury Lane in 1778:
the tragic hero wore a mixture of eye-catching
styles and an obligatory head-dress of feathers.
(Courtesy of the Theatre Museum, London)   243

11 William Congreve, *The Way of the World*, 1700:
Mrs Pitt as Lady Wishfort in act 3, in a print from
Congreve's *Works*, 1776. (Courtesy of the
Newberry Library, Chicago)   267

12 The stage of the Theatre Royal, Covent Garden
(1732) as seen at the time of the Fitzgiggo price
riot during Thomas Arne's opera *Artaxerxes*
in 1763. The playhouse is bigger, but the doors
and boxes still face an apron stage, with more
chandeliers hanging over it. (Courtesy of the
Harvard Theatre Collection)   276

13 Richard Brinsley Sheridan, *The School for Scandal*,
1777: the screen scene (4.3) at Drury Lane: the
apron is still prominent and the shadows suggest
new lighting.   300

14 The interior of the Theatre Royal, Covent Garden
in 1810: stage doors remain, but the picture-frame
proscenium has arrived. (Courtesy of the Harvard
Theatre Collection)   306

15 Dion Boucicault, *The Colleen Bawn*, the Adelphi
Theatre, 1860: on the rock Danny is shot, while in
the water Eily is drowning. (Courtesy of the Mander
and Mitchenson Theatre Collection)   323

16 W. B. Yeats, *At the Hawks's Well*, 1916: costume
design for the Guardian of the Well by Edmund
Dulac.   370

17 Samuel Beckett, *Waiting for Godot*, 1953, the first
English production directed by Peter Hall at the
Arts Theatre in 1955. (Photograph by Houston
Rogers, courtesy of the Theatre Museum, London)   386

Preface

The English Stage: A History of Drama and Performance traces a persistent institution through its many changes in style and convention, focusing chiefly on issues of performance as seen in particular plays.

The secret of many an interesting play – and of the special event its production represents – is lost in the past, and must remain so, because in one sense no play really survives its own day, its performance being dead as soon as it ends. Yet in another sense, each new performance, each revival, ensures that something of the original life of the play is still alive. Re-creation of that life is the concern of drama study, and certainly of an historical survey. It is a matter of focus, of seeing where the text carries within itself signs of the original event. The dedicated student of drama is in the business of theatrical birth and rebirth.

To seek to recover the circumstances of staging a play is also to insist upon looking for its vitality. A play lives in its ability to create something of an electric circuit between the actor and his audience, and this interchange also reflects the relationship of the theatre and society, between the implicit role of the stage and the community that nourishes it. It follows as the night the day that the merits of a play may not be fully understood without a sense of how it worked, or failed to work, when it was played under the conditions for which it was written.

The present inquiry therefore aims to pay more than lip-service to the notion of drama as performance, and to make more than a gesture towards the idea of theatre as a composite art, one that mixes music and mime, dance and song, painting and design, poetry and narrative, and much else. It is precation and response, and seeks out evidence of the manipulation of the audience and its powers of perception. A play acquires life according to the nature and possibilities of its staging methods, but always together with the innumerable conventions and devices, extrinsic and intrinsic, that make up its elements. What passes between actor and spectator on the occasion of a performance is a compound of a multitude of forces – mostly traditions and expectations, but also the anticipated contributions and innovations of the playwright, the actors and other theatre artists.

In the mode of stagecraft at work in any play or period, four insistent principles belonging to the art of drama claim special attention:

(1) *The audience's role* in the creative act of theatre is an indispensable factor in the equation that makes drama possible.
(2) *The physical medium* of performance – the acting area, its shape and space, the stage structure, the playhouse and its size – affects the kind of acting and the response to it.
(3) The style of *the actors' performance* absolutely determines the success or failure of the work as a whole, and whether its purpose has been fulfilled and its point and purpose perceived.
(4) *The written play* is subject to the pressures of past ways and means, the tyrannical expectations of the audience, and the strengths and weaknesses of the human factor in the artistic undertaking.

In short, all drama is subject to a body of aesthetic laws for performance and communication. These are generally brought unquestioned to a theatrical event as part of the common baggage of all parties to the play – author, actor and audience – and imply their general consent if the business of the theatre and the play is to go forward. Each contributor is associated with certain kinds of conventions, and the following condensed list may be helpful as a guide to the spectrum of conventional possibilities:

(1) *The author's rules*, governing:
  – the play's form and style, and its musical content.

- the play's genre: comedy, tragedy, etc.; masque, mime, etc.
- the degree of reality implied: natural, symbolic/poetic or ritualistic.
- the play's plot and structure.
- the forms of language, devices of speech and dialogue.

(2) *The actor's signals*, transmitted in performance through:
- his mode of performance: naturalistic, representational, etc.
- movement, gesture, facial expression (for characterization).
- manner and tone of speech: realistic, ritualistic.
- costume, mask, make-up; props, décor, setting, lighting.
- a physical acting area or playhouse, his spatial workplace (arena, thrust or proscenium stage).

(3) *The audience's expectations*, born of:
- its place and time.
- its cultural experience and assumptions.
- its political, religious, economic persuasions.
- its kind and degree of imaginative perception.

In a recent Hamlyn lecture Richard Eyre, Director of the Royal National Theatre, summarized the function of convention by asserting that the theatre 'thrives on metaphor; things stand *for* things rather than being the thing itself, a room can become a world, a group of characters a whole society' (4 July 1991). Decoding a text that is for the most part encoded unconsciously and passively is the obvious task of the actor, and it is also the implied duty of the student of drama.

The book, finally, is indebted to a variety of artists as well as scholars: it is a mistake to ignore the practical discoveries made by actors, directors and designers. The important mixture of interests these silent contributors represent makes a last point: living theatre has always been nourished by disparate voices, and where an advance in the study and practice of drama has been evident in the last few years, it has often been a consequence of the coming together of the artist and the scholar in a joint enterprise. It would be pleasing if the present undertaking were to make a contribution of this kind.

Acknowledgments

In the preparation and writing of this study I am grateful to many unseen contributors over the years, not least to my students – without whom nothing. But to be brief and to the point, my particular thanks are due to my friends and colleagues, David Bevington, Douglas Cole, Alan Dessen and Homer Swander, who from time to time have lent their generous support and advice over the long period of the book's gestation. My warm gratitude is also extended to my helpers and mediators at the Cambridge University Press, Victoria Cooper, Teresa Sheppard and Sarah Stanton, to whom from the beginning I have owed a great deal of practical assistance, sensitive suggestion and courteous guidance in matters of choice, emphasis and structure.

Medieval drama, secular and religious

Popular drama and the importance of community

The popular religious and folk drama which begins the story of the English stage demands the basic elements needed for any dramatic activity: actors, spectators and a space in which the play can be performed and seen. By this a 'convention' has already been created in which the audience has access to the world of the drama and can share the experience that lies at the heart of performance. An audience needs the actor to speak for it, but an actor cannot speak for it unless he has its consent, the two making a mutual bond of the most mysterious and fundamental kind. Moreover, if shared experience is important to dramatic activity, so too is the community that makes it possible and from which the activity springs. The more closely knit the group, the better an audience it makes. Popular drama particularly serves its community, and can only be understood in its social role.

Many details in this chapter remain shadowy and conjectural, but the drama of the fourteenth century certainly served its community, while evidently enjoying the licence of art. Released to a degree from reality, it invited thinking and feeling on another level than the mundane, and wonderfully expanded the imagination. In this, it could be businesslike, seeking and supplying information, or it could be recreational, extending experience with only pleasure as its apparent purpose. The stage can teach and it can please, and still be intricately tied to the life of its community. It used to be argued that for centuries life in England was starved of all dramatic activity. It is true that the early Church decided from the first century to suppress what few vestiges of drama the Roman civilization had left, damning the hellish arts of feigning and face-painting, and citing Deuteronomy, for example, in support of its case against actors and their costume disguises:

> The woman shall not wear that which pertaineth unto a man, neither shall a man put on a woman's garment: for all that do so are abomination unto the Lord thy God.
>
> (22.5)

However, up to 1000 AD forms of theatrical activity persisted, and, finding its own channels, the native drama grew robust. Minstrels and strolling players, story-tellers and entertainers of every kind, needed no tradition of playwriting, no institutionalized stage, in order to flourish. The processions and pageants, tournaments and mummings, and the generous way these were presented, reflect the dramatic impulse of the age.

A sense of their contribution to the community also strengthens the view that the great Corpus Christi cycles were unique dramatic achievements in their own right. They used to be thought of as drama in a state of evolution, constituting a primitive dinosaur of human activity that had yet to be tamed, a rough and ready thing that only waited to be refined and polished to become the great drama of the English renaissance. When certain unidentified writers of the Middle Ages – probably clerics – wrote scripts for the festival of Corpus Christi, they wrote for the people they knew. The religious plays of the medieval period were indeed a legitimate drama, determined by their own content and shape. Nor did they merely wither away, but were at their height when the Church and the authorities put a stop to them. New productions of these plays in recent years have confirmed that they represented an extraordinary achievement in all departments of dramatic art: they are completely viable as good theatre and they exemplify how a community can answer its own needs in dramatic terms.

Mummers' plays and street theatre

The centre of dramatic and quasi-dramatic activity in the Middle Ages was not in London, but, significantly, in the country at large. The village green and town square provided natural arenas for the unlocalized *platea* [Latin: 'wide street' or open acting space] round which spectators gathered. In such acting areas the performer reckoned to hold the attention of his audience almost without scenery and with a minimum of props. As early as the tenth century elementary props and costumes were in modest use. For the *Quem quaeritis?* trope in Winchester Cathedral, the *Regularis Concordia* of St Ethelwold (*c.* 965) instructs 'four brethren' to wear copes and carry palms as if they were the women looking for Christ's tomb. When in later years drama was performed in the banquet hall of some great manor house, a more domestic content called for the use of simple props and settings, and the long, slow growth of drama as 'illusion' had begun. Otherwise the drama in English at its inception seemed to enjoy the freedom of creating and communicating virtually without the need of realistic illusion.

Religious and community drama, as we shall see, drew upon a host of ready 'amateurs' – willing clergy and parishioners and guildsmen who became actors for the time being. But folk entertainment also flourished with the aid of many itinerant performers who may be loosely grouped according to the kind of entertainment they had to offer:

(1) The acrobats and jugglers, tumblers and rope-dancers, wrestlers and animal trainers, were the forerunners of what is today the circus. The peddlers and mountebanks came with them, and the hawkers and hucksters who inhabit markets and fairgrounds the world over. In *Bartholomew Fair* (1614) Ben Jonson supplied a rich picture of such people.

(2) The sword and morris dancers, the clowns and buffoons, jesters and fools, performing often scurrilous antics, are found on the doubtful margins of many forms of carnival and comic entertainment. It is interesting that the Italian word *buffa* and the early French *buffon* [jest] both also embrace the idea of pantomime and morris dance.

(3) Ballad-singers and tale-tellers, named in Old English as *gleemen* and in Old French as *jongleurs*, were the minstrels found throughout Europe at this time. Singing and

story-telling were from the beginning almost one and the same, and the combination of music and drama provided a mutual reinforcement of expression that magically established the imaginative tone of the performance and the spirit of its reception.

(4) What were known later to Thomas Dekker as the 'strowlers' [country players] were probably early professional actors not far removed from vagrants and vagabonds. They were people who wandered the country performing as and where they could, although they survived into the nineteenth century as the strolling players of Charles Dickens's acquaintance. These strollers and street mimes were key figures in the early history of the theatre, and, together with the performers attached to noble houses, lead us directly to the forms of established stage which made possible the rapid development of a professional drama in the sixteenth century.

Three features of medieval street theatre call attention to themselves. First, all the performers named above were itinerant and found everywhere. Rovers all, they ensured that many forms of embryonic dramatic activity should spread quickly from town to town and country to country. If music, passing beyond language barriers, is the international language, then drama had its beginnings in the same company.

Second, although the players no doubt spiced their shows with pantomime and clowning, which would have encouraged and widened their universal appeal, their work arguably fell within a great oral tradition. An oral tradition implies that, without a written script, a song or a story is passed on from place to place and age to age, and seems by such means to perpetuate itself; and the intimacy implicit in the style and nature of oral performance made it immediately responsive to its audience, encouraging rather than inhibiting change. Thus the problem, and the interest, of much medieval drama lies in its inherently *unstable text*.

Finally, street entertainment also acquired a curiously ritual quality, whereby the expectations of the people were no doubt gratified by its repetition from performance to performance. This norm of anticipation may have been apparent in the ceremonial events that occurred in town or village. These were the pageants or processions that attended weddings, funerals and other Church occasions, and festivities and celebrations occasioned by local legends and seasonal rites and customs. Such local and community occasions were socially distinct from the revels associated with royal visits and coronations, which were celebrated at great expense with highly ornamented carriages and floats. Extraordinary events on public record, like those of the celebration of the victory of Edward I over the Scots in 1298, the coronation of Richard II in 1377 or the arrival in London of the Spanish princess Catherine of Aragon in 1501, were occasions for building elaborate symbolic tableaux.

The origins of the English folk plays are lost in time, but we have some idea what they were like because a few were preserved in written form into the eighteenth and nineteenth centuries: these are the secular *mummers' plays*. The phrase 'to go a-mumming' dates back to at least the fifteenth century, but the plays are certainly earlier, since in its mixture of dumb show, lively action and wild clowning mumming embodied the death and rebirth of the seasons. Mummers' plays were found with popular variations all over England and Scotland – they were so widespread, in fact, that it is impossible to hypothesize a common source for them.

Although mummers' plays were not sponsored by the Church, they were probably associated with Christmas or Easter, both festive holidays which corresponded with the seasonal changes of the countryside. A play would often begin with a cry that was partly a charge to the spectators, partly an announcement of intent: 'Ring, a ring!' (from Heptonstall, Yorkshire) or 'Room, a room!' elsewhere (Shakespeare includes the line, 'A hall, a hall, give room!' in *Romeo and Juliet*, 1.5.26, when Capulet welcomes the visitors to his ball). Whether ring or room, the notion of an acting space and a theatrical relationship with an audience is implicit.

In spite of the corruptions and variations of every kind that might be expected from an oral tradition, the 'plot' of the mummers' plays remained much the same. In the Oxfordshire *St George's Play* (recorded for the first time in 1853) the hero would step forward into the circle and announce himself, as did everyone else, in rhyming couplets of the most ragged kind:

> I am St George of Merry England,
> Bring in the morris-men, bring in our band.

The spectators would draw in, and the ritualistic repetitiveness of such introductions arose from the need to alert an audience to its proper reaction. St George was a Christian knight confronted by his enemy – in some plays the Dragon,

> I am the Dragon, here are my jaws;
> I am the Dragon, here are my claws ...

and in others the champion of the Turks,

> Here come I, the Turkish Knight,
> Come from the Turkish land to fight ...

The action culminated in a mighty combat, in which either George or his foe is slain. If George, he will be revived by the 'Doctor', who first announces that he can cure 'the itch, the stitch, the palsy and the gout' before working his medicine and his magic on the hero.

The occasion is magic in other ways too. An extraordinary variety of characters, some ritualistic and festive, and others touched with popular symbolism, may chance to introduce themselves in the course of the play with the same forthright announcement of their presence, and with the same blunt invitation to the crowd to take them and their disguises as it finds them. Some of these characters even become lightly involved with the more solemn issues of living and dying. In Oxfordshire an unmistakable Father Christmas was one such, and another was Beelzebub, perhaps carrying a club and a frying-pan. Giant Blunderbore, Old King Cole complete with wooden leg and Captain Slasher with sword and pistol are all good for a fight or a romp. The genial, 'come-one-come-all' spirit of the performance does not preach in any way, and taking up a collection in a frying-pan at the end of the performance must have seemed entirely appropriate.

Along with the St George plays, there were several other early forms of folk drama that also introduced a theme of death and resurrection, offered in the spirit of ebullient comic revelry. A *Sword Dance Play*, dating from at least the tenth century, might be seen during the Christmas season to mark the defeat of winter by summer, something in which the performers, dressed in white and splendidly decorated with ribbons, began with balletic steps dancing over and around swords laid on the ground, and ended with a fight in which one of the dancers might expect to be slain – sometimes representing the village 'Parson'. It then took the grotesque efforts of 'The Bessy', a clown-figure dressed in women's clothing, to bring him quickly to life with the help of the ever-available Doctor – in one instance by making him sneeze.

Just as popular during the May games were the *Robin Hood Plays*, performed to celebrate the return of spring. In these the colourful folk hero of legend, always on the side of the poor, was King of the May. Robin would step out and usually began his play with the lines,

> Now stand ye forth, my merry men all,
>   And hark what I shall say;
> Of an adventure I shall you tell,
>   The which befell this other day.

His play would enact a battle joined with the enemy for the occasion, perhaps Friar Tuck, or perhaps the infamous Sheriff of Nottingham. Every time, a rousing fight erupted at the centre of the comic action, and a violent death was followed by a rapid resurrection.

Mumming troupes travelled from village to village, creating truly an itinerant form of theatre. Everywhere the spirit of 'let's-put-on-a-play' seemed to run through their entertainments, and the longevity of this curious tradition proves that the mummers' plays contained within them the seeds of what makes drama work and street theatre successful.

The Church and its liturgical drama

The Church stood at the centre of life in the Middle Ages, like the church building itself in town or village. It spoke for the community, and only through the Church might the people know something of music and painting, literature and drama. It is a matter of great importance for the history of the English stage that the Church recognized drama as a force to be harnessed and chose to use it to teach the people about the Scriptures and to glorify God. It is a pleasant irony that the very institution that had stamped out the vestiges of drama left by the Roman occupation was itself to encourage a new, popular and far more vigorous theatre.

The powerful ingredients of its ritual observance appeared in everything the Church did, in the splendour of its colourful robes and vestments, the glory of its processions, the beauty of its choral singing and the conduct of its forms of worship. It ordained the occasions for its ritual around the calendar, so that it might carry a significance greater than itself and belong to the life of the community in the passing of the seasons. On special occasions – and especially at Christmas and Easter – it carefully added the mysticism of its liturgies [public rites and services], already suffused with such embellishments as candlelight, incense, music and the Latin language. The structure of the building itself, designed to hold a compact congregation, with a central nave leading to a choir [that part used by the singers] and chancel [that part used by the clergy], and usually flanked by pulpit and lectern, provided an excellent natural theatre, as T. S. Eliot and Christopher Fry reminded audiences in the twentieth century.

Paradoxically, however vast the subject and profound the content, the actual theatrical mode of presentation of drama in church by clerics in the tenth century was familiar and personal, the opposite of what might have been expected. And in the fourteenth century the pageant plays of the Corpus Christi cycles, which told the story of man's relationship with God and embraced immense issues, were played on surprisingly small stages by local players, by 'amateurs' of the best kind. As a result of this, the plays in performance retained an intimacy with their audiences which determined much of their style. The new drama of the Church thrived because it sprang from, and spoke directly to, its community, which was its congregation.

The Latin drama of the Church after the tenth century was rooted in the Mass. From another position, O. B. Hardison, Jr insisted in *Christian Rite and Christian Drama in the Middle Ages* (1965) that the Mass contained 'all the elements necessary to secular performances,' and he asked,

> Should church vestments then, with their elaborate symbolic meanings, be considered costumes? Should the paten, chalice, sindon, sudarium, candles, and thurible be considered stage properties? Should the nave, chancel, presbyterium, and altar of the church be considered a stage, and its windows, statues, images, and ornaments a 'setting'?
>
> (79)

He and others have found it possible to answer yes.

A ceremony which, according to Anglican literature, declared its intention '*to show forth*' the death of Christ had already admitted to a substantial theatrical bent by using 'show forth' in the sense of 'display' or 'exhibit'. What was sacred turned for support to secular resources and forms, while what was profane was soon to acquire strength from the mysteries of the Church. The result was a prodigious extension of its simple liturgies and liturgical tropes [in medieval drama, verbal elaborations of the liturgy] when the great Corpus Christi cycles were written.

By the sixth century, as a result of the guidelines in Pope Gregory the Great's *Antiphonarium*, Gregorian liturgies, sung and chanted in Latin, called for the participants to take opposite sides and already gave the service a dramatic shape with two viewpoints. By the tenth century, the visual elements of procession and pageantry helped to illustrate the message of the service, and words were added to the singing in order to extend their meaning. At Christmas such a trope might tell the story of Joseph or Herod, the Three Shepherds, the Magi, and at Easter the story of Lazarus, the Three Marys or Christ in the Garden of Gethsemane. Each trope would end with a song of praise, like the *Te Deum laudamus*, and so the sacred drama concluded appropriately when the congregation joined in.

Since the content of the liturgy was taken from the Scriptures, it told a story as a *lectio* [lesson], and this was performed during the office of Matins [the service of morning prayer]. (The style may be heard today in modern recordings of the

seventeenth-century Venetian Vespers [the evening prayers].)
But the liturgy was *sung*, and should be thought of as musical
drama, the text serving as a *libretto* to the singing, with its
words carried along on the melody. The chief medium was
the voice, and the drama progressed when the chanting,
usually rendered by the single voice of the precentor [leader]
in counterpoint with the choir, was answered by voices that
were 'responsorial' [more supportive] or 'antiphonal' [more
like an answer]. It then proceeded by adding to or repeating
the theme. There was little attempt at verisimilitude, but some
sense of difference between characters could be conveyed by
modulating voices to suggest different speakers.

Over six hundred years there were hundreds of versions of
the Easter trope known as the *Quem quaeritis?* or the *Visitatio
Sepulchri*, which began as a monastic exercise. One example
from the Swiss abbey of St Gall by Lake Constance dates
from *c.* 950, and the earliest in England, found in Winchester
Cathedral, has been assigned the last third of the tenth
century. The basis is from the Gospel according to St Mark,
which tells of the three Marys who wish to anoint Christ's
body after the Crucifixion:

> And entering into the sepulchre, they saw a young man
> sitting on the right side, clothed in a long white garment;
> and they were afrighted. And he saith unto them, Be not
> afrighted: Ye seek Jesus of Nazareth, which was crucified:
> he is risen; he is not here; behold the place where they laid
> him.
>
> (Mark, 16.5–6)

In the simplest performance, four lines in Latin tell the story.
When the Angel turns the three Marys away from the tomb
with the news that Christ has risen from the dead, their grief
turns to joy:

THE ANGEL. Quem quaeritis in sepulchro, O Christicolae?
[*Whom do you seek in the tomb, O Christians?*]

THE WOMEN. Iesum Nazarenum crucifixum, O Caelicola.
[*Jesus of Nazareth who was crucified, O heavenly one.*]

THE ANGEL. Non est hic, surrexit sicut praedixerat.
　　　　　　Ite, nuntiate quia surrexit de sepulchro.

[*He is not here; He has risen even as He said before.
Go; proclaim He has risen from the grave.*]

All sing 'Alleluia!', and the *Te Deum* completes the musical performance.

In *c.* 967 Ethelwold, Bishop of Winchester, issued a remarkable set of rules for the conduct of the singing and playing of the *Quem quaeritis?* in Benedictine houses. This was his *Regularis Concordia*, a document that may be thought of as the first piece of directorial commentary in English, and this too contributes to our picture of early performance. Here is the part of it that is relevant to the text above, with italics to draw attention to some of its advanced performance signals:

> While the third lesson is being chanted, let four brethren vest themselves. Let one of these, vested in an alb, enter *as though to take part in the service* [or: *as if doing something else*], and let him approach the sepulchre *without attracting attention* and sit there quietly with a palm in his hand. While the third respond is chanted, let the remaining three follow, and let them all, vested in copes, bearing in their hands thuribles with incense, and *stepping delicately as those who seek something*, approach the sepulchre. These things are done in imitation of the angel sitting in the monument, and the women with spices coming to anoint the body of Jesus. When therefore he who sits there beholds the three approach him *like folk lost and seeking something*, let him begin in a dulcet voice of medium pitch to sing *Quem quaeritis*. And when he has sung it to the end, let the three reply in unison *Ihesum Nazarenum* ...

The alb [Latin *albus*, white] ensured that the Angel appeared in symbolic white, and the repeated suggestion of 'as though' to a degree expected an impersonation of real life. And after the three women had turned to the choir and sung their 'Alleluia' at Winchester, another development followed when the Angel, 'as if recalling' them, chanted the anthem *Venite et videte locum* [Come and see the place]:

> And saying this, let him rise and lift the veil, and show them the place bare of the Cross, but only the cloths laid there in which the Cross was wrapped. And when they have seen this, let them set down the thuribles which they bare in that same sepulchre, and *take the cloth, and hold it*

up in the face of the clergy, and *as if to demonstrate that the Lord has risen* and is no longer wrapped therein, let them sing the anthem *Surrexit Dominus de sepulchro*, and lay the cloth upon the altar ...

(translation by E. K.Chambers in *The Medieval Stage* (1903), vol. II)

More than just to direct movement and gesture, Ethelwold's business with the property cloth causes it to acquire a symbolic quality and intensity. The magic cloth makes its point first when it is seen to be cast away and then when it is flourished. All in all, through music, costume, gesture, voice and props, he appears to be prompting a response to the biblical narrative as if to an audience, and this little drama ended appropriately with the injunction that 'all the bells chime out together'.

The playlet of *The Three Marys* brought a powerful sense of life and actuality to the Easter message. It did not take much to do this: the plot was at a minimum, and impersonation was more ritualistic than real; the singing was still in Latin, which few of the people would have understood; all the women were played by a celibate priesthood dressed in clerical copes, and differences of character and gender were ignored; nor in the neutral staging (in which the available space represented any place) was there a need for any scenic setting or property. Yet the possibility of all these dramatic ingredients was present in the ritual, with hints of mime and movement latent in the symbolism of the earthly tribulation and the heavenly answer, together with implied amazement and joy in the repetition of '*surrexit*' [He has risen] and the likely display of grave-cloths as the emotional peak of the exchange. The anthem and the music presumably swelled from *piano* to *forte*, and was accompanied by the ringing of the church bell. The element of *sharing the performance through worship* governed the thinking behind the dramatic iconography and the theatrical arrangements, the whole making a beautiful statement of feeling.

From our knowledge of the features of the medieval church building it is also possible to guess at some of the movements of the players. In order that the three Marys should seem to represent the ordinary people, they may later have proceeded through an expectant congregation, as in a monastic church like that of Fleury in France two centuries later, probably entering the nave from the west and walking to the steps of the altar, where the voice of the Angel, singing his lines from a higher place, would halt them. Many churches contained an Easter sepulchre in replica usually situated to the north side of the chancel, or even set up on the altar, and the Marys would turn to this before they displayed the grave-cloths. Some versions included the disciples Peter and John, in which case they might repeat the pattern before Christ revealed His presence.

What began as a simple action grew more elaborate as new scenes were added. In Dublin, for example, the *Quem Quaeritis?* also had the three Marys hurrying to John and Peter with the news, so that they could join in the search. The scene in Gethsemane in which Jesus was mistaken for a gardener was also popular, as was that of the wayfarers to Emmaus. The appearance of such tropes all over Europe indicates that the dramatic demonstration of the Scripture was successful as a way of teaching and of sharing the sacred moment.

The Anglo-French *mystères* were even more distinctively 'plays' than the liturgical tropes, and they are commonly regarded as transitional because they mixed dramatic features from the past with elements yet to come – singing rendered in Church Latin woven with dialogue spoken in the Anglo-Norman vernacular, and sublime liturgical material from the Mass with elements drawn from popular street performance. Two twelfth century plays of this kind survive, although both are unfortunately incomplete: *Le Mystère d'Adam* (c. 1150) and *La Seinte Resureccion* (c. 1175). Both are punctuated from time to time by commentaries in the form of liturgical responsories sung on the order *'chorus cantet'* [let the choir sing].

Le Mystère d'Adam tells the story of Adam and Eve, Cain and Abel and the Fall of Man; it concludes with prophecies of the coming of Christ the Redeemer – all this before the final appearance of a merry gang of devils who chase everyone off to Hell. The play anticipates some of the plot and structure, as well as the character and detail, found later in the cycle plays.

It also embodies in Latin a most elaborate set of stage directions that point to the possible beginnings of Tudor staging. These suggest that the play was originally performed on a platform outside a church, and that the churchyard was kept for an acting space with the church doors used both as a fixed 'backdrop' and as a permanent entrance for the actors. However, it is evident that Satan and his devils, unlike the other characters, also enjoyed the freedom of the whole arena, and made good use of it as a way of getting as close as possible to the spectators.

The opening direction, which contains especially symbolic suggestions, is cited at length, and again the italics draw attention to what is significant:

> Paradise shall be set *in a fairly high place*; curtains and silk cloths shall be hung around it, at such a height that the persons who shall be in Paradise can be seen from the shoulders upwards. Fragrant flowers and leaves shall be planted there; there shall also be various trees with fruit hanging on them, *so that it looks a very pleasant place*.
>
> Then shall come God the Saviour wearing a dalmatic [a white robe], and Adam and Eve shall be stationed in front of him. *Adam shall wear a red tunic*, but *Eve a woman's garment in white with a white silk scarf*; and they shall both stand in front of God – Adam, however, nearer to God with a calm countenance, *Eve with face lowered*. Adam shall be well trained not to answer too quickly nor too slowly ...
>
> Whenever anyone shall speak of Paradise, he shall look towards it and *point it out with his hand*.

Something of a symbolic setting was offered here, with Paradise located apart and higher up, and the actors required to assist the audience's perception of it with their gestures. This Paradise was dressed to please the eye, especially since Hell Mouth was set on the opposite side of the same acting space, looking like the great jaws of an animal. With the help of its devils, Hell belched smoke and represented pandemonium itself by the banging of 'cauldrons and kettles', an effect that became standard. The costuming was also symbolic in a simple way, with Adam dressed in red to signify his nobility and manhood, and Eve in white to indicate her innocence and modesty, which was reflected also in the gesture of lowering her face. These two shortly suffered a costume change when they took off their fine clothes and put on 'poor clothes sewn with figleaves'.

After showing Adam and Eve the way to Paradise, God made his exit significantly through the church doors, looking like some mighty bishop. Then, possibly during the temptation of Eve and the business with the apple, the main acting area came alive with devils, anticipating simultaneous staging [using a single space for more than one place], a technique afterwards found in the Elizabethan playhouse. The intriguing stage direction reads: 'Meanwhile devils shall run about the places.' Here the important words in Latin are *per plateas* [plural], suggesting that there was more than one acting area, and that while any prominent piece of action, like the quarrel of Adam and Eve over the apple, or their laborious cultivation of the land after leaving Paradise, or Satan's planting of thorns and thistles in their field, was centre stage and at the centre of attention, a substantial secondary action was also possible. One such area was evidently near the audience, since Satan, and no doubt his devils too, were instructed to 'run around among the spectators'.

In all this, Paradise, Hell and Heaven were symbolically represented by three separate stage locations: Adam and Eve had their base in Paradise, God's departure into the church marked the direction to Heaven and Satan passed freely between Hell and Paradise. Nothing could be simpler, and it was a pattern of staging that was repeated from play to play. When the actors occupied the neutral space between these three focal points, the imagination of the audience was granted the freedom to wander spatially and temporally; even then, place and time were of no importance until they were specifically identified by the passage of actors across the stage. When that happened, the neutral and central area, encroaching provocatively upon the space where the spectators stood, would also symbolize the Earth itself and all those who inhabited it.

The Corpus Christi plays

In England the national drama of the Middle Ages sprang from native soil and knew virtually nothing of the classical drama of the Greeks and Romans. The native drama grew to prodigious proportions over a period of two hundred years. It remained a religious drama, an act of faith, so that one problem is to estimate how much of devotional participation was in fact carried over into its secular presentation. The English stage early demonstrated its genius for compelling and workable dramaturgy, and for a remarkably inventive stagecraft, both by undertaking the task of dramatizing the copious materials of the Bible and by making them responsive to local needs and feelings. That creative achievement, in spite of recent developments still largely an unexplored territory for both scholars and actors, resides principally in the vast and impressive cycles of plays that probably arose from and are related to the Feast of Corpus Christi. This feast was celebrated in late May or June and the plays were possibly played at any time during the summer.

Because of the involvement of many people in the production of the plays, and because of their great range of material from both Old and New Testaments, the tendency is to think of the Corpus Christi plays as panoramic and untidy, if not actually loose in intention and structure. It is true that whole communities contributed to the plays, and that they covered an extraordinary sweep of subjects from the Creation, Adam's disobedience and Fall and the stories of Cain and Abel, Noah and Abraham; then the Nativity, Joseph and Mary's flight into Egypt and the Massacre of the Innocents; Christ's entry into Jerusalem, the Last Supper and the Crucifixion; the Harrowing of Hell, the Resurrection and finally Doomsday. Nevertheless, the Feast of Corpus Christi, instituted to celebrate the Eucharist [the sacrament of Holy Communion which consecrated the bread and the wine] as a memorial to the wonders of God, is the possible immediate source of *the unity and purpose* of the cycles, although they no doubt owed a great deal to the complete and indivisible vision of the Church year and its cycle of life and death. In the sequence of the plays this sacrament supplies a dramatic beginning-middle-and-end, with the Passion and the Resurrection urging a climax upon a sacred drama. In other words, all the plays drive to a point, no matter how various their subjects and style, nor how often they were rewritten. The intention of the plays was to exhibit the nature of man and the purpose of life, resolved at the last on the Day of Judgment. The spirit of Corpus Christi and the design of the plays were all one.

Two separate sequences of events came together to start the plays on their two-hundred year history:

(1) The doctrine of the transubstantiation of Christ was promulgated in 1215 and celebrated locally at Liège in 1246. In the Eucharist the congregation partook of the bread and the wine, so giving form to the idea of uniting the human and the divine. In 1264 Pope Urban IV proposed to extend the Feast to the whole Church and in 1311 Clement V finally confirmed it at the Council of Vienna.

(2) In 1244 the Bishop of Lincoln (Robert Grosseteste) prohibited the participation of the clergy in *'ludi theatrales'* [theatrical games or performances]: this amounted to preventing performances in church and opened the way for secular elements to appear.

The Council of Vienna decreed that the Feast of Corpus Christi should be celebrated on the Thursday after Trinity Sunday (seven weeks after Easter, ten days after Whitsun, therefore in late May or June, and close to the longest days of the year), and this feast joined the others in determining the rhythm of the year. Thus *the play* called Corpus Christi became an outward manifestation of the Feast, bringing a special excitement to the community every summer.

This outline does not convey the widespread popularity the new drama enjoyed. This was the first time in England that a form of theatre had been created which included a wider range of ranks and classes in medieval society. Furthermore, although the services of learned clerks helped put together the many playlets needed for the new festival, the plays were in the vernacular, not in Latin. Of foremost importance, the vast cosmic vision of this drama had to be presented in manageable sizes and digestible gobbets without losing a sense of the whole. Nor can any simple account do

1 The pageant wagon as a 'processional' presentation: a *tableau vivant* of the Nativity in the Triumph of Isabella, Brussels, 1615; an angel sits on the roof.

more than hint at the power now vested in the new actors and craftsmen coming from outside the Church, ordinary people evidently anxious to seize the possibilities of a native drama. They especially experimented with those basic street-theatre conventions of non-realistic performance – the imaginative management of ideas in neutral place and time, and the manipulation of the perception and response of a familiar audience.

Of a hundred or more towns in the British Isles which enjoyed the annual festival presentation we know of less than a dozen, and of these only four have the bulk of the text of their plays extant:

(1) *York*, whose cycle was written in stages probably beginning *c.* 1350. There were forty-eight plays and the performance lasted one day only. If some were written by a monk from St Mary's Abbey, he has been conveniently named 'The York Realist'; but they are more likely to have been the composite work of several authors, revised over the years. The method of presentation was '*processional*', i.e., the plays were performed on pageant wagons [movable stages] travelling from station to station [places appointed for stopping] where the spectators waited. For many years it was assumed that the forty-eight plays assembled at 4.30 am on Toft Green, processing along a route consisting of twelve stations where each play was presented in turn. It has recently been pointed out that this would call for an unlikely 576 performances finishing at 2.15 am the next morning, and that without immaculate timing and plays of equal length the wagons would stop and start like cars in a traffic jam. It is also possible therefore that the procession was only one of tableaux presented on wagons which finally assembled in the Pavement, York's market-place, for a complete performance.

(2) *Wakefield*. Although it is not certain that it is from Wakefield, this cycle is also known as the *Towneley* plays, after the family who owned them. They were probably written in the fifteenth century, and consisted of thirty plays. 'The Wakefield Master' has been adopted as the name of the author of a handful of the plays distinguished

by their metre and style. References in the dialogue to a 'kyrk' [church] suggest that this cycle was performed on scaffolds in front of a church, that is, stationary at a *single station* in 'mansions' [houses designed for performance], with some of the action possibly taking place between the scaffolds. Large scenic items (a tower for God, a hill for Christ to pray, a table and benches for the disciples) support this theory.

(3) *Chester*, whose cycle consisted of twenty-five plays possibly first written in the fifteenth century and performed for three days at Whitsun. The latest author was probably a single editor or reviser, since the plays are composed consistently in eight–line stanzas. This cycle was thought to have been played on *processional* pageant wagons, although the fact that the plays differ greatly in length would have disrupted the flow of the pageants.

(4) *N-Town*, a cycle possibly from Lincoln (Lincolnshire) or Bury St Edmunds (Suffolk), since the language indicates their origin in an eastern county. The plays are also sometimes called after a previous owner, Robert *Hegge*, and sometimes known as the *Ludus Coventriae* from an early misreading of the manuscript. This group of plays was first called 'N-Town' by W. W. Greg from a clue found in the final address to the audience:

> A sunday next yf that we may
> At vj [6] of the belle we gynne oure play
> In N. towne wherfore we pray
> That god now be youre Spede.

One conjecture is that the designation 'N' [for the Latin *nomen*, 'name'] assumed that any company of strolling players would merely substitute the name of the next town on their itinerary, although the idea that a Corpus Christi cycle would be in the hands of such a group is very questionable. A second, more likely, solution is that announcements were made in surrounding villages inviting people to travel to a central location for the performance. The cycle consists of forty-two plays written in the middle of the fifteenth century, possibly revised by one author. These plays differ from the Corpus Christi cycles and are unusual for introducing abstract virtues as characters (Contemplacio, Veritas, Misericordia, Iusticia, Pax and others) and are thought to have had a *'single station'* presentation, with the audience moving from play to play and some of the scenes 'clustered' according to their use of a single *locus* [place, locality] like Heaven, Hell or Paradise.

The methods of staging and the ways of setting up the large number of stages may be summarized as:

(1) *Processional staging*. The pageants could be mounted on wagons and pulled round the town. The idea was no doubt borrowed from the customary processions of both Church and state, in which allegorical tableaux were displayed in a parade for all to see. By this method the spectators remained in their places and the plays would pass in sequence in front of their eyes (thereby incidentally requiring the doubling of major characters like God, Satan and Jesus, who appear in more than one play). In the Chester *Breviarye* (1595) the pageant stage is described:

> These pagiantes or cariage was a highe place made like ahowse wth ij [two] rowmes beinge open on ye tope the lower rowme they apparrelled & dressed them selues, and in the higher roume they played.

This arrangement has been disputed, and certainly there was more to a pageant than a tiring-room with a platform on top. If the pageant was built on two levels, resembling a double-decker bus, the levels could suggest Ptolemy's division of the world and seem to represent vertically Earth and Hell, or Heaven and Earth, as in the York Mercers' Play with its angels and devils on stage simultaneously. The pageant stage was also richly painted and decorated; the Coventry records for 1440 even mention 'cloth to lap about the pajent'. If it was furnished with traps, pulleys and winches, it began to resemble a house of illusions, and apparently had the capability of creating effects that smacked of the supernatural: the Flood would be suggested by water poured from above and Hell would be conjured up with noise and smoke, fireworks and flames.

(2) *Mansion staging*. If the stages were set horizontally in a

semicircle (possibly also in a full circle with the audience inside), they were 'mansions' [houses or booths], possibly arranged in the market-place or against the great west door of the church. In this way the plays could be viewed by many people simultaneously, making the audience more mobile than the wagons. This system originated from the way houses were set round the walls inside the church, or on either side of the nave. The nine mansions for the pasion play at Valenciennes in 1547 were arranged neatly from left to right to represent Hell, Limbo, the Golden Gate, a House of Bishops, a Palace, Jerusalem, the Temple, Nazareth and Paradise, with Hell opposite to Heaven, a common arrangement.

The *platea*, the acting area in front of each mansion, acquired special importance in mansion staging, where the static, frontal view of the mansion might otherwise have distanced the play from the spectators. In the N-Town play of the Trial of Christ, an unusual stage direction suggests the probability of the actors' exciting use of the *platea* when a messenger is instructed to 'come into the place running and crying "Tidings! Tidings!" and so round about the place, "Jesu of Nazareth is taken! Jesu of Nazareth is taken!"'

When E. Martin Browne revived the York plays for the Festival of Britain in 1951, he decided to present them in mansion form for the convenience of modern seating. The great ruin of the north wall of St Mary's Abbey, with its arches and bays and clerestory windows, had 'its own power to stir the imagination, and to produce the Mystery Plays before it would be to add like to like' (Browne, *Two in One* (1981), 185). In this way the grass in front supplied the *platea* for the plays, and from the high windows the players in Heaven looked down upon the mortals who inhabited the Earth below. It turned out that this mock mansion staging had the great advantage of speed and continuity in performance: scenes could be dovetailed as the focus shifted from one play to the next, and on the great grass acting area, crowd choreography permitted exciting shifts of focus and direction. Incidentally, Browne also reported that the alliterations and assonances of the plays' Middle English verse, which daunted a good many of the actors, proved to be theatrically effective: spoken without the use of microphones over great distances, the lines were 'the instruments by which the actor can catch the attention and push home the point' and 'truly express character and yet carry clearly' (189).

(3) *Staging in the round*, with the actor at the centre of the circle. This was a third arrangement, found chiefly in Cornwall, that associated with the 'rounds', the earthworks that may still be seen in St Just. The Cornish rounds were great stone and earthen amphitheatres, some 120 feet across, which may have been built in the first place as military fortifications. Arranged with scaffolds and tents set around a central *platea* for the actors, and with terraces on the sides of the circle for the spectators, they provided a convenient theatre. Luckily we have the plan and some of the details of performance in the round from *The Castle of Perseverance* (1425), discussed in the next chapter.

The plays possessed, and profited from, an unusual feature. Addressed to the citizenry, they were also mounted and performed by them, and by the later fourteenth century the festival procession and the pageantry associated with it were arranged and financed by *the guilds*. Only the great medieval trade guilds had the money, the resources and the organization for this task. The procedure was for each guild to ask its mayor and corporation to assign to it one, or part of one, of the plays. The guild then took on the responsibility, with some pride, of planning the production, designing and building of its pageant or mansion-stage and casting and rehearsing the parts. A selection of such assignments from York in 1415 shows that the authorities often attempted to match the craft of each guild to an appropriate theme in the plays, and no doubt the guild chosen was pleased to exhibit its skills. Thereafter, long tradition assured it its place in the total scheme:

The play	assigned to	*the guild*
The Creation of the Earth		The plasterers
Building the Ark		The shipwrights

Noah and the Flood	The fishmongers and mariners
Adoration of the Shepherds (with the star over Bethlehem)	The chandlers [candle-makers]
The Adoration of the Magi	The goldsmiths and goldbeaters
The Flight into Egypt	The marshals [stablemen and farriers]
The Last Supper	The bakers
The Crucifixion	The pinners [nail-makers] and painters
The Mortification of Christ	The butchers and poulterers

In other corporation accounts interesting entries are to be found that start the imagination: the skinners may present the play of Adam and Eve (who wore white leather costumes), the fishmongers the play of Jonah and the Whale, the dyers the Division of the Red Sea, the vintners the Marriage at Cana, the cooks the Harrowing of Hell (where the din of pots and pans was an anticipated feature). The guilds undertook their tasks in a devoted, if not competitive, spirit.

With so many plays and so many parts, almost everybody in the community was involved in the preparation and presentation of the festival, and a pageant-master was elected probably to oversee the work and arrange the order of the procession. He also collected and dispensed the 'pageant-silver' levied upon each guildsman, a sum varying between a penny and four pence. The tax was necessary because the decoration of the pageants was costly (£8 8s was paid to build Noah's ark at Hull in 1494), and the actors were paid for both rehearsal and performance. It is of interest that the guilds chose to spend according to the value of the parts in the performance rather than their importance in the Scriptures (at Coventry in 1490 God was paid 2s, the same as Pilate's Wife, but less than King Herod, who was paid 3s 4d).

There is also evidence at York that the guildsmen were jealous of their standards as actors, and on 3 April 1476 the Council Book has an entry of unusual interest. It seems that the best actors were required to act as judges of the rest:

> That yerely in the tyme of lentyn there shall be called afore the maire [mayor] for the tyme being iiij [four] of the moste

connyng [skilful] discrete [wise] and able players within this Citie, to serche, here, and examen all the plaiers and plaies and pagentes thrughoute all the artificers [craftsmen] belonging to Corpus Xti Plaie. And all suche as thay shall fynde sufficiant in personne and connyng, to the honour of the Citie and worship of the saide Craftes, for to admitte and able [prepare]; and all other insufficiant personnes, either in connyng, voice, or personne, to discharge, ammove, and avoide.

Before the event, the banns [proclamation] announcing the plays would be read in the streets by a town crier or herald, as in York in 1415:

Oiez &c. We comand of ye Kynges behalue and ye Mair and ye Shirefs of yis Citee yat no mann go armed in yis Citee with swerdes ne with Carlill-axes, ne none othir defences in distorbaunce of ye Kingis pees and ye play, or hynderyng of ye processioun of Corpore Christi ... of payne of forfaiture of yaire wapen and inprisonment of yaire bodys.

[*The authorities were worried about the danger of the unusually large crowds gathering in their towns and cities.*]

And yat men yat brynges furth pacentes [pageants] yat yai [they] play at the places yat is assigned yerfore and nowere elles, of ye payne of forfaiture to be raysed yat is ordayned yerfore, yat is to say xl^s [11s].

[*The planning of the performances was so complicated that it was a serious matter if the sequence was broken.*]

... And that euery player that shall play be redy in his pagiaunt at convenyant tyme, that is to say, at the myd howre betwix iiijth and vth of the cloke in the mornynge [4.30 am], and then all oyer pageantz fast followyng ilk one after oyer as yer course is, without tarieng.

[*Quite a military operation, with the troops 'standing to' at first light, especially since in the first play God had to create light.*]

The years during which the Corpus Christi plays flourished taught important lessons about practical theatre. Whether in pageant or mansion, the actor enjoyed the liberty of playing on a stage that could be *localized and unlocalized* at will.

When localized, its *locus* might be a particular room or house identified by a scenic prop like a throne or an altar. If the actor played within the intended *locus*, he became a character in the scene. If he stepped outside, perhaps to the *platea*, he was a player with a player's licence and might be anywhere. None the less, the *locus* was not realistic in any modern sense: the pageant or mansion telescoped space and merely represented its scene iconographically by visual symbols that were instantly recognizable. This sort of staging ensured a strong, if simple, impact and the full participation of an audience that had acquired the habit of seeing iconographically.

The symbols did their own magic work. A character wearing an appropriate costume located the scene for his audience and also suggested his purpose. Joseph and Mary were immediately known, and their arrival in Bethlehem was confirmed by the presence of a traditional prop like a manger. Meanwhile on the other side of the space three shepherds, or three Kings, would *simultaneously* by their pantomime indicate their distance from Bethlehem, and establish their intentions towards the central event. The medieval stage also accomplished great leaps in time, as when Noah with his ark at York suddenly announced,

> A hundred winters, well I know,
> Are gone since I this work have wrought.

It has sometimes been argued that the medieval drama had as one of its chief purposes to give actuality to divine happenings, and no doubt there were moments when a realistic detail kept the audience all agog, but the theatre of non-illusion had the power of being both realistic and ineffable at the same time, if need be. The distinction of the unlocalized acting area, the empty space that was the chief glory of the medieval stage, lay in its ability to specify or to banish time and place at will.

Not long after, in *An Apology for Poetry* (c. 1581), Sir Philip Sidney castigated those who neglected the unity of place:

> ... you shall have Asia of the one side, and Afric of the other, and so many other under-kingdoms, that the player, when he cometh in, must ever begin with telling where he is, or else the tale will not be conceived. Now you shall have three ladies walk to gather flowers: and then we must

believe the stage to be a garden. By and by we hear news of
shipwreck in the same place: and then we are to blame if we
accept it not for a rock ...

Following Aristotle's unity of time, he also protested the
absurdity of representing the passage of more than one day. It
was already too late: the licence of what had become Tudor
staging was accepted everywhere by actor and audience alike;
and, as for the authors, Shakespeare and his contemporaries
took pleasure in a useful convention.

In matters of *costume* the actors playing supernatural
figures got special attention. Angels wore wigs, as suggested
by records like, 'paid for a pound of hemp to mend the angels'
heads, 4^d'. At Leicester, they were particular about painted
wings for their angels; elsewhere, haloes were given promi-
nence. God achieved impersonality by wearing a gilded mask,
and the requirement is on record for 'a face and hair for the
Father'. Flying entrances and exits were possible with the aid
of pulleys and winches in those plays which involved an
ascent to Heaven. At York and elsewhere, Adam and Eve
(both played by men) were accorded a touch of realism in
their costuming, and their 'flesh-colour, close-fitting coats
and hose' made of white leather suggested their nudity, while
keeping at bay any possibility of sexual impropriety. Devils
wore leather suits, and horns, snouts and claws added to the
effect. In the Garden of Eden Satan would seem to be villainy
itself when he was given 'a serpent form with yellow hair
upon his head', but Cornwall gave him 'a virgin face' and the
Norwich grocers specified a tail. At Coventry, an element of
symbolism was seen in the costumes of Christ's torturers,
who wore 'jackets of black buckram ... with nails and dice
upon them'. There are also many hints of the way the popular
imagination worked: at Norwich, Adam had 'a rib coloured
red' and Herod carried the blood of the innocents upon him
by wearing a pair of red gloves. In the Judgment plays the
damned went to Hell in black and the saved to Heaven in
white.

This emblematic dressing matched the décor of the stage
itself. In the Wakefield play of Jacob, the River Jordan was
evidently a property dividing the stage, and in the Pharaoh

play the stage was divided by the Red Sea, possibly represented by a red cloth. With a flowery Paradise and a fiery
Hell, and with its tricks of blood and thunder, pageant or
mansion presented a colourful and eye-catching picture, and
contemporary illustrations suggest that good use was made of
the best decorative arts of the age.

The liturgical drama was sung in Latin and the cycle plays
were spoken in the vernacular, but in the latter *music and song*
were widely used to dramatic effect; if there were no minstrels' Guild, waits or minstrels were hired. In York the
minstrels eventually produced the play of Herod and the
Magi because trumpets were called for to augment the pomp
of the alien King, who in N-Town orders the trumpeters to
'blowe up a good blast'. Fanfares of horns, symbolizing the
breath of life, were wanted for the Shepherd's play at Chester,
and on the direction '*hic cantabunt organa*' [here instruments
will play] jubilant bells rang out in Coventry and Wakefield
for the Purification of Mary. The N-Town Assumption was
assisted by the angelic sounds of cithara [lyre] and organ (the
portable kind), suggesting that musical instruments themselves
had symbolic value, here of the ethereal. In the Wakefield
Prophets' play David foretells the Incarnation of Christ by
holding a harp as a symbol of the Crucifixion.

Another feature of the medieval stage is worth a special
mention. Its audience was not troubled when Noah prayed to
the Trinity, or Herod swore by Mahomet. The players
delighted in *anachronism*, a feature which is also characteristic
of the Tudor and Jacobean drama to come, and which is not
unknown as a device on the twentieth-century stage
(Thornton Wilder's *The Skin of Our Teeth* is built upon it,
for example, as are recent concept productions of Shakespeare
by Michael Bogdanov). Anachronism is not a sign of ignor-
ance; it can be a direct and effective method of making a
dramatic point, almost a convention in its own right. When
Pontius Pilate called himself 'regent' and behaved like a
medieval potentate, when his Roman soldiers marched on
stage in medieval armour to the sound of pipe and tabor, and
when Caiaphas, Annas and the rabbis robed themselves in
mitres and tabards of scarlet like Catholic bishops, at a stroke
the players were drawing vivid, even satirical, comparisons

between the past and the present. The actor hit another kind of target when God appeared on high dressed like the Pope, or when Mary Magdalen entered like a wimpled lady attired in the height of fashion.

Time is known by what happens in it, and thinking was untroubled in the fourteenth century when the stage insisted that all human activity took place in a pattern of eternal time. By such means it brought past, present and future into the same time span, and so related them. Above all, anachronism was at its most powerful when it was at its most familiar. When the Shepherds preparing to visit Jesus in the manger made a deliberate switch from their local dialect to the language of the Scriptures, anachronism inspired a dramatic insight and achieved a true *coup de théâtre*. As those living in the present perceived the past, so the past could speak to the present. From another perspective, what in *The Play Called Corpus Christi* (1966) V. A. Kolve has called the plays' 'larger rhythms' (100) are to be seen in the way the Old Testament prepares us for the New, with the sacrifice of Abel, or Isaac, prefiguring the Passion, and Noah's building of the Ark against the Flood looking towards Christ's salvation of the world.

The Corpus Christi plays inaugurated a new style in the language of performance from Church Latin to the vernacular, a momentous advance for the future of the drama in English. Latin had made the drama universal and interchangeable, but also solemn, abstract and remote; the vernacular simplified and localized it, and made it personal and familiar. Although music and song pervaded the plays and the alliterative verse form of the dialogue stiffened their expression and admitted a rather operatic quality to the style of performance, the lines belonged essentially to everyday speech, not intonation or song. Some of it may have echoed the preacher's voice in his sermons and homilies, but with lay actors, men known intimately within the community and speaking in the idiom of the district, rich with local reference and common lore, the English drama took on another kind of vitality and popularity.

There is at this time no theory of *acting*, and other than the gestic suggestions in the poetry of the lines when they convey feeling, there are few clues about the manner of acting. However, given that men or boys played the female parts throughout the period, some degree of unreal, stylized performance may be assumed, with possibly a quality of clear, emphatic speaking and strong gesture designed to point and reinforce the lines. A hint may be taken from a tenth-century liturgy, a playlet of *The Three Marys* which was accompanied by directions to the clerics who were to play the parts. The following lines and gestures were given to Mary Magdalen:

> (*Here she turns to the men with her arms extended*) O my brothers! (*Here to the women*) O my sisters! Where is my hope? (*Here she beats her breast*) Where is my consolation? (*Here she raises her hands*) Where is my whole well-being? (*Here, head inclined, she throws herself at Christ's feet*) O my Master!

These directions convey some sense of the expected formality of the performance by their simple stylization, and add a pleasing dignity to the emotion. It is possible that when liturgical Latin was replaced by the vernacular, a more natural form of acting followed.

The point was made some years ago by A. W. Pollard (in *English Miracle Plays, Moralities and Interludes* (1927)), that the most interesting characters in the plays are those about which the Bible has little or nothing to say; in other words, Scripture has obligingly left some parts to the imagination of the actor and his audience. It is these characters who are quick to acquire local and more natural characteristics, and many of them a quality of humour; their speech betrays their non-biblical origins and their behaviour indicates the popularity with which they were viewed by their audiences. Especially noteworthy are the following characters:

– *The ploughboy* who introduces the Cain and Abel play at Wakefield. This 'Boy' is the type of impertinent servant found throughout Roman and Renaissance drama, and provides a good match for Cain, who is presented as the type of English farmer, albeit a bad-tempered one. In the original the Boy is called 'Pikeharnes', someone who robs a dead body of its armour. When Cain calls for help with his team of plough horses (probably the real thing, brought as close to the stage as street and pageant would allow), Pikeharnes, always ready with an aside, expresses the audience's contempt for his master:

> Godys forbot, that ever thou thrife!
> [May God forbid that ever you should thrive!]

- *Noah's wife* in the play of the Flood, especially at Chester, Newcastle and Wakefield. In refusing to leave her 'gossipps' and enter the Ark at the earnest behest of her husband, she takes on the appearance of a shrew, and, since she was played by a man, Mrs Noah was something of an early pantomime dame and a caricature of all shrews. When she is finally pulled aboard (presumably from the street up to the pageant level), she retaliates with a blow that lands on the righteous Noah:

> NOYE. Welckome, wiffe, into this botte.
> NOYE's WIFFE. Have thou that for thy note!
> NOYE. Ha, ha! marye, this is hotte!

- *Pharaoh*, who swells into the braggart King of Egypt when confronted by Moses and the Israelites in the York cycle. In the face of each plague, Pharaoh swears and struts and blusters, and his favourite oath is 'Go hence to the devil of hell!' The audience no doubt enjoyed watching one of its favourite characters being provoked as matters went from bad to worse.
- *Herod* from The Slaughter of the Innocents grew into the noisy tyrant whom Hamlet condemns for his manner of speaking. In the Coventry play his lines include, 'I stampe! I stare [glare]! ... I rent [rend]! I rawe [rave]!' with the famous direction, *'Erode ragis in the pagond [pageant] and in the strete also'*, and from this we may deduce that his pride and anger were full of comic bluster. His fate was to be hauled off to Hell by devils.
- In some cycles *Pilate* acquires an interesting degree of humanity when he sympathizes with Christ. At Wakefield, Pilate is the image of evil, but elsewhere he tries to deal with the politics of the situation shrewdly, and grows weary of the vindictiveness and hypocrisy of the priests who accuse Christ.

These characters, among others, are distinguished by their freedom from scriptural constraints, and thrive on the liberties they take with familiar Bible stories. It is possible their manner of acting was also less restrained.

Many details of *everyday realism* are scattered through the plays, setting the profane among what is deeply sacred, and colouring the sacred with what is familiar. These popular elements may be divided into four broad kinds:

(1) Direct and natural details that would have been immediately recognizable by the audience.
(2) Moments of tenderness and pathos to which the audience could make a sympathetic response.
(3) The realistic exhibition of violence and cruelty chosen to reflect the audience's notion of barbarism.
(4) Elements of ribaldry and clowning, with touches of satire and caricature from common life.

In every case the massive theme of the play in question is subjected to teasing forces which both reduce and enlarge it. The reduction made the material accessible, no doubt, but the treatment also served to manipulate the audience's perception in order to intensify or expand it.

The natural details range from references to the weather ('Lord, what these weders ar cold!' is the cry heard from the shepherds of the Nativity) and what the common people wore, cooked and ate, to wider topics like the enclosure of land and the collection of taxes. Actual places are sometimes mentioned, as when Christ's torturer at Chester is claimed as the best to be had from there to London, and when the devils at Wakefield name a particular street in their preparations for Doomsday ('Let us go to our doom up Watling Street'). In York, differences of rank are signalled when Herod in his personal vanity calls for his valet to arrange his dress, Pilate prefers to wash his hands in warm water and his wife betrays her snobbery by the way she speaks to the Beadle. The shepherds' gifts to Jesus at York are wonderfully unpretentious: 'a brooch with a bell of tin', 'two cob nuts ... upon a band' and 'an horn spoon ... will harbour forty peas'.

The plays of the Fall make much of the business with the

tree in the Garden of Eden. At York, under Satan's persistent persuasion, Eve's curiosity about the apple induces laughter:

> SATAN. Eat it safely you may ...
> EVE.   Is this sooth that thou says?
> SATAN. Yea; why believe not me?
>   I would by no kind of ways
>   Tell ought but truth to thee.
> EVE.   Then will I to thy teaching trust,
>   And take this fruit unto our food.
> SATAN. Bite boldly on; be not abashed.

> (trans. J.S.Purvis from *The York Cycle of Mystery Plays* (1957))

To the reader Satan may seem to steal the scene, but in performance all eyes are on Eve as the reluctance behind her reluctance to take the apple invites the expected mockery of the weakness of the female sex.

Moments of natural human feeling were not hard to find and exploit in the Bible stories. The play of *Abraham and Isaac* at Chester was particularly moving, as it was at Brome, and the sketchy account in Genesis 22 encouraged invention. A good deal of time is given to establishing the loving relationship between father and son, and since neither of them may rebel against authority, the tension they share unifies the action. The expression of sorrow by the father who must sacrifice his child is heard implicitly in:

> Make thee ready, my dear darling,
> For we must do a little thing.

And when Abraham tells the boy he must die, Isaac's pleas for mercy ring true:

> If I have trespassed in any degree,
> With a yard [stick] you may beat me.

The child also cries pathetically for his mother:

> Would God my mother were here with me!
> She would kneel down upon her knee,
> Praying you, father, if it may be,
>   For to save my life.

> (trans. Pollard, *English Miracle Plays and Interludes*)

He finally asks his father's blessing before he is slain. This kind of dialogue lengthened the suspense before the crisis, as well as assisted the actors in their task of drawing the audience into the strong emotion of the situation. Yet for all the tragic tension and divine anguish, the purpose of the play was to focus on Abraham's faith and God's reward and end on a note of joy and reconciliation.

At Chester in the play of *The Slaughter of the Innocents* the ranting of Herod is set off against the protests of the women whose children and babies are being killed by his soldiers. The cruelty exhibited in this play was present throughout the drama of the period, and the Continent supplied vivid examples of the beheading of John the Baptist, the mutilation and burning of Saint Barbara, the torture of Saint Apollonia, the racking and grilling of Saint Denis, the stoning of the woman taken in adultery, the hanging of Judas and more. In such scenes of pain and torture the use of dummies and the simulation of blood enabled the violence to reach inordinate proportions, and the impulse to unnerve the spectators was of the same kind that attracts audiences to horror films today, by projecting realistic images beyond the normal experience. The paintings of Bosch and Brueghel suggest something of the same purpose.

Yet even this cruelty was eclipsed by that of *The Crucifixion* itself, the dramatic pinnacle of the cycles. No fewer than four of the York plays are concerned with this event, from the binding and scourging to the nailing on the cross. However, there is little biblical authority for the extraordinary detail with which the Crucifixion was dramatized; the simple statement *crucifixerunt* [they crucified him] became therefore another starting point for vivid dramatization. The torture begins as soon as Pilate gives the order for execution to his soldiers:

> Let us drive to him dreadfully with dashes;
> All red with our rods we array him
> And rend him.

They mock 'his lordship' with the crown of thorns:

> Now press to him tightly with this thick thorn.
> Lo, it holds so to his head that the brains out fall.

With great attention to detail they nail Him to the cross, only to find that the holes bored in the wood are too far apart, so that His arms and legs must be first stretched with ropes:

> A rope shall rive him down,
> Though all sinews go asunder.

The heavy cross was heavier still with the weight of a man, and presented a genuine problem in lifting it from the ground and then lowering it into a hole. Yet this too was made to serve the drama:

> set him by the mortice here,
> And let him fall in all at once.
> For sure that pain shall have no peer.
>
> (trans. J. S. Purvis from *The York Cycle of Mystery Plays*)

The players here are aiming at an unusual degree of verisimilitude.

The brutality of these scenes alone did not make up their strength. They are painful in their unusual length, perhaps because over the years the dialogue grew longer to meet the needs of the complicated business of the Crucifixion; and although at York in the early fifteenth century they were shortened, the soldiers' lines are also breathlessly stichomythic, broken in their flow only by two longer, sober speeches by Christ. The action is also more impressive for being spoken 'in character' – coldly and objectively, as the soldiers get on with the job. When they cast lots for Christ's clothes, the same callous indifference to what is happening again sharpens the point. Finally, the elements of comic mockery heard in the soldiers' lines make it more unbearable by the disarming distance that humour lends to the central action – as in Shakespeare at his best.

The element of humour in sacred plays should not be surprising. After Christmas, there had long been a tradition – a vestige, no doubt, of the Roman Saturnalia – of the choirboys' Feast of the Boy Bishop and his clownish attendants, and the Feast of Fools or the Feast of Asses permitted subdeacons and other lesser clergy to make fun of the Church and its rituals. On these special occasions, nobody objected to the practice of their ringing the church bells in the wrong

order, wearing ridiculous vestments or singing out of tune.
None of this inspired blasphemy, but it certainly encouraged
parody; and so it was in the cycle plays. Nor were such
dignitaries of the Church as friars and nuns privileged against
laughter, as the poems and tales of the period abundantly
confirm. Religious solemnity was a post-Reformation trait,
and in the literature that preceded it comic material could turn
up unexpectedly anywhere.

In the cycles, laughter begins with the temptation of Eve,
and grows apace as soon as Paradise is lost. Once out of the
Garden, Adam and Eve assume the parts of a much-married
couple, and are quickly into a spat about who was responsible
for the Fall. Cain chooses to quarrel with his impertinent
ploughboy, who in turn curses both his master and the
audience. Comedy naturally embraces the stubborn character
of Noah's Wife, played in drag, and makes thorough use of a
tyrannical King Herod ('*Hic Herod pompabit*' [Here Herod
pomps]) and of Pilate too, foolish when he is drunk. The
buffoonery reaches a peak in the behaviour of Satan and his
devils, who appear to have risked stealing any scene they
played in. For the Harrowing of Hell at York, provision was
made for six good and six bad spirits, and, at the Last
Judgment, twelve angels and good spirits were set off by ten
bad spirits and devils. On these occasions the devils perhaps
saw their roles as rather those of grimacing circus clowns than
that of frightening figures intended to fetch down judgment
on sinners.

The unique quality of humour in the plays may be best
seen in the irreverent fun had even when dealing with a sacred
doctrine like that surrounding the Immaculate Conception.
At York, the elderly Joseph expresses ironic surprise at the
arrival of Mary's baby, after he was apparently unable to
beget a child himself. He enters wearily, convinced that he has
been cuckolded:

> For shame what shall I say,
> That thusgates now in my old days
> Has wedded a young wench to my wife,
> And may not well stride over two straws?
>
> (trans. J. S. Purvis from *The York Cycle of Mystery Plays*)

At Coventry, the pair fight, and, at N-Town, a comic character, Den the Summoner, attempts on behalf of the bishop to
try Joseph and Mary for infidelity. In the manner of a street
actor, he first calls for space to perform ('Avoid, sirs, and let
my lord the bishop come'), and then *the pageant of the Trial
of Joseph and Mary is brought into the place'*. Clowning
proliferates when he demands payment and threatens the
audience with his 'great rough tooth' if they refuse him.

Nevertheless, it is easy to misunderstand the nature of the
comic material in the plays, particularly in those, like Noah
and the Shepherds, which seem to have a predominantly
humorous tone. The entire cycle was seen as 'comedy' – a
divine comedy of rebirth. If the stage seems to display
irreverence, it may be that modern sentimentality, not medieval belief, is at fault.

The Wakefield *Second Shepherds' Play* (c. 1450) is the best-
known of the cycle plays; it is constantly anthologized, and
not without reason. Here it may pull together some outstanding features of the Corpus Christi drama.

The play first demonstrates that the stage could respond to
a popular and secular need, since more than two-thirds of its
text is given to material that springs from the clowning of folk
drama and catches the spirit of its place and time. The play is
rich in local colour: the actors speak in a familiar north
midland dialect, full of the idiom of speech and local proverb,
and they immediately suggest that the characters are not
unlike people in the Yorkshire audience itself. They show that
they know the wolds and moors intimately: it was good sheep
country, but the climate and conditions of work made it far
from benign. This was to be a chilly Yorkshire Nativity, yet
the play also works as a fully integrated Christian celebration.

The subject is The Adoration of the Shepherds, but
although the spectators had just seen the play of the Annun-
ciation and heard Mary sing the Magnificat, at first there is no
hint of the Bible story in the way it begins, although glancing
references to the sacred drama to come slyly remind the
audience it is watching a Nativity play. The actors begin by
offering to produce, not the customary three, but four
shepherds. Moreover they enter, not as the traditional group,

but separately, so that they introduce a degree of individual difference. And each shepherd first addresses the audience, suggesting from the beginning that his primary role is to speak to the spectators, his fellow countrymen. Thus the First Shepherd complains bitterly about the cold weather (an implicit stage direction for pantomime), his poor clothing (a signal for visual realism), his weak legs and frost-bitten fingers (more signals for the actor) and the system of taxation or 'purveyance' by which the feudal landlord took his payment in kind. No Palestinians these: the three are contemporary Yorkshiremen, and their lines are colloquial and alive with anachronistic oaths like 'Christ's cross me speed' and 'Christ's curse'.

If expectation demanded that the Angel next appear and show them the way to Bethlehem, it was delightfully frustrated. A fourth figure enters, suspiciously wrapped in a large cloak; however, he is not the Angel, but one Mak, a sheep-thief who manages to plant the notions that his wife Gill has a propensity for giving birth and that his house is full of infants:

> And ilk [each] yere that commys to man
> She bringys furth a lakan [baby] –
> And, som yeres, two.

The comic plotting and the knockabout business is in the robust English tradition, and with this unabashed foreshadowing both of Mak's plan to steal a sheep and of the Nativity, already the audience is able to join in the dramatic strategy. The shepherds settle to sleep having carefully arranged Mak between them for safety's sake.

What follows tells a good deal about the use of space on the medieval pageant or mansion-stage. The pace of the play picks up as Mak and Gill's stratagem develops. Entrances and exits follow more quickly upon one another, and the action chops between the two locations of moor and cottage with disarming speed. Gill's lines invite broad farcical business, especially since she is played by a man. Only after a good deal of slapstick does the Angel appear and sing *'Gloria in excelsis'*, the song changing the mood of the audience and introducing the next part of the play.

The parallelism in the play between the sacred and the

profane leaves the modern audience with some seemingly impossible equations. If Mak with his remarks about his wife prefigures Joseph, does this mean that Gill played in drag was a grotesque version of the Virgin Mary, also of course played by a male? Was the sheep itself, swaddled ridiculously in its cradle, thought of as the Lamb of God? The leaps of irony are nothing short of acrobatic.

The Corpus Christi or mystery plays were suppressed between 1530 and 1590. In 1534 Henry VIII broke with the Roman Church, and the controversy over its doctrines began. These doctrines were embodied in the plays themselves, and when Elizabeth came to the throne in 1558, the process of political censorship followed, slowed down only by the affection in which the people held them. The Archbishop of York (Edmund Grindal) and his Dean (Matthew Hutton) succeeded in their efforts to prohibit them, and last performances in the north are recorded in York in 1569, Chester in 1575, Wakefield in 1576 and Coventry in 1579. Elizabeth's Star Chamber completed the ban in 1589.

Nevertheless, the condemnation of the cycle plays by the authorities was a defeat for the Church of major proportions. It lost a powerful ally in the drama, when there might have been popular religious forms developing alongside the vigorous commercial theatre of the Elizabethans. As it was, actors had to find other kinds of stage, which they managed to do in London, first, possibly, by setting up wagons and booths in the inns of Islington and Whitechapel. It was not long before interest in the drama called for the building of playhouses designed to meet its particular needs. Yet none of this could have happened without the earlier experience of the medieval performance conventions, and the true legacy of the medieval drama is to be found in the common theatrical expectations held by player and spectator alike.

2

The early morality play

A definition reflecting purpose

If there was an intellectual 'play of ideas' in the Middle Ages it was the morality play, of which about sixty examples are extant. It was a form that dramatized a concept as much as it provided entertainment. The term is reserved chiefly for those plays of the fifteenth century that presented the virtues and vices of man in their struggle for the possession of his soul. It was once assumed to have been developed from the fourth century *Psychomachia* [the war of the soul], a poem by the Christian poet Prudentius that recounted an heroic contest between the Seven Cardinal Virtues and the Seven Deadly Sins. The morality play was written and performed contemporaneously with the Corpus Christi plays, but was not directly dependent upon the Bible or the Church for its content. In its own day it was known as 'a moral', 'a moral play' or 'a moral interlude', but any modern definition must turn upon what it does and how it does it. The earlier morality has been named 'repentance drama' because it was primarily homiletic – like the sermon, a vehicle for moral teaching.

The title of a morality usually suggested its central concern, and its themes were few and often repeated: the slight shift of emphasis held the dramatic charge each time. It might cover the stages in the life of man from childhood to maturity (as in *Mundus et Infans*) or the contest for his soul between the forces of good and evil (as in *Wisdom*, in which Christ is in open conflict with Lucifer); in *Mankind* man is put on trial for his sins; and *Everyman* is a pilgrimage which begins at the end of man's life, so to speak, in order to dramatize the inevitability of mortality and the judgment that awaits him. However, as it shook off the influence of the Church during the Tudor period

40

[1485–1603], the form became increasingly secular, broadening its audience to provide entertainment for the Court, changing its purpose for more aristocratic spectators in order to focus on political targets and the ways of government and finally merging with the more popular forms of comedy, tragedy and history associated with the Elizabethan stage.

The morality pursued its purpose by working with *abstract* characters that conveyed an *allegorical* story. Happily the struggle of good and evil automatically built a bold, confrontational dramatic structure: the morality was essentially a form of 'debate' (to choose a word now in widespread use among scholars) and the forthright conflict of human attitudes and intentions supplied the distinctive conventions and devices of its stagecraft.

(1) *Characters*. It was necessary to personify and humanize the virtues and vices, while depicting them with exaggeration in black-and-white terms, sharpening their differences and codifying their roles to meet the needs of both stage and pulpit.

(2) *Plotting*. Although irony was possible in the telling, the story was set out as an arrangement of events that would drive to a point, serve a moral end and leave intact an audience's sense of right and wrong, and good and evil. Formally, therefore, every morality was a 'comedy'.

If its topics inclined towards the abstract, performance itself could be vividly human and particular, for it was by no means a dry business to dramatize the personal choices in life. It would also be a mistake not to recognize that in spite of its apparently mechanical system the morality play was also a poetic drama with unpredictable power to lift its audience to an exalted plane of imagination and feeling: to this day *Everyman*, for example, can hold an audience enraptured.

Staging in the round

Notions of stagecraft implicit in these plays point to straightforward dramatization of the story, but staging could permit the performance to extend its limitations of space and time, take on lively, protean qualities and finally transcend itself. The unadorned stage of indefinite time and place can be smooth and quick in operation, seamless in scene building and powerful in impact. On the medieval stage less may well have meant more.

Any attempt at reconstructing a performance of an outdoor morality play (for example, *The Castle of Perseverance*) or an indoor one (for example, *Mankind*) takes us back to the first principles of staging, with few of the scenic devices needed for certain of the mystery plays contemporary with them. Yet morality staging also constitutes an invitation to be loose and flexible in performance, and modern notions of theatrical illusion are out of place. The tradition of playing out of doors persisted in one form or another, and town squares and market-places, village greens and courtyards all provided the space needed for popular public performance. The issue of a medieval theatre-in-the-round is still in dispute, but what evidence there is points to the likelihood that playing in the round, with the actors occupying a *platea* that could be surrounded by spectators, thrived on the proximity of an involved audience crowding round the players. Playing in the round naturally determined the patterns of movement and conventions of stage action, but the 'roundness' in morality performance introduced an effect greater than that of mere convenience. As in the Elizabethan theatre, the form of playing that called for an audience all around the actor contained within itself a powerful element of ceremonial and ritual. The roundness suggested the world itself: it made of the platform stage or other acting area a microcosm which enclosed its human inhabitants. It encour-aged a degree of symbolism in the arrangement of the action: the acting space, the *platea*, became a battleground for the forces of light and darkness, with man himself caught in the middle. The stage became a moral arena. *The Castle of Perseverance* is the outstanding example of this form of staging.

The Castle of Perseverance

This is the earliest extant and complete morality play. It dates from the early years of the fifteenth century and was evidently

played in Lincolnshire. It was intended for outdoor performance in the round and embodies many of the features later
displayed by the best of the morality plays. It was unusually
long by English standards, over 3,600 lines, and managed to
embrace most of the themes of sin and redemption. In every
sense Humanum Genus (also named 'Mankind') is at the
centre of the play, which traces his busy progress from birth
to death and ends with divine judgment itself.

It is possible to deduce a good deal of detail about the
presentation of the play from particulars in the text and
connected with it.

(1) The original Macro text opens with the 'banns' [procla-
mation] spoken by two heralds who announce what is to
come:

> 1 VEXILLATOR [flagbearer]. [W]e purpose us to playe
> This day sevenenyt, before you in syth [sight],
> At_____on the grene, in ryal [royal] aray ...

> 2 VEXILLATOR.. Ye manly men of_____, ther
> Crist save you all! ...
> Now, mery be all_____, and wel mote
> [may] ye cheve [thrive],
> All oure feythful frendys, ther faire mote ye fall
> [befall]!

The three blank spaces were probably left in order that
the heralds should insert the name of the town or village
where they were, as with the 'N-town' plays which
summoned prospective spectators to come to another,
central and presumably nearby location.

(2) The performance was to begin at 9.00 am and take place
'on the green'. The heralds were also pleased to make the
point that the play was to be in costume with theatrical
props.

(3) The play has an uncommonly large number (thirty-six) of
its personified characters. Since there were so many, the
players were probably professionals who could double
and treble the parts.

(4) In their lengthy announcement the two heralds first salute
the audience and proceed to introduce the subject of the

play, even reviewing the virtues and vices who were to confront Mankind:

> The case of oure coming, you to declare,
> Every man in himself forsothe [truly] he it may find;
> Whou [how] Mankinde into this werld born is ful bare
> And bare schal beried be at his last ende.

The subject is frankly stated, and if the last two of these four lines recount the argument, the others alert the playgoers to the role they are expected to play: an interesting ratio between narrative and manipulation, between the tale and the teller.

(5) A graphic diagram of the stage arrangements survives, and the instructions written on it are unusually full, although still open to speculation. It shows Mankind's castle raised on stilts with a little bed beneath it. The castle is surrounded by the awesome powers that govern his existence – indeed, Mankind seems to be permanently under threat and in a state of siege. As if in combat with the castle, three scaffolds are set symbolically around the acting place in order to display the conventional trio known as the World, the Flesh and the Devil – each according to custom with a little group of Deadly Sins as companions – together with two more scaffolds for Covetousness and God the Father, five in all.

(6) The words written round the drawing indicate that there is a barrier surrounding the castle and the acting area, which some believe to have been a ditch with water, enhancing the scenic picture of a castle complete with its moat. These instructions have been variously interpreted: it is possible that a physical barrier was erected round the acting space, not so much to keep out distracting spectators or gatecrashers, as to supply an effective theatrical and symbolic frame for the action. A ditch around the castle would have been a useful theatrical and allegorical feature: at one time Sloth, for example, tries to fill it with a spade to destroy its protective powers.

The performance of *The Castle of Perseverance* is less of a puzzle. In the arena, Mankind, having been born naked and

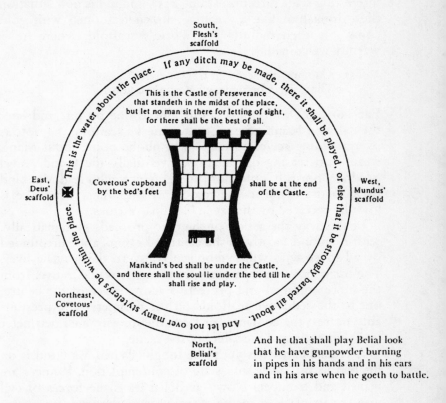

The four daughters shall be clad in mantles: Mercy in white, Righteousness in red altogether, Truth in sad green, and Peace all in black; and they shall play in the place all together till they bring up the soul.

2 The plan for *The Castle of Perseverance* (early fifteenth century), appended to the manuscript.

weak, makes his appearance propped up by a Good Angel on one side and a Bad Angel on the other. As may be expected, it is the latter who shows him the temptations of Lust-Liking [Pleasure] and Folly, and these two evidently share the

scaffold set up for the World. They complete their seduction
of Mankind with the help of music (*'Pipe up mu[sic]'* is the
interesting stage direction at line 455), and in his new situation
they dress him like a wealthy citizen festooned with gold
coins. He then mounts the World's scaffold, where he is
warmly welcomed:

> Cum up, my servaunt trew as stel!
> Thou schalt be riche, whereso thou goo ...

Each of the Deadly Sins is introduced one by one and later
they all join Mankind on Covetousness's scaffold: the riotous
overcrowding seems to make a symbolic point about Man's
steadily increasing degradation. Eventually the Good Angel
produces Shrift [Confession] and Penance, who lead Mankind
back to the castle in the middle of the arena, where he is
joyfully received by the seven Cardinal Virtues.

In this way the action of the play proceeds systematically,
with Mankind mostly at the centre of events and surrounded
by all those who will symbolically govern the way he lives.
The basic movement patterns are themselves illustrative: from
the more confined and protective acting space of the centre,
out to the seductive scaffolds on the perimeter and presumably nearest the audience, or from the unrestrained perimeter
into the centre and the safety of the castle.

A crucial battle has yet to be fought. When Mankind is on
his bed in the castle in a state of contemplation, banners are
waved and trumpets blown as Belial leads the forces of evil
into the attack. Perhaps he charges across the arena on horseback with his lance at the ready as in the joust: the directions
on the drawing indicate that he 'shall have gunpowder
burning in pipes in his hands and in his ears and in his arse'.
However, on reaching the Castle, each Vice is repulsed by an
appropriate Virtue dressed like a lady and bearing a rose,
emblematic of Christ's blood and the Passion.

Covetousness bribes a now ageing Mankind with riches
from his 'cupboard' (carefully named in the drawing) and
tricks him into avarice, taken to be the worst sin of old age. In
his final feeble condition, he is easily enticed from the protection of the castle, so that the actor is able to introduce touches
of realism and render his part human:

> I ginne to waxyn hory and olde;
> My bake ginneth to bowe and bende ...

So it is that Death makes his inevitable appearance – an entrance no less thrilling for being anticipated – and forthwith summons Mankind, who falls dying on his bed. A little humour infects the irony when his wealth is given to the World's servant, the boy Garcio, who cannot believe his luck, and when little Anima, Mankind's soul, who has been hidden all the while beneath the bed, now creeps out, presumably dressed in black, praying for forgiveness of his sins, only to be carried off to Hell by the Bad Angel.

The four daughters of God, Mercy, Truth, Righteousness and Peace, each in a symbolically coloured mantle of white, green, red or black (carefully indicated on the drawing), enter the acting space, kneel before God sitting on his throne [*Pater sedens in trono*] on his scaffold, and plead for divine mercy. The play ends when God shows His mercy, and the audience is reminded of the play's message:

> Thus endith oure gamys.
> To save you fro sinninge ...

Altogether a scene of incessant activity, yet with a purposeful structure based on man's uncertain progress and final decline, until the sense of the play is transparent.

The visual mode of allegory

The style of *The Castle of Perseverance* is generally one that is solemn and dignified, as befits an account of man's soul torn between good and evil and preparing to face Judgment Day. Nevertheless, within the constraints of the Scriptures, popular elements of comedy crept in. Among the Vices, wry details of dress and behaviour are deliberately provocative, and their noisy wails and complaints when they are flogged are intended for laughter. The immoderate bearing and boasting of the World, the Flesh and the Devil are comic in tone, and certain characters, like the Detraccio [Backbiter] lend themselves to the performance of a jester or a clown. Such Vices increasingly become figures of fun, and the mainstay of the popular stage. Yet this is another demonstration of that tradition in English theatre of serio-comic performance set in a tragic context, later exhibited in the surprising elements of farce in Marlowe's *Doctor Faustus* and the disturbing ironies of Shakespeare's Fool in *King Lear*. These phenomena signal a profoundly important mode of dramatic perception which permits complete contrasts of style within the whole, with the consequent increase in objectivity. The audience accepted comedy and farce in a devoutly serious play because laughter was an inseparable part of the dramatic process of manipulating its response, and this process was heavily dependent upon a stage of visual *allegory*.

The term 'allegory' derives from a Greek word meaning 'saying something in another way', and literary criticism has led us to think of allegory as a verbal metaphor pointing to a meaning beyond that of the obvious one; in its literary forms it has been applied particularly to poetry and shorter fiction, since in a true allegory the whole work must be written in the chosen mode of double meaning, and all of it perceived on the assumed level of literary obliqueness. Thus Bunyan's *The Pilgrim's Progress* offered the rare example of a long work which tells its tale of Christian's progress (in a manner not unlike that of a morality play) completely within the abstract limits established by the author from the beginning.

Yet some years ago, in *English Drama from Early Times to the Elizabethans* (1950), A. P. Rossiter invited us to consider allegory as 'picture-thinking' rather than as a demand to decode meanings, as vision rather than thought.

> When it is effective, thinking or contemplation is itself visual: there is an intuitive apprehension of significances, rather than an intellectual de-coding.

(96)

For a later generation, Marshall McLuhan advanced this idea to suggest that we think inclusively in *Gestalten* [patterns], not by some analytic dissociation of our senses. 'Consciousness is not a verbal process', he declared in *Understanding Media* (1964):

> Consciousness is regarded as the mark of a rational being,

yet there is nothing lineal or sequential about the total field
of awareness that exists in any moment of consciousness.

(87)

Allegorical drama insists that allegory on the stage also
manifests itself in 'irrational' ways, and is unlikely to respond
to a process of verbal analysis.

By the nature of theatre and the conventions of the play
performed within it, drama must always stay within its
prepared and agreed frame, a condition which is at the heart
of the ritual of dramatic performance in the first place. In the
case of a morality play, the actors impersonate characters that
are themselves impersonations, and the action of the play, and
where it is supposed to take place, must consistently pursue
and support the allegorical assumption. When he watches the
play, the spectator perceives double – he sees both what is in
front of his nose and what he is invited by convention to see
of significance beyond this. Of the double image thus engendered, part may be deadly serious, and part may be risible,
and the consequence is that at any time the audience may be
free to laugh and free to think, simultaneously if necessary.

Inclusiveness was a fundamental prerequisite of the morality play experience, and its allegorical mode, constantly
inviting comparisons that were extensions of the material,
permitted the spectator to extend his viewpoint and expand
his mind. In *The Castle of Perseverance* some of the costumes
were made emblematic by their colour, with Truth in 'sad
green', Mercy in white, Righteousness in red, and so on. But
white was also the colour of purity and innocence, and red
was also emblematic of Christ's blood shed for mankind. The
conflicts in the story, those between the Good and Bad
Angels, between man's greed and his hope of Heaven, and
many others, lead the imagination to many pertinent situations that touch ordinary life.

Allegorical doubleness worked well for drama and the
stage. In *The Castle of Perseverance* man is like a castle
besieged, yet with realistic mines and an actual fire under its
walls; good and evil fight to the death, and an actual figure of
Death, dressed in funereal black and looking suitably frightening, stands ready at the end. In the many conflicts of the

plot we sense the insistent and repeated impulse towards allegory. These conflicts are essential to performance: they made lively acting possible, set the imagination alight and saved a sober play from dullness. The figurative details flow unceasingly, whether it is an impertinent young Garcio inheriting Mankind's treasure, or a pathetic little Anima whipped from the grave and swept off to Hell.

Early localizing

From *The Castle of Perseverance* we also learn about scaffolds, thrones and houses, each of which bears a special significance in the fifteenth century. When the World is on his scaffold, he certainly sits on a chair:

> Now I sitte in my semly sale [fine hall];
> I trotte and tremle [quiver] in my trew trone,

and this image of an abstract force for evil ensconced within his assigned realm suggests that the whole acting space was set about by similar thrones placed on the circle of scaffolds that the performance plan depicts. Later, there is the further evidence of Covetousness, who invites Mankind to 'sit up ryth [right] here in this se [seat]', whereupon Mankind climbs up and joins him.

Now a curtained scaffold that conceals a particular throne, decorated appropriately and readily identified with a major character, is a workable and attractive idea. It leads smoothly to the conception of scenic 'houses' – places for the actors identified and set within the acting space, and possibly representing a castle or a whole city with its battlements. They may be related to the Stations of the Cross set inside the church, the formal mansions of the cycle plays, and again to the scenic structures erected as if for localizing purposes in the presentation of the Court masques. They will reappear in the next chapter when particular stage localities are wanted in the interludes and pageants of the sixteenth century – three tents for the principals in *Jacob and Esau* (1558), a bower for Melissa in *Misogonus* (c. 1560) or a bawdy house for Wantonness in *Wit and Wisdom* (c. 1579). The idea is given support by a near-contemporary reference to 'apte howses of paynted canvas and properties incident' in the Revels Office accounts of Queen Elizabeth (1571–89). To furnish these, it is likely that there were early scene makers who framed and fashioned the canvas.

If two or more such 'locations' are called for in a play, it is but a short step to the later concept of 'multiple staging' of the kind commonplace in Elizabethan and Jacobean production. When this occurs, the paradoxical effect of multiplying location is one of shrinking space and telescoping time.

Mankind

Exactly half-way through the performance of *Mankind*, three clownish rascals, New Guise, Nowadays and Nought, announce that they are going to take up a collection from the house, and fifty years after *The Castle of Perseverance* it seems that companies of players were everywhere making a success of plays with morality themes. The appeal was to a wider audience, and much of the script is scatological and full of broad entertainment supplied by the play's bunch of rogues and clowns, with their obscene singing and dancing, their slapstick and knockabout. For the rest, the story is a simple morality with Mercy and Titivillus as Mankind's good and bad angels, so to speak, and Mercy finally winning him over with the promise of salvation. At the end the play's moral purpose is as strong as ever.

Realistic details invigorate the dialogue – it is rich with references to winter and cold weather, and the characters owe more to human models and succeed as recognizable human types. At the centre of the play, Mankind is seen as a local farmer carrying a sack of grain and a spade as his personal props – he is an honest working man whom the devil Titivillus torments by burying a plank of wood in the earth Mankind is ploughing and stealing off with his sack of grain. Only when Mankind has lost his temper at his ill luck does he sink into the conventional pattern of temptation and sin: then it is that New Guise helps him to new clothes, and to put him in the fashion cuts his coat ridiculously short. Finally Mankind falls into a state of despair, even ignoring his former advisor Mercy, who now imitates the priest who comes to shrive Mankind before it is too late.

The script is totally workable. The props are simple and the dialogue calls for nothing specific in staging. Unlike that of *The Castle of Perseverance*, *Mankind*'s acting area, whether a booth stage set in a town square or the empty space in the middle of a Tudor hall, would have served if flanked by a door or a curtain to provide an approximation to an entrance and an exit. No scenic background is needed – there is no 'location'. The only requirement repeatedly implied in the lines is one of *intimacy* between actor and audience, and if there is a certain lack of plot, the play made up for it with a great deal of business implicit in the exchanges with the spectator. From the start Mercy addresses the audience directly as if it is fully participating and uses the actual names of ten citizens in Cambridgeshire: whether these gentlemen were real or not, nothing is more calculated to startle a spectator than to make him aware that the aesthetic gap between the stage and the real world has suddenly shrunk.

Almost no formal entrances and exits distance the action and separate the stage from its audience: in *Mankind* the term 'enter' is not used. Entrances and exits probably occur among the spectators in such a way as to minimize any formality. The three comics perform their first dance, with minstrels accompanying them, apparently in order to demonstrate what sinners look like, but since they are already in the acting space they have no real need to 'enter', and certainly not to 'make an entrance'. Thus New Guise jumps in the ring and calls for a dance:

> Ande how [ho!], minstrellys, pley the comyn trace
> [common dance]!
> Ley on with thy ballys [switch] till his bely breste [burst]!

They simply begin with a wild dance, two of them urging on the third. Later, the three are in some other part of the space, eavesdropping on the serious encounter beween Mercy and Mankind, so that their comedy is in counterpoint with the moral tenor of the lines: the spectator's eye has no difficulty in taking in both scenes at the same time. Then Nowadays pushes his way into the circle with a peremptory 'Make rom, sers!' and they invite the audience to join them in singing an obscene song by repeating each line. Finally Nowadays again calls on the audience to 'make space', this time for Titivillus in his devil's mask and tail.

Palpable as he is, this merry devil explains to the audience, 'Ever I goo invisibull' – possibly suggesting at this point a change to a new and more derisory acting style, and indicating that the spectator is to share the Devil's view and see more than Mankind can. This game is given a demonstration when at line 589 Mankind falls asleep and snores. Then Titivillus whispers the idea into his ear that Mercy has been hanged for a horsethief, and in so doing compels the spectator to share the conspiracy of lies with him, making him villain and victim both:

> Not a worde, I charge yow, peyn of forty pens!
> A praty [crafty] game shall be schewde yow, or ye go hens.

The audience must have rather enjoyed its double role, if not the actual duplicity itself.

Indoor performance and the Tudor hall

Performance in a hall is not infrequently mentioned in morality play texts, and most moralities were played in the great hall of a local guildhall or manor house before its lord or squire. *Fulgens and Lucrece* (c. 1497) and *The Four Elements* (c. 1517) both mention such a hall. Such a place was the hub of the wealthy house, in regular use for the eating of meals and the social recreation of the well-born family.

The usual Tudor hall or great chamber was about fifty feet long and thirty feet wide, a comfortable size for the performance of a play, although the specific dimensions and the geometry of the rectangle imposed new rules on its writing and performance. While the commanding qualities of intimacy and ritualism were carried over from playing in the round, different architectural conditions, together with torchlight performance at night, were imposed on the drama and controlled how it was perceived.

The rectangular shape of the Tudor hall, with doors or an entry of sorts at each end (Medwall's *Nature* (c. 1501), mentions the 'dorys') and with heavy refectory tables ranged round the sides, not only provided a central acting space, but also introduced for the first time the possibility of a focal point for the actors at either end of the room. The matter is complicated because one end embodied a screen which masked the passage from an exterior door to the kitchen or buttery and traditionally had two doors leading into the main part of the hall, while the other end was situated near the raised dais that was provided for the high table. A fireplace was also usual in the side wall of such a hall, and one such is referred to in *John John* (c. 1529).

The matter is further complicated by other external evidence. When Plautus's *Aulularia* was played in Cambridge before Queen Elizabeth in 1564, such a stage extended across the nave of King's College Chapel, the side chapels serving as two houses for the play (John Nichols, *The Progresses and Public Processions of Queen Elizabeth* (1788) names 'a great stage containing the breadth of the church from one side to the other, that the chappels might serve for houses'). And when the Queen visited Christ Church, Oxford in 1566, the hall was set with a raised stage at the end opposite to the high table.

All this suggests that there were no firm rules about the arrangement of the acting area inside a great hall at this date. Nevertheless, in imagining a common setting for a morality play, some scholars have shown an inclination to anticipate the thrust stage of the Elizabethan playhouse platform with its twin upstage doors, and have gone so far as to supply a curtained platform and a pair of doors in front of the hall screen of the Tudor manor house, with the hint of a tiring house behind it. Nevertheless, until James Burbage's Theatre of 1576, no playing space that we know of in England boasted a permanent stage platform. It would be fair to say that frontal or end staging of any kind seems to have been unnecessary to plays of this period, whereas the flexibility of playing in the round remained an asset in itself. As long as the Tudor hall remained right for size, accoustics and visibility it served for many years.

Emerging conventions

During the fifteenth century the morality stage adopted many elements of theatre that had graced the earlier drama: the acting and clowning, the costumes and pageantry, the minstrels and their popular music. The period also saw the rapid development of important conventions which were tested and found useful.

The sermon in the play, its didactic underpinning, urged the morality form towards analogy and allegory; if preachers used parables, so did a drama morally conditioned to point up a firm message. The result could be at its worst an assembly of allegorical platitudes and characters imprisoned in abstraction, or at its best it could reflect a vitality belonging to its time. For one instance, the figure of Death could remain the commonplace *memento mori* of the Middle Ages, or, cleverly deployed, it could terrifyingly recall the fullness of youth and beauty in the life it denied, as when Death stops Everyman short while he is having a good time and thinking least of his mortality. The allegorical stage could capture images that were overwhelmingly emotional, yet also thought-provoking; supporting a religious theme, yet answering a full community need.

In the conventions of morality characterization, abstract notions of vice and virtue limited any three-dimensional qualities, but this negative burden could be redressed and balanced in several ways, as *Everyman* demonstrates. The arrangement of the characters could be illuminating in itself, just as Everyman's friends are true or false each in his own way. An individual character might seem more realistic than abstract, as in *Everyman* where Fellowship, Kindred and Cousin acquire human qualities that are rounded and recognizable. The relationship of two characters could be dramatically alive, like that between Everyman and Good Deeds whose intimacy grows stronger as they near the grave together. It is no surprise that successful anthropomorphic characters (if abstract, but living, characters may be so called) have persisted from Ben Jonson to Charles Dickens.

Yet the greatest strength in a morality play lay always in the central part. The character usually had a name like 'Mankind',

'Everyman' or 'Youth', and he was the human being whose
weaknesses and temptations were understandable and with
whose humanity an audience could identify. His progress
throughout the play held it together as a dramatic structure.
This kind of 'Everyman' was soon to grow to become
Faustus, and even to acquire another sublime dimension in
the role of a Lear or a Prospero.

The mode of this drama was still nevertheless independent
of 'illusion' and did not require acceptance of the story as a
reality, the stage as an actual location or the scene as a
particular place and time. All the acting conventions found
within the writing contributed, however, to a sense of con-
temporaneity in the performance of the play: the use of
prologue or presenter to establish a bridge with the stage;
repeated address to the audience; the frank and open narration
of the plot; the simple announcement that someone was about
to enter; the periodic and conscious reference to the idea of
performance in the way that is now called 'metadramatic'; and
other features of this kind which made the spectator feel
accountable for what was taking place. This mode of performance also induced the sense that the action of the play is here
and now.

The achievement of *Everyman*

The Dutch *Elckerlijk* was translated into English as *Everyman*
(c. 1495) and proved to be the finest of the moralities, straightforward in staging and powerful in its simplicity. It is unlike
Mankind: it eschews the customary banter with the audience
and as a result it forgoes much of the usual humour; but what
it loses in comedy it gains in solemnity. Its tone is sober as if
the stage has accepted the challenge of a sacramental mission:
it keeps firmly in sight its theme of the divine law and the
responsibilities of a Christian, and, like *The Castle of Perseverance*, it presents a spiritual allegory of the sinner about to meet
his Maker. However, the coming of death and the moment of
dying are subjects of universal and undying appeal, and the
play never loses its grip on what is real and human.

The play is totally stageworthy and has stood the test of time. Props are few – an account book, a knotted scourge, a robe of contrition, a crucifix. Staging is simple – an open space with a throne for God, who must sit 'in the hye sete celestiall'; this is placed in or near the 'hous of salvacion' where Everyman will make confession; and his grave may be suggested by a box or a trap. But essentially this space is unlocalized, as if the action takes place in Everyman's head and the spectator's mind.

The play also remains more workable than other moralities because of its adept use of its central character. The human decline into sin and a catalogue of transgressions are commonplace, but Everyman's slow, belated recognition of the frailty of his body and the unsatisfactory state of his soul is all-pervasive. As a play about the instant of death, the theme had to be expanded and treated retrospectively, so that after a long prologue by a Messenger and then by God, the audience is granted a kind of extended flashback of human experience instead of what might otherwise have been a tedious preacher's warning of mortality. Thus the play rehearses Everyman's past as if it were a painful journey to the grave and Judgment Day, the pilgrimage of life and death, the knowledge of which the audience shares moment by moment as a foretaste of what is to come. Every time Everyman is spoken of by name, each spectator hears 'every man' and assumes that he is addressed individually.

When Everyman enters, he is first seen through the eyes of a brisk and businesslike Death. This Everyman is evidently pleased with himself (some modern directors go farther and show him drunk) and he is 'gaily' [colourfully] dressed, wearing clothing that will later be significantly changed to the penitentially drab tones of the 'garment of sorowe'. The style is pointedly colloquial, and every line reflects the intended performance:

> DETHE. Everyman, stande still! Whider arte thou goinge
> Thus gaily? Hast thou thy Maker forgete?
> EVERYMAN. Why asketh thou?

Everyman is told how to dress and how to walk, then is accosted unexpectedly and stopped in his tracks; yet this line is so effective that it could also be delivered as a whisper in the ear with equally striking force. By watching Everyman fulfil these early instructions the audience sees him behave with almost amusing predictability.

The pace of life and the urgency of death are captured in the action and structure of the play. The arrival of Death as a character comes as a surprise and a shock, and on 'I am Dethe' Everyman realizes to whom he is talking and his fear grows quickly. The audience sees and hears his mortal panic, and the sensation is one of the acute pressure of time:

> – To give a rekeninge, longer laiser [leisure] I crave!
> – Full unredy I am suche rekeninge to give.
> – Now, gentill Deth, spare me till tomorowe.
> – And also my writinge is full unredy.

The reiterations continue, until finally Everyman's complaints all come together: 'The time passeth. Lorde, helpe, that all wrought!' He is in anguish at the passing of time, but the audience sees that Death has already left him to his own slim resources.

Everyman's relationship with his sins is presented in lively little scenes and each one is made to seem human. Fellowship, Kindred, Cousin and Goods are like hypocritical friends, and not the regular gang of vices. The meeting with Fellowship comes across naturally, with voices neatly in contrast, Fellowship spirited, Everyman dispirited:

> Everyman, good morowe, by this daye!
> Sir, why lokest thou so piteously?

Each in turn refuses to accompany Everyman to the grave: Kindred offers his servant in his place; Cousin protests, 'I have the crampe in my to'; and Goods is afraid that he is 'too britell, I may not endure'. Unusually, they achieve realistic qualities without the application of farcical devices, and the basic seriousness of the play is consistent and sustained – a matter of importance if the play is speaking for the Church about the sacraments, especially about making amends for sin by doing penance through contrition, confession, satisfaction and absolution.

By the insistent repetition of the words 'journey', 'voyage', 'pilgrimage', the illusion is given that Everyman is more on the move about the stage than he is. But the process to the grave is carefully enacted step by step, and, as always, the audience enjoys the anticipation of the inevitable. Good Deeds, at first weak and lying 'colde in the grounde', replaces Goods, and Knowledge replaces Fellowship – two sisters who will stand on either side of Everyman when he prays and does penance. When he grows tired ('Alas, I am so faint I may not stande!'), Beauty and Strength fall away, followed by Discretion, then by Five Wits ('Everyman, my leve now of the I take. I will folowe the other'). Like Faustus's last moments, Everyman's are spread thin, as if his end, being predestined, must be witnessed in slow motion. Dying is an act caught in suspension as the focus narrows and concentrates exclusively on a focal character seen increasingly as lonely and alone, and therefore on the audience's sense of mortality. Only Good Deeds stays with him to the grave, until 'aungelles singe' and an Aungell welcomes him to Heaven – with offers of a comparable salvation to everyone who has witnessed Everyman's story.

Everyman is now part of the modern repertoire. Since William Poel revived it in 1901, H. Walford Davies has set it to music (1904) and it has been played as an opera (1915). Since 1950, the Dutch version has been presented annually in Delft. The most famous of all treatments was Max Reinhardt's for the Salzburg Festival, where the name of Jedermann [Everyman] was made to echo eerily from every roof and tower in the city. This was Hugo von Hofmannsthal's poetic version of 1911 played nearly every year after 1920, the open air performances developing in characteristic Reinhardt style with each new production. His Everyman became a wealthy burgher, and Beauty became his mistress; he gained a mother who pathetically followed his coffin at the funeral. New characters named the Thin and Fat Cousins were developed to broaden the comedy, and Mammon was introduced especially to emphasize the motif of material acquisitiveness. The production in the Domplatz before Salzburg Cathedral, while in no way recalling medieval stagecraft, is nevertheless still a gratifying echo of the play's popular origins in the fifteenth century.

3

The Tudor interlude

A perplexing name

Some of the plays known as moralities were also 'interludes'. It is not known how the interlude came to be called its awkward name, but most scholars believe that it implies a play performed in an interval or intermission during a social occasion like a banquet, so that it is virtually synonymous with 'an entertainment'. The occasion might be a celebration in the private house of a noble lord or a city gentleman, or in a mayoral hall; or it might mark a feast day for a college or an Inn of Court. As a technical term it does not in any way define a genre, nor describe its content or purpose. Instead, many of the plays presented during the middle of the sixteenth century are lumped together as interludes, even though they display a variety of staging elements that persisted from earlier religious and morality drama. They also embrace many of the sub-genres that became common in later Elizabethan theatre, for example, the history or chronicle play, comedy and farce, and tragedy and tragi-comedy. If these plays had anything in common, it was that their authors wrote from outside the Church. The type is to be defined by its individual constituents, sometimes moral, sometimes allegorical, sometimes neither. It may be concluded that 'interlude' is an umbrella term under which is found almost any secular Tudor play.

There is more that complicates any picture of the Tudor interlude. It can take its nourishment from a variety of accessible dramatic forms, any of which may affect its stagecraft:

(1) *The English morality play*, whose patterns are still to be seen in plays as late as Marlowe's *Doctor Faustus* (c. 1588).

Glynne Wickham coins the term 'moral interlude' to suggest a frequent commitment to a theme of moral order (*Shakespeare's Dramatic Heritage* (1969), 26).

(2) *The native folk drama*, with its mumming tradition of plays about champions, challenges and combats, and its joyful inclusion of ballad singing and rustic dances.

(3) *The Roman drama* of Plautus, Terence and Seneca, the familiar classics read and performed in Latin by boys and young men in school and university.

(4) The material of *French farce*, mixed freely with a native knockabout, clowning performance. A certain quality of hearty realism is especially present in the plays of John Heywood, for example, in *The Pardoner and the Friar* and *John John*.

That said, the plays conveniently grouped in this chapter are as heterogeneous as the name 'interlude' itself. *Fulgens and Lucrece* and *Magnificence* were labelled interludes, but *John John* and *Gammer Gurton's Needle* were offered as comedies, and *Cambises* and *Gorboduc* as tragedies. These plays reflect the capricious diversity of the drama that falls into the sixteenth century, a period of gestation subject to every wind that blew. Any definition of an interlude should suggest the following qualities that tend to recur:

(1) A broad element of *inventive unreality* in the treatment, paradoxically manifested by the play's awareness of the real presence of its audience; this is the spirit behind the 'intimate' or reciprocal entertainment found in modern music hall, cabaret and revue.

(2) Relatively *uncomplicated staging* with few scenic requirements; flexibility, adaptability and mobility are the watchwords for production.

(3) The possibility of *music, song and dance*, all characteristic expressions of the unreal, intimate mode, and formally associated later with the masque, the sophisticated form of balletic musical entertainment that developed at Court in the later years of the century.

(4) *Symbolic costumes and properties*: extravagant dress would suggest godless prodigality, a beggar would display his

rags, a rich man hug his money bags, a vain man flaunt his frills and feathers.

(5) Bold, *two-dimensional characterization* that was quickly identifiable and calling for an instant response. This also made casting simple and doubling possible. (The development of individual characterization is one of the astonishing changes at the end of the century.)

The occasion and the spirit: *Fulgens and Lucrece*

Although its author, Henry Medwall (*fl.* 1490), was a clerk in holy orders, the performance of *Fulgens and Lucrece* (*c.* 1497) was secular, and the play in itself almost defines the term 'interlude': eating and drinking are mentioned frequently, and a banquet appears to be suspended in order that Part I may be played, after which Part II is performed 'aboute Suppere' – presumably after the last course – on the same day. However, in this play the spirit of occasion is felt in its conspicuous informality, and although the story of Medwall's play is set in the past, it seems to take place in the present because it is alive with touches of improvisation. The author was chaplain to John Morton, Archbishop of Canterbury, in whose household improvising a play was a popular pastime. Thomas More grew up in that household, and according to William Roper in his *Life of Sir Thomas More* (1626) would 'sodenly somtymes stepp in among the players, and never studyinge for the matter, make a parte of his owne there presently among them, which made the onlookers more sport than all the players beside'.

In the interlude, like the morality play, the form of a 'debate' was common, and in *Fulgens and Lucrece* that between the rich nobleman Cornelius and the virtuous gentleman Gaius Flaminius eventually controls the action in Part II. Nevertheless, this is only a small part of the whole, and the free-wheeling comic characters 'A' and 'B' dominate two-thirds of Part I. They are there primarily to catch the attention of the audience and amuse it, but in the event their sub-plot, in which they woo the servant girl Joan, not only parodies the main plot, it may even usurp it.

Fulgens and Lucrece begins when someone unannounced actually jumps up from the audience crying, 'For Goddis will!', and then pushes through the crowd:

> What meane ye, syrs, to stond so still?
> Have ye not etyn and your fill,
> And payd nothinge therfore?

'What are you waiting for?' is his theme. He spots someone he knows who tells him there is to be a play and before you know it, Medwall has created two characters, 'A' and 'B'.

> A. Shall there be a play?
> B. Ye, for certeyn.
> A. By my trouth, therof am I glad and fayn,
>   And ye will me beleve.
>   Of all the worlde I love suche sport ...

A and B then proceed to introduce the story of the play. Medwall has chosen to label these two nondescript players simply 'A' and 'B', and they are well named: in a sense, they are nobody and everybody. Moreover, they are both in and out of the play, now as actors and now as spectators. They belong to a drama of improvisation.

Improvisation informs the process of performance, and notwithstanding the *'intrat'* [let him enter] and *'exeat'* [let him go out] in the script – and at one point in English *'Avoyde the place A'* – the clowns seem to enter from the audience or from behind it, often speaking (*'dicens'*) directly to those around them as they do so:

> – What meane ye, syrs?
> – But how say you, syrs?
> – What now, syrs? How goth the game?

On one occasion B enters by knocking, perhaps on a door. A says, 'I here hym knocke' and then invites someone in the audience to see who it is – 'One of you go loke' – so that the audience seems always to be involved in the action. This role for A and B keeps the two clowns at the centre of the performance, to the point where they are not only 'presenters' or chorus figures in some degree detached from the proceedings, but also spectators themselves, seeing with the eyes of the audience, and, when they become servants to the suitors, characters too.

Of this comic duo, it is B, fractionally more the insider, who speaks fifty-six lines of what used to be called 'the argument' of the story. Fulgens is a Roman senator, the hand of whose incomparable daughter Lucrece is sought in marriage by both a rich patrician, Publius Cornelius, and a virtuous plebeian, Gaius Flaminius. Fulgens has decided to give Lucrece the choice of a husband, and she says that she will have the more noble of the two. B even anticipates which suitor will win. Everything seems rather predictable, until, having drained the play of suspense, Medwall has A disagree with the expected outcome. This development has the force of keeping A and B in a brisk and stimulating – a consciously metadramatic – relationship with the audience.

B is next employed to announce the entrance of Fulgens. Again, the manner in which B speaks has more to do with signalling the mode of the performance than with any story, and the importance of the principal player is by that much diminished.

> B. Pees, no moo wordes, for now they come,
> The plears [players] bene evyn here at hand.
> A. So thei be, so help me God and halydome [domesday],
> I pray you, tell me where I shall stand.
> B. Mary, stand evyn here by me, I warand.
> Geve rome there, syrs, for God avowe
> Thei wold come in if thei myght for you.

There are no less than twelve lines of this kind before Fulgens comes in, and when he does, it is with the direction '*Intrat* Fulgens, *dicens*', suggesting that he makes his entrance speaking from outside the hall with little ceremony.

Nevertheless A and B finally enter the story as servants, and it is this that prompts a great block of new business, and wooing 'gentyll Jone', Lucrece's maid, introduces a new dimension of style and purpose to the action. The scenes of wooing this boy actor-maid are a simple parody of the main plot of wooing her boy actor-mistress, and done at a vigorous, physical level, constituting a burlesque device of a kind that was subsequently to enliven the Elizabethan stage time and again. '*Come in the maydyn*' is the cue for an attempted kiss by B, and 'Tusshe, I pray you, let me go' is her response. He eventually manages to embrace this 'flowre of the frying pane', and '*et osculabitur*' [and he shall kiss] is the direction at the very moment that A enters for the classic triangular interruption of farce. At the height of a mock chivalric altercation in which B throws down his glove to A in a challenge, Joan trusses them up with their arms behind their backs and pushes staves probably between their elbows, 'thorow here', so that their duel takes on the appearance of a cockfight. The scene ends when clever Joan declares that she is betrothed to another, whereupon she beats them both.

This comic scene lasts some four hundred lines and in its burlesque tends artfully to distract the spectator from the main plot. However, the didactic spirit of the morality play finally returns and Cornelius and Flaminius warmly dispute whether the source of true nobility lies in high birth or in virtuous conduct. Lucrece will choose the latter. This more consequential material is likely to be played centre stage – ironically on the spot where the clowns had a moment before been in laughable physical contention. The serious tone of the debate is even relieved by music and dancing, and the play is brought to a conclusion, not by Fulgens or Lucrece, but by further comic banter from A and B.

The improvisational mode

Improvisation or extemporizing on the stage permits the actors themselves to take charge of the action. Thereby it lessens the importance of the plotting, and places greater emphasis on the pleasures of the journey rather than its destination. The improvisational spirit in medieval drama manifested itself in several ways:

(1) *In forms of speech.* To provide the right words for improvised performance seems to be a contradiction; however, in *Fulgens and Lucrece* A and B speak in '*rime couée*,' a short, colloquial stanza form mixing six and eight syllable lines. When the principal characters speak,

3 *Fulgens and Lucrece, c.* 1497: frontispiece from the facsimile in the Huntington Library, California; the costumes are not in Roman style, but in that contemporary with the printed play (*c.* 1520).

this easy style is replaced for contrast by the more formal and dignified rhyme-royal stanza of seven regular decasyllabic lines rhyming ababbcc.

(2) *In the staging and setting.* Like most interludes, *Fulgens and Lucrece* needs no scenic or other stage devices, and this freedom, together with the spatial licence granted by the Tudor hall, encouraged the less restricted and disciplined performance that prompts informality and improvisation.

(3) *In frequent address to the audience,* as if the external

relationship between actor and spectator should take precedence over the workings of the internal story. Singing songs to the audience is in the same spontaneous spirit.

(4) *In a realistic vein of comedy.* The lighter spirit of vulgar realism often lent the moral ingredient of the play its vigour. In the case of *Fulgens and Lucrece*, the serious subject is a formal 'disputacyon of noblenes', as the title page insists, but the debate takes up only four hundred lines of a total 2,353, and by far the more entertaining part of the play is supplied by A and B, lowlife characters who are essentially outside the story proper.

(5) *In horseplay and clowning.* In a clown show all the emphasis is on the actor, and the special skills of the medieval clown were evidently in high demand. Audiences also anticipated the regular appearance of the 'Vice', a character who was, like any clown, partly outside the main action. As will be seen, he thrived dramatically by taking different forms: it has even been suggested that he was a composite of the Deadly Sins, and had in his make-up a strong streak of the Devil. Yet in performance he suggested a delightful ambivalence, since while the sober side of the spectator wanted the Vice to get his just deserts, another side wanted him to get off scot-free, and he consequently hung between an aesthetic Hell and Heaven. The Vice has been called a 'goblin jester', and goblin humour crackles in many Elizabethan villains.

Although the spirit of immediacy is, in the nature of the art, present in every age of drama, it is strongly felt in the Tudor interludes. In this vein of ribald comic anecdote, rich in bawdy asides, homespun stage props and coarse stage business, are the lively plays of John Heywood (*c.* 1497–1580), who described himself as 'of mad merry mirth', and his contemporary Bishop John Bale reported on his time spent arranging Court entertainments that involved music and dancing, plays and pageants. Heywood was the probable author of four comedies performed in the 1520s: *The Pardoner and the Friar, The Play of Love, The Play of the*

Weather and *John John the Husband*. Of equal interest, the comedy of *The Four P's* has also been attributed to him.

The drama seeks new fields: *Magnificence* and politics

An art form that could as readily embrace a vulgar farce as a moral debate was wonderfully serviceable and responsive, and so the new drama must have seemed in the sixteenth century. Before the century had ended, the stage had tried out much that it knew from past literature, testing the power of performance to handle history and politics, comedy and tragedy. On the ecclesiastical and political tidal wave that floated the Protestant churches, the stage, using morality play patterns of debate and allegory and satire, lent itself naturally to doctrinal issues and controversies, and thrived on the politics of Church and state.

John Skelton (1460–1529) has one surviving play, *Magnificence* (c. 1516), which is often taken to be an indirect criticism of the young King Henry VIII and the worldly politics of Cardinal Wolsey and his influence over the Court; but the shadows of all men of birth and power, as well as of King and chancellor, are to be seen behind its satire about rule and corruption, and the play's political target is a wide one. It carries the title-page description, 'a goodly interlude, and a mery', but when it cautions against prodigality and the advice of false friends, it aims its barbs at the Court and its courtiers. Its hero, Magnificence, is 'a noble prince of might', but in the idiom of the morality stage his figure also denotes a general concept of statesmanship, ranging between splendid munificence and petty vanity.

It is a long play of 2,567 lines, and an outline of the action suggests a little of the wealth of stageworthy ideas that follow one upon another. At the outset, Magnificence is surrounded by people who incline towards virtue; he speaks with noble rhetoric. When Measure leaves him, and when Fancy in the guise of 'Largesse' and bearing a forged letter of introduction takes his place, the prince's former dignity leaves him. He is now beset by Counterfeit Countenance, Crafty Conveyance, Cloaked Collusion and Courtly Abusion, rogues and hypocrites every one. Skelton thereupon grants this ugly crew some thirty minutes of intrigue and comedy for them to make themselves known to the audience and form a conspiracy. To assist an audience who must tolerate a great deal of doubling among the actors, nearly all the characters are identified by distinctive speech and manner, as well as by prop and costume. Countenance probably wears a mask; Conveyance carries his forgeries; Collusion walks up and down *'cum elato aspectu'* [with a haughty expression] and wears a long cloak; Courtly Abusion makes his entrance virtually singing and dancing, and is a gallant who is very pleased with his appearance:

> My hair busheth
> So pleasantly,
> My robe rusheth [flows]
> So ruttingly [dashingly] ...

There are thirteen stanzas in this vein, each a gift to the comedian lucky enough to get the part.

When Magnificence is seen again, a new note of arrogance is in his voice:

> For now, sirs, I am like as a prince should be:
> I have wealth at will, largesse and liberty.

Abusion offers him princely pleasures, including a mistress, 'a lusty lass' with 'veins as azure indy blue', skin 'lily white' and 'lips ruddy as the cherry'. But retribution hurries on, and it is not long before Fancy, now dressed as a fool, enters sobbing to announce the loss of Magnificence's wealth.

On the stage, there follows an immediate change in the style, and the spirit of the morality play returns with a rush. Adversity enters like Death in *Everyman*, an ominous figure who speaks now at considerable length in heavy couplets. The stage direction reads, *'Here Magnificence is beaten down and spoiled from all his goods and raiment'*, and Adversity apparently achieves this with a wave of his hand. Poverty makes his grim appearance, ragged and diseased, and carries his victim and sets him down *'super locum stratum'* [on a place for a bed], possibly on a cloth or on straw. Moaning on the ground and now in rags, Magnificence is the epitome of wretchedness.

It is then that Skelton devises one of his strongest dramatic contrasts, in order to remind the audience sharply of how things were at the beginning of the play:

> MAGNIFICENCE. Alas my folly, alas my wanton will!
> I may no more speak till I have wept my fill.
> (*Enter* LIBERTY)
> LIBERTY (*sings*). With yea marry, sirs, thus should it be:
> I kissed her sweet, and she kissed me;
> I danced the darling on my knee; ... etc.

As Magnificence grovels on the floor, his former associate Liberty appears to trip over his body, and, addressing the spectators, asks with surprise, 'Who is that?' When a horn summons Liberty to his next assignment, it is as if the whole story will be repeated elsewhere, in some other court, on some other stage.

Magnificence must pass through a state of despair and even attempt suicide (Mischief shortly enters with halter and knife) before he is finally, but not unexpectedly, saved. The end comes somewhat abruptly at the hands of the *deus ex machina* figure of Good Hope, who, with the help of Redress, Circumspection and Perseverance, exchange Magnificence's rags for a symbolic garment of grace. This drama is shapely in a modern way, and could even be arranged as if it were a play in five acts, rising to an emotional crisis before its emphatic dénouement.

In spite of the play's length, the marks of its stageworthiness are visible on almost every page. Three of its features are especially characteristic of medieval performance:

(1) It contains a striking example of Tudor *doubling*, whereby a script calling for eighteen parts could be satisfied by five players: this was facilitated by the many moments of soliloquy, which give actors going off-stage time to change, and by the practice of having an on-stage character describe another about to enter and then draw attention to him with a deictic word like 'yond' or 'lo' ('But yond commeth ...').

(2) *Consciousness of performance* is constantly present. There are six references to the acting area as the 'place', which appears to have been all the available space inside some great hall (probably set for a banquet, since Folly must

enter *'beating on tables'*): London's Merchant Taylor's Hall has been suggested. There are repeated addresses to the audience, on one occasion even asking it to stand back. Above all, implicit directions to the actor are ongoing, and in the Folio text numerous explicit stage directions are included both in Latin and in English. Skelton provides an extraordinary example of business detail when Magnificence reads his forged letter:

> *Here let him make as if he were reading the letter silently. Meanwhile let* COUNTERFEIT COUNTENANCE *come on singing, who on seeing* MAGNIFICENCE *should softly retreat on tiptoe. At the right moment, after a while, let* COUNTER-FEIT COUNTENANCE *approach again looking out and calling from a distance, and* FANCY *motions silence with his hand.*

> (trans. Paula Neuss)

(3) More than all this is the evidence of *aural variety* built into the sequences in the play. The choice of verse form and an appropriate language are used to match the differences between characters and suit the development of the action, and this is felt from the start. A solemn Latinate opening of four–stress rhyme-royal stanzas promotes the appearance of Magnificence with his 'noble port and fame'; with the entrance of Fancy, colloquial couplets lighten the tone in preparation for the conspiracy of the vices. 'Skeltonics', occasional bits of two–stress rhyming doggerel, are the basis for a loose verse style for which the poet is well known, and they serve his play-writing well when he needs to suggest corruption in the Court through a more vulgar, racy speech and behaviour. Skelton's unusual lines regularly indicate that he is experimenting with a new way to help his actor do his work and get another response from his audience.

Old bottles, new wine: politics and history

The drama, child of fantasy and vision, is capable of endless enterprises of the imagination, and in the pursuit of a political theme, is quick to mix fact with fiction. In the sixteenth century it did not hesitate to combine a moral purpose with the history of an actual King, finding that imagination and truth draw strength from one another, and it is not hard to see where the stage's licence to bend history might make political points in dramatic form.

Under the patronage of the Lord Chancellor, Thomas Cromwell, Bishop John Bale (1495–1563) was the author of twenty and more plays, most of them lost. In *King John*, which was acted before Thomas Cranmer, the Archbishop of Canterbury, at Christmas, 1538, Bale made the remarkable experiment of dipping into a period of the remote past (some four hundred years earlier) in order to bolster his fierce promotion of the contemporary Protestant cause. There is not much in the history of King John to support Henry VIII's case for becoming the head of the Church in England, but this was Bale's grand design: the first history play in English drama was presented in the belief that the reign of King John saw the start of 'the putting down of the bishop of Rome', and so the stage managed to overlay the abstract allegory of personified characters with the more compelling representation of historical figures.

Summoning the three estates of the Nobility, the Clergy and the Law to a Parliament, King John announces that he will assert the supremacy of the English throne over the Roman Church in the matter of the Pope's appointment of the Archbishop of Canterbury. The conflict between King and Pope is nicely theatricalized when towards the end of the first part the Vice characters of Usurped Power, Private Wealth and Sedition exit in order to make a rapid change of costume, and return soon after dressed as the Pope, Cardinal Pandulph (the papal legate) and Stephen Langton (the new archbishop); the Vice Dissimulation also turns into first the monk Raymundus and then the poisoner Simon of Swynsett. By this device, doubling and disguising in this play constitute an ingenious method of overtly demonstrating hypocrisy. When the imposing figure of Imperial Majesty (representing Henry VIII himself) enters to put affairs to rights, the play is seen as more a foregone conclusion than a debate, more of a morality than a true history, but this matters less than that it introduces the fascinating possibility of using the stage to make an allegory of actuality. In its day its audience spotted with surprise and delight the figures it had known before only as historical hearsay, and felt that contemporary politics was being paraded across the stage before its eyes.

The great morality play of the Scottish theatre was Lindsay's panoramic *Satire of the Three Estates*, performed at Linlithgow, near Edinburgh, in 1540. Sir David Lindsay (1490–1555) was an official of the Scottish Court, and the title of his play suggests his sweeping intention of attacking corruption in all parts of society. Its central character, King Humanity, is first shown enthroned on a scaffold in the traditional way, and the play begins with his seduction by Lady Sensuality and her waiting-women. This is the first of several subversive attacks upon man and his government, during which, in a mock baptism, three Vices change their image from Deceit, Flattery and Falsehood to Discretion, Devotion and Sapience in order to become the King's treasurer, counsellor and secretary. The play ends predictably with the three estates in the stocks, the unfrocking of the ecclesiastics and, with a roll of drums, the merry hanging of the Vices.

Like *John John the Husband* and *King John*, *A Satire of the Three Estates* is written as a metrical medley, chiefly done in springing four–beat couplets, with an abundance of song and dance and comic business punctuating the more solemn scenes of Court corruption. In terms of broad farce and low comedy, indeed, irrepressible portraits of Pardoner, Friar and Parson, Tailor, Souter [cobbler] and their termagant wives enliven the action. The Tudor trick of using a costume change to make a sharp moral point, as seen in *King John*, is also frequent in *A Satire of the Three Estates*: Flattery is disguised as the Friar, but when his habit is pulled off, he is shown to be in fool's motley; when the Prioress's habit is removed, the gaudy colours of a harlot are revealed; and the true trappings of the Spiritual Estate, represented by Bishop, Abbot and Parson, are also shown to be motley. The device of unexpectedly switching costumes makes for arresting stagecraft, and it becomes less a way of suggesting a disguise or of helping the actor play more than one part, common enough in plays of this period, than of dramatically disclosing, explaining and giving depth to a character's identity.

Beside such theatrical ingenuity, this play exhibits another characteristic of popular drama at this time, that of direct address to the audience, and it was this, among other qualities in the text, that persuaded Tyrone Guthrie to produce the play in the large, square, open auditorium of the Assembly Hall of the Scottish Kirk for the first Edinburgh Festival in 1948. The play was adapted by Robert Kemp and has been revived several times in later years. In his autobiography, *A Life in the Theatre* (1959), Guthrie wrote of the difficulties of presenting the play in a modern theatre:

> Scene after scene seemed absolutely unplayable on a proscenium stage, almost meaningless in terms of 'dramatic illusion'; but seemed at the same time to offer fascinating possibilities.

(306)

Inside the Assembly Hall he therefore decided to build a platform that could be thrust into the middle of the spectators, who were thereby disposed on three sides of the actors. The result was a theatrical experience that was new to modern audiences:

> All the time, but unemphatically and by inference, each member of the audience was being ceaselessly reminded that he was not lost in an illusion, was not at the Court of King Humanity in sixteenth-century Scotland, but was in fact a member of a large audience, taking part, 'assisting' as the French very properly put it, in a performance, a participant in a ritual.

(311)

The comic dimension: *Ralph Roister Doister, Gammer Gurton's Needle*

The persistent form throughout the Tudor period was comedy. It permitted the steady introduction of the vernacular to the stage, and encouraged the more genial and ironic observation of people and society that has often been the lifeblood of popular theatre. It sought new material where it could find it. At a time when the Roman New Comedy of

Plautus and Terence was pleasing new readers and audiences in school and university, the burgeoning Tudor stage discovered in it a source of dramatic life that offered a world of fresh ideas and directions fairly free of the moralizing imperative. One of the side-effects of this recharging of energy was the perhaps unfortunate stereotyping of character and situation, and it is hard to understand why Tudor playwrights adopted such mechanical elements of a drama so alien in time and place. Nevertheless, the fixed characters and wooden plotting of Roman comedy finally did nothing to suppress the native English spirit.

Ralph Roister Doister (c. 1553) is the only certain surviving play of Nicholas Udall (1505–56), headmaster of Eton and Westminster, and it was at one time assumed to have been written for a group of his boys. Following Renaissance thinking about classical forms, the play is divided into five acts and broken into scenes according to the entrance of characters; it also manages to a degree a unity of time and place – in the manner of the Roman theatre the scene is a street in front of the house which is the play's focus of attention. But it cannot be said that these restraints greatly affected the dramatic structure of the action, which lopes along at its own pace towards a resolution, and is otherwise full of the verbal wit, instrumental music, singing and slapstick of its own cheerful devising.

The part of Ralph Roister Doister is borrowed boldly from Plautus's braggart in *Miles Gloriosus* and Terence's Thraso in *Eunuchus*, but, although the character is a 'type' and his situation mechanical, the happy spirit of London's lowlife is inextricably woven through the action. Ralph is an English coward ('to roister' meant 'to bluster'): 'All the day long is he facing and craking [swaggering and bragging] / Of his great actes in fighting and fraymaking', but he is really only 'as fierce as a Cottssold lyon' [as brave as a Cotswold sheep]. He is the epitome of vanity, believing all women to be in love with him, and he decides to woo the widow Dame Christian Custance, but only because she is wealthy and he needs the money (the notion that she is 'worthe a thousande pounde' is used like a refrain in 1.2). He is aided and abetted by Matthew Merrygreek, who combines the Roman part of parasite

('Greek' implied cunning) and that of the comic Vice from the English morality, living by his wits and playing all the parts as necessary. Thus Matthew flatters his master brazenly and adopts the outrageous ruse of saying that everyone has likened Ralph to the heroes of old.

The play is sprinkled with strong comic scenes involving Matthew's trickery and treachery, including such jokes as Ralph's performance as the great lover of the servant's hall in 1.2, the burlesque of a burial and the mock requiem Matthew chants for his lovesick master in 3.3 and the mispunctuated love-letter he reads aloud in 3.4. More interesting, however, are the lowlife characters of the play, all appropriately named in order to establish their obvious personae: the gullible old nurse Madge Mumblecrust and the maidservants Tibet Talkapace and Annot Alyface (possibly 'Ale-face'), gossips all. Add to these Ralph's servants, Dobinet Doughty and Harpax, and several others, and the stage is soon peopled with comic 'background' figures commenting on the main events, not unlike a chorus of Dorset villagers in Thomas Hardy. The fourth act erupts into a fracas between, on one side, Ralph and Matthew with their servants carrying gun and drum, and, on the other, the boys playing women armed with all the paraphernalia of the kitchen: distaff, broom, poker, skimmer, firefork and spit. The image of this bizarre and diminutive crew got up in pots and pans was doubtlessly hilarious on its own, but there was more to come.

The preparation for battle betrays a certain difference of opinion among the masters:

> RAFE ROYSTER. On therfore, marche forwarde, – soft, stay
> a whyle yet.
> MATHEW MERYGREEKE. On.
> RAFE ROYSTER.   Tary.
> MATHEW MERYGREEKE.   Forth.
> RAFE ROYSTER.   Back.
> MATHEW MERYGREEKE.   On.
> RAFE ROYSTER..   Soft.

After this display of cowardice, it is not surprising that the women rout the men in a noisy scrimmage, an open invitation to general improvisation; whereupon Ralph decides that the Widow must have slain her first husband, and beats a hasty retreat whimpering, 'Slee else whom she will, by Gog she shall not slee mee'.

Gammer Gurton's Needle (c. 1553) prints on its title-page the encouraging superscription, 'A Right Pithy, Pleasant, and Merry Comedy', which neatly embodies what it was trying to be, and no more. This interlude is among the few to have received more than one professional production since it was successfully revived by the Birmingham Rep. in 1959. *Gammer Gurton* emanated from Christ's College, Cambridge, had its origins in Terence and was written by a Mr S. who declared himself Master of Art, and so it is surprising to find that its central character is a grotesque caricature of a village goody, old mother Gurton, and that its whole plot turns upon the loss of a needle.

The play is again superficially touched by the classical influence: scenes are arranged according to the five–act convention and a gesture is made towards a unity of time and place, the scene being a single street between two houses. However, the only Roman character type is that of the parasite Diccon, who in any case is more recognizable as the familiar Vice, pretending here to be a Bedlam beggar who haunts the English countryside. The rest of the comedy builds upon the bunch of rustics made up of Gammer Gurton, her contentious neighbour Dame Chat, her simple servants Hodge, Tyb and Cock, Dr Rat the curate and Master Bailey the officer of the law – each observed in good detail. As for the search for the needle, lost when Hodge needed to have his breeches mended, this is the lamest of excuses for embroidering an attractive comic tapestry. From the beginning the Prologue announces what happened to the precious needle, so that the audience is never troubled on that score. It is in the detail of ordinary human behaviour, albeit of a rude and homespun crew, that the play lives.

It displays all the marks of popular theatre. Like a chorus speaking in solo address to the audience, the first of a series that keeps the audience one jump ahead of the comic action, Diccon prepares the necessary background of information, and at the same time seems to stage-manage the action and instruct the players in the style and tone they should adopt. In all his travels, he says, he has never before seen what he has seen in this house – implying, of course, what the audience is going to see:

> Syghing and sobbing, they weepe and they wayle,
> I marvell in my mynd, what the devill they ayle ...

These lines make the first of many shrewd comments on the little world of village life and, in the trivial matter of the lost needle, what is apparently important to it.

When Diccon asks Hodge what is making Gammer Gurton and her maid Tyb frown, he considers that 'tys theyr dayly looke, / They coure [cower] so over the coles, theyr eyes be bleard with smooke'. This is one of a host of realistic details that fill out the human picture and provide a natural justification for rural speech and acting. In order to arrive at an account of how the needle was lost, the audience has to know about the rent in Hodge's trousers, Tom Tankard's cow, Gyb the cat and a whole menagerie of farm animals, and all before Tyb comes out with the terrible news:

> HODGE. Gogs woundes Tyb, my Gammer has never lost
>   her neele?
> TYB. Her neele.
> HODGE. Her neele?
> TYB. Her neele by Him that made me, it is true Hodge I tell
>   thee.

The exchange urges its own timing and escalation of feeling: in the servants' exact inflexions of speech, the silly needle is magnified beyond price and Hodge's distress knows no bounds. In act 3 the old women enjoy a free-for-all of smiting, biting, scratching and clawing. Nearly forgotten, the search for the needle has to wait.

All the devices of farce are mustered to sweep the action up and along. Songs are scattered through the play, and at one time, between acts 2 and 3, Diccon calls for musicians to 'pype upp your fiddles'. Comic business builds and the dialogue reaches a kind of zany crescendo: when the touches of realism are no longer wanted, they are cheerfully thrown out. In this atmosphere any moralizing has evaporated: these lightweight characters are for exhibition, not correction. Yet the audience is confidently left to enjoy a pleasant perspective on rural community life and on the human condition as a whole. The cause of all the trouble, the needle itself, is finally recovered from Hodge's trousers, where it has lodged all the time, and the call goes out for general celebration and a drink in the alehouse. At the end, Dame Chat's alehouse in this way becomes both fiction and reality.

The Vice and his importance

Diccon 'the Bedlam', not Hodge, not Gammer Gurton, is at the heart of *Gammer Gurton's Needle*, and a new, indigenous dramatic form is evident, one centred upon a key element present in the interlude – that of the Vice, the supreme comic intriguer and the master of deceit. Following his double-talk to the boy Prince Edward in Shakespeare's *Richard III*, the evil Duke of Gloucester lightly compares himself in an aside to the audience with 'the formal [i.e., conventional] Vice, Iniquity' (3.1.82), and to Prince Hal in *I Henry IV* Falstaff is 'that reverend vice, that grey iniquity, that father ruffian, that vanity in years' (2.4.447–9). Elizabethan audiences took the point immediately. The Vice was at the protagonist's elbow, working with him and against him, and in his intimacy with the audience, troubling and yet also entertaining.

When the variety of comic vices in the morality plays – popular figures all – began to disappear from the stage, their lack was supplied by a single creature who met the persistent need for a comic rogue, and this figure acquired a popularity that only the comic stage could explain. For all his moralistic origins, the Vice was a genial rascal, and serving as he did the convenient role of schemer and plot director, he was seen less as an embodiment of the Devil than as a dramatically useful figure of fun. He became a special kind of clown who, to the general delight, always spoke frankly to his audience about what he planned to do next, and seemed to draw the house into an extra-dramatic conspiracy that allowed the spectator to make his maximum contribution to the performance. In his time, the Vice was in this way a rare gift to the comic playwright.

Thus in John Heywood's *The Play of the Weather* (c. 1520), the Vice Merry-Report assumes the role of Jupiter's messenger to those who complain about the weather, and thereby seems to direct a good deal of the action himself, introducing each new character and having a joke with the audience about the play it is watching. This Vice is more of a mischievous gadfly, a well-meaning joker, and less the sinister tempter. Yet with his own farcical perspective the Vice was popular enough to appear also in more serious drama, even in tragedy, and in *Appius and Virginia* (c. 1559), which was offered to its audiences as a 'tragicall comedie', the Vice Haphazard helps the wicked judge Appius to seduce the chaste Virginia – and at the end is hanged for his trouble. About ten years later, Thomas Preston's bloodthirsty *Cambises* was superscribed 'A lamentable tragedy mixedful of pleasant mirth', which suggests how well everyone concerned appreciated the services rendered by the treacherous Vice Ambidexter and his scenes of horseplay with the soldiers Huf, Ruf and Snuf and the country yokels Hob and Lob. In this tragedy, moreover, Ambidexter is absurdly dressed for this work – he enters 'with an olde capcase on his hed, an olde pail about his hips for harnes [armour], a scummer [ladle] and a potlid by his side, and a rake on his shoulder'.

The presence of this uniquely English clown in many plays of different genres had the effect of secularizing the morality and deflating the more pompous and bombastic of the interludes. The vestiges of the Vice's role that recur through Elizabethan and Jacobean drama in major and in minor characters, in an Iago or an Autolycus, are surely the result of qualities that reside in the nature of his performance and were not easy to eradicate. His enduring popularity also encouraged the professional success of such popular clowns as Richard (Dick) Tarlton (d. 1588), favourite of Queen Elizabeth, and Will Kempe (d. after 1603), for a time in Shakespeare's company and famous for his jigs and a celebrated morris dance from London to Norwich.

The tragic dimension: *Cambises, Gorboduc*

The tragic form lent itself better than the comic to the dramatization of political matter and permitted the stage to expound solemn lessons in 'policy' [government]. The Tudor playhouse was in a good position to supply 'a mirror for magistrates' [an example for rulers] concerning the fall of princes, and since drama can work obliquely, it ran less risk of giving offence. As a source of tragic form and emotionally charged speech, some academic playwrights, those from the schools, Inns of Court and universities, coveted the work of the Roman Seneca, whose plays eventually became available in a complete English translation in 1581. However, native conventions were not easily suppressed, and new troupes of players were in no position to ignore practices established by popular acclaim. So in the tragic treatment of romantic stories and legends from history and the Bible playwrights shamelessly included the familiar Vice and did not hesitate to invent comic material. In *An Apology for Poetry* (1580), Sir Philip Sidney blasted the product of this way of 'mingling Kings and Clownes' as 'mungrell Tragy-comedie', but something of this mixture pervaded English drama for many years to come.

The appeal of the Stoic tragedian Seneca is not far to seek, since he drew lustily upon Greek mythology for themes of sensational sex and violence – incest and adultery, murder and revenge. *Gorboduc* (c. 1561) was a first attempt at Elizabethan Seneca, and *Jocasta* from Gray's Inn and *Gismond of Salerne* from the Inner Temple (both c. 1566) followed soon after. Seneca's was a closet drama constructed to a five-act formula, and today we find his characterization flat and his rhetoric inflated. However, some of the new playwrights of a quickly expanding stage found their needs answered by the long sententious choruses punctuating his plotting and the lurid horrors moralistically deployed. Unfortunately the physical violence was decorously kept off-stage and (to invoke Alan Downer's immortal comment in *The British Drama* (1950)) 'reported by longwinded messengers with a passion for detail'.

It so happens that *Gorboduc* was almost contemporary with a popular mongrel tragedy, *Cambises*, and to set these side by side is to gain an insight into the concoction that made up the Tudor interlude and the Elizabethan taste in tragedy.

Cambises (1569) by Thomas Preston (1537–98) has the formal title *A lamentable tragedy mixed ful of pleasant mirth*, *conteyning the life of Cambises King of Percia* (the printed page reads like a promotion). If inspiration for the play came from Seneca's dramatic arrangements for the tragic fall of a wicked King, it showed a notable lack of classical decorum and made no attempt to keep its thrills discreetly off-stage. One gory incident follows another, nearly all in full view of the audience, so that this story of a notorious tyrant makes a somewhat distracted progress towards his retribution: the sermon is lost in the sensationalism. The details give a fair idea of the spirit of the popular tragic stage at this time.

The unworthy judge Sisamnes meets his death in a way that is both conventional and innovative: Cambises calls for his executioner, and the stage direction reads, *'Smite him in the neck with a sword to signify his death.'* The contradiction here between the directions 'smite' and 'signify', between the real and the allusive, suggests an impressionistic stage. Yet when the King's counsellor Praxaspes cries, 'How he doth bleed!', the effect is more real than allusive, and this thinking is supported a little later when the death of Cambises's brother Smirdis calls for *'A little bladder of vinegar prikt'* – the vinegar presumably made from red wine. The whole gruesome action is completed only when Cambises gives the order to 'pull his skin over his eares to make his death more vile' – for 'ears' the second quarto has 'eyes' – and even then it is felt necessary to spell this out with another stage direction, *'Flay him with a false skin'*. On another occasion the King in his cups decides to shoot an arrow through the heart of his counsellor's young son, and then has it cut out to prove that he managed to hit his target; the distraught mother runs in so that in tears and grief the parents may carry off their dead child. The bloodbath continues until Cambises himself meets a grisly end by making an entrance *'without a gown'* to reveal *'a sword thrust up into his side, bleeding'*. After he has lain a while 'gasping here on ground' and regretting his misdeeds, he finally expires to the further direction, *'Here let him quake and stir'*, in the vivid throes of a theatrical death for one last sensation.

If Cambises's name was a byword for bloody tyranny, the play's roaring fourteeners [lines of seven iambic feet] worked hard with their rhyming couplets to build up the emotions of the spectator: this was the style Falstaff made infamous by remarking in mockery that he would 'speak in passion ... in King Cambyses' vein' (*I Henry IV*, 2.4.382). However, where Seneca had used his bloodthirsty bombast to *compensate* for what was missing on the stage, *Cambises* used the ranting vein as a *supplement* to his realistic obscenities.

Yet this same play could also include the delicate scene of Cambises in love with his prospective Queen. The abstract figures of Venus and Cupid make a symbolic entrance, and Cupid shoots his arrow to the poetic suggestion of 'blowing buds', 'the sweet smell of musk white rose' and 'chirping birds', the whole effect completed by the music of 'lute and cittern [guitar]' playing in 'heavenly harmony'. The King calls for additional music to accompany his wedding banquet, although in the event the festivities are as much heard as noises off, as may be assumed from Ambidexter's report:

> Running at tilt, justing, with running at the ring,
> Masking and mumming, with eche kinde of thing,
> Such dauncing, such singing, with musicall harmony.

Again, the mixture is a balance of realism and allusion.

Monarch and goddess hold the stage side by side in this kind of drama, together with lowlife creatures like the comic soldiery represented by Huf, Ruf and Snuf. Yet the Vice Ambidexter – his name precisely suggesting his double-dealing and trickery – has a remarkable function over and above the entertainment he provides by clowning and horse-play. An audience is unable to avoid the startling impact of his zany appearance following each bloody horror: he jokes with the audience after Sisamnes has been skinned and a child's heart cut out, and he cannot forbear laughing at, or with, the audience after Smirdis is butchered. Ambidexter's presence in this black farce of a tragedy raises issues about a Tudor actor's ability to work simultaneously on the level of an audience's reality and on the level of the play's fantasy, and the way he plays points to the author's success in balancing contradictory moods to create an early form of dark comedy. Thomas Preston has been named as the first of university half-wits, but it may be that he was among the Elizabethan avant-garde, tailoring his material to the popular taste.

After *Cambises*, the Senecan *Gorboduc, or Ferrex and Porrex* may be more admired for what it was trying to do than for what it achieved. It was written by two young lawyers, Thomas Sackville (1536–1608) and Thomas Norton (*fl.* 1560), soon to be members of Elizabeth's Parliament. The occasion was a Christmas celebration by the Inner Temple, and the play was intended as a cautionary tale based on legendary English history, warning of the civil anarchy that could follow an unresolved succession to the throne, a constant concern of Protestant politics during Elizabeth's reign.

The production of *Gorboduc* was evidently a lavish one and a great success: it was repeated before the new Queen Elizabeth and later praised by Sidney in a famous neo-classical plaudit as 'full of stately speeches and well sounding phrases, clyming to the height of Seneca his stile, and as full of notable moralitie, which it doth most delightfully teach, and so obtayne the very end of poesie' (51–2). Following Castelve-tro's misinterpretation of Aristotle, he cavils only a little at the play's loss, for all its reportage, of the unities of place and time. For it is a bloodlessly bloody story, in which brother kills brother, mother kills son, the people kill the King and Queen, and the nobility kill the people – civil chaos indeed – but all done decorously in words. Here is a sufficiency of plot, all of a kind in tone and unbending in observing the unity of action, but the characters can only talk about it, since nothing happens on stage.

Nevertheless, this play presented the emergent stage with several elements of great importance for the future:

(1) *Blank verse*. Where *Cambises* was shackled by its couplets, *Gorboduc* enjoyed the possibilities of a new freedom and flow of speech in its unrhymed lines. The blank penta-meters not only came closer to the English bisyllabic accent in ordinary speech, but permitted the sort of flexibility in voice, gesture and movement that the stage needed. It was the serviceable verse form that Shakespeare and his contemporaries later used and developed.

(2) *Choruses*. 'Four ancient and sage men of Britain' make up the Chorus of the play. Unfortunately they are totally

automatic and, unlike the choruses in Greek tragedy, they
are largely without character and quite unrelated to the
action. In order that their words should be distinctive,
they return to rhyming, but find little to say that has not
already been made perfectly clear. Nevertheless, the idea
that stage dialogue might be varied by role and function,
that action might be broken and stopped for reflection
and that certain sentiments might be given the special
force of such separation, constituted an interesting new
departure for writers to come.

(3) *Dumb show*. Each chorus is linked to a short pantomime
that precedes each act, and *Gorboduc* is the first play in
English to employ this characteristically Elizabethan
dramatic device. The dumb show is not found in Seneca,
but it may have been copied from the *intermedio* [in
Italy, a musical piece performed between the acts of a
play]. It was acted to music and consisted of a brief
allegorical masque intended to summarize and emphasize
the moral and symbolic purpose of the action to come; it
could even add a touch of mystery to the proceedings –
as it did when Claudius watched the dumb show in
Hamlet. It certainly brought pageantry and panache to
the tragic stage, while at the same time the heightened
manner of the acting made its dramatic context, the scene
that surrounded the dumb show, seem more realistic
than it was.

(4) *Instrumental music*. Music is a staple of all medieval
drama, but *Gorboduc* is unusual in specifically calling for
six different intruments, selected to match the content of
each dumb show and to determine the mood and atmosphere of the subsequent scene. They are:

> (act 1) *violins*: for the opening dumb show showing a
> faggot of sticks that could not be broken when
> fastened together.
> (act 2) *cornets*: for a dumb show showing a King poisoned
> by his courtiers with a cup of gold.
> (act 3) *flutes*: for a dumb show made up of a troupe of
> mourners all in black processing three times round
> the stage.
> (act 4) *hautboys*: for a dumb show of furies who rise from

> Hell [presumably a trap] and drive before them a
> King and Queen who have slain their children.
> (act 5)   *drums and flutes*: for a dumb show of a company of
> harquebusiers and other armed men in order of
> battle.

This evidence shows an awareness of the power of appropriate music to prompt a response to the play at each
stage, and so help to shape the play as a whole.

(5) *Drama as opera.* Together these dramatic elements add up
to an effect of major consequence for performance, and
suggest that the developing mode is at bottom operatic.
This is felt not just in the use of music, but in the
persistence of a non-colloquial speech heard on the level
of song. The insistent choruses and extended harangues
and tirades by so many counsellors in *Gorboduc* are
supported by a rhetoric sustained beyond the needs of
dialogue and interaction, and seem akin to hymn, aria and
dirge. The new vogue of tragic interlude leans towards
what modern criticism identifies as poetic drama.

A note on casting, disguising and doubling

The title-page of *Cambises* (printed 1569) apportions thirty-
eight parts among eight players, and if this tells us something
about the spirit of unrealism in which the Tudor drama was
produced, it also points to Preston's ingenuity in organizing
his cast and the new professionalism of travelling companies
and the English stage.

The title-page of the printed play is sometimes revealing,
since it was not unusual for it to advertise its play by
suggesting the facility with which it could be performed.
After listing a cast of no less than twenty-one, the anonymous
King Darius (c. 1559) adds the advice, 'Six persons may easily
play it'. The title-page of John Phillips's *Patient and Meek
Grissell* (c. 1561, printed 1569) claims that 'eight persons may
easily play this commody'. Some printers even suggest how
the doubling may be managed, and John Pickering's *Horestes*
(printed 1567) has twenty-six parts in which it is recom-

mended that one player may play no fewer than seven parts, and two others five each. Nevertheless, even allowing for a printer's business inclination to exaggerate, doubling of characters other than the principal was evidently the common practice. In some instances, like *Gorboduc* at the Inner Temple, no such restrictions applied, but most Tudor plays could be performed by six actors, the probable number in an adult company.

The widespread characteristic of doubling the parts in an Elizabethan play worked in combination with the device of changing the name and usually the costume of a character in the course of performance, a practice that dates back to the previous century. In Henry Medwall's morality play *Nature* (c. 1495), the Deadly Sins assume aliases and probably new clothes to make a moral point; in *Mundus et Infans* (c. 1508), Infans enjoys seven changes to portray the ages of man; in *Magnificence* (c. 1513), the hypocritical Vices change their clothes with their names; and in *Respublica* (c. 1553) Avarice soon becomes the more respectable 'Policy'. David Bevington finds that a pattern of what he calls 'suppression and alternation' is the practice, whereby the play suppresses one character in order to bring on another, or have an actor alternate between two contrasting roles (*From 'Mankind' to Marlowe* (1962)).

Disguising in the play and doubling in the performance are arguably expedients that are two of a kind, for just as the former forges a link between the part and the player, the latter ties the playwright to the company for which he is writing. These matters grow in importance as the professional stage expands and develops.

4

The Elizabethan theatre

Professional players and boys' companies

Strolling players who made a precarious living by travelling from one town or village to another multiplied in the sixteenth century, as the vigorous growth in the number of plays suggests. Working from a stage made of 'boards and barrel heads', it was possible for four or five men to set up shop and without ado announce their programme as soon as they arrived at a likely place that promised a responsive audience. In town and country alike the new drama received a welcome. Yet in 1572 itinerant players were everywhere troubled by the restrictive Statute of the Realm, Elizabeth 14, in which Parliament revised the laws against rogues and vagabonds to include 'all fencers, bearwards, common players in interludes, and minstrels, not belonging to any Baron of this Realm, or towards any other honourable personage of greater degree'. However, the players were fortunate to have some influential institutions and agencies which promoted their advancement and lent them respectability in the face of civic and religious opposition, and it so happened that Elizabeth's repressive law had the opposite effect from that intended, and actually increased the number of professional players and companies at a critical moment. These agencies may be summarized:

(1) The patronage of the *Court* itself finally ensured the survival of the art of drama. The King or Queen customarily kept at command a consort of musicians and a company of interlude players, while it seems that the Master and Children of the Chapel Royal were in regular demand and the call for new plays never ceased.

(2) The *Inns of Court* allowed its young lawyers to write and

act, as did the Universities of Oxford and Cambridge their young scholars. Later the so-called 'University Wits' introduced a learned, but notably fresh, quality into the new drama. Playwrights who were able to draw upon exciting material from rediscovered classical (Roman) sources and the elegance of Renaissance Italy brought to the stage a quality of culture that pleased their specialist audiences immensely.

(3) Above all, the *nobility* emulated the Court in furnishing their houses with servant companies and chapel boys, and this had the good consequence of spreading important patronage where it was needed. Groups of players hastened to win the protection of a noble patron, as did, for example, James Burbage and his men, who wrote to the Earl of Leicester in the same year as the 1572 decree and asked, not for his money, but to wear his livery – 'when we shall have occasion to travel amongst our friends, as we do usually once a year, and as other noblemen's players do, and have done in time past'.

The respectable professional element on the English stage properly begins with the boys' companies, those acting groups associated with school or church whose work was first advanced by the Court. Only after the arrival of the first permanent playhouse in London in 1576 could the adult companies assume the leadership. It is a curious story, and begins with the belief that a young gentleman's education should include music and drama. In his late play *The Staple of News* (1625) Ben Jonson could write,

> They make all their scholars playboys! Is't not a fine sight to see all our children made interluders? Do we pay our money for this? We send them to learn their grammar and their Terence and they learn their playbooks!

However, in 1592 the Oxford playwright William Gager had been engaged in a typical quarrel over the public presentation of plays, and offered his reasons why university scholars should learn to act:

> to try their voices and confirm [strengthen] their memories; to frame [control] their speech; to conform them to

> convenient action [suitable behaviour]; to try what metal is
> in every one, and of what disposition they are of; whereby
> never any one amongst us, that I know was made the
> worse, many have been much the better.

The traditional training of the boys as choristers and musicians for royal and sacred occasions set a standard of good stage performance that throughout the period remained a factor for the men's companies to reckon with.

The history of the boys' companies goes back to the fourteenth century, and in the sixteenth they progressed strongly under Henry VIII and Elizabeth. The Children of St Paul's were taught by John Redford and Sebastian Westcott, and in the 1580s produced several plays by John Lyly; after a lapse they returned to the stage under Edward Peers for several years after 1601. The Children of the Chapel Royal prospered and in 1580 divided into two, the London and Windsor branches. They enjoyed a succession of gifted masters (William Cornish, Richard Edwards, William Hunnis, Richard Farrant) who developed their stage work, offering about two productions a year and persuading major playwrights like Jonson, Marston, Middleton and Chapman to write for them.

Their persistent success long after the adult companies were established seems strange: it is not possible to ignore the continuing approval they received from the Court and the general public, and the support of many heavyweight playwrights. The boys' training in the arts of rhetoric and debate, in music and dance, and singing and acting, also ensured that new forms of light comedy, alive with physical display, and sporting a deft way with quip and quibble, suited their skills. Moreover, the boys' talents were also in demand in the adult companies, and where before any actor might play a woman, in Elizabeth's time boys were increasingly used as specialists in female roles.

A sense of what the boys could do is important for an understanding of how they managed the women's parts in later Elizabethan and Jacobean plays. The virtuosity needed for playing a Portia or a Rosalind may be explained, yet the casting of a Lady Macbeth or a Cleopatra is more surprising: we may deduce that their author took pains to colour in a tone or an emotion verbally and to provide special incidents and even whole scenes to exhibit the outward expression of, say, coquetry or passion. Nevertheless, the debate continues: some scholars (who may be called the illusionists) believe that the boys acted naturally and realistically, and were convincing in their parts; others (the formalists) think that the non-realistic mode of the Elizabethan stage permitted a detached, stylized, even burlesque, style of acting.

Private and public playhouses

The two or three chapel companies performed in 'private' playhouses, although this term was unknown before the seventeenth century. The private playhouses flourished as *indoor* theatres alongside the 'public' playhouses, and two were built in the old monasteries of Blackfriars, near St Paul's, which opened in 1575, and Whitefriars, where the children played after 1608. The Cockpit or Phoenix in Drury Lane opened in 1616 and housed several adult companies.

The Blackfriars is of special interest because it was here that the King's Men later produced Shakespeare's last plays. In the 1580s it was typically a fashionable house where the Children of the Chapel Royal performed perhaps twice weekly for high prices before a smaller and higher class audience, which no doubt included the gentlemen from the Inns of Court situated nearby. The men's companies were always troubled by the competition from the boys, concerned that bad weather could affect the business of their open-air playhouses. As a consequence James Burbage in 1596 leased and adapted rooms in Blackfriars, and, since plays from the public playhouse were to be transferred there, he probably tried to make the private interior as like the public one as possible. It turned out that his company, the Lord Chamberlain's Men, were not permitted to play there, and so on his death his son Richard leased it to the Children of the Chapel Royal until 1608, when, under James I, the renamed King's Men could take it over.

There were significant differences between the public and private playhouses: the latter had a limited capacity and a more confined and covered space, together with a more cultured, coterie audience. Together, these ensured a different dramatic product. In a better acoustical setting the boys improved the quality of the music, which was played before, during and after the performance, and instrumental music regularly punctuated a performance. Along with orchestral music came the general dramatic use of dancing and masquing. Plays were seen in candlelight, and artificial lighting, although inflexible by today's standards, enhanced the element of spectacle and raised the possibility of scenic effects: the Revels accounts suggest an increasing elaboration of visual devices, and in later years masque-like scenes were more common in the plays. With their flying machinery and half-darkened stages, the private theatres especially encouraged on-stage shows, magical effects and scenic decorations (rather than scenery itself).

It followed naturally that the wealthier adult companies should want their own playhouses. John Braynes and his brother-in-law the actor James Burbage had evidently erected 'skaffoldes' in the Red Lion inn at Stepney in 1567, and this must have given them some ideas about stage design, and the event that precipitated the erection of purpose-built public playhouses came in 1574, when the mayor and aldermen of the City of London decreed that no innkeeper 'within the Liberties of this City' [areas outside the City under its jurisdiction] might house a play without their permission. In order to allow Leicester's Men to develop their plans, Burbage in 1576 built a playhouse in Shoreditch in the Liberty of Holywell outside the City. He called it 'The Theatre' [from the Greek for 'a place for seeing'], a name of ancient lineage which has stuck.

Little is known about this first playhouse. Taking its arena shape from the great halls and galleries Burbage was familiar with, he added a raised platform on scaffolds and set it against a tiring-room wall, which also provided a convenient façade of doors and balcony, as well as permitting the central hanging of a divided arras or cloth. Burbage's Theatre was an immediate success, and the fact that it was used by other companies and exchanged plays with other playhouses in its subsequent twenty years of life suggests that, in its rudiments, the formula suited everyone. By the time John de Witt visited London in 1596 he was able to record the existence of four handsome new playhouses. In the north lay the Theatre with its immediate rival nearby, the Curtain (1577), its name possibly derived, not from any stage curtain, something unknown for a hundred years, but from *courtine*, a 'small court'. In the Liberty of the Clink on the South Bank of the river, Philip Henslowe's Rose (1587) flourished under Edward Alleyn as its leading actor, and a little to the west Francis Langley soon after built the Swan (1595). Others would follow quickly: also on the South Bank, the first Globe (1598), built from the timbers of his father's Theatre, flourished under Richard Burbage as leader of the Lord Chamberlain's Men, and, to the north in the Liberty of Finsbury, the Fortune (1599), this time square in shape. By the end of the century the professional companies had several homes of their own.

The companies grew in wealth and strength. Henslowe's *Diary* advises us that the Admiral's Men at the Rose enjoyed a succession of over two hundred plays between 1594 and 1597; it was in use until its lease expired in 1605. When the Chamberlain's Men were settled in their new Globe, and with Shakespeare as their principal writer, they may have exceeded even this rate of production. The incentives were frankly commercial. A good actor would expect to become a 'sharer' and a businessman, and have a vested interest in each production.

Now more than ever, the players and their authors had to know their audiences and their tastes. It was one of the smaller miracles of the age that so much of the new drama was created for the 'public' playhouses, where audiences were truly heterogeneous: the public stage of the Elizabethans enjoyed a common touch that saved it from academic pretentiousness and upper-class preciousness.

The essential Elizabethan playhouse

It is axiomatic that the physical playhouse dictates much of the style and process, and many of the conventions and devices, of the performances played in it. The Elizabethan play tends to be simple, direct and sensory, and demands and suffers little 'dramatic illusion', in the way that this uncomfortable term is generally understood. The Elizabethan actor is not acting to himself or to another actor, as in much modern illusionistic theatre, but unabashedly to and for the audience in front of him to secure its maximum participation in the shaping of the occasion and the making of the play.

The basic dimensions and design of the Elizabethan public playhouse were acceptable enough for the same pattern to continue into the seventeenth century with only minor cosmetic changes. The following is a bald summary of its elements:

(1) The *shape* was round or polygonal. By this shape the medieval spirit of theatre-in-the-round and arena playing was strongly sustained, and implied a shared, generally ritualistic mode of drama that affected the playing and the response. Many scenes embody this element of ritual, like Faustus's pact with the Devil in *Doctor Faustus*, and the reconciliation of Leontes and Hermione at the end of *The Winter's Tale*.

(2) The *outside diameter* of the playhouse was nevertheless relatively small, suggesting that a quality of intimacy between actor and audience was taken for granted. Recent excavations have proved that the Rose was the smallest of the known houses, its outside diameter being about 74 feet and the inner about 50 feet; the Fortune, according to Henslowe's contract with the builder Peter Street, is known to have been 80 feet wide, with a 50 feet interior; and there are now geometrical conjectures applied to the remains of the Globe that it may have been up to 100 feet wide, with a 75 feet inside dimension. Yet all these are still small by modern commercial standards.

(3) Three *galleries* on three levels, or storeys, built round the arena afforded seating for those prepared to pay another penny more than those standing in the 'pit'. For a price one of the galleries also provided a selected area close to the stage (the 'lords' room'), while other gentlemen sat

on the stage itself. Such galleries as these brought the capacity of the Swan to 3,000 (de Witt's estimate), yet still allowed the spectators to be at no great distance from the action, and all around, below and above the actor.

(4)   The acting area consisted chiefly of a *platform* about 5 feet high and, according to Henslowe's contract for the Fortune, 43 feet wide 'to extend to the middle of the yard' – i.e., about 27 feet deep and open on three sides, 'thrust' boldly into the auditorium. This extraordinary acting space was therefore well over 1,000 square feet, and that encouraged direct address to the audience in the shape of soliloquy and aside, prologue and epilogue, and accounts for the impulse of the actor to step out of character and be himself.

(5)   The platform stage had at least one simple *trap*, probably placed in the centre and suitable for effects of unexpected appearance and disappearance. This was a stage device that has proved itself to this day to be the most convenient arrangement for the introduction of ghosts and other supernatural and spectacular images.

(6)   On the upstage side of the platform lay the *tiring house* and green room for the actors, concealed by a *façade* which itself was immensely serviceable. It supported a balcony and doors and what might be needed to hang a banner or a backcloth. Without being scenically representational, it encouraged symbolic decoration, especially since it suggested a domestic building with doors and windows, or else a throne room, a gatehouse or a castle wall to begin with.

(7)   According to the drawing of the Swan, a pair of symmetrical *doors* balanced one another on either side of the façade, and provided for the majority of entrances. They would also ensure that the general direction of movement on the platform was upstage-downstage, north to south and back, as it were, often governing the manner of entrance and exit, and the arrangement of onstage characters in a scene, making the centre of the house and the audience itself the apparent point of attack.

(8)   If and when a *curtain* was hung centrally between the

doors, perhaps suspended from the balcony above, the area behind it automatically created the *discovery-space* associated with the curtained booth-stages of medieval times.

(9) The existence of a *balcony* overlooking the stage, a continuation of the second level gallery across the fourth side of the arena, proved to be a useful facility to playwright and actor alike. A higher physical level in performance permitted a semi-representational picture image like that of a city wall or battlement, and also allowed the actor to play to his fellow on the space below him, and vice versa.

(10) A painted *'shadow or cover'* – also known as 'the heavens' because it was coloured blue and spangled with stars – was erected (and possibly supported by pillars as in the de Witt sketch) above as much of the stage as possible, probably intended to protect the costumes in wet weather, and perhaps the actors too. However, the roof above the stage was also the best way to store and conceal the machinery needed for flying the spectacular devices increasingly expected of a production.

(11) Finally, and to return to first principles, the fact that the playhouse was *without a roof* is a reminder that all plays presented therein were subject to the remarkable 'daylight convention', there being no artificial lighting. More of this below (see 101).

Here certainly is a case where one picture is worth more than a thousand words, but unfortunately the only picture of the interior of an Elizabethan playhouse is the rather poor drawing of the Swan Theatre known as the de Witt sketch. This, however, fills in the essential outlines.

The *private* playhouses were, however, roofed, with important differences in lighting conventions that little by little prompted magical effects of feeling and illusion. Otherwise their plays were bound to conform to the smaller size and rectangular shape of the halls or buildings they occupied: Blackfriars was 66 feet by 46 feet, with its platform at one end ('end staging') and its seating for about six hundred probably in the middle and on three sides.

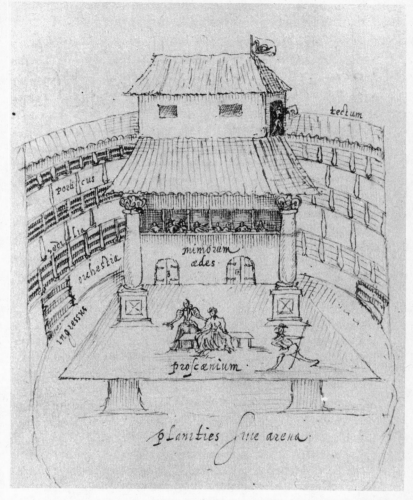

4 The well-known de Witt sketch of the Swan Theatre, *c.* 1596: the only contemporary picture of the interior of an Elizabethan playhouse.

Features of the new stagecraft

Victorian critics believed that the Elizabethan play was trying for visual illusion and verisimilitude. As late as 1918 James Agate, London's leading theatre critic, was arguing that these must be maintained at all costs: 'It is vital to the art of the actor that he shall *keep his frame*, and that there shall be no point of contact between him and the spectator' (*Buzz, Buzz! Essays on the Theatre*). He had misunderstood the nature of open stagecraft. It is true that a bare stage is never entirely without character: as soon as the actor entered it could be a bedroom or a battlefield, and men bearing flags and banners could turn the open platform into Tamburlaine's empire or Lear's Kingdom. Nevertheless, the Elizabethan actor was quite at home on an open stage, playing almost in the round and thrust into the world of the audience. To appear real was never the first thing on his mind and the bare Elizabethan stage was an ideal vehicle for the promotion of *a different kind of drama*.

It is possible to isolate a few of its general features:

(1) *An absence of scenery*, with two doors set symmetrically in the façade, meant that the platform could virtually disappear before the eyes and the scene on stage need not be localized. The absence of scenery also denoted the absence of time, or at least its extreme elasticity, as in the last scene of *Doctor Faustus* where the eleventh hour is made to seem like eternity. Place and time remained unimportant until the one or the other was called for. This might be done by the specific appearance of a character whose location was known, by an indicative prop (a throne, a tomb) set on the stage or by a simple cue line like 'Now, Hal, what time of day is it, lad?'

Even then, some scenes carried a dual location, as in *Richard III* when Richard and Richmond both have their tents on the same stage, and 'simultaneous staging' on the large multi-centred Elizabethan platform could take many forms. An upstage door, or any other solid physical feature of the stage, could unexpectedly be made to seem a realistic item, like the door to Shylock's house in *The Merchant of Venice*, but the neutrality of the empty platform at the same time permitted the unreal make-believe of the folk tale to grow according to a different set of laws, the real and the unreal co-existing. A designated location could also fade into oblivion after it had served its turn, as when Lear's heath dissolves into the symbolic wilderness of his imagination and madness.

The late Victorian theory of a 'traverse curtain' hung between pillars and behind which scenery could be changed is now discounted, together with notions of a pattern of 'alternating' scenes devised to make use of it.

(2) None of this means that some *scenic pieces* were not called for on occasion, as they were on the medieval pageant wagon. In Henslowe's *Diary*, the important account books kept by the theatre owner and manager Philip Henslowe for 1592–1602, he kept a note of painted cloths, including a 'city of Rome' for *Doctor Faustus*, scenic props like a mossy bank and 'one cauldron for the Jew' in Marlowe's *The Jew of Malta*, and other items of a realistic nature including severed heads and blood in 'bladders' and 'vials' – presumably from a sheep's gather. Even then, these spectacular devices did not necessarily localize a scene or provide scenic illusion: Henslowe's props, touched with residual symbolism though they may be, were the nuts and bolts of practical performance on an empty stage.

Since there was no curtain or means of a modern stage 'blackout', the actors themselves had to bring on and take off any props or scenic pieces, and if a death occurred on the stage, they had also to remove the body.

(3) During performance *music* could be all-pervasive. It was vocal or instrumental, and the singers and musicians, thought to have occupied an upper balcony as they did above the screen of a Tudor banqueting hall, were visible to the spectators. Thus while music or song could serve the mood or atmosphere of a scene as in the cinema today, again it pretended to no illusion. Solemn or supernatural, pastoral or romantic, the music consciously assisted the work of the stage, and the audience knew it. The Renaissance fusion of the arts found a genial home on the Elizabethan stage, which accordingly acquired a little of the spirit of modern ballet and opera.

(4) Less certain are the stage *effects*. Since battles, fights and skirmishes were created more by playing musical instruments than by playing soldiers, even the chronicle plays

had their musical additions. Armies would march on and off, however diminished in number by the exigencies of casting, to the sound of a sennet on drums and trumpets or cornets, a warrior might join arms to the sound of a flourish or a tucket and forces might engage to the alarums of clashing cymbals, trumpet blasts and rolling drums.

Hautboys in Elizabethan times were shrill and reedy in sound, but when not in use during a banquet, their piercing notes served well for eerie supernatural effects – the appearance of apparitions, the imminence of death. Thunder was created with a 'thunder barrel' and the rolling of cannon balls in wood, and after that invention knew no bounds. 'A peal of shot', bells and fireworks and cannon, all had their uses, and sometimes to disastrous effect, as the King's Men knew when the thatched roof of the Globe caught alight from the cannon fire during a performance of *Henry VIII* in 1613.

(5) As indications of dramatic purpose, *costumes* played a greater part in a production than scenic devices, and the emphasis was more on the actor's person than upon the visual scene. In particular, entries, pageants and processions were splendid affairs, but if the plays were rich in royal coronations and princely funerals, as they often were, they presented a special problem of authenticity and detail, since performances enjoyed the intimacy of the close-up. Henslowe's costs show that the costumes were expensive, and it has been suggested that the company's patron and his family supplied the actors with their cast-offs. Elizabeth's Master of the Revels was authorized to retain tailors and drapers, mercers and furriers.

The wardrobe no doubt saved costs to some extent by keeping its costumes for the most part contemporary – the performances were in 'modern dress' – and, as in the medieval drama, anachronism on the stage was never questioned. Without shame, Caesar spoke of plucking ope his doublet and Cleopatra asked for her lace to be cut. Anachronism should still be considered an important convention in Elizabethan production, since it would have the immediate visual effect of equating stage time and real time, as well as assisting the spectator to step into the same world as that of the characters in the play he was watching.

As the *features in the private theatres* differed, so performance there brought about modification in their physical and aesthetic effects. The principal difference lay in the loss of the daylight convention, since the private playhouse and its stage were lit by torchlight and candlelight, thus diminishing the impact of scenes of pretended darkness. In the public playhouse the audience shared the imagined imposition of darkness with the players, just as in *A Midsummer Night's Dream* the spectator is 'invisible' along with Oberon and Puck at the expense of the lovers. Otherwise the need for artificial lighting stimulated visual spectacle and encouraged the playwright to devise processions and ceremonies, dumb shows and tableaux. John Marston, writing in 1599 for St Paul's Boys, was fond of such shows, and the second part of *Antonio and Mellida* calls for several eye-catching moments – blood-stained arms and swords caught in the light of torches, a torchlit funeral procession set about by streamers, and tapers carried at midnight to light Antonio to his father's tomb dressed in his nightgown and nightcap.

The theatrical change of key in the private playhouses is also noticeable from the increase in the number of scenes of 'masquing', and it is apparent that the spirit and purpose of the drama changes as the stage introduces more spectacle, music and song. Not that an enhanced visual and aural dimension need ignore the drama's thematic concerns, but it is hard not to suspect that some non-verbal elements are prompted by showmanship. As the mode of the drama increasingly reflects the visual elements of the masques of Inigo Jones and the elaborate entertainments of the Stuart Court, the immediacy and directness of the Tudor years fade.

The straightforward and artless conventions and devices of the Elizabethan stage all point to the special *actor–audience relationship* the drama enjoyed in those years. The open-handed and unselfconscious compact between two partners in a common creative enterprise encouraged prologues and inductions and other stylistic stratagems like asides and soliloquies (together with a host of half-asides and near-soliloquies). Indeed, any sort of address to the house must have seemed strikingly natural against much of the stage-bound rhetorical speech of the period. Direct address helped define character and reiterate theme, but its primary purpose was to put the actor into immediate touch with his listeners at critical moments in the action, like the shower of semi-comic asides given by Marlowe to Barabas in his earlier scenes in *The Jew of Malta*. In all this, again, the logic of realistic illusion is missing, never considered.

It followed that *characters* could range between the realistic and the unreal. They could be withdrawn into their play, or half in and half out, like the medieval Vice. They could be 'high' or 'low', the interior and distant figures of tragedy or the bolder, extroverted figures of farce. They could be as abstract as morality figures (Luxury, Revenge, Pride, and the like) and narrowly stereotyped to meet the needs of two-dimensional allegorical performance. Yet they could also meet the needs of two-dimensional comic performance, like Jonson's 'humours', characters who showed a single exaggerated facet of human nature (for example, the braggadocio, the gull, the usurer). When an actor assumed a disguise or a multiple role, like Hal in *I Henry IV*, who must play both roisterer and politician, or Edgar in *King Lear*, who must play both the son of a duke and Poor Tom the Bedlam beggar, he could change instantly.

The mode of performance and perception is usually found in overt cues in the *dialogue*. As a rule of thumb, prose was reserved for the comic and the prosaic characters, verse for the nobility and those with a passion to tear or a high-minded sentiment to impart. T. S. Eliot made the general point that in Elizabethan drama the poetry almost sensuously exhibits and displays its thought and feeling in the colour and sound of the words, and in a verse drama especially, much depends upon the style of the individual writer for the satisfactory performance of the play on the stage.

In a drama licensed for the unreal, it is not surprising to find its *plotting* to be incredible, even outrageous. *Pace* Philip Sidney, a young prince could fall in love, have a baby, who can be lost, grow up, fall in love and be ready to have another, 'and all this in two hours space'. However, in structure, the method was straightforward enough, and followed the plain narrative procedure of placing one brick upon another until the house was built and the story told. A simple change of fortunes for good or ill (like the *'peripeteia'* [reversal] of Greek tragedy) might constitute the only complication.

Sidney's criticism was that the drama appeared to care little for the unity of action, and dared to 'mingle Kings and clowns' and 'match hornpipes and funerals'. The freedom of this stage could juxtapose violently contrasting ideas, and this is nowhere better exemplified than in the development in Elizabethan drama of the *sub-plot*, a pregnant device which by coincidence or parallelism was woven with the main plot, reflecting and expanding the purpose and theme of the action. The sub-plot, which was as open to abuse as any device, was in fact a triumph of Elizabethan stagecraft. It is embryonic in the parody of Faustus's servant Wagner, who in *Doctor Faustus* tries to imitate his master, bind the Clown to him for seven years and raise a pair of devils of his own. It reaches aesthetic heights in Shakespeare's *The Merchant of Venice*, where the tensions of the trial for Antonio's pound of flesh are echoed and eclipsed by Portia's gentler trials in amorous Belmont engineered to test her lovers.

In an unfamiliar theatrical world of shows, the number of ways to exhibit and explore the allegorical and symbolic in performance defeats our full comprehension of the dramatic mode. *Dumb shows* are sprinkled freely through the plays, serving not so much to interrupt and divert the flow of the drama as to focus and lift it on to another plane. To be vividly understood, the dumb show was played wordlessly in a style more exaggerated than the play it illustrated. A *play-within-the-play* in the same way could arrest attention by its abrupt change of style in speech and music, while reinforcing the substance of the host play; at the end of Kyd's *The Spanish Tragedy*, for example, Hieronimo's play-within, *Soliman and Perseda*, is electrically transformed when the principals die in earnest and the audience finds that fact and fiction have been shockingly confused. Moreover, many scenes were conceived almost as tableaux. Thus they are scattered through Marlowe's *Tamburlaine*, clustering to make a point especially at the end, when 'the scourge of God' must die. There is more than a touch of magic in the air when in mourning black Mercade descends on the last act of Shakespeare's *Love's Labour's Lost* like the figure of Death himself, directing a change in the costumes of the actors, the mood of the scene and the tone of the drama.

The University Wits and their experiments

The English stage owes a great deal to the so-called 'University Wits', the name given to a group of young men from Oxford and Cambridge who in the years 1585–95 chose to experiment with a range of different kinds of play from pastoral comedy to revenge tragedy. However, if they brought to their writing a new professionalism, it sprang more from their scholarly reading and less from their experience of the stage and exposure to the public. In Part II of the anonymous Cambridge play *The Return from Parnassus* (1601) 'Burbage' and 'Kemp' give a mock interview to the cousins Philomusus and Ingenioso, two young college graduates who want to be playwrights, and they are warned, 'Few of the university men pen plays well; they smell too much of that writer Ovid, and that writer Metamorphosis, and talk too much of Proserpina and Jupiter.' The eternal opposites of the stage world, the literary and the theatrical, are both amusingly confounded here. Nevertheless, the University Wits were alive to the opportunities of the moment, and as free spirits they opened up a variety of avenues in subject and technique for the playwrights who followed them.

This was particularly true of their comedy in the years before the end of the sixteenth century. Although at this time intellectual arguments for comedy were still defensive, with audiences it was the most popular genre, quickly multiplying its methods and modes, and running the gamut from pastoral romance to hard satire. Yet no potentially tragic material was quite free from the mixtures dear to the Elizabethans, and, with its lovers and its clowns, much of it is on the edge of 'mongrel tragi-comedy', or what Lyly in his Prologue to *Midas* calls 'a mingle-mangle'. Plato's idea that serious matters cannot be understood without some laughter was readily accepted, and echoed by Sidney in his *Apology for Poetry*: 'As in geometry, the oblique must be known as well as the right, and in arithmetic, the odd as well as the even.'

In addition, the self-reflexive quality of medieval drama, the sense of theatre-as-game in which a play was for all to share, happily lingered on.

The elegant *John Lyly* (1554?-1606), Oxford author of the seductively stylistic novel *Euphues* (1578), wrote his plays for the Earl of Oxford's St Paul's Boys, and aimed them, not at the popular stage, but at the Queen and a sophisticated, courtly audience. As a result he has been labelled a 'dramatist's dramatist'. Yet Lyly was immensely important for the future of English drama because for the stage he pioneered a dialogue in prose and introduced without a qualm the notion that artificiality and stylization were admissible on the stage, particularly the form of rhetoric associated with the celebrated style 'Euphuism' that so enchanted Polonius. With its alliterative word games, its pointed and balanced similes and antitheses, the style on the face of it seems too shallow and verbal, incapable of holding an audience in the theatre. In drama the style is the play, and in Lyly it is apparently so clockwork, so measured and methodical, that it could never take a spectator by the throat in performance. Yet this may be the wrong way to look at it. That the playwright preferred to offer a fragile courtly entertainment played by a child's company suggests that he was matching a style to the spirit of his audience and the level of his players, and creating for his comedies of romantic love a delicate unisex of the tongue.

Strangely, in conditions of performance, the style promises (for the plays are rarely produced) to do something else and offer to transport the spectator to a dream world. The Prologue to *Sappho and Phao* beseeches the Queen to let him work on her fancy:

> We all, and I on knee for all, entreat that your Highness imagine yourself to be in a deep dream, that staying the

conclusion, in your rising your Majesty vouchsafe but to say, *And so you awaked.*

Swaying to its internal rhythms like the dancers in a graceful pavan, the style exudes an hypnotic quality that could enthral its audience on another level, that of a masque-like dream, a theatrical allegory in part made up of the figures of classical mythology. That being so, Lyly needs none of the muscularity of the blank verse with which Shakespeare could animate actor and character. Instead, the witty offsetting of thoughts and ideas in Euphuism could be as exhilarating as argument or as seductive as sleep.

Of Elizabethan stagecraft little is to be learned from Lyly. There are a few explicit calls for song, but almost no stage directions. *Campaspe* (c. 1583) is a shadowy story of the rivalry between Alexander the Great, in love with the eponymous slave-girl, and one Apelles sent to paint her portrait. The comedy uses the classical five-act structure, and the way the stage is set round the Athenian market-place with houses for the King's palace and the painter's studio and a tub for Diogenes suggests multiple staging of the familiar kind, together with an arrangment of symbols of royalty, art and philosophy. Lyly's has been called 'a stage for allegory'. The mildly allegorical *Endymion* (c. 1588) has the moonstruck mortal of the title offer himself as worshipper of Cynthia, immortal goddess of the moon. The play is an early image of an abstract and timeless pastoral world in which mortal may rub shoulders with immortal, and if in its day the play gracefully intended Cynthia to represent the Queen herself, it acquired a special edge, and afforded its Court audience a pleasant and witty fantasy.

Gallathea (c. 1584) is of a different interest because it is the first Elizabethan comedy to have a boy actor play a girl who disguises herself as a boy, with the complications implicit in the device, and since Gallathea and Phillida are two girls who, in order to avoid a virgin sacrifice to Neptune, are both so disguised, the complications are deliciously compounded. It is typical that the two should fall in love with one another, each thinking the other a boy, which presents a problem that only the goddess Venus can resolve. Here again, mortal may mingle with immortal, and lovers and clowns sport themselves in a fantastic world of nymphs and fairies, as in *A Midsummer Night's Dream*.

When the equivocations of the style reflect the complexity of a single figure, *Gallathea* displays a stronger sense of performance than Lyly's other plays. It enjoys an occasional salvo of asides, as in 2.1 where the two girls have lines that speak what is in their heads and imply a fine sense of their comic behaviour as boys ('I fear I should make a curtsy instead of a leg'). In act 2 the two girls juggle a pair of matching soliloquies in which their feelings are captured by the mechanical balance of their lines:

> GALLATHEA. How now, Gallathea, miserable Gallathea ...
> PHILLIDA.   Poor Phillida, curse the time of thy birth ...

The duplication is more aural than visual when the see-saw of the thoughts is heard, with Gallathea vexed by the inequity of the outward and the inward views, and Phillida (like Rosalind later) cursing the unsuitability of her doublet and hose as a support for her racing emotions. Gallathea's preference of sacrifice over slavery, of drowning over servitude, is nicely bracketed with Phillida's despair at being wrongly dressed for the occasion and at wanting what she may not have. The alternations and undulations finally dissolve into the ridiculous self-contradictions of a Launcelot Gobbo: 'I will – I dare not; thou must – I cannot.' The achievement of the parallelism of Gallathea and Phillida is in matching two complete characters and their attitudes, for such twinning is comic in itself. When the two girls successively stand centre stage, the cloning amounts to clowning.

In the hands of the Cambridge man *Robert Greene* (*c.* 1560–92), the stage returned to a brisk, popular folk comedy, mixing pastoral myth and romantic adventure with country jests and fairy magic. Of importance here, Greene's work from the beginning smacks strongly of the stage. A first play, *The Comical History of Alphonsus, King of Aragon* (*c.* 1587), is alive with directions and detail that derive from the prompt-copy and are essentially authorial. The play opens with an induction in the professional way it means to go on, beginning impressively, '*After you have sounded thrice, let Venus be let down from the top of the stage, and when she is down, say: . . .*' And soon after comes, '*Enter Melpomene, Clio, Erato, with their sisters, playing all upon sundry instruments, Calliope only excepted, who coming last, hangeth down the head, and plays not of her instrument.*' Greene has an instinct for directing, and makes his thinking known.

His last play, *The Scottish History of James the Fourth* (*c.* 1591), is no less rich in detail, and the induction begins, '*Music playing within. Enter after Oberon, King of Fairies, an Antic, who dance about a tomb placed conveniently on the stage; out of the which suddenly starts up, as they dance, Bohan, a Scot, attired like a Redesdale man, from whom the Antic flies. Oberon manet.*' One may question the presence of the King of the Fairies in a chronicle play, but *James IV* is less of a history and more of a romance, one in which two noble young ladies, Dorothea and Ida, inhabit an idealized, sylvan world taken from Cinthio. The text is rich in suggestions for costume and dance, specifying a jig or a hornpipe or a round; it is particularly striking in its concern for spatial arrangement and movement, with unusual notations like '*aloof*', '*stands aside*', '*spying him*', '*descend down*', '*overhears*', '*approaching*', '*march over*'; and occasionally it offers a more demanding direction of an histrionic nature like '*they all are in a muse*'.

Friar Bacon and Friar Bungay (*c.* 1589), also called 'a history', is even more of a generic hotchpotch, but it also deserves attention for its wealth of authorial directions for performance. It embodies the popular concoction of the time and pairs Kings and emperors with rustic clowns and country wenches. It also mixes a degree of patriotic and moralistic sentiment, here associated with the story of a Griselda-like romantic heroine, with magic shows and spectacle. The play also prolongs the life of the Vice by distributing his favourite characteristics between two rascals, Miles and Rafe, and cannot forbear to retain a merry devil or two from some former street entertainment. Yet what emerges from this mixture is a trim double plot (not just a main and a sub-plot). The first is well-focused on the courtly lovers, Edward and Lacy, in their rivalry for the affections of Margaret, the fair maid of Fressingfield, and the second on the rival magicians,

Friars Bacon and Bungay, and their attempts to outdo one another.

It has been suggested that much of the multiple plotting in this play was induced by the apparent need to double so many parts while using only one-third the number of actors, but this is a chicken-and-egg argument, and Greene manages to achieve dramatic unity of purpose and action by marching the two stories shoulder to shoulder through the play, so that at the end Edward's nobility in stepping aside for Lacy is echoed by Friar Bacon's desire to break his magic glass and forswear his necromantic powers: 'Think Mercy sits where Justice holds her seat.' Some of the credit for this unity in performance may be ascribed to Greene's success with double and multiple staging, so that any confusion caused by the divers styles was possibly resolved by the agency of the neutral stage, well able to encompass the crowded action in two or three areas simultaneously.

Scene 6 is notable for its flexible handling of several conflicting centres of interest. The audience is also to understand that the first pair are in Bacon's lodgings in Oxford, and the second in Fressingfield in Suffolk. Moreover, when the two parties are established in two separate areas of the stage, the Oxford party may look in Bacon's magic glass and 'see' the other. If all this seems ham-fisted as stagecraft, the transitions in the scene are characteristically smooth, and betray no strain in the writing. Greene's is a joyful stage which is untroubled by realism and the need to convince. In scene 9 he conjures a 'tree leav'd with refined gold', a 'dragon shooting fire' and then a magic feast, before, in scene 11, drawing the 'study' curtains (now become a kind of wizard's cloak) and disclosing a spectacular brazen head. This is theatre as magic show, justified, no doubt, in a play about two rival magicians, but otherwise a case of uninhibited theatricality.

From Oxford, *George Peele* (c. 1552–97) offered *The Old Wives' Tale* (c. 1590), which may be set beside *Friar Bacon* as an even more restless and extravagant mixture of romantic folk tale and madcap farce that also manages to snatch a kind of unity from variety by making use of an easy induction, but one of no less than 135 lines – a lengthy section of a play of only 970 – an induction that is actually a 'frame' for the action of the story to come. As Madge, wife to Clunch the Smith, entertains three pages, Antic, Frolic and Fantastic, with food and drink and all good cheer, they are to be (like Christopher Sly in *The Taming of the Shrew*) the on-stage audience which listens and watches as she tells her tale. They settle down to eat a meal of cheese and pudding, once or twice a dog barks off-stage and everyone sings a chorus of a popular ditty: the realistic details of simple life in a peasant cottage are a clever prelude to the fantastic story to follow, a sort of licence for the audience to indulge the pleasures of the incredible by making it conscious that it is indulging itself. From time to time the 'narrative' is stopped for Madge to correct her memory or answer a question, which adds to the relaxed realism of the frame and even suggests that the performance of the play must be better than the telling of the tale. In this the mixture of myth and magic, all perpetrated in a self-reflexive mood of fun and jest, is so unbelievable that its very disconnections may well be the source of the play's humour and charm.

Conventions in *The Spanish Tragedy*

With *Thomas Kyd* (1558?-94?) professional English stagecraft took a leap forward and English tragedy found a shape. His play *The Spanish Tragedy* (c. 1587), together with Marlowe's *Tamburlaine* and the opening of Henslowe's Rose, made this date particularly memorable for the English stage. *The Spanish Tragedy* was a piece of exceptionally successful theatre of the macabre, and its leading part was probably played by the great Edward Alleyn at the Rose; it was subsequently revived at the Fortune and remained popular for many years, as its frequent parodying confirms. With this play English drama finally completed the shift from the narrative to the dramatic mode in a process of visual realization that persists throughout the action.

The play is a grisly tragedy of revenge whose theme of guilt

and retribution is rather overshadowed by its mechanics: it
has a frenzied revenger for a hero and a heady sequence of
physical and visual horrors marks out its progress by hangings
and stabbings in full view of the audience. It also drew upon
the new taste for Seneca and his mixture of revenge ingredients
that included sententious choruses, restless ghosts, allegorical
dumb shows and an inclination towards tableaux. However,
Seneca's was a literary treatment of sin, despair and violent
death, and offered a self-conscious verbal style made up of
long, bombastic speeches closer to narrative poetry than
dramatic rhetoric; for his part, Kyd made sure that every set
piece matched the character speaking it, and balanced a
soliloquy with the activity of the scene in which it was placed.
He knew that studied artificiality may be useful, but that it has
to obey the laws of theatrical stimulus and response. And Kyd
also brought a dead stage to life by making Seneca's bloodbath
palpable and his rhetoric *visual*: after Andrea's Ghost narrates
the story of his death, the audience sees eight murders and
suicides, and is entertained by several scenes of madness and
one of biting out one's tongue. Chris Dyer's design for the
production at the National Theatre in 1982 captured this
gruesome world by dressing the stage with chains, gallows
and instruments of torture.

As Seneca's hand grows faint in *The Spanish Tragedy*, the
play appears to be a great exhibition of stage devices and
stratagems of Kyd's own invention as he coins new ways of
telling his story. The text of 1592 is thick with what must have
been the author's directions, interpolated to ensure that what
was staged was as he wanted it, and these are seen not only in
the big effects (*'she runs lunatic'*, *'she stabs herself'*), but also
in the more subtle ones (*'she, in going in, lets fall her glove'*,
'staring him in the face'). In the larger arrangement of the
plot, revenge repeatedly provides the simplest fuel for the
action: in a dishonourable fight Balthazar has killed Andrea,
who now needs revenge, as does Bel-imperia, his betrothed;
offering to help her, Horatio wins her love, and Balthazar and
Lorenzo seek their revenge on him; thus these two kill
Horatio by a dishonourable hanging, so that his father
Hieronimo also wants revenge; accordingly, when Hieronimo
kills Balthazar, both Andrea and Horatio are revenged. Yet

even this dogged sequence of revenges acquires qualities of original stagecraft.

To increase the tension within the machinery of the plot, Kyd supplies touches of parallelism and parody through lesser characters like the villains Villuppo and Pedringano (who is dispatched, 3.6, in a moment of bantering black humour with a jest on his lips like Macheath on the gallows), and has Horatio echo Andreas as Hieronimo echoes the Viceroy of Portugal, so that the stage seems imbued with kindred dangers revolving upon themselves. When the play opens with a supernatural induction in which the gory Ghost of Andrea, speaking gory words ('Here falls a body scinder'd [sundered] from his head ...') and seated beside the figure of hideous Revenge itself, these two remain on-stage throughout the performance to frame the play and lend the stage the illusion that the audience is watching *itself* watch the sequence of horror. And as the real audience watches Hieronimo arrange his revenge through the sly agency of a play-within-a-play in the last act, it is doubly horrified to discover that the players are killing each other in earnest, so that the sense of theatre and the sense of real life are at the end unnervingly muddled. Following the text, Michael Bogdanov's 1982 production used four different languages for the play-within, so that the effect of Babel added to the noise and confusion of the butchery.

Set against a diabolic villain of Machiavellian persuasion, one Lorenzo, the protagonist Hieronimo is the revenger who over a period of time runs mad with grief, and this provides the occasions for Kyd to make his Senecan perorations into acceptable peaks of rage and anguish. More than this, the scenes of madness actually add to the suspense of the story by introducing moments of procrastination that apparently appealed to the author of *Hamlet*. Hieronimo's soliloquies are full and frequent, but manage to symbolize the cruelty of an unjust society while suggesting with a certain degree of realism a private mind an audience can enter. Again, Kyd succeeds in matching rhetorical character with visual action, and supplies personal props to help him: in 3.12 Hieronimo enters '*with a poniard in one hand, and a rope in the other*', the tokens of suicide, apparently determined to stab or hang

himself or both. Soon after, he makes one entrance after
another, searching everywhere by torchlight in the night, and
digging with his dagger to 'rip the bowels of the earth' to find
his son's remains and 'show his deadly wounds'. Ironically he
is conscious of stage daylight when he cries,

> Was I so mad to bid you light your torches now?
> Light me your torches at the mid of noon.

The scene of Horatio's murder (2.4) deserves attention for its
confident handling of the detail of the sensational. First, the
horrors to come are prepared by the contrasting tone of a
sensual love scene between Horatio and Bel-imperia. On the
daylight stage the dark night invokes an ambiguously
amorous and fearful mood, with love ironically tinged with
evil as the treacherous servant Pedringano chooses to betray
the lovers. Horatio has a silver tongue:

> Now that the night begins with sable wings
> To overcloud the brightness of the sun,
> And that in darkness pleasures may be done,
> Come Bel-imperia, let us to the bower ...

While Bel-imperia's heart 'foretells me some mischance',
Horatio continues unwittingly to paint the night blacker still:
the stars 'hold back their twinkling shine' and the moon 'hides
herself to pleasure us'. And before disaster descends on them
as they sit in 'these leavy bowers', Kyd meticulously directs
what they must do erotically with their hands, feet, lips and
arms. Finally, looking passionately into the lady's eyes,
Horatio offers to make love to her:

> O stay awhile and I will die with thee.

The sexual pun on death is nicely placed to cue the ironic
entrance of the little band of villains who come to murder
him.

It is then that the same flowery bower that stimulated their
love supplies the very gibbet to hang Horatio before he is
stabbed, the rope and the knife used in that order – a version
of common hanging and drawing that anyone who paid a
gruesome visit to Tyburn would recognize for its popular
theatrical value. The property 'arbour' was probably an arch

The Spanish Tragedie:
OR,
Hieronimo is mad againe.

Containing the lamentable end of *Don Horatio*, and
Belimperia; with the pittifull death of *Hieronimo*.

Newly corrected, amended, and enlarged with new
Additions of the *Painters* part, and others, as
it hath of late been diuers times acted.

LONDON,
Printed by W. White, for I. White and T. Langley,
and are to be sold at their Shop ouer against the
Sarazens head without New-gate. 1615.

5   Thomas Kyd, *The Spanish Tragedy*, c. 1587: the title-page of the
1615 edition. The scene in the woodcut is of 2.4, the murder of
Horatio in the arbour.

of lattice (decorated with leaves and looking a bit like the 'tree' referred to later in the play), sturdy yet portable for convenient hangings; it possibly did double duty when Pedringano was hanged in 3.6. Such a prop is sketched on the title-page of the edition of 1615, where Hieronimo from his bed finds Horatio hanging, while Bel-imperia is pulled away by Lorenzo in a mask.

The deed is done in front of Bel-imperia's eyes, and her screams for help as she is dragged off are the 'outcries' that pluck Hieronimo from his 'naked bed', clad in his nightshirt and bearing a torch in the imaginary darkness – altogether a full, material moment of terror demonstrated, witnessed and felt.

The screams also pluck on the next scene, which smoothly follows its predecessor, and against the backdrop of so much spectacle offers the actor Alleyn the rich opportunity of his first bravura soliloquy. Hieronimo staggers about in the dark, the audience holding its breath until he finds the hanging body and cuts it down, the father first recognizing his son's clothing and then discovering his identity. After all the noise, his voice is incisively quiet as he addresses his 'sweet lovely rose':

O heavens, why made you night to cover sin?

He embraces his son's corpse, and the picture of his grief is enhanced by the entrance of his wife Isabella. She closes Horatio's staring eyes, and the father exhibits a 'handkercher besmear'd with blood' – dipping a handkerchief in the victim's blood was a practice at public executions. J. R. Mulryne in his edition of the play also suggests that this object was the same 'scarf' that Bel-imperia gave to Andrea to wear in battle, thus seeming to make Horatio into Andrea's double on stage, and also that it was the 'bloody napkin' that Hieronimo treasures to the end as a token of his revenge. Together the mother and father take up the mutilated body, and to Isabella's plaintive rhymes and Hieronimo's formal lament intoned in Latin with sword ritualistically held to his chest, the unhappy parents close out an unforgettable scene and leave the stage to the agonized chorus figure of Andrea.

The liberal exhibition of blood, in which letters are written as if the most natural substance in the world; an extravagant sequence of mad scenes (3.8, 3.9) in which Isabella follows Hieronimo in his derangement before taking her own life with a flourish (4.2); and the preliminary ritual of a macabre marriage in dumb show in which the nuptial torches are quenched by blood (3.15) – all precede the more lavish bloodshed to come. General slaughter makes up Hieronimo's masque *Soliman and Perseda*, in which the principals of the play-within are with ominous predictability played by the principals of the main play. If by the time of this last act the real audience is besotted by bloodthirstiness, it now watches the royal party of the King of Spain watch the carnage with a fresh face of horror, as it witnesses the pretence of murder made actual. In the theatrical progress of the play the audience has seen a dramatic concoction of theatrical shows, in which it has watched an on-stage audience watch a dumb show, and then another of villains watch a love scene of their intended victims; at the same time it has been aware of everything on stage and off being watched by the chorus of Andreas and Revenge. So it is entirely appropriate that this savage climax of sensation upon sensation is presented in the context and spirit of a masque, among the most theatrically artificial and synthetic of forms. When at his last appearance the Ghost coolly adds up the number of the dead, the encapsulated monstrosities are given their final seal of distancing, packaged in the theatrical frame in which they began.

So much for the theatrical imagination. The mode of late Elizabethan theatre, with its absence of scenery and its heavy emphasis upon bold stage conventions, greatly encouraged new plays, and the University Wits took every advantage of the situation. Lyly's extension of multiple staging derived directly from the medieval practice of setting mansions and houses around a neutral area, but, floating on his delicate lines, his plays gracefully espoused its timelessness and place-lessness, and sweetly generated his pastoral, allegorical world. Greene and Peele exploited the liberal stage more extrava-gantly, their lusty folk comedy and wild romanticism spin-ning an exuberant theatrical magic. Kyd's professionalism filled his tragic stage with grisly images to balance a new rhetoric, and he pumped up his audience's reactions with a relentless string of dramatic devices: ghostly observers, vengeful monologues and sundry orchestrated sensations including the dumb show, the play-within and the masque. It was altogether a theatre of high spirits and wide choices, all in pursuit of an exciting new stagecraft. Christopher Marlowe had yet to show what could be done with it.

5

Marlowe's stagecraft

Marlowe's theatre: the discovery of the Rose, 1989

In 1587 Philip Henslowe opened his Rose playhouse in Rose Alley, Maiden Lane (on the South Bank in the Liberty of the Clink) and, associated initially with the immensely successful productions of *The Spanish Tragedy*, *Tamburlaine* and *The Jew of Malta*, it was no doubt the centre of theatrical attention. It is likely that all of Marlowe's plays were first played there, and it could be thought of as 'Marlowe's theatre'. It possibly also introduced Greene's *Friar Bacon and Friar Bungay* in 1589 and Shakespeare's apprentice plays '*harey the vj*' and '*titus and ondronicus*' (as Henslowe's diary has them) in *c*. 1592. In 1594 Henslowe combined Strange's Men and the Admiral's Men into a new company, with his son-in-law the great Edward Alleyn as their leading actor, and this company played its repertory at the Rose until 1600. At that time hot competition from the new Globe less than 100 yards away forced Henslowe to move to the Fortune which he built on the other side of the river, and he let the lease of the Rose expire. By 1606 it had been pulled down.

Four hundred years later the foundations of the Rose were unearthed, making it the first Elizabethan theatre about which there is sure evidence of shape and size. If the design of a theatre is the unique pointer to the ways a playwright assumed his play would work, the Rose should tell us about Marlowe. The foundations were different from expectations. Henslowe had referred to the estate of the 'Little Rose', but with a 72 foot outside diameter (compared with the Fortune's 80 feet and the Globe's probable 100 feet) the Rose had half the space of the Globe and, with its tiring house inside the frame of the building, it was truly compact. It also had fourteen sides, not the anticipated eight, and was irregular in shape to boot. The stage jutted about two-fifths into the yard, like Inigo Jones's Court theatres, and faced south, giving it more sun and light than had the stage of the Globe, which seems to have faced north-east. At its maximum width it was 36 feet 9 inches, tapering to 26 feet 10 inches, and was 16 feet 5 inches deep, yielding an acting area of 490 square feet. There was no evidence of stage-posts or traps, but nothing to suggest that a balcony, with discovery-space below, did not exist.

In 1592, presumably in the light of experience, Henslowe made some changes. He enlarged the stage end, moving the wall 6 feet 10 inches further north, so increasing the size of the yard and galleries, and bringing the capacity of the house up from 2,000 to 2,425. He also thereby increased the depth and thrust of the stage to 18 feet 4 inches, which offered an acting area of 533 square feet. From the evidence of the footings and a drip-line from the thatch, it is likely that stage posts were added at the front of the stage, suggesting that a stage roof or 'shadow' was built.

In the last analysis, all assumptions about the details of the Rose and its productions are speculative, but within the general parameters of surmise there seems no doubt that the stage had twin doors, indicated in many plays simply as '*at one door*' and '*at the other door*', sometimes suggesting an automatic contrast between the characters using the entrances. Between the doors the call for Horatio's 'bower' in *The Spanish Tragedy*, a 'counting house' for Barabas in *The Jew of Malta* and the 'study' in *Doctor Faustus* was evidently satisfied by a discovery-space, which could on occasion introduce the magic theatrical element of a dumb show or other pleasant surprise, as when Hieronimo '*knocks up the curtain*' for his play-within in *The Spanish Tragedy*.

The common term '*above*' in *The Spanish Tragedy*, *Tamburlaine*, *Titus Andronicus* and other plays indicates the certain use of a balcony over the stage, always in relation to activity on the main stage below: in *2 Tamburlaine*, 5.2, the balcony represents the walls of Babylon, upon which the Governor appears with his officers and defies the demand of Theridamas and Techelles to yield the city, whereupon '*they scale the walls*' and Tamburlaine himself enters below in his chariot to give the order to shackle the Governor:

> Go, bind the villain – he shall hang in chains
> Upon the ruins of this conquered town.

and a moment later:

> Go draw him up,
> Hang him in chains upon the city walls
> And let my soldiers shoot the slave to death.

The shooting proceeds, and it is not difficult to imagine how the two levels could vividly accommodate all this business, including the burning of holy books in a fire on the stage shortly after.

A trapdoor (or two) on the large stage space may also be assumed, enabling the Ghost of Andrea to return to Hell at the end of *The Spanish Tragedy*. It also supplied a home for the devils in *Doctor Faustus* and an appropriate exit for Faustus's long-anticipated descent into Hell. And it conveniently provided a 'loathsome pit' and 'this unhallow'd and blood-stained hole' for several bodies in *Titus Andronicus*, 2.3. The trap was another magical device, inherited from the medieval pageant wagon, that the theatre has adopted as its own for ever.

Marlowe's early sense of theatre

Christopher Marlowe (1564–93) was a Cambridge poet and the greatest of the University Wits, but beguiling problems of Renaissance morality and individualism have distracted scholars from the technical advances found in his plays. An ambitious overreacher he may have been, and he may have projected his own personality into his extravagant heroes, but like any other playwright he was confronted with the immediate demands of a challenging new playhouse of limited dramatic precedent. For this reason alone his success is of significance in the history of the stage.

Ben Jonson's identification of Marlowe's contribution as his 'mighty line' also indicated the vocal qualities called for by the colour and excess of its rhetoric, suffused with figures and patterns, and heavy with imposing names and allusions to classical myth: John Russell Brown has remarked that Hamlet's advice to the Players, that they speak 'trippingly on the tongue', was not appropriate for Marlowe. Thomas Nashe wrote of 'the swelling bombast of bragging blank-verse', although Michael Drayton, more kindly in his epitaph to Marlowe, declared his poetry to be 'all air and fire'. The ranting of Marlowe's lines has historically been linked with the majestic acting style of Edward Alleyn (1566–1626), something of a barn-stormer who capped his reputation as the mad Hieronimo by playing the giant characters Tamburlaine, Barabas and Faustus. His name, like Tamburlaine's, is synonymous with the extremes of formal acting and declamatory, operatic speech: in 1597 Joseph Hall wrote of his 'stalking steps' and 'thundering threats', and, thinking of Alleyn's performance as Tamburlaine, Jonson in *Timber* scathingly referred to 'the scenical strutting, and furious vociferation' of 'the late age'. Nevertheless, excess of colour is also a source of vocal monotony, while unduly rich speech makes for static movement, the two together dulling the attention, and the perception, of the spectator – something Marlowe himself realized in his later plays when he manipulated more subtly the iambics he wrote for Edward II and Faustus.

The insistence of Marlowe's poetry, and its immensely ritualistic rhetoric, points to a telling factor that lies behind his stagecraft, that he was still writing for an essentially ritualistic theatre. For his is not, in the end, a moralistic theatre: the Good and Bad Angels who hover through *Doctor Faustus* are somewhat grotesque morality figures left over from an earlier time, but even in this play Marlowe is not so much moralizing as exploring: he lets the drama itself do any teaching, and his characters' addresses to the audience are not those of the author as preacher, but as presenter. His towering stage heroes are therefore to be seen as characters set up for exhibition, and they provide focal points for his scrutiny, as well as the driving energy behind his dramatic voyages of discovery. In Marlowe there is a final concern with the nature of sin and redemption, reflecting the cycle plays from which his drama springs, and while it is difficult to find much that is

humanly realistic in a Tamburlaine or a Barabas, it is easy to
see that Faustus is more of an observed human being than,
say, Mankind or Everyman.

We may pass over Marlowe's first play *Dido, Queen of
Carthage* (c. 1585), if only because he probably shared the
authorship with Thomas Nashe the pamphleteer (1567–1601)
and because it was written for the Children of the Chapel
Royal and their private audience at the Blackfriars. It is worth
observing that the young Marlowe is already alive to the
possibilities of a formal stage, but the play has more narration
than characterization. It is the unconscionable Tamburlaine
who heads the extraordinary procession of Marlowe's gross
sinners and heretics, and it is frequently maintained that his
extravagance is relieved by a certain sense of submerged
comedy. The recurring mode of Marlowe's drama is that of
curiously ironic satire, in which the tone is in every case made
more persistently ambivalent – and gratefully more natural –
by touches of black humour. This emerges in *Tamburlaine*
chiefly in relentlessly jeering at the tyrant's enemies and
captives – the taunting of the weak Mycetes, King of Persia, in
the first act, and after he has been carefully exhibited *'in great
pomp'*, the ironic mockery accorded Bajazeth, Emperor of the
Turks, in the third. However, this humour does little to
reconcile an audience to an unlovely hero, and the success of
Marlowe's stagecraft turns on other, more notable, contributions to the new theatre.

Tamburlaine the Great

Marlowe was twenty-three when in 1587 he wrote *Tamburlaine the Great* for the small stage of the Rose. In this play he
has hardly mastered his medium, and the scenes march
relentlessly on to the platform one after another to parade
Tamburlaine's victories and the wretches he has conquered.
Marlowe repeatedly crowds his stage with oriental emperors,
kings and lords, and in Part I he is fond of adding *'and others'*
to his opening direction (in Part II this becomes *'and their
train'*), as if he wanted to make sure no one was omitted. Yet

with all its excesses, *Tamburlaine* embodies Marlowe's exuberant spirit of youth, and, apart from the subject he dares to offer, it speaks clearly of his gifts as a new writer for the public playhouse. In Henslowe's inventory for the Lord Admiral's Men, his diary records some of Tamburlaine's colourful clothing, including a 'coat with copper lace' and 'breeches of crimson velvet'. From the moment in scene 2 that Tamburlaine discards his shepherd's weeds for armour, every theatrical device of music, prop and sumptuous costume is brought into play. However, there seems to be nothing planned or premeditated about the work, and its stylistic flights are spontaneous and intuitive. Henslowe indicates that Part I was an instant success, and according to its Prologue the consequence was that Marlowe wrote Part II without hesitation.

To look briefly at Part I, the Prologue immediately announces the challenge of the play:

> From jigging veins of rhyming mother-wits
> And such conceits as clownage keeps in pay,
> We'll lead you to the stately tent of war ...

This is also a declaration of a new programme for the theatre, which is now to be taken seriously. Be that as it may, Marlowe shows little care for dramatic plot or shape, and in telling the story of the rise of a Scythian shepherd to be emperor, *Tamburlaine* presents a picture of unbridled megalomania in a series of audacious adventures that resemble a narrative poem delivered in salvos. And if the mode of the play does not quite belong to drama, it consists of processional pageantry in which its scenes assume the appearance of *tableaux vivants*, or emblematic shows and images.

Particular scenes that are almost tableaux best convey the sense of Marlovian ritual pageantry. From Part I, the scene in which the rival Queens Zabina and Zenocrate wear the imperial crowns of the two emperors Bajazeth and Tamburlaine while they and their armies do battle off-stage (3.3) is such a one. On a stage set about with crowned kings and imperious 'bassoes' [bashaws or commanders] gloriously costumed, the two women sit side by side – presumably on thrones upstage centre – and taunt one another:

> ZABINA.   Base concubine, must thou be placed by me
> That am the empress of the mighty Turk?
> ZENOCRATE. Disdainful Turkess and unreverend boss,
> Callest thou me concubine, that am betrothed
> Unto the great and mighty Tamburlaine?

This is a static arrangement, and such ceremoniousness belies the pace of the action, but the formal mirror effect of the echoing lines is strikingly theatrical, for while the catlike ladies mechanically spit and slash at one another with words, the real business of doing war and defeating Bajazeth and his army is taking place off-stage, however conveniently for the theatre.

Act 4 opens with a theatrical consciousness of colour that is unusual for any period, and in 4.2 a Messenger carefully explains the meaning of the colours with which, with appalling calculation, Tamburlaine is in the habit of terrorizing the citizens of any city of his choice over a three-day siege:

> The first day when he pitcheth down his tents,
> White is their hue, and on his silver crest
> A snowy feather spangled white he bears,
> To signify the mildness of his mind
> That, satiate with spoil, refuseth blood;
> But when Aurora mounts the second time,
> As red as scarlet is his furniture –
> Then must his kindled wrath be quenched with blood,
> Not sparing any that can manage arms;
> But if these threats move not submission,
> Black are his colours, black pavilion,
> His spear, his shield, his horse, his armour, plumes,
> And jetty feathers menace death and hell . . .

By the ingenious device of changing the colour of costume and décor, terror is transferred from the stage to the audience and back again in the scenes that follow (4.2, 4.4, 5.1), while Tamburlaine processes through each colour-coded phase of his siege of Damascus. The stage image passes from the chivalric milk-white of his flags of mercy to the bloody scarlet of his threats in 4.4,

> Now hang our bloody colours by Damascus,
> Reflexing hues of blood upon their heads

> While they walk quivering on their city walls,
> Half dead for fear before they feel my wrath.

So to the final menace and evil of his coal-black tents before his attack.

It is while wearing his white plumes that Tamburlaine has his prisoner Bajazeth exhibited and fed scraps of food in a cage like an animal, the cage itself an emblem, and then delights in climbing over his body to reach his throne, there using him as a footstool (4.2). The prop is strongly symbolic of the barbarian monster's methods and of his savage mind, and the scenic picture reveals him as grotesquely larger than life. In Part II the parallel scene is 4.3, where a brace of deposed kings, with bits in their mouths like horses and whipped on by Tamburlaine, draw him in his chariot across the stage to his cry, 'Holla, ye pampered jades of Asia!'

When Tamburlaine is costumed in his unrelenting black, the Governor of Damascus in desperation sends a deputation of four virgins to beg for mercy, whereupon the tyrant promptly orders them to be put to the sword and their 'carcasses' hung upon the city walls. This dark scene makes yet another statement about Tamburlaine's infamy, but this time, with dizzying effect, the ugly symbolism persists even when at the next moment, as drunk with love as with blood, he suddenly changes his tune in soliloquy and speaks an almost lyrical ode to his Queen:

> Ah fair Zenocrate, divine Zenocrate!
> Fair is too foul an epithet for thee.

The mind is intended to boggle at the shocking juxtaposition and the outrageous discord that discloses Tamburlaine's two sides so violently. In Peter Hall's production at the National Theatre in 1976 Albert Finney as Tamburlaine here introduced a note of lunacy into his voice as he spoke.

Black comedy: *The Jew of Malta*

In this play the Marlovian gift for creating extravagant theatre turned to comedy. Just as *The Jew of Malta* (c. 1590) is memorable for its daring content, it is also important for its staging experiments – another leap in both genre and technique. With Barabas its supremely Machiavellian villain, a stereotype of the Jew verging on the grotesque in mind and appearance, and his equally Machiavellian Turkish slave Ithamore ('We are villains both'), there never was a compact so deliciously evil as that in 2.3 in which they join forces against the Christian powers of Malta:

> BARABAS. First, be thou void of these affections,
> Compassion, love, vain hope, and heartless fear;
> Be moved at nothing, see thou pity none ...

The mood of the play is black indeed, and whether this villain loses his money or his daughter, he displays no feeling other than rage, so that the audience is never allowed to feel pity for him. It has troubled some playgoers that the play should change its tone to farce during act 2; but it is in the intractable nature of black humour that it can only grow more farcical as it grows blacker.

The religious and moral satire apart, the assault by excess upon the audience's defences begins from the start. A withering Prologue from 'Machevil' (Marlowe's felicitous spelling and presumed pronunciation of the name) in which he refers to 'a Jew, / Who smiles to see how full his bags are crammed' runs straight into the discovery announced by '*Enter* BARABAS *in his counting-house, with heaps of gold before him*' – and it is most appropriate that Machevil himself draws the curtain that discloses his creature. Barabas talks directly to the audience as he counts his chinking coins; he complains of the labour ('What a trouble 'tis to count this trash!') as he greedily fills his 'steel-barred coffers'; and he dreams about 'bags of fiery opals, sapphires, amethysts' while not forgetting to check the wind that carries his wealth to his shores. As he sits, merchants bring reports that his ships are safe and a deputation of fellow Jews summons him to the Senate. In all, it is an initial demonstration, a striking tableau, of the villain at work and play – a figure to laugh at and to fear – with the unseen presence of the sinister Machevil, it is assumed, lurking not far away.

Other discovery scenes occur later in this play: in 4.1 Friar

Bernadine is discovered asleep, only to be woken to be strangled and propped up for Friar Jacomo to find, and in 5.5 the outrageous final scene of the cauldron may well have used the discovery-space. However, it is more impressive that the play also made frequent use of the 'above', Marlowe first employing a balcony in 2.1 to suggest the window of Barabas's house from which his daughter Abigail might throw down his bags of gold, and then probably using the upper level in 5.1 so that his body might appear to be *'thrown down'* over the walls of the city. In 5.5 Barabas prepares his monstrous device for the Hell-like boiling alive of his Christian victim to the memorable injunction, *'Enter with a hammer above, very busy'*, and a moment later the direction *'the cable cut, a cauldron discovered'* (with a steamy Barabas cooking in it) suggests a procedure to simulate the way in which he might seem to fall sensationally from one level to another into his own trap. Henslowe supplies 'j cauderme [cauldron] for the Jewe', but it does not seem necessary for modern scholarship to speculate in much detail on how such spectacular illusions and effects were managed by the ingenious professionals of the time.

Outstanding in this play is Marlowe's use of the 'aside' (a direction found inconsistently in the quarto of 1633, but liberally inserted, sometimes also with italics in the text, by every editor since). It is associated chiefly with Barabas and it is used almost from the beginning and in nearly every scene, suggesting that as a device it constituted a major technique of performance by which the spectator was compelled to assume a special relationship with the Jew: the actor takes the audience into his confidence and, as it were, incriminates his auditors in some gross and unspecified conspiracy of evil. For the actor himself, the aside assists the work of Barabas as he reveals himself as an hypocrite and impostor, and prepares the spectator to receive him in his later disguises. Finally, it has the additional function of presenting a play on two levels, since speech after speech is capped by a seeming contradiction, forcing the audience to be alert to the duplicity of the society it is shown. An aside always urges an audience to watch two plays at the same time.

The aside may be a quick throw-away remark tagged on to

the end of a line, so that it first sharpens awareness of the character of Barabas and his role, and the abundance of such asides that establish a relationship with the audience has been thought to link him with the comic Vice of medieval times:

> If anything shall there concern our state,
> Assure yourselves I'll look – *unto myself.* [*aside*]

And it may also constitute a regular barrage of commentary flung directly at the house that jerks the stage alive with irony and deceit. In a lengthy exchange of double-talk the two levels of the play are intimately associated, not just with the mutual hatred of Christian and Jew, but with the behaviour of society at large.

The play had not been professionally produced in London for over forty years when Clifford Williams directed it at the Aldwych Theatre for the Royal Shakespeare Company in 1964, and the curiously comic flavour of its excesses pleased an audience recently acquainted with the post-war theatre of the absurd.

Only Marlowe's next play, *The Massacre at Paris* (c. 1592), had more excesses. Its grisly subject was the bloody purge of thousands of French Protestants twenty years before and known as the Massacre of St Bartholomew, for which Marlowe offered a series of some two dozen individual murders performed on-stage in a sampling sequence that increased in pace towards the end, a 'snapshot' method of representing the bloodbath.

Doctor Faustus: experiment in form, style and staging

Marlowe's last two plays, *Edward II* and *Doctor Faustus*, both dated *c.* 1592, have proved to be enduring in performance, which has confirmed in them his growing skills as a playwright in the short time before his early death in 1593. *Edward II* is among the earliest of history plays, and interest is less in its management of the stage than in its use of Holinshed's *Chronicles* and its management of a new genre.

Even then, the choice of a weak and capricious tyrant for a protagonist suggests that Marlowe was not so much interested in putting history on the stage as in using the stage to dramatize a human tragedy. He takes liberties with events in order to project a character-study of the self-deluding Edward in relation to his favourites and set against his Queen and the Machiavellian traitor Mortimer. Any new stagecraft is confined to the devising of pitiful, manipulative speeches when the King is deposed, and the ironic manner and shocking exhibition of his murder.

After its success in its own day, *Edward II* lay dormant for three centuries because of its homosexual content, and has been revived in London only since Brecht reworked it in Munich in 1924 and Joan Littlewood took it up again in her Theatre Workshop in 1956. The enduring legend of Faustus, on the other hand, seems never to have wanted for audiences: the play was in demand throughout the Stuart period, and after Cromwell's time Pepys took his wife to see it. In the eighteenth and nineteenth centuries it was apparently lost in harlequinades and pantomimes (which may say something about the latent comedy of its theme) until Irving attempted a version at the Lyceum in 1885. Following some thirty professional productions since the Second World War, it is now 'in the repertory'.

The reason for its longevity is not far to seek. Much of *Doctor Faustus* is a sophisticated play of ideas dealing in salvation and damnation, thus mixing the concerns of the Christian cycle plays with the medieval moralities. Faustus is a morality Everyman, as identified by his Good and Bad Angels, but one who shows recognizably human traits, not least in being subjected to a spiritual and psychological conflict of mind as he hurries to his fearful end. Yet in the heresy of selling one's soul to the Devil lies an audience appeal that at once conjures the mysteries of medieval superstition and speaks for the Renaissance spirit of dissent and rebellion. Above all, in his gross apostasy Faustus's story constitutes one of the great myths, and Marlowe gives him a stage treatment that is full of humour and humanity while it simultaneously creates a timeless ritual of sin and terror.

Characteristically, Marlowe obeys no dramatic laws except

those his subject demands. He ignores the unities of time, place and action, in particular freely juggling stage and real time in order to hasten or slow down the performance, so controlling the audience's degree and kind of attention. Thus a speech of twenty-eight lines by a Chorus figure directly plunges the house into 'the form of Faustus' fortunes' from his birth and his schooling to the time of his maturity and his passion for black magic. Then this Chorus suddenly draws back the upstage discovery curtain, a favourite ruse with Marlowe, and reveals like a specimen for inspection the man himself *'in his study'* practising his black arts. In soliloquy Faustus spices this business with learned argument in a speech of sixty-two lines mixed of English, Latin, Greek and the Bible before he bids 'Divinity, adieu!' for 'a world of profit and delight'. Next, a madcap twenty-four years make up the bulk of the play: the story of his temptation by Mephostophilis, the pact with the Devil and the bizarre comedy of his sins. Finally the merry-go-round stops for the last hour of Faustus's life before he is dragged off to Hell. He meets his end in famous lines that in their gestic and vocal magniloquence catch the spirit of an overwhelmingly climactic moment to crown the play. The action has again stayed more or less with a single giant figure, one ambivalently sympathetic and unsympthetic to the troubled spectator, and it now ends with an explosion of compassion and accord, altogether in a tragic vein.

The 'temptation' of the early scenes in which Faustus chooses to sin is presented with striking ritualism. Like a hangman the Chorus exhibits his victim before his execution, and returns throughout the play to advance the story and teach its lesson dispassionately to the end. Then Marlowe has the idea of visiting Faustus with the two Angels, the first from one door and the second from the other – formally and symmetrically.

> GOOD ANGEL. O Faustus, lay that damned book aside
>   And gaze not on it lest it tempt thy soul ...
> BAD ANGEL. Go forward, Faustus, in that famous art
>   Wherein all nature's treasury is contain'd ...

They speak starkly in conflict, seeming to articulate what is in his mind and dramatizing his conscience as if the choice between good and evil were his, so immediately clarifying the issue for the audience.

All this prepares the stage for the first alarming appearance of Lucifer and his devils in scene 3 (using the B-text of 1616; this important effect is missing from the A-text of 1604). They enter *'above'* to the sound of *'thunder'*, so that they look down upon Faustus and the audience in their mortal sphere – the stage and the playhouse – and seem to guide the action. Moreover, their presence ensures that the audience hears everything Faustus says through Satanic ears. Thus when the stage is verbally cloaked in 'the gloomy shadow of the night' (3.1), Faustus draws a circle on the floor like a magician casting a spell, an action determined absolutely by Lucifer, because he can be seen as if pulling the strings of his puppet; there follows more thunder.

Mephostophilis is next commanded to return in the likeness of 'an old Franciscan friar'. It was a medieval commonplace that the Devil could appear in holy orders looking suitably pious, and by presenting this image on the stage Marlowe casts a keen ironic light on the Devil's role as Faustus's mock confessor. For Mephostophilis seems to try to stop Faustus in his headlong flight to damnation by fearfully speaking the truth about the consequences of sin, while actually encouraging him to emulate the 'aspiring pride and insolence' (line 70) of Lucifer before his fall.

Scene 4 interpolates a moment of slapstick (and a touch of parody that anticipates Faustus's future dealings) when his servant Wagner plays the Devil to Robin the clown and has two devils, essentially figures of fun from the medieval stage, chase him noisily round the platform. This, together with a last wrangle between the two Angels that mixes the ridiculous and the sublime precedes the principal business of Marlowe's sensational scene 5, to which he devotes the anticipated sorcery of the occult. There seems to be no limit to the theatrical panache with which Mephostophilis urges Faustus to 'stab his arm' and 'bind his soul'. He must write his bequest in blood, and for one startling, concentrated moment this miraculously congeals, so helping the audience pause and focus on the issue before Mephostophilis adds to the picture

The Tragicall Hiſtoy of the Life and Death, *of* Doctor Fauſtus.

With new Additions.

Written by *Ch. Mar.*

LONDON,
Printed for *Iohn Wright*, and are to be ſold at his ſhop without
Newgate, at the ſigne of the Bible. 1620.

6 Christopher Marlowe, *Doctor Faustus, c.* 1592: the title-page of the Quarto of 1624. Faustus draws his magic circle to protect himself before conjuring the Devil (scene 3).

by entering with a 'chafer of fire' to make the blood flow again. Faustus completes the work with a final blasphemy on his lips: *'Consummatum est'* were the last words of Christ on the Cross. Even then Faustus is brought up short again by the words *'Homo fuge!'* inscribed on his arm, but the hesitation serves only for Mephostophilis to have his devils adorn his victim in *'crowns and rich apparel'*. The ritual thus concludes with Faustus reading the Devil's covenant and its conditions when he is dressed in glorious array, the casuistic scholar who was until now seen only in solemn black here transformed into a colourful popinjay.

This transformation is the beginning of the play's descent into farce – the black comedy of its central scenes. Dressed like a lord, Faustus calls for a wife, and promptly *'with fireworks'* a devil enters dressed like a woman, a sure signal for laughter. Then, following another visit from the Good and Bad Angels, Marlowe arranges a near-burlesque parade of the Seven Deadly Sins, with Pride significantly in the van and led by a piper: the tragic psychodrama of a lost soul is reduced to a mocking display. The frivolous scenes (lines 8–18) that follow are commonly condemned by literary critics, but in Tudor performance they would have been central to what has been called 'the comedy of evil', reflecting as they do the madly illogical nature of sin. These scenes, now pursued on a lower level of comic performance, show Faustus playing tricks on the Pope and boxing his ears, throwing fireworks among the friars and conjuring magic for the Emperor and the Duke and Duchess of Vanholt. They also contain a farcical episode like that in which Faustus teases a horse courser [dealer], and the general corruption of the text suggests that in performance other such scenes may have been introduced at random. But at all times Faustus is visually accompanied, indeed shadowed and haunted, by Mephostophilis and his devils. In their perverse way the central scenes pleasure the audience while they dramatize the way in which Faustus pleasures his ego.

The richest moment of quasi-comedy is kept for last. In scene 18 the Scholars whom Faustus has been impressing ask him to conjure Helen of Troy, a request worth something in any public theatre. So Mephostophilis escorts her to music and '*she passeth over the stage*', a common direction that is generally taken to mean that the actor enters by one door, circles the platform without speaking and leaves by the other. The moment is enhanced when Faustus stabs his arm again and, heard by a grateful house, pleads to see Helen once more. So Helen enters again, '*passing over between two Cupids*' (in the B-text), and this time she obliges him with a kiss:

> Sweet Helen, make me immortal with a kiss.
> Her lips suck forth my soul: see where it flies!

In the context of the play's inevitability, Faustus's apostrophe to Helen is breathtaking in its irony. Still Helen has not spoken, and she has no need: Faustus's portentous lines have exchanged his heavenly immortality for a kiss from a phantom of the theatre. At this point, with the sensuousness of these words echoing in his ears, the spectator's sympathy with Faustus may be at its strongest. Helen in her terrible beauty is symbolic of man's lust at its most ineffable and elusive: she is fleeting and demonic, and she quickly appears and disappears – indeed, she is no more than a boy actor. The scene is rounded off on the one side by the pious image of an Old Man who seems to represent holy wisdom, and on the other by the sight of a howling and grimacing troupe of dancing devils. Helen's scene makes visible on stage the ugly chaos of the irrational, and Faustus's flirtation with Hell.

For its final moments *Doctor Faustus* returns in scene 19 to the ritualism with which it began, although the action is now well interlaced with the personal tribulations of its protagonist. Witnessed (in the B-text) from '*above*' by the forces of Hell, visited for a last time by the Angels '*at several* [i.e., different] *doors*', 'the jaws of Hell' are to seem to open while Marlowe has the Bad Angel describe 'that vast perpetual torture-house'. Some think the stage-trap provided this, but the stage would achieve a tidy visual echo if Hell were shown to be lurking in the discovery-space that previously served as Faustus's study. Once again Faustus is virtually alone as the clock strikes the eleventh hour and gives his cue to speak in soliloquy the agony of his thoughts in his last hour on earth. His speech constitutes an extraordinary stream-of-consciousness for its day, one that is alive with the movement of mind and body: 'O, I'll leap up ... Who pulls me down?' The clock strikes three times, and time is suddenly all-important, and yet in the divine scheme of things is finally of no account.

The devils return with '*thunder and lightning*' to haul him screaming off to Hell ('I'll burn my books!'). In *Astrologaster* (1620), John Mellon supplied an account of this grotesque moment in the play when he described how 'the shag-haired devils run roaring over the stage with squibs in their mouths, while drummers make thunder in the tiring-house, and the twelve-penny hirelings make artificial lightning in their heavens' (31). The spirit of Marlowe's tragi-comic stage may be sensed in that picture, as the Scholars, chorus-like, remain to supply the closing abhorrent vision of Faustus's limbs 'all torn asunder' in a hellish death.

Marlowe was the first of the true stage professionals. At the Rose he ventured a massive exhibition of a play: for *Tamburlaine* he had the stage sense to muster every effect of symbolic staging in order to dress out his colourful image of a despot, and in doing so he created a ritual pageant of a drama thundering in sound and ablaze in spectacle. Yet only the change in the hero's attitude after the death of Zenocrate redeemed the play's two-dimensional quality. In *The Jew of Malta* the monstrous opening *tableau vivant* of Barabas in his counting-house was one of Marlowe's many uses of the discovery-space or gallery to present a symbolic set piece, which in this play culminated in an actual representation of an infernal boiling in oil. Yet this play too was another potential excursion into a cul-de-sac, this time to be unexpectedly saved by flirting with farce. In *Doctor Faustus* Marlowe brought together all his favourite devices – the stagecraft of the discovery-space, the sweep of his language and the spice of slapstick and humour – in order to confound the audience's contempt for his hero with a thoughtful sympathy. In this play Marlowe set a wealth of *external* effects in brilliant accord with its *internal* scrutiny of the human spirit.

6

Shakespeare's practice

The study of Shakespeare's stagecraft

The strategy in this chapter will be different: it will not survey the plays of William Shakespeare (1564–1616), but the way he worked as a man of the theatre. If he is not representative, he shows the parameters of Elizabethan stagecraft and to what extraordinary ends the stage and its conventions could be put. He repeatedly demonstrates how to generate dramatic energy from non-dramatic material and how to govern the perceptions and responses of an audience. The challenge is to understand the shared experience of a Shakespeare play.

Criticism always generalizes in trying to tame the live theatre experience, but in performance a play is from the first a specific attack on the senses and perceptions in terms of the immense particularity of its medium. For example, where verbal criticism usefully *identifies* the animal imagery in *King Lear*, the playgoer must *see* man as beast, *see* Edgar as a mad beggar. Edgar declares his intentions:

> To take the basest and most poorest shape
> That ever penury, in contempt of man,
> Brought near to beast; my face I'll grime with filth,
> Blanket my loins, elf all my hairs in knots ...   (2.3.7–10)

There is much more: the playwright is describing in great detail how the actor is to disguise himself and how he is to feel. Why does Shakespeare say all this? Because he expects the spectator's ears and then his eyes to make a double contribution, the verbal imagination first drawing upon the memory or experience of Bedlam beggars, and anticipating what is to be enacted, before the sensational actuality of

References are to the New Arden edition of Shakespeare's plays (1951–82).

Edgar's performance itself. Moreover, when Poor Tom takes the stage in 3.4, the actor's physical synthesis of Edgar's original instructions will include the new dimension of the actor's interpretation, and also, since the audience knows that Edgar is only pretending madness, their ironic theatricality. At a play an audience does not see words, nor does it hear them; it always sees and hears what, in all their complication, they stand for.

An audience is not passive, and as a gifted playwright Shakespeare knew this instinctively. He constantly used his stagecraft to keep his audience busy by prompting, anticipating and mixing its reactions, mostly with apparently unpredictable results. The spectator ought to hate Shylock, but he is not permitted to; he ought to laugh at Rosalind, but his ridicule is modified to include sympathy. Shakespeare is the master playmaker, and it is through his manipulation of the stage and its devices that he can manipulate the audience's contribution. The audience may listen to Hamlet's soliloquy on whether to live or die, but Shakespeare also insists that the spectator is aware that Claudius and Polonius are eavesdropping behind an arras, so adding a political meaning to what he is saying, and places on the same stage a girl at her prayers in order to wrap the whole situation in a mantle of religion and human feeling.

Throughout this period the actor is never playing to himself, and rarely to the other actors: he is usually playing openly and unashamedly to the audience. When Macduff is told that his wife and children have been murdered, his repetition 'All my pretty ones?' – 'Did you say all?' – 'All?' – 'What, all my pretty chickens ... ?' (*Macbeth*, 4.3.216–9) certainly allows the actor to imitate the sounds of grief in a variation of tones, but the repeated 'all' is primarily heard by the house as if it were a howl intended to involve everyone in Macduff's pain. This kind of dramatic writing uses to the utmost the essential Elizabethan stage outlined in chapter 4. Its features are listed there – especially the close proximity of its audience, which encouraged a range of voice work from a whisper to a roar and inducing qualities of ritual performance; its large open platform permitting either the solitude of a soliloquy or the pageantry possible on a loaded stage; the strong attacking entrances and the depth of movement into the house of a 'thrust' stage prompted by the upstage doors; the spatial freedom of its great open platform, inviting the simultaneous use of different centres of interest and rapid changes of scene and mood. With these simple but indispensable features Shakespeare devised his theatre games, juggling space and time, mixing the real and the unreal.

Signs in the script, signals from the stage

'Semiotics' is from a useful Greek word, recently fashionable, signifying the study of signals, signs and symbols, and this section has to do with some of these in Shakespeare. One of the actor's tasks is to decode his lines, in order to discover, often by trial and error, what their signs and directions, explicit or hidden, expect of him. In performance, he is also concerned with the business of transmitting these as signals from the stage to the audience. In this lengthy circuit from text to stage, and from stage to audience and back again, there is room for the creative contribution of the many people involved, so that there is even more room for error and the compounding of error; but that is what makes live performance endlessly fascinating.

In Shakespeare explicit directions for *gesture* and *movement* are rare, but what few there are (whether written by the playwright or by the book-holder watching the performance) make signals that are usually highly significant. When the lovers – and the audience – return to reality with the morning lark after the night's adventures in *A Midsummer Night's Dream*, the Folio direction is insistent: '*Horns and they wake. Shout within, they all start up*' (4.1.137), and the play must change its atmosphere and direction. When Coriolanus makes the fatal choice between his mother and his erstwhile enemy Aufidius, the famous stage direction is highly pointed: he '*holds her by the hand silent*' (*Coriolanus*, 5.3.182); no matter that Shakespeare had this from North's *Plutarch*, with a sceptical Aufidius watching him Coriolanus's gesture marks the crux of the play. When in *The Tempest* Ariel leads

Ferdinand on to the stage as if by magic, the direction is particularly stimulating: *'Enter Ferdinand and Ariel, invisible, playing and singing'* (1.2.376), since the paradoxical direction 'invisible' indicates how Ariel is to act, perhaps what he is to wear and also how other characters are to react to him.

Nevertheless, the bulk of Shakespeare's signs to the actor are implicit in the lines. Examples of this are legion, since every line carries within it some suggestion of how it is to be seen or heard, and therefore how it is to be spoken or matched with gesture and movement. Some signs are buried less deeply than others, and it may be surmised therefore that these are not to be ignored. In *Othello* the Moor's lines over the sleeping Desdemona change from the abstract to the particular, from a verbal image to a physical action:

> when I have pluck'd the rose,
> I cannot give it vital growth again,
> It must needs wither; I'll smell it on the tree,
> A balmy breath, that doth almost persuade
> Justice herself to break her sword.
>
> (5.2.13–17)

From this the actor can tell precisely when Othello is to kiss Desdemona, and how and where; and the audience also knows that he is in love with his wife in spite of his purpose to kill her. And when he speaks over her dead body a few minutes later, his thoughts of burning hellfire are changed to convey to the audience by a speaking gesture her chill life-lessness:

> when we shall meet at count,
> This look of thine will hurl my soul from heaven,
> And fiends will snatch at it: cold, cold, my girl,
> Even like thy chastity.
>
> (5.2.274–7)

It is not possible for Othello to say the words 'cold, cold' without touching her and conveying how close to her he is. Another kiss perhaps? For the first kiss Desdemona was alive, for the second dead, but Othello's feeling for her was constant.

A line may be alive with gesture for the actor as well as rich in dramatic meaning for the spectator, often echoing other

parts of the play. From the scene of Lear's awakening (*King
Lear*, 4.7), a range of remarkably simple gestures is laden with
implication for the relationship between Lear and Cordelia
and for the play as a whole:

> O my dear father! Restoration hang
> Thy medicine on my lips ...
>
> (26–7)
>
> [she kisses him]
>
> Was this a face
> To be oppos'd against the warring winds?
>
> (31–2)
>
> [she caresses his head]
>
> I will not swear these are my hands: let's see;
> I feel this pin prick ...
>
> (55–6)
>
> [he examines his hands]
>
> O! look upon me, Sir,
> And hold your hand in benediction o'er me.
> No, Sir, you must not kneel.
>
> (57–9)
>
> [they both kneel]
>
> Be your tears wet? Yes, faith. I pray, weep not.
>
> (71)
>
> [he touches her cheeks]

Although these lines suggest gestures that are completely
natural, each seems symbolic too, each making a statement far
bigger than itself and together helping to elevate the whole
scene into one of sublime ritual.

So it is that by repetition and unusual staging certain
gestures may acquire symbolic and even ritualistic status,
and kneeling is one of these. With Lear and Cordelia
kneeling centre stage, father to daughter and daughter to
father, the visual picture is sufficiently topsy-turvy for the
scene to draw attention less to the duties owed by a subject
than to the bond between parent and child. Something of
the same effect is achieved in *Coriolanus* when Caius

Martius, echoing the former scene when he had defeated Corioli, kneels to his mother Volumnia outside Rome ('Sink, my knee, i'th'earth', (5.3.50)) only to have her respond unnaturally by kneeling to her son ('What's this? Your knees to me?' (56–7)), since she is now ironically the suppliant begging him to spare the city.

As with gesture, so with the actor's movement across the stage. Because on the great space of the Elizabethan platform a significant entrance may be missed, another actor already there will frequently remark it – 'See where he comes' – 'Here comes Romeo' – 'Here's goodly gear' – 'O God she comes' – 'Here comes the lady': all these instances are from the first two acts of *Romeo and Juliet*. And since on certain significant occasions Shakespeare may intend an actor to make his way downstage from an upstage door for some 20 or 30 feet, these warnings are also signals that the audience should observe the character's demeanour closely. When Tybalt wishes to pick a fight with Romeo, he ignores Mercutio's taunts, and firmly signals Romeo's entrance:

> TYBALT. Well, peace be with you, sir, here comes my man.
>
> (3.1.55)

The audience is here surprised to see a different Romeo, a man who has just married Juliet, who is Tybalt's cousin, and Romeo's long entrance is to indicate his new reluctance to fight. He responds to Tybalt's challenge of 'villain' in a tone not heard before:

> ROMEO. Tybalt, the reason that I have to love thee
> Doth much excuse the appertaining rage
> To such a greeting: villain am I none,
> Therefore farewell. I see thou knowest me not.
>
> (61–4)

From the evidence of these measured lines it is possible to introduce a pause of misgiving before Romeo speaks, and another of astonishment before Tybalt replies. The pace has changed. Everyone on and off the stage is agog at the new direction the action has taken, and therafter the lines are strong with implicit directions for the gesture and movement that leads to the inevitable sword-fight: Tybalt's 'turn and draw', Mercutio's 'will you walk?'

Equally, Shakespeare may take advantage of an exit, as when in *Troilus and Cressida* Cressida has been turned over to the Greeks and leaves the stage under the jaundiced eye of Ulysses:

> NESTOR. A woman of quick sense.
> ULYSSES.   Fie, fie upon her!
> There's language in her eye, her cheek, her lip –
> Nay, her foot speaks; her wanton spirits look out
> At every joint and motive of her body.
>
> (4.5.54–7)

It is for the audience to look at Cressida's protracted departure upstage and decide whether Ulysses's sarcastic words better describe her attitude and manner of walking or his own spite and manner of thinking.

Sometimes Shakespeare's words for movement are so sparse that only the test of performance can determine how the actor should speak and move for maximum effect. At the end of *King Lear*, both Quarto and Folio editions have '*Enter Lear with Cordelia in his arms*' (5.3.256) accompanied by the repeated words 'Howl, howl, howl' (four times in the Quartos). This line marks a moment of supreme intensity, signalling not only the sound of the King's voice, but also its location: first off-stage, then on his entrance and finally after his passage through the crowd, which falls back and freezes (a gesture anticipating 'O! you are men of stones'). For the last 'howl' the actor is probably at a position at the foot of the platform for the intimacy of his own feather-and-button death scene. It is almost as if Lear is offering the spectators Cordelia's body like a sacrifice, and accusing the audience of her death.

Shakespeare never neglects the simple but direct visual signals for audience response that *costume* and *colour* can make. In the first scenes of *Hamlet* the Prince is alone in wearing the 'customary suits of solemn black' among a colourful court. At the opening of *All's Well That Ends Well* the whole assembly is '*all in black*', inviting the audience to seek the multiple reasons for it. Conversely, Marcade's news of the death of the King of France at the end of *Love's Labour's Lost* precipitates a bitter-sweet ending, and the cast exchanges its summer colours for sombre black after 'The scene begins to cloud' (5.2.714). Before the battle of Agincourt in *Henry V*, the King borrows Sir Thomas Erpingham's cloak (4.1.24) to visit the camp at night in disguise; in this way he covers his handsome armour and majestic insignia, and seems to put himself on an equal footing with his soldiers; indeed, the tone and style of those middle scenes in prose bring a wholly new and more human perspective to the play. The trick is effectively repeated in *Coriolanus* when Caius Martius attempts to humble himself in his pursuit of 'voices' [votes] by covering his splendid uniform with 'a gown of humility' (2.3.41): Shakespeare has turned North's lucky mistranslation of *'une robe simple'* to theatrical advantage and ironically presented the citizens with a veritable wolf in sheep's clothing.

Shakespeare often allows for three costume changes for his principals, and these flag the dramatic progress of the character through his play, even in comedy. Malvolio in *Twelfth Night* makes a wonderful ascent from puritanical black to the vanity of yellow stockings and cross-garters (3.4); but he also makes a stop on the way to appear in the traditional nightgown and nightcap for the drinking scene (2.3), and we may imagine his final appearance when he emerges from the 'hideous darkness' of his prison (5.1): every change is in violent contrast to the severe costume he wore at the beginning. Hamlet too must exchange his 'nighted colour' for a 'doublet all unbrac'd' and 'stockings foul'd' (2.1), as Ophelia reports his appearance, so preparing the audience for the mad Hamlet; and, following his adventure at sea, he will reappear at Ophelia's grave (5.1) with a 'sea-gown scarf'd about' him like a newly freed spirit. The tragic hero who best illustrates the changing pattern of his play is Lear, whose royal crown and ermine change to the 'unbonneted' and 'bare-headed' figure who tears off his clothes on the heath with 'Off, off, you lendings!' (3.4.111) and exchanges his crown for Capell's fantastic dress of wild flowers (4.6.80); his last costume, however, is neither despotic nor preposterous: at the moment of his return to sanity and humility the Doctor reports that they put 'fresh garments' on him (4.7.22), and the implication is that these should convey his pathetic simplicity and a new honesty.

As with costumes, so with *properties*: they are few, but carefully selected and powerful in their symbolism. Yorick's skull (*Hamlet*, 5.1) is thrown up for a joke from Ophelia's open grave by the Gravedigger, then seen by Hamlet as a symbol of mortality first as Yorick's skull and then as the Queen's and finally as his own; while all the time the audience remembers whose innocent grave is being dug. The incident is thereby given a compelling immediacy, and one prop of this order serves many purposes. In *Twelfth Night* Olivia's veil serves for her nun-like mourning, for her game with Viola when she is first sent as Orsino's messenger Cesario and for flirting with her ('we will draw the curtain and show you the picture' (1.5.235–6)).

In the history plays certain items take on emblematic qualities: in *Macbeth* the throne that bedevils Macbeth carries a monumental meaning for the audience, as Banquo ominously suggests: 'Thou hast it now' (3.1.1); as a set piece it doubtless stood prominently upstage centre, either pushed out or flown from above ('creaking throne comes down, the boys to please' is Jonson's scornful comment in the Prologue to *Every Man in His Humour* (16)). The crown shines out in every play that disputes the monarchy, and in *2 Henry IV* its misuse by the Prince makes it the centre of the play's debate on kingship (4.5).

Nowhere do these royal emblems work to greater effect than in the deposition scene in *Richard II*, 4.1. When Richard enters, Bolingbroke may be presumed to be sitting on the throne in order that Richard should kneel to him in ceremonial submission; but soon after this the usurper is required to come down and stand on equal footing with the one he has deposed:

> Give me the crown. Here, cousin, seize the crown.
> Here, cousin,
> On this side my hand, and on that side thine ...
>
> (181–3)

The repetition nicely suggests that Bolingbroke is wary of a trick and hesitates before he leaves the throne. Eventually, however, the two men symbolically hold the crown between them, and it appears to change hands during the subsequent imagery of the 'two buckets' – except that within a few lines there are strong hints that Richard has in fact refused to part with it. Shakespeare has ingeniously provided several different, even ambiguous, ways to conduct this scene. Richard may have temporarily leaped back on to the throne and even replaced the crown on his head, all to bring into sharp focus, at this moment of crisis, the importance of both of these powerfully strategic props.

Music, *song* and *dance* also provide signals to the audience, sometimes separately, often together. Some thirty-two of Shakespeare's plays call for music and he has more than three hundred musical directions. Trumpets, hautboys, sackbuts and drums indicate royal or noble entries, marches and processions, while strings and lutes provide for more domestic occasions like banquets that have singing to accompany them. Hautboys may also serve a particularly dramatic function, as in *Antony and Cleopatra*, 4.3.11, where the famous Folio direction *'Music of the hoboys is under the stage'* marks the ominous passing of the night before the Battle of Actium. Unfortunately, however, most of the time there is no hint of which instruments are employed, only that *'music plays'*. In *The Merchant of Venice* Lorenzo calls for music to enhance the sweet atmosphere of Belmont (5.1.68), or in *King Lear* the Doctor whispers 'Louder the music there!' (4.7.25) in order to awaken the King from his madness – and it subtly helps to change the mood of the whole play. In *The Winter's Tale* the magic revival of Hermione suggests a fusion of all the arts when Paulina, in the role of high priestess, cries, 'Music, awake her; strike!' (5.3.98).

With their additional verbal qualities Shakespeare's *songs* have a far wider range of specific dramatic uses, but they are always there for a purpose, comic or tragic. Bottom's pretty song about woodland birds beginning 'The ousel cock, so black of hue' (*A Midsummer Night's Dream*, 3.1.120) may be suitable for a wood near Athens, but hardly for Bottom's rough voice in a state of panic – but then this is the song that must wake Titania from her flowery bed. In *Much Ado about*

Nothing, 2.3.62, Balthasar's 'Sigh no more, ladies, sigh no more, / Men were deceivers ever' is the ironic ditty that is intended to change Benedick's misogynistic state of mind, as well as touch the theme of the whole play.

With the songs in the tragedies Shakespeare again regularly achieves dramatic relevance, so that a song that extends the audience's impression of the character singing it also deepens its understanding of the situation. In *Hamlet*, 4.5, Ophelia's gently bawdy singing is a conventional sign of her madness when she enters '*distracted*' (F) or '*playing on a lute, with her hair down singing*' (Q1), but she has no fewer than five songs: the one about a dead lover is addressed to the Queen, the second about a seducer is sung to Claudius, one is for Laertes about their dead father (a lament mixed with a love song), and for herself there is a snatch of a popular ballad and another of a song of unrequited love: in a deft and ingenious survey Ophelia's songs manage ironically to take in every major character in the play. In *Othello*, 4.3, Desdemona's pathetic willow song of love scorned was evidently a popular piece that would have been well known to everyone, and here it is sung without accompaniment, broken up naturally, half remembered, half forgotten, so that its manner of singing exactly catches her simplicity and innocence, making intensely human the monster of Othello's imagination just before her murder.

The *dances* belong chiefly to the elements of masque in the plays, but, like the music, a dance vividly reflects the spirit, and often the theme, of its play. A court dance, like the pavan or the galliard, stately or elegant, conveniently buttresses Capulet's party in *Romeo and Juliet*, 1.5, so that it is against somewhat restrained but happy dancing that the passion of the young lovers is first seen and Tybalt's deadly threats are heard:

> Now by the stock and honour of my kin,
> To strike him dead I hold it not a sin.

(57–8)

The coranto is used to fine effect in *All's Well That Ends Well* when Helena restores the dying King of France to health, and in 2.3 the two of them are able to make their entrance with this running and springing dance to the complete surprise of the Court.

With all these signals Shakespeare engages an audience's eyes and ears in many different ways, yet fused in the imagination, they illuminate one another and extend their own meaning. They also have the power to contradict one another, as will appear, so that in their fission the play may also be charged and ignited from scene to scene.

Conventions of place and time

Shakespeare wrote essentially 'one-set' and 'one-act' plays. Much of the academic division of the script into acts and scenes was done in the seventeenth century, and was completed by Nicholas Rowe in 1709. The division of the plays for *location* followed soon after during the eighteenth century, and in 1790 Edmund Malone was pleased to announce a location for every scene in Shakespeare. However, the Elizabethan stage had nothing that could today be called scenery. A prop like a throne or a bed, or the keys hanging at a gaoler's waist, helped to localize the stage temporarily, and if a sense of location were otherwise needed, a word or two supplied it. When in *Much Ado about Nothing*, 2.3.4, Benedick asks for a book to be brought 'hither to me in the orchard', the thought of a location is planted in the mind of the audience, and the way the actors behave in the scene completes the idea of an orchard: there is no need for the stage to be dressed with bushes and trees, and eavesdropping can take place perfectly well without them.

However, most of the time there is no 'place' at all, and it is this factor that encouraged outstanding effects of pace and continuity in production, as modern directors like William Poel and Granville Barker were to discover afresh. Indeed, most of Shakespeare's scenes work best in a condition of placelessness. For a street-fight there was no need to localize a street, and a battle may be fought without a battlefield. Lovers may find themselves in a wood near Athens or Lear drag himself on to a heath, but the vagueness of the location is significant in itself. Nor is there any reason to ask where a soliloquy is spoken: it is all, literally, in the mind. In a world of self-conscious theatre, of so-called 'metatheatre', there is always a hidden joke in a line like Rosalind's 'Well, this is the Forest of Arden!' because all that is seen is the same old stage, and Gloucester's 'When shall I come to th' top of that same hill?' is an explicit joke because on the stage itself a character, Edgar, also knows that it is only a stage. And when a character who has identified a location exits, the location exits with him, just as the Witches in *Macbeth* take the wind and the rain with them wherever they go. In *Othello*, 4.3, it seems that only when Othello, Lodovico and their attendants have left Desdemona's bedchamber can she undress for bed, but of course it is only because Desdemona undresses that her bedchamber materializes.

As with place, so with *time*: there are no clocks in the forest, nor on Shakespeare's stage – not, that is, until the audience is reminded of time. Then, like Puff in Sheridan's *The Critic* which opens with a clock striking 'to beget an awful attention in the audience' (2.2), Shakespeare makes the most of it: Juliet's father suddenly announces that she must marry Paris on Wednesday, the Provost in *Measure for Measure* shocks the audience by proclaiming that Claudio will die at four o'clock the next morning and in *All's Well That Ends Well* everything – the substitution of Helena in Bertram's bed, the gulling of Parolles – converges on the fateful hour of midnight.

Shakespeare's late romances, played at Whitehall or the Blackfriars, especially employed spectacular *lighting effects*, probably imitating the visual marvels of Inigo Jones's 'pictures with light and motion' created after 1605 by coloured transparencies and dozens of torches and candles. The experiments with spectacular lighting are found especially in Jupiter's descent on an eagle to thunder and lightning and throwing a thunderbolt in *Cymbeline*, 5.4, in the magnificent masque of the goddesses in *The Tempest*, 4.1 and in Queen Katherine's visionary dream in *Henry VIII*, 4.2, all written at about the same time as Jones's dazzling inventions for the masque of *Oberon* (1611).

Torches and lanterns, sometimes a nightgown, sometimes

the gestures of 'treading softly' or groping in the dark, supply the clue that the audience is witnessing a *night scene*. The astonishing fact is that the plays are full of references to night, and that some dozen of them embody major scenes of darkness. Indeed, one thinks of whole plays, *Romeo and Juliet, A Midsummer Night's Dream, Much Ado about Nothing, All's Well That Ends Well, Othello* and *Macbeth*, as plays essentially of the night. Yet in both the public and private playhouses the general lighting did not change, so that, paradoxically, a call for light implied darkness, and when a character was supposed to be able to see nothing, the spectator could see everything. Shakespeare made excellent use of this convention in such a comedy as *A Midsummer Night's Dream* in which the audience deliciously shares with Puck his magic gift of seeing in the dark when the lovers want a sword fight:

> LYSANDER. Where art thou, proud Demetrius?
> Speak thou now.
> PUCK. Here, villain, drawn and ready.
> Where art thou?
>
> (3.2.400 ff.)

This metatheatrical effect of lighting in-the-head continued for more than two hundred years, well exploited by comedies like Goldsmith's *She Stoops to Conquer* in its scene of mistaken identities on Crackskull Common.

The freedom of an empty and unlocalized stage inspired *eavesdropping* scenes in some twenty plays of Shakespeare, and *Much Ado about Nothing* has five such scenes, providing almost a dramatic motif in themselves. *Love's Labour's Lost*, 4.3, manages a multiple eavesdropping scene pattern in which the four lovers overhear one another as each breaks his compact to abstain from the thought of women. This scene also offers a gloriously physical moment of comedy as they chase from place to place around the platform. In *Twelfth Night*, 2.5, the gulling of Malvolio by Toby, Andrew and Fabian is perhaps the funniest eavesdropping scene of this sort. The tragedies, too, are spiced by scenes of spying, as when in *Hamlet*, 3.1, the King and Polonius overhear the Prince and Ophelia, and in *Othello*, 4.1, Iago has the Moor think he has overheard Cassio's treachery. It may be that the

King and Polonius hide behind an arras, and Othello behind a pillar, but neither scenic prop is necessary to the success of this curious convention, since eavesdropping facilitates the performance of a play-within-a-play with the help of simultaneous staging.

Simultaneous staging allows the stage to carry on two actions at once, where in a more realistic drama these would be separated in a temporal sequence by their different locations. The famous instance in early Shakespeare occurs in *Richard III*, 5.3, the scene of the Battle of Bosworth Field which begins with the entrance of the King and his injunction, 'Here pitch our tent'; this is followed at line 18 by the entrance of his rival Richmond who proceeds to speak of his own tent; and after due time has been allowed for the tents to be pitched probably symmetrically near the two doors in the façade, the two leaders finally withdraw into them on the same stage. In about the same year (1593) *Romeo and Juliet* devised a street scene with Romeo, Benvolio and Mercutio (1.4) that merged into the scene of Capulet's ball (1.5) by introducing the arresting stage direction, '*They march about the stage, and Servingmen come forth with napkins.*' The implication here is that the Montagues do not in fact leave the stage, but their movement changes the scene from outdoors to indoors when the Capulet servants enter with preparations for the banquet.

It is this effortless licence with space on the Elizabethan platform that enabled Shakespeare to experiment with so many visually absorbing scenes in which space itself was expressive in joining or dividing the actors. In *Romeo and Juliet*, 2.5, Juliet impatiently addresses her audience in something of a comic soliloquy, criticizing the tardiness of the Nurse who brings news of her wedding to Romeo:

> But old folks, many feign as they were dead –
> Unwieldy, slow, heavy, and pale as lead.

(16–17)

She says this at the very moment when the Nurse is making her entrance and ironically feigning weariness. At the next moment the Nurse escapes the ardent Juliet at her heels in order to speak a comic aside to the house at the girl's expense:

> Jesu, what haste. Can you not stay awhile?
> Do you not see that I am out of breath?
>
> (29–30)

The full length of the platform from the upstage door to the middle of the house is here used to play the young off against the old.

Romeo and Juliet is an early play, but at the end of his career Shakespeare was still testing the dramatic possibilities of space on his stage, and in *The Winter's Tale*, 1.2, he encapsulates the progress of Leontes's jealousy by judiciously distributing his characters at a distance from one another. When Leontes asks Hermione to persuade Polixenes to stay (line 27), she does so in some fifty lines without interruption by her silent husband – because he is elsewhere on the stage, seen to be spying on her. When Leontes rejoins Hermione and Polixenes, he separates from them at line 108 in order to speak in soliloquy or to his son while they continue their pleasantries in silent pantomime for some forty more lines, also somewhere else on the stage. By such a device the audience has the living sense of how the eye can deceive the mind and a disastrous misinterpretation be made. When Leontes is finally alone with his son, he is a lonely and miserable figure indeed:

> Inch-thick, knee-deep; o'er head and ears a fork'd one ...
>
> (186)

Space divorced from place and time can be eloquent.

Talking to the audience, role-playing and non-illusion

Spatial matters are closely linked with the kind of speaking practised on the Shakespearian stage. Shakespeare manipulated the blank verse line as no poet before or after him: his lines live as song or as natural speech, and have the power to make the actor speaking them respond in gesture and movement big and little – they are alive kinetically like 'gestic poetry', as Brecht would say, guiding the eye of the audience

by its ear. Shakespeare's sense of stage speech is as much
spatial as it is vocal, and in this he is instinctively concerned
with the conventions of theatrical style and communication.
Entrance and exit are carefully prefigured in speech, and when
he decides to isolate a single figure, usually in soliloquy, it is
impossible to fault his timing – Macbeth's moments alone
with an audience all come in the earlier part of his play when
his mind is struggling with itself and the audience needs to
share his problem; Othello has no soliloquy in the first part of
his play where he is to be seen as a suspect public figure in
Venice and Cyprus, and to Iago's eight he is granted three,
but only in the second half of the play after he has become
terribly vulnerable and the audience is intended to pity him.
Shakespeare was here writing for the actor in his fundamental
relationship with the spectator.

Soliloquy and *aside* did not come into the language as
technical terms until the eighteenth century, but drawing the
audience into the action was implicit in many of the lines
Shakespeare habitually wrote: the actor might not be speaking
strictly in soliloquy, but some elements of his speech could be
directly addressed to the house, even if it meant losing some
of a character's fictional identity. The set piece soliloquy is
obviously intended as a vocal high point when a Prince Hal or
a Hamlet presents to the audience matters important to the
progress of the play or to defining his character; yet at such
times his speech, while being intimately and realistically
delivered, may have become unrealistic and theatrical.

Sometimes lines are heard in a limbo between direct and
indirect address, between the real and the unreal, like these of
Macbeth's to Lady Macbeth after the murder of Duncan:

> MACBETH. But wherefore could not I pronounce 'Amen'?
> I had most need of blessing, and 'Amen'
> Stuck in my throat.
> LADY MACBETH.   These deeds must not be thought
> After these ways: so, it will make us mad.
> MACBETH. Methought, I heard a voice cry, 'Sleep no more!
> Macbeth does murther Sleep,' – the innocent
> Sleep;
> Sleep, that knits up the ravell'd sleave of care ...
> (2.2.30–6)

In this 'dialogue' the actors speak in carefully contrasted ways, Lady Macbeth uttering an urgent and prosaic injunction and Macbeth almost intoning a rhythmic, repetitive verse which changes into the dreamy, unnatural speech of a man distraught. His lines are apparently addressed in part to his wife, in part to himself, but as they grow universal in import they are essentially delivered also to the audience with whom he shares his feelings. Nor are such lines without their sense of movement across the stage, and Macbeth drifts away from his wife as his speech grows more profound and more painful.

Soliloquy and its many forms give immense power to the actor on the thrust stage – Hamlet has some two hundred lines spoken to the house, and in the event it is not possible to distinguish in his lines what belongs to the 'plot' and what to the 'character' – what speaks for Shakespeare the playwright both directly and obliquely. On occasion the personal and the impersonal sides to soliloquy may confuse its audience, as when at the beginning of *Troilus and Cressida* Cressida seems to speak of herself at the same time as she is used as a presenter of one of the issues of the play:

> Men prize the thing ungain'd more than it is.
> That she was never yet that ever knew
> Love got so sweet as when desire did sue ...
>
> (1.3.294–6)

Commentators may be forgiven for having found this an unsavoury sentiment in the mouth of a young woman and a mark of the place assigned to Cressida by history, but its delivery in soliloquy, in rhyme and in sonnet form points to the fact that this is also an impersonal, choric statement that remains to be tested in the play to come.

3 Henry VI managed to pair off an abstract 'Son that hath killed his Father' with a 'Father that hath killed his son': they enter, according to the Folio text, at separate doors each with a body and continue their lives apart. When they exit they give the impression of doing so with one another's bodies:

> SON.   Was ever son so rued a fathers's death?
> FATHER.   Was ever father so bemoan'd his son?
> KING HENRY. Was ever King so griev'd for subjects' woe?
>
> (2.5.109–11)

The presence of the King makes this a kind of 'triple aside', but the unusual stagecraft highlights the simple symbolism of the King's reflection upon the atrocities of civil war. At a critical point in *Hamlet* ten years later, Shakespeare dares to set up two soliloquies almost in parallel: when Claudius is at prayer ('O, my offence is rank' (3.3.36)), Hamlet comes upon him as if unexpectedly ('Now might I do it pat' (73)), thus effectively equating the two speakers and urging a Christian perspective on the issue of revenge.

Clowns habitually speak directly to the audience, reflecting their strange power over the house and the special licence that releases them from the more restrictive conventions of the stage. The Shakespearian clowns gather up scraps left by the long history of the species, from the *servus* of Roman comedy, the tumblers and minstrels of the Middle Ages, the Vice from the morality plays and the *zanni* of the Italian *commedia dell'arte*. The fact that the clown regularly steers his audience through the play, offering comment and criticism as he goes, controlling its response, maintaining a proper comic distance from the action and all the while providing the broad entertainment that is uniquely clowning, suggests that it is a mistake to regard him as just another character. Unlike a character, the clown can be ageless like Feste, sexless like Puck and wise beyond belief like Lear's Fool, but like a character he may appear young or old like the Gobbos, may react to the other sex like Touchstone and Lavatch and sometimes seem stupid like Launce and Bottom. Sometimes he is so important to his play that he assumes the role of a character enjoying clown characteristics: so it is with Hamlet, who plays the role of a clown for the bitter purposes of his tragedy. In the unparalleled case of Falstaff, a major clown turns into a completed character over the passage of two or three plays and ceases to enjoy his initial freedom.

The grey areas of non-illusion on Shakespeare's stage are elusive, but they are unmistakable in their frequency, presenting modern productions with problems of convention today's audiences find awkward. Prologues and inductions, characters as presenters and role-players, tableaux and plays-within-plays, choruses and on-stage audiences, sub-plots and allegorical offshoots, are all the manifestations of 'metatheatre'. This is a convenient, if prickly, term adopted in recent years to indicate the sort of stagecraft that is less concerned with the story a play is telling than with the carefully self-conscious way it is presented. Most of Shakespeare's plots do not stand up to realistic scrutiny and rarely expect an audience to believe what it sees. The metatheatrical stage cries out, 'Let's put on a play!' and its conventions tempt the spectator to share in the creative act. Again and again Shakespeare introduced a major character who virtually 'managed' the action of a scene or of the play like a presenter: Puck and Petruchio, Rosalind and the Duke of Vienna (in *Measure for Measure*), Hamlet, Iago and Prospero are like this.

As in the case of Cressida, an actor could find himself in a part that could be intensely realistic at one moment, and stripped of personality altogether at the next. The ramifications of this are endless, and the term *'role-playing'* has been adopted as an umbrella word to cover the many instances. It was axiomatic in Victorian melodrama that the actor should not play the role, but play the actor playing the role, and Shakespeare would have agreed with Brecht's arguments that the actor had a dual responsibility in being both character and performer. However, literary criticism has in the past been attracted by the complexity of a character when what was intended as a double role has been taken as evidence of psychological depth. Is the villain Iago motivated by a confusing mixture of realistic reasons for disliking Othello, or is he simply playing the symbolic role of the Devil with less and less need to explain himself?

This approach to characterization produces apparently irrational results. Enobarbus, the drunken soldier in *Antony and Cleopatra*, is the amazing choice of character to deliver the breath-taking eulogy of Cleopatra beginning, 'The barge she sat in, like a burnish'd throne ... ' (2.2.191); the monster Caliban is the character in *The Tempest* who helps to conjure the magic of Prospero's island with the lyrical lines beginning, 'The isle is full of noises, / Sounds and sweet airs ... ' (3.2.133–4). Sometimes the role-playing is made formally explicit: Oberon cries, 'I am invisible' (*A Midsummer Night's Dream*, 2.1.186) as the spectators join him in overseeing the adventures of the night, Edgar declares, 'Edgar I nothing am' (*King Lear*, 2.3.21) before he impersonates Poor Tom, and Prospero instructs Ariel, 'Be subject to / No sight but thine and mine' (*The Tempest*, 1.2.302–3) as the two of them prepare to tease Caliban and those who are shipwrecked.

Richard of Gloucester can 'change shapes with Proteus for advantages' (*3 Henry VI*, 3.2.192) and in *Richard III* proceeds to do so when he plays the hypocrite again and again. In *1 Henry IV* Prince Hal is prepared to play the prodigal son and yet at the outset confesses to the spectators (who know the facts of the matter) that he will 'make offence a skill, / Redeeming time when men think least I will' (1.2.211–12), his astonishing opening scene revealing him as playing the roistering youth expected of him and also providing a chorus figure commentating upon his historical role. In *All's Well That Ends Well* the enigmatic Helena, to some extent echoing the choric role of Cressida, must realistically act the modest girl who conceals her love for Bertram, and yet speak for the true feelings of all women who want men they cannot have as husbands. Shakespeare this time supplies her with rhyming couplets to shift the level of her performance from the real to the fantastic, beginning with her first sonnet-soliloquy, 'Our remedies oft in ourselves do lie ... ' (1.1.212); when she speaks in couplets again, to cure the King of France (2.1) and choose a husband (2.3), it is not possible or necessary to separate the reality from her dream.

The play-within

In a performance of a play by Shakespeare there was always a suggestion that its audience was watching, as it were, two plays, one tracing the story-line of an inner plot and another of the activity framing it, so providing a bridge between the fiction and the real world. The experience of the play, therefore, lay not in the audience's response to the story alone, but also in the way it was manipulated by the deliberate conventionality of the stage. Stylistic jumps and mixtures resulting from the juxtaposition of the inner scene with choric soliloquy, pageant masque, dumb show or play-within in many combinations, spark the intelligence and imagination into activity. The price of achieving this is to forgo the realistic illusion that later naturalistic playwrights held dear. There is strong doubt whether the Elizabethans would have understood the idea of 'illusion' at all.

Symptoms of the two levels of perception induced by a self-conscious theatre are seen in a variety of devices, for example, in the use of an *on-stage audience*, that is, characters introduced into a scene to guide the reaction of the house to what is going on. After the murder of Duncan (*Macbeth*, 2.3), Malcolm and Donalbain watch Macbeth in fear and thus provide the hushed reflective aftermath that echoes the apprehension of the real audience. Those who form an on-stage audience can react and speak for the house, like Lodovico and the Venetian attendants who witness Othello's abuse of his wife:

> My lord, this would not be believ'd in Venice,
> Though I should swear I saw 't.
>
> (*Othello*, 4.1.237–8),

or the Citizens in *Coriolanus* who remain suspicious of Caius Marcius's motives when he seeks their votes. Unlike those in *Julius Caesar*, these Citizens are not a mob; they approach and speak in groups of two and three, and as individuals they represent different views; like the audience itself watching this political tragedy, they must seem a thoughtful judiciary. But whether the spectator agrees or disagrees with the on-stage reaction, the device either focuses his perception or works for him ironically – giving him two messages to absorb.

These effects of an on-stage, representative audience mean rather more when they occur in conjunction with the clever device of the *play-within-the-play*. In *Love's Labour's Lost*, 5.2, the ludicrous pageant of the Nine Worthies parades all the clowns of the comedy as heroes of antiquity in order to ridicule the bookish learning exalted by the noble gentlemen of Navarre and their pseudo academy. In *A Midsummer Night's Dream*, act 5, the clown-mechanicals of the comedy produce the 'very tragical mirth' of 'Pyramus and Thisbe' to round out the romantic nonsense of the night with an uproarious parody of the extravagant passions of the play's young lovers. *The Taming of the Shrew* frames the whole story of Petruchio's boisterous wooing of the unwomanly Kate with another story, that of the intoxicated tinker Christopher Sly, so that the manner of the courtship, and especially Kate's final submissiveness, are ironically coloured by the audience's awareness that it is all a drunken dream; if a production is prepared to admit the Epilogue from the parallel script of *The Taming of a Shrew*, which supplies Sly with a page-boy as a 'wife' to take to bed, the frame-play carries an even greater irony, since the Kate of the inner play was, after all, only a boy actor all the time.

Such obvious plays-within as these do not diminish the power of those that are more subtle. The scenes of the artificial, pastoral lovers Silvius and Phebe, as witnessed by Rosalind in *As You Like It*, are there to enhance her perception – and the spectator's – of mismanaged love, and the words used by the old shepherd Corin invite her and the spectator to bring them into the main plot and 'see a pageant truly play'd'. The action of withdrawing from the scene like spectators, as well as Rosalind's agreement to 'prove a busy actor in their play', all insist that these players are themselves to become an on-stage audience, and that they will witness a play-within whose radical change in diction and style will warn the audience that a dramatic comparison is afoot. It is a special delight when an on-stage spectator steps into the play-within, as does Rosalind.

The best-known and most complicated play-within is the mousetrap play in *Hamlet*, 3.2, 'The Murder of Gonzago'. Again a contrast in verse style sets the play-within apart from the drama that surrounds it, and indeed makes the main plot seem more intense and realistic by the comparison. But this is the Prince's stratagem to reveal the guilt of the King, and occurs at the crisis of the action for the character and the audience. Nevertheless, the significance of the device is magnified in performance when it is seen that not only are the King and Queen on the throne watching their parodistic doubles in the Player King and Queen, but also that Hamlet and his surrogate Horatio are watching the throne; moreover, because of the intrusive behaviour of Hamlet (who in fact breaks the tension himself before the end of the play-within) the real audience is also watching *him*. Thus there are, in a sense, three plays-within to watch on-stage simultaneously. Not to be forgotten is the astonished on-stage audience of courtiers who provide the natural and uninformed reaction to the triple centres of action on the stage, and it is probably this group that guides the real audience to the progress of the scene and the success or failure of Hamlet's trick. All in all, in this extraordinary scene the audience is required to feel four lines of tension and to exercise four pairs of eyes.

Even so, the mousetrap scene is also preceded by a *dumb show* intended to prepare the audience for the action to come and to free its attention to carry out all this watching of watchers. When at the outset Claudius sees the dumb show grotesquely mimic his murder of King Hamlet, all the players and their watchers are in place and the game may begin. The dumb show served as a useful device for dramatic foreshadowing, performed to music in a highly stylized manner, and probably a little enigmatically. In *A Midsummer Night's Dream*, the Mechanicals even precede their burlesque of Pyramus and Thisbe with a delightfully silly little dumb show at 5.1.125. However, Shakespeare did not make as much use of this device as his contemporaries, like John Marston in *The Malcontent* and John Webster in *The Duchess of Malfi*.

Over half of Shakespeare's plays make some use of ritual pageantry. In the last scene of *Love's Labour's Lost* the flirtatious mumming of the Muscovites' dance and the ludicrous pageant of the Nine Worthies together cast the little world of love and learning in the Court of Navarre into comic perspective. The shows of Ghosts in *Richard III* and of Kings in *Macbeth* fix and affirm the historical import of their tragedies. The elements of masque introduced into the late romances, *Cymbeline*, *Pericles* and *The Tempest*, succeed in drenching their fantasies in a brilliant allegorical light. And it is possible in *The Winter's Tale* to see the figure of Time the Chorus also as the 'presenter' of the last scenes of the play, as if they were a grand sequence of scenes leading towards the final reconciliation; for this he has Paulina as his priestess to release the 'dead' Hermione from his toils: ''Tis time' (5.3.99), she says, as her music strikes up and the play closes movingly in a scene of beauty and grandeur.

Modern commentators have found it a little puzzling, but totally engaging, that Shakespeare's stage commonly comments self-reflexively on its own methods. *A Midsummer Night's Dream* is possibly the most metatheatrical of Shakespeare's plays, and Quince the producer of 'Pyramus and Thisbe' stops in mid-rehearsal (and at the mid-point of the whole play) to remind everyone concerned of the problems of dramatic illusion. One is 'to bring the moonlight into a chamber; for you know, Pyramus and Thisbe meet by moonlight ...' (3.1.46–7). After much inept debating by the assembled clowns about the possibility of having a real moon shine through the casement window (weather permitting), Quince finally comes up with a simple solution:

> Or else one must come in with a bush of thorns and a lantern, and say he comes to disfigure or to present the person of Moonshine ...
>
> (55–7)

Quince is evidently a symbolist, although he fails to recognize that a proliferation of lunar emblems in the arms of Starveling the tailor may be as dramatically distracting as any attempt to capture real moonlight for the play.

The comic range

The poetic indications of self-conscious dramaturgy occur in all types of play. In the chronicle plays, Shakespeare makes good use of the audience's general foreknowledge of the facts of history, although in *Henry IV* it is striking that the Prince's plans to direct his own story almost go awry when the theatrical vitality of Falstaff unshakably persists – the rebel Hotspur is historical and can be dispatched at the proper time, but the fat knight is an invented creature of the theatre who will not readily be banished. Metatheatrical scenes also abound in the tragedies. One of the more bizarre occurs in *King Lear*, 4.6, where the blinded and blood-stained Gloucester decides to take his own life and throw himself from

Dover Cliff. He and his son make a long, grotesque entrance
to centre stage in a scene of unequalled irony and ambiguity:

> GLOUCESTER. When shall I come to th' top of that same
>   hill?
> EDGAR.   You do climb up it now. Look how we
>   labour.
> GLOUCESTER. Methinks the ground is even.
> EDGAR.   Horrible steep.
>
>   (1–4)

The result is wonderfully ambivalent: Gloucester's death-wish
is pitiable, but Edgar's cure for pessimism evokes the laughter
of the theatre of the absurd.

There are few, if any, of Shakespeare's histories and tragedies that do not embody comic or farcical elements of one
kind or another. In the case of *Romeo and Juliet*, hardly a
scene escapes its injection of laughter, as if this tragedy of
young love needs insulation from incipient sentimentality.
The theory that comic intruders in the tragedies (Hamlet's
Gravediggers, Lear's Fool, Macbeth's Porter, Cleopatra's
Countryman, and so on) constitute 'comic relief' for the
audience is these days an exploded idea – if anything, they
tend to intensify and revitalize the situation. Even Desdemona's purity is accentuated by the earthy normality of Emilia:
soon to die for her fidelity, Desdemona wonders whether she
is different from other wives:

> DESDEMONA. Wouldst thou do such a thing for all the
>   world?
> EMILIA.   The world is a huge thing, it is a great price,
>   For a small vice.
>
>   (*Othello*, 4.3.67–9)

The sudden shift of perspective controls the spectator's attention, but does nothing to lower the tension.

Nevertheless, in comedy proper all its forms from low farce
to idyllic romance, from satire to serious problem comedy,
seem to sanction a special freedom for metatheatrical games-
manship, and generate a positive spectrum of styles and
manoeuvres in comedy light and dark. The signs and signals
from script and stage may be of the simplest *comic
incongruity*. *A Midsummer Night's Dream* contrives to have

the highest embroiled with the lowest, and the Queen of the Fairies is outrageously paired with Bottom the weaver wearing his ass's head. In *Much Ado about Nothing* the characters chosen to witness the villainy of Conrade and Borachio and bear the grave responsibility of saving the marriage of Hero and Claudio, and indeed rescuing the whole play from disaster, are none other than the clown Dogberry and his comic Watch, all hopelessly incompetent. The puritan Malvolio in *Twelfth Night*, initially clothed in sombre black, must for his ambition wear a laughably garish costume, and cap this by splitting his poker-face with a smile. In *Measure for Measure* Pompey the clown and tapster to Mistress Overdone's grim brothel must for his sins do his time in gaol as, of all things, assistant to the executioner Abhorson:

> ABHORSON. A bawd, sir? Fie upon him, he will discredit
>   our mystery.
> PROVOST.   Go to, sir, you weigh equally: a feather will
>   turn the scale.

(4.2.26–9)

When such an earthy clown in his motley wields his mortal axe, the audience will perhaps speculate upon the appropriateness, and not the incongruity, of Death the Jester.

In spite of such wild incongruities, Shakespeare's special gift in romantic comedy is to seek the delicate *balance between ridicule and sympathy*. In their contexts Caliban and Malvolio remain ambiguously grey rather than black. In the case of Shylock, whose image for an audience hovers between his villainy and its justification, the imponderable balance of sympathies has to this day made *The Merchant of Venice* one of the most controversial of comedies, and great actors have variously tried to overcome the character's ambivalence – in 1970 Laurence Olivier left the trial scene of act 4 with such a sob that it seemed to echo to the end of the play. In another vein, Falstaff naturally prompts many broad jokes deriving from his great girth – when asked on Gadshill to put his ear to the ground, he replies, 'Have you any levers to lift me up again, being down?' (*1 Henry IV*, 2.2.34). However, his frank discourse on honour in battle ('How if honour prick me off when I am come on?', 5.1.130) is totally endearing, and prepares the audience for the pathos of his rejection by the new King in Part II.

In the lighter romantic comedies, the balance between the audience's acceptance and rejection of a character is even more crucial. In her doublet and hose as Ganymede in *As You Like It* Rosalind is mostly a figure of fun as she finds it difficult to catch Orlando's attention, but in the end, in spite of her comic pretence that she has 'counterfeited', her swoon at the sight of his bloody napkin (4.3.156) must be taken as genuine, made all the more touching because Celia and Oliver are far too interested in one another to see her growing alarm. Reversing this pattern, Viola in *Twelfth Night* risks too much sympathy for her unrequited love for Orsino – until in 3.4 she finds herself entangled in one of the funniest sword-fights in drama when as the page Cesario she is challenged by Andrew Aguecheek, an effeminate man confronted by a girl in man's clothing.

One of Shakespeare's more elusive comic techniques is *the shifting of audience perspective* occasioned by having it leap from one level of perception to another. This is the true comic extension of the Elizabethan fashion for mixing kings and clowns. For example, *A Midsummer Night's Dream* has four kinds of lovers, three of them deviating preposterously from the natural norm of speech and behaviour established at the outset by Theseus and Hippolyta: the overwrought young lovers of Athens appear to be 'abnormal' (to choose a distinguishing term), the immortals Oberon and Titania to be 'supernatural' and the burlesque lovers Pyramus and Thisbe to be ludicrously 'subnormal'. With the consent of the audience, this delightful play proceeds by alternating extremes of style and subject, the contrasts in themselves signalling where each is fit for the audience's ridicule. *As You Like It* is another comedy with at least four pairs of lovers, all in lively juxtaposition. And in *Twelfth Night* Olivia has an even wider variety of 'suitors' – Orsino, Viola/Cesario, Malvolio and Andrew – and, though comic in herself, she is also the catalyst who exposes the comedy in them, the comic assortment designed to grant an audience the distance and the freedom to laugh.

Boy actresses

The English stage had no use for women in its productions until the Restoration of Charles II in 1660, and, as we saw, boys from the chapel companies were chosen by the adult companies for the young female parts. James Shirley (1596–1666) has some seven or eight plays in which a boy actor playing a girl disguises herself as a shepherd or a page, but no playwright makes more varied comic use of the boy-girl-boy transposition than Shakespeare. It is as if this convention offered him a special opportunity to set in conflict the realities of the playhouse with what is unreal in his play.

The following are the five comedies of Shakespeare in which his boy actresses disguise themselves as boys:

- In *The Two Gentlemen of Verona* Julia becomes the page Sebastian to follow her lover Proteus, a source of pathos.

- In *The Merchant of Venice* Portia disguises herself as a doctor of law to outwit Shylock, and suggests that in matters of wit and compassion women are more competent than men. (Shylock's daughter Jessica also disguises herself as a boy for a more conventional elopement with Lorenzo.)

- In *As You Like It* the banished Rosalind disguises herself as the shepherd Ganymede to protect her cousin Celia in the Forest of Arden, and so discovers and reveals the restrictions society imposes on her sex.

- In *Twelfth Night* Viola becomes the page Cesario in order to join the household of Orsino whom she loves, but to her grief she must deliver his amorous messages to her own rival; at the same time, conveniently for the plot, her male attire makes her the identical twin of her brother Sebastian.

- In *Cymbeline* Imogen, in another pathetic situation, disguises herself as Fidele, another page-boy, to escape the anger of her husband Posthumus.

Unlike the bawdy breeches parts of Restoration comedy, which permitted actresses to wear clothes that revealed their gender, and their legs, there could be no titillation in Shakespeare's sexual transformations. Nor could there have been much prudery, since he wrote at least five female parts that required a pregnant appearance: Jaquenetta, Doll Tearsheet, Helena, Juliet in *Measure for Measure* and Hermione. Nevertheless, Shakespeare was principally concerned to explore female sensibility, not her anatomy: Portia in a court of law finds herself in a man's world, Viola at the side of the man she loves must hide her feelings, Rosalind trapped like a prisoner by her disguise must find new ways to promote her amorous relationship with Orlando.

The sex change in *As You Like It* provides a notable opportunity for Shakespeare to play a metatheatrical game with his audience. He dares to proliferate the number of images of Rosalind the boy-actress that the spectator is required to keep in mind. First the audience is frequently reminded of Rosalind's true sex by Celia's teasing:

> Good my complexion! Dost thou think though I am caparisoned like a man I have a doublet and hose in my disposition?
>
> (3.2.191–3)

Again, when she hears that the stranger who is pinning verses to her on the trees is none other than the shy Orlando, her first response is, 'Alas the day, what shall I do with my doublet and hose?' (215). Her best moment comes when as Ganymede she suggests to Orlando that she play the part of Rosalind in order to cure him of his lovesickness, and from then on the audience must conjure four images of 'Rosalind' in its imagination: the boy actor, the girl character, the girl disguised as a boy and the girl of Orlando's expectations.

When in 4.1 she offers to be his Rosalind 'in a more coming-on disposition' (107), she takes the opportunity to act out a mock-marriage with him, herself playing the parts of both the bride and the priest and so creating a fifth and sixth Rosalind. In her several roles her voices accordingly become as varied as her actions, and the dialogue becomes a convoluted challenge to an audience's perception:

> No, no, Orlando, men are April when they woo, December when they wed. Maids are May when they are maids, but the sky changes when they are wives.
>
> (138–41)

It is for the player and the audience to decide which of the Rosalinds is speaking these lines, and it may be that the last sentiment belongs to the boy-actor speaking in aside through all the disguise and pretence. She has not finished, indeed, and when she proceeds to play a harridan of a wife in as shocking a way as she can, an audience may well think that in testing her lover she has gone too far.

Shakespeare's techniques refined beyond belief the work of his predecessors. The basis of his stagecraft begins with the minutiae of words chosen for the actor's gesture and movement, along with indications of his use of props, costume and kindred elements. In his exercise of stage space and time, light and darkness and indefinite location, he reveals a little of his special gift for engaging his audience. By his manipulation of the range of conventions that belong to a non-realistic stage, especially in comedy, he guides and controls the progress of the story. But the tale is less important than the telling. Shakespeare's deployment of kinds of characters, their choric function, their role-playing, the use of bi-level disguise for the female parts and much more, becomes part of his strategy for eliciting an audience's response and prompting its participation.

Shakespeare's stage innovations also include the arrangement and structure of his scenes and episodes that direct the audience's mood and perception. A term from the Greek to describe this has been suggested: *'parataxis'* [the marshalling and order of troops for battle]. The sequence and especially the juxtaposition of each scene is never concerned with its imaginary location, always with its impact and meaning in performance, and as the story unfolds, the rapid and continuous succession of scenes in itself creates a rhythm and spirit in the action.

Scenes may proceed in parallel: for example, passing between Greek and Trojan camp in *Troilus and Cressida*, setting the King's scenes beside Gloucester's in *King Lear*, leaping from Egypt to Rome in *Antony and Cleopatra*. They may proceed in contrast: providing the discord between court and tavern in *1 Henry IV* and the clash between the public occasion and the private moment in *Romeo and Juliet*, 3.1,2 –

Romeo banished from Verona leaves the busy platform just as Juliet enters on her lonely balcony to pray for him to come to her: 'Gallop apace, you fiery footed steeds'. While the shifts and transitions from crowd to isolated figure, from formal blocking to informal behaviour, from high state to low society, create the tension and excitement of the play, the ordering of the scenes, like ironic echoes or shadows, is designed to trigger and stimulate audience perception and bring the spectator the pleasure of fitting the pieces together for a complete experience.

7

Ben Jonson's comic stagecraft

The brave new world of Jacobean drama

Ben Jonson (1572–1637), better than Shakespeare, helps put in perspective the eruption of Jacobean theatre, especially in its daring explorations and imaginative adventures in comedy. Jonson's career spans the reign of James I (1603–25), during which time he attacked the lack of direction he thought he saw in the legacy of Elizabethan tragedy and comedy, and tried to reform their loose romantic propensities. If he failed to impose a new classicism upon Jacobean tragedy, he set new artistic standards of control and purpose for its comedy. In the seventeenth century the genius of Shakespeare was disregarded and Jonson had more influence on English drama than any other playwright for the next hundred and fifty years.

The basic physical factors governing Jacobean drama remained much like those of the previous century. The absence of any visual backing on the stage remained unchanged and the emphasis fell as before on the presence of the actor. The platform stage of the Jacobean public or private theatre was still as neutral and therefore as mercurial as the imagination would allow, and locality and the clock or the calendar, where they were called for, were still implicit in the character and his lines. There was nothing approximating to modern stage realism, not even the development of more introspective characterization, to suggest that the interaction between actor and spectator was not as open and non-illusionistic as it always had been. An audience was still invited to go to the play, not to escape into some other world of pretence and dream, but to help build and share in a candidly theatrical event.

The Jacobean stage witnessed wide experiment with ever bolder plotting in hyperbolical comic intrigue or tragic revenge, often given added piquancy by the use of exotic locations peopled by Italianate men and women, especially Machiavellian monsters. Its tragedy was marked by ingenious horrors and excessive blood and violence. Character could be grotesquely distorted for either comic or tragic reasons and the stage abounded in outlandish comic types and cynical tyrants and Satanic villains. The drama enjoyed a theatrical excess unlike that of any other age, with music and song, ornate dumb shows, magnificent processionals, flamboyant plays-within and stage spectacles of every kind.

Jacobean acting naturally echoed its extravagant stage. In any genre an actor might play two or more roles, and even role-play within a single characterization. Child actors still performed adult drama in the strangely 'burlesque' or deviate mode that was acceptable at this time. Since women remained excluded from the stage, boys still played the female parts, and in the hands of a Shakespeare or a Shirley could slip in and out of their adopted sex as easily as in and out of their disguises, boys behaving like girls and girls like boys. An element of preposterous puppetry lay behind this sort of performance.

Ben Jonson and the concept of comedy: *Every Man in His Humour*

Jonson was at the heart of this dramatic excitement, especially in its audacious methods of illuminating reality. He risked following Sidney and ran counter to the romantic fashions of the popular Elizabethan stage, including Shakespeare's. In his Prologue to *Every Man in His Humour* (first performed in 1598, although probably not spoken on that occasion since the play was presented by the very Lord Chamberlain's Men he seemed to be attacking), he betrayed his scorn for the happy audiences whose 'delight' could be 'purchased' by disregarding the classical unities, a theme he took up again in the Prologue to *Volpone* in 1606. Throughout his career he was a persistent audience-baiter, even in a comedy as late as *The Staple of News*, presented in 1626, setting on the stage four noisy lady gossips as representative spectators.

In *Every Man in His Humour* he ridiculed the play that broke the unity of time:

> To make a child now swaddled to proceed
> Man, and then shoot up in one beard and weed
> Past threescore years.

>   (7–9)

He was equally hard on the play that used words and cheap effects as a substitute for the unity of place:

> Where neither Chorus wafts you o'er the seas,
> Nor creaking throne comes down, the boys to please

>   (15–16)

Jonson's distaste for the spectacle of his contemporaries and his general opposition to the use of stage machinery and scenic effects are well known; they are also part of his appeal for neo-classical standards. In his own practice he made little use of the stage levels and spatial effects found in Marlowe and Shakespeare, and preferred his drama to stand or fall on what was heard, not on what was seen. Nevertheless, plays like *Volpone* and *The Alchemist* went on to use the dramatic unities as rarely before on the English stage – to create a claustrophobic prison of the stage space, the chosen room, in which the action is supposed to take place. His idea of 'place' was all but metaphysical and his plays were arranged like wheels-within-wheels, plays-within-plays, with the audience looking from without at a stage-within-a-stage, where the fools and gulls of the play were usually ensnared.

Behind this lay Jonson's greater intentions for his new theatre. In the *Every Man out of His Humour* (1599) Prologue he offered a self-confident prescription for a better stagecraft and a more effective drama based, in these famous lines, on

> deeds and language such as men do use,
> And persons such as comedy would choose
> When she would show an image of the times.

>   (21–3)

Jonson is echoing Cicero, whom Cordatus 'the author's friend' in *Every Man out of His Humour* quotes: '*imitatio vitae, speculum consuetudinus, imago veritatis*' [imitation of life, mirror of the times, image of truth]. If this sounds like realism, it is realism without stage illusion and the image is a distorted one. Indeed, Jonson brazenly departs from realism in order to drive home his points, and creates his comic satire by an impudent mode of characterization, suggesting a spectrum of degrees of reality through which comic drama may pass. In the same way the rattling pace of the action in his comedy is something of a stage convention, an unnatural whirl of events, as if the audience is to be denied a chance to question the unreasonableness of the comic intrigue. The spectator may no longer expect to be wooed by cool, sweet verses, but seized by the neck and shaken.

In the Induction to *Every Man out of His Humour* Jonson again assumes the role of instructor and is more specific about his intentions. By putting himself on the stage in the character of the irrepressible Asper, 'eager and constant in reproof', he seeks to enter into a contract with his audience, and fires off the next of his comments on the theory of drama. This time he defines his kind of characterization, and conveys his early sense of the comic stage as one peopled by eccentrics. His particular contribution is his well-known metaphorical transfer of the medieval medical analysis of the personality to the 'humours' of practical stage characterization:

> As when some one peculiar quality
> Doth so possess a man that it doth draw
> All his affects, his spirits, and his powers,
> In their confluctions, all to run one way;
> This may be truly said to be a humour.

> (105–9)

A show-stopper in *Every Man in His Humour* was the boastful captain Bobadilla (Bobadill), who is granted the cant of a fencing master and a swearer of dainty oaths, but he is above all the teller of outrageous stories about his prowess, albeit conveyed with the false modesty of a gentleman: 'I could have slain them all, but I delight not in murder' (4.5.49–50). However, the method by which a playwright pins down a comic character as a type also risks the danger of depicting him as a cartoon, and such creatures can be mechanical and chilling. The system may not easily admit the contradictions that exist within real people, and with some few exceptions Jonson's characters, especially his women, lack the humanity that is generally found in Shakespeare's comic fools.

The audience does not ask whether such two-dimensional characters are realistic or true to life, only whether they are actable and stageworthy, and Jonson's are eminently so. There is a place for a flat character in a certain kind of comedy, and especially in a play that intends a crowded gallery of busy creatures: Jonson regularly called for casts of fifteen to twenty, with *Bartholomew Fair* coming in at well over thirty. Flat, 'cardboard', 'two-dimensional' characters are appropriate in the farcical situations associated with Roman comedy, which dealt in authoritarian fathers and prodigal sons, surrounded by rascally servants. Of this kind is Jonson's tribe of gulls, fools and braggarts, creatures of vanity and greed, assembled with a view to passing quick moral judgments on human folly and affectation.

Jonson's work was continually experimental, and his first comic success, *Every Man in His Humour*, was cleverly revised for the collection of his plays published as his *Works* some years later in 1616, with the result that there are two versions of the play, which side by side reveal the growth of his sense of a comic stage. In the characterization of the revised version Jonson observes his people more closely, and a stereotypical, bull-headed father in the first version (Lorenzo Senior) becomes in the second the much more sympathetic Old Kno'well worn with care over his wild son Edward. The passionately jealous Thorello becomes a more subtly self-deluding Kitely full of doubt and hesitation (later to be a favourite part with David Garrick in the eighteenth century, and Kean and Macready in the nineteenth). If these characters are 'humours', whether genuine or affected, they are not grotesquely so, and their new subtlety made them more actable. Satirical comedy may in this way embrace human comedy.

When in his revision Jonson shifts the action of the comedy

from Florence to London, from the conventional world of Italian comedy to something essentially English, he is also publishing a manifesto for dramatic change. There are many silent changes of location assumed in the play, from house to street to tavern and more, but there are no changes of setting that matter. However, the change to London was a prescription to scour the streets and taverns known for figures familiar to author, actor and audience alike. The play with its beggars of Moorfields and musters [military assemblies] at Mile End, the porters and carmen of Thames street and Custom House quay, and many more local types, is the first of his comedies that radiates a sense of teeming London life. Like other city dramatists, Jonson taught himself to manipulate a Rabelaisian world, a circle of merchants and rogues, Puritans and roaring boys, pimps and whores and a host of others, each with his appropriate attitude and values, and each speaking the appropriate tongue. Through the artistry and drive of *Every Man in His Humour*, the spirit of Jonson's London takes hold.

The mature comedies: *Volpone, The Alchemist*

When in five brisk weeks Jonson devised and wrote *Volpone* (1606) for the King's Men at the Globe, he was still thinking in terms of Italianate satire and applying the classical rules he understood best. Jacobean London was only faintly visible in the play's English travellers, especially the pompous Sir Politic Would-Be and the insufferable Lady Would-Be, his wife. The target was instead the acquisitive society of Renaissance Venice in all its glitter and corruption. The images of greed Jonson believed to be universal and his zeal as a reformer – 'to mix profit with your pleasure', according to the Prologue – were undiminished. His focus in this play was upon an unconscionable rascal who is a *magnifico* of Venice and a monster of a voluptuary, and he is surrounded and complemented by creatures who are extensions of his own bestiality: his parasite Mosca and a bizarre trio made up of a dwarf, an eunuch and an hermaphrodite. The audience soon meets this repulsive little bunch when in 1.2 they present their master with a grotesque entertainment, a 'sport', of their own devising. Thereupon Volpone declares that he will pretend to be a dying man in order to swindle the predators who are drawn to his deathbed, and the stage is set for a black, not to say macabre, comedy.

At the Old Vic in 1968 Tyrone Guthrie had his cast wear animal masks (and study their roles at the London Zoo): he was responding as a director to the imperatives in the text that at one level of perception the audience should be made aware of animals of prey. Aesop and the medieval fabliaux led Jonson to name his hero 'fox' and his servant 'fly', and to imagine Voltore, Corbaccio and Corvino ('vulture', 'crow' and 'raven') as carrion birds who descend upon a dying carcass. To these figures of masquerade Jonson added qualities of performance that recall the farcical *vecchii* [old men like Pantalone and Dottore] masks of the Italian *commedia dell'arte*, and Mosca inherits some basic qualities of the *zanni* [clowns], especially of Scapino. From the technical point of view of a dramatized allegory, the playwright's inventive fancy was irrepressible.

Jonson also achieved a *quasi* unity of place, since the comic action revolves for much of the time round Volpone's house and presence. On his couch he is thrust out on to the platform to receive his rapacious visitors in his pretended sickness, and also to enact the seduction of Celia. When he takes to the street as a mountebank his scaffold is erected on much the same spot, at which time the audience seems to be part of the on-stage crowd. When he is finally '*brought in, as impotent*' (4.6.20) to the Senate for his trial, he is once again seen on his couch. For all it is a bare stage, the effect of Volpone's domination is to concentrate and rivet the action and, supported by a unity of time in which the story takes place in less than a day (from morning to afternoon), what began as the single suggestion of a fox's den retains its sinister confines to the end.

From the explosion of Volpone's notorious opening line when he rises from a sumptuous bed to greet the day, and, after Mosca perhaps throws back the discovery-curtain, to greet his gold, the ears are assaulted by hyperbolic poetry and its unconcealed blasphemy:

> Good morning to the day; and, next, my gold!
> Open the shrine, that I may see my saint.
> Hail the world's soul, and mine!
>
> (1.1.1–3)

From there on, it is a rare quality of ironic poetic theatre that grips the spectator.

Jonson's skill with a rich comic situation was never better than when Volpone and Mosca have moments of by-play at the expense of their victims, and when in their gleeful asides they seem to share their delight with the spectator. The playwright's stagecraft is overwhelming when Volpone plays the disguiser. Like many others of Jonson's comic leads – Truewit in *Every Man in His Humour*, Subtle in *The Alchemist* – Volpone is gifted with a singular histrionic sense that he imparts vividly to his audience and that Jonson uses to turn much of the action into something of a play-within-a-play. Volpone revels in his role as an actor and scrutinizes his mirror; he delights in the use of costume and make-up, wrapping himself in his foxy furs and nightcaps, and gumming up his eyes with ointment. Above all, he glories in the different voices he assumes as a dying man, a mountebank, an ardent lover or an officer of the law. This is how the text conveys the way he must greet Voltore, when his first victim is about to enter:

> Now, my feigned cough, my phthisic, and my gout,
> My apoplexy, palsie, and catarrhs,
> Help, with your forced functions, this my posture,
> Wherein, this three year, I have milked their hopes.
> He comes, I hear him – uh! uh! uh! uh! O –
>
> (1.2.125–9)

As an impostor Volpone is from the beginning venomously self-confident. Every knock brings another predator, and with each new entrance Volpone's performance changes, while Mosca, another of Jonson's actors, plays off one fool against another. By the time of Corvino's entrance, Volpone has almost gasped his last breath, but one feeble claw is able to revive sufficiently to reach out and grasp the pearl and the diamond he is offered.

The visit of the beauteous Lady Would-Be, 'madam with

the everlasting voice', fussing with her ruff, her hair and her powder, and forever chastising her maidservants, proves less attractive to Volpone than he had expected, so that, ironically, he must feign sickness even more energetically in self-defence. However, when Corvino has been persuaded to prostitute his lovely young wife Celia, Volpone for balance and contrast leaps from his couch on her entrance a lover 'fresh', 'hot' and 'high' (3.7.156–7). And Jonson introduces a sly irony when, to prove to Corvino that Volpone is too far gone to hear anything spoken to him, Mosca gleefully takes the opportunity to insult his master with words that come perilously close to what he really feels:

> The pox approach, and add to your diseases,
> If it would send you hence the sooner, sir.

> (1.5.52–3)

Jonson returned wholly to the London scene with *The Alchemist* (1610), and this play competes with *Volpone* as his most popular comedy. The subject is again the world of greed, and he invents a perfect vehicle to show that money makes fools of everyone. At the same time the play projects his particular vision of teeming London life in all its idiom and colour. The play was first presented by the King's Men at either the Globe or the Blackfriars, where a wide platform allowed the spatial freedom to suggest virtually a single location, inside or just outside Lovewit's house. The spectator is intermittently reminded where the scene is, and the playing time also seems to cover the actual duration of the action. In this fashion the single drive of a well-fabricated plot, taken with continuity at a quick pace, is all that is needed to grip the house, and the unities serve Jonsonian comedy to perfection, granting his material an irresistible energy and urgency.

The Alchemist is the story of a huge deception. Jeremy the butler makes use of his master's house (conveniently located near Blackfriars) in his absence. It is to provide a convenient base for one Doctor Subtle, a quack pretending to be an alchemist, together with his punk Doll Common and himself in the guise of Captain Face, to practise confidence tricks on any boobies they can pick up in the City. Versed in all the appropriate jargon, they offer to tell fortunes, raise super-natural spirits and, to top it all, turn base metal into gold – they have put it out that they have discovered the secret of the apocryphal 'philosopher's stone', which in the play becomes a symbol for the greed and fantasies of wealth shared by villain and victim alike. It is their intention to fleece anyone who comes, and then share the spoils among themselves.

The play gets off to a cracking start with a roaring quarrel between the two rogues, who enter at a dash for a short, fast and oblique exposition scene:

> FACE. Believe't, I will.
> SUBTLE.   Thy worst. I fart at thee.
> DOLL. Ha'you your wits? Why, gentlemen! For love –

Bit by bit the initial information needed by an audience emerges, but all in the process of a brawl in which the curt, abusive lines speak for the violence of the exchange. The sense that Subtle is chasing Face with a bottle of vitriol is present in a hint in the dialogue – a hint interpreted otherwise by Guthrie in his modern dress production at the Old Vic in 1962, when Leo McKern as Subtle threatened Face and the spectator with a brimming chamber pot. Jonson has begun at a level of vulgarity which can descend no lower, although Doll's protests are not at what they are saying, rather at the racket they are making. And while her interpolations suggest that she is trying to restrain them, they also mark the growth of a crescendo over a period of some five minutes. At the peak, like Beckett's tramps in *Waiting for Godot*, they are mechanically shouting one-word insults: 'Cheater – Bawd – Cow-herd – Conjurer – Cut-purse – Witch', until Doll explodes with, 'O, me! We are ruined! Lost!' (106–8).

The three are scarcely reconciled when a bell announces the arrival of their first victim. Immediately their attitudes undergo a transformation: Face tells Subtle to put on his 'robes', Doll hides herself and Face goes to let the caller in, while all the time the audience is left to wonder what trick has in fact been planned. So the disguising and the play-acting begins with this apparent play-within-a-play, already making the audience party to a knavish conspiracy. And so for the audience the play itself can begin.

With each new entrance another gull arrives and the mercurial stage and its chameleon actors spring into another frantic scenario of deception. And what a gallery of characters Jonson has gathered! The shy clerk Dapper, who wants a familiar spirit to help him to a winning streak as a gambler, is persuaded that he is blessed with the Queen of the Fairies for an aunt; the audience learns that none other than Doll Common is to appear in this part, but it has to wait for the anticipated encounter until the last act. Abel Drugger is a slow-witted seller of tobacco who wants astrology to help him set up shop; this was a part that David Garrick took to himself, inventing new business, for over thirty years. Other visitors are a brace of sanctimonious Puritans from Amsterdam, Ananias and Tribulation Wholesome, one Pertinax Surly, a card-sharper and Kastril, a roaring boy who wishes to be a courtier and learn how to quarrel. But perhaps Jonson's most notable creation is the voluptuary Sir Epicure Mammon, a gross and gullible knight who dreams of wealth, food and women – hence calling up another apt role for Doll.

Sir Epicure is also a man of grand words, so that the verse lines that roll from his mouth are themselves a gross mockery of good poetry. He makes his first entrance thus:

> Come on, sir. Now, you set your foot on shore
> In *novo orbe* [the new world]; here's the rich Peru ...
>
> (2.1.1–2)

and he turns the bare platform into a luxurious palace by a performance to match the language. He minces and swaggers across the breadth of the stage in an outrageous exhibition of self-admiration:

> I will have ... my glasses,
> Cut in more subtle angles, to disperse
> And multiply the figures, as I walk
> Naked between my succubae.
>
> (2.2.41, 45–8)

The audience hears the fantasy, but sees the reality. With such material, scene after scene catches fire in performance.

If the audience to *The Alchemist* is drawn into the conspiracy, a quality of playful theatricality pervades the action from the beginning. With their quick changes of costume and assumed voices, Face, Subtle and Doll, like Volpone and Mosca, are glorious role-players as well as impostors. Moreover, their gulls are also in one way or another seen to be acting out their dreams, dressing themselves up and adopting new attitudes. The play all but anticipates Jean Genêt's house of illusions in *Le Balcon* (1956), with the comparable intention of embracing all of society in its grotesque picture of human fantasizing. And Jonson's playfulness extends to the end, where in his last line Face cheekily suggests that the audience he is addressing could be among his next victims, just as Genêt's Madame Irma sends the audience home as if they are her clients at the brothel.

The achievement of *Bartholomew Fair*

In satirical comedy Jonson discovered his strengths on the public stage. In 1603 in *Sejanus* he had attempted a classical Roman history for the King's Men which did not impress, and in 1611 he tried his hand again with another story of a Roman conspiracy in *Cataline* with even less success. Both had an excessive number of characters. Both were in blank verse and both were classically constructed as unrelieved tragedy. His subsequent achievement with *Bartholomew Fair* soon after in 1614 suggests that he at last settled for what he knew best.

This play marks the ultimate development of humours comedy and is a remarkable achievement in Jonsonian stagecraft. Played by the Lady Elizabeth's Men, it was among the first plays to be produced at the new Hope Theatre, opened by Henslowe in 1614 on the site of the Bear Garden on Bankside. For a play about an extremely popular, not to say vulgar, festival, this location was wholly appropriate: the Hope was a dual purpose playhouse where every so often bull- or bear-baiting would replace the performance of plays. To make this possible, the stage was built on trestles and had no stage-posts. The builder's contract is clear, and insists upon

> a stage to be carried or taken away, and to stand upon
> trestles good substantial and sufficient for the carrying and
> bearing of such a stage ... [Also] the heavens all over the
> said stage, to be borne or carried without any posts or
> supporters to be fixed or set upon the said stage.

(Glynne Wickham, *Early English Stages*, vol. II, Part II (1972))

Moreover, when Jonson had his Stage-Keeper sweep the stage
for apples 'for the bears within' and had his Book-Holder
[prompter] remark the 'special decorum' of playing in this
theatre, 'the place being as dirty as Smithfield [the site of the
Fair], and as stinking every whit' (Induction, 52, 160–2), he
wanted his audience from the outset to be aware of where
they were, and frequent references subsequently sustain this
awareness.

Bartholomew Fair was the annual three-day cloth fair held
every August in Smithfield, the market-place just outside
London. Since this place was owned by the Priory of St
Bartholomew, it had a reputation for dispensing miracles
along with a great deal to eat, drink and enjoy in the way of
games and shows. It was a holiday, and drew a cross-section
of London society to satisfy the needs of any city comedy,
and some of those who make it up are listed in the little
pamphlet *Bartholomew Faire* (1641):

> Hither resort people of all sorts, high and low, rich and
> poor, from cities, towns, and countries; of all sects, Papists,
> Atheists, Anabaptists, and Brownists: and of all conditions,
> good and bad, virtuous and vicious, knaves and fools,
> cuckolds and cuckoldmakers, bawds, and whores, pimps
> and panders, rogues and rascals, the little loud-one and the
> witty wanton.

Symbolically this fair represented London, if not England.
More than this, as it became the magnet for every kind of
fraud and trickery, it was also the place where any vice might
be exhibited and exposed. Moreover, since the action of
Jonson's comedy touches only a single visit, he again achieves
the unity of time. The large neutral platform was able to
accommodate a number of makeshift booths and any number
of visitors moving around them, and, in the Elizabethan way,
as they came and went the scene could change and yet remain

the same. Thus the play almost manages the unity of place as
well, so that the location of the scene is readily identified with
the occasion of the Fair.

Such a comedy cried out to be blessed with a large number
of characters, and although Jonson was adept at individua-
lizing his creatures by their idiomatic speech and appropriate
cant, the problem was to create the life of the Fair without
turning so many parts to caricature. He did it by building his
cast in groups or 'families', which put together become the
microcosm of London he sought, and what seems to be an
unruly mob of people, intended to catch the Fair's general
atmosphere of hurly-burly and confusion, in performance is
less random because of their distinguishing marks of speech
and behaviour.

An obvious division of the cast recognizes the difference
between those who are part of the Fair, plying their
customary trades, the crowd of vendors and dealers,
hawkers and entertainers, thieves and cutpurses, bawds and
pimps, and those who are the visitors. The first group awaits
its quarry, the second varies in its purpose for going to the
Fair, and accordingly subdivides by class and calling. In the
upper class, Bartholomew Cokes, the spoiled young booby
and the Fair's ideal customer who buys everything he can, is
an Esquire of Middlesex, and with his servant and tutor
Humphrey Wasp, sister Dame Overdo and Grace his betrothed, he leads a group of the gentry. To this class is
added the wife-hunting gentlemen adventurers, Winwife and
Quarlous, and Grace's guardian, the zealous Justice Adam
Overdo, a respectable magistrate who has disguised himself
as Mad Arthur of Bradley in order to spy on the 'enormities'
practised at the Fair. Proctor [lawyer] John Littlewit of
Paul's, together with his pretty wife Win-the-Fight ('She has
as little wit as her husband, it seems') and her Puritan
mother Dame Purecraft and the Puritan Zeal-of-the-Land
Busy, the Dame's gluttonous suitor, are solid bourgeois
citizens. These are also the 'Banbury-bloods' [Puritans] of
the City who have 'come a pig-hunting' (3.2.96): the reason
Busy gives for eating two-and-a-half servings of roast pork
is 'to profess our hate and loathing of Judaism' (1.6.94).
When they are not identified by, say, their religious hypoc-

risy, the social and family relationships of these visitors link them together.

Yet Jonson has another, more powerful, structural device to bind his play dramatically. The comic action proceeds by careful stages, which slowly fill the empty platform and simultaneously draw the audience into the business of the Fair. It comes as no surprise that a play by Ben Jonson opens with an induction, but *Bartholomew Fair* introduces a Stage-Keeper sweeping an empty stage and speaking in soliloquy as if he is one of the spectators – a particularly effective device on a thrust stage nearly surrounded by the expectant crowd of spectators. Moreover, by criticizing what they are about to see, he tries to ingratiate himself with the house and so close the aesthetic gap still further. The Stage-Keeper is suitably sceptical of this new-fangled comedy, and the Book-Holder who follows him offers the audience a contract: if it will kindly give the play its attention, the playwright will delight everyone and offend none.

With that, the play appears to begin again by stepping back into the middle-class world of the Littlewits, whose eight characters are introduced by another soliloquy. They are preparing to go to the Fair, which makes of them a play-within-a-play at the outset, the audience observing them from without or within as it pleases. The visitors to the Fair are in their own way spectators and eavesdroppers whose asides in any case add to the spirit of play-acting and the conscious game of creating an illusion. But Jonson has not finished with the preparation of his structural footings, since with act 2 and a third soliloquy the play appears to begin yet again: Overdo introduces himself in his disguise as he is preparing to spy on what he and the audience are about to see, so inviting it to share the role of a pompous on-stage busybody and reveal yet another curtain of illusion.

It is only when these outer and inner circles of reality are established that the assembled company is allowed to set foot in the Fair, and when the Fair proper is presented it is with a resounding blast of words from Lantern Leatherhead the hobbyhorse-seller quarrelling with Joan Trash the ginger-bread-woman and accompanied by the street-cries of London. They drag their wares in with them and set up their

booths and stalls, but it is not long before the entrance of
Ursula the pig-woman, a sweating giantess of a bawd who
dominates the scene 'all fire and fat'. She confesses with pride,
'I do water the ground in knots as I go, like a great garden-
pot' (2.2.51–2) and berates her tapster for not widening the
sides of her chair. Hers is also a perfect giant of a comic part
to play in drag, as it was in the first production. In act 2
Ursula's stall becomes the centre of life at the Fair.

For a minute or two in 4.6 Jonson arranges that Wasp,
Busy and Overdo, the representatives of education, religion
and the law, are sitting in a row in the stocks – exhibited and
chastised together in a grotesque and distorted image of their
unfortunate humours. And the play is rich in other satirical
incidents that challenge propriety, as when in 4.4 the learned
and testy Wasp is caught up in the horse-dealer Knockem's
game of vapours (in which each speaker must contradict the
last that spoke), and in 4.5 Punk Alice enters beating the
Justice's wife for stealing her pitch:

> A mischief on you, they are such as you are, that undo us,
> and take our trade from us, with your tuft taffeta haunches.
>
> (4.5.64–6)

Not till the end is Justice Overdo shocked to discover his
wife, along with Win, drunk and dressed like a whore. But the
most outrageous development comes when Jonson reveals the
inmost circle of his game of illusions and presents a puppet-
play. All the visitors to the Fair are assembled to watch at this
finale, but it is chiefly the excited, totally absorbed reaction of
the naive Cokes that is heard: teased by Lanthorn Leatherhead
the puppeteer, he takes the wooden puppets to be live actors
and the vulgarized love story of Hero and Leander to be real.
Finally comes the anticipated entrance of none other than
Brother Busy, also drunk, condemning like the Puritan he is
all 'stage-players, rhymers and morrice-dancers':

> Hold thy peace, thy scurrility, shut up thy mouth, thy
> profession is damnable, and in pleading for it, thou dost
> plead for Baal.
>
> (5.5.17–20)

So much was to be expected, but Jonson holds his trump

till last. As the 'disputation' proceeds, Leatherhead, who was working the puppets all along, cleverly begins to answer Busy's charges through the voice of one of his puppets:

> BUSY.   ... you are an abomination: for the male, among you, putteth on the apparel of the female, and the female of the male.
> PUPPET DIONYSIUS. *You lie, you lie, you lie abominably.*
> COKES.   Good, by my troth, he hath given him the lie thrice.
> PUPPET DIONYSIUS.. *It is your old stale argument against the players, but it will not hold against the puppets; for we have neither male nor female amongst us. And that thou may'st see, if thou wilt, like a malicious purbling zeal as thou art!*
>
> *[The Puppet takes up his garment.]* (5.5. 91–9)

This example is light on stage business and movement, but heavy on irony. The Puritans had always denounced the playhouse for having boys play women, confusing the real with the illusory; now to denounce wooden puppets on a similar charge was doubly to confound this obvious distinction by which all drama must work. Like Cokes, Busy muddles what is real and what is unreal, so that the two are depicted as being equally simple-minded.

The Restoration could not have enough of *Bartholomew Fair*. For Samuel Pepys it was 'the best comedy in the world' (*Diary*, 2 August, 1664) and Thomas Shadwell thought it 'one of the wittiest plays in the world' (Preface to *The Humourists*, 1668). It was also praised by John Dryden for its realism, for 'those very things that are daily spoken or practised in the fair' (*A Defence of the Essay of Dramatic Poesy*, 1668). However, with the development of changeable scenery and the loss of the pace and freedom of an open platform, this multifaceted comedy raised many problems of production; and the middle-class audiences of the eighteenth and nine-teenth centuries found that the very realism that had pleased Dryden was too much to stomach. The play was not per-formed again until Montagu Summers's revival in 1921 (when Ursula was again played by a man, the large Roy Byford).

In recent years the difficulty has been to strike the right balance between authenticity and modernity – between what the author wanted and what an audience could make sense of. Since the production by George Devine for the Old Vic in 1950, the practice has been to stuff the stage with people and props, all the trappings of the Fair with its bustle, noise and vulgarity: in this way at least the spirit of the occasion could be staged and seen. When in 1969 Terry Hands for the Royal Shakespeare Company tried a knockabout and deliberately anachronistic clown show, and when in 1978 Michael Bog-danov, targeting the more cynical and commercial side of the play, turned the Young Vic into a modern-dress circus, and in the same summer Peter Barnes, emphasizing class differences, turned the Round House into a Jacobean-cum-Victorian fair-ground of doubtful identity, the signal was one of loss of confidence in the playwright. None of these productions, incidentally, used the Induction to pursue the wheels-within-wheels arrangement of the play's structure.

Jonson was to go on in later life to write several lesser comedies for the King's Men: *The Devil Is an Ass* (1616), *The Staple of News* (1626), *The New Inn* (1629), *The Magnetic Lady* (1632) and *The Tale of a Tub* (1633). Each continued his wrangle with his audience, but none nudged or wooed it into the theatrical fray as his best comedies had succeeded in doing. In epistles and inductions, prologues and epilogues, it is evident that he was tormented throughout his career by the demanding presence of the 'judicious spectator', and that it was irksome that his chosen vocation compelled him to confront the audiences he often appeared to despise. This may also account for some part of his criticism of the more and more elaborate scenes and machines that naturally attracted an audience's attention to the masques for the Court (see chapter 8). At all events, his contribution to the developing art of the stage did not lie in the direction of decoration and spectacle, and although he was careful to furnish his own stage directions in his masques and his plays, his interest in plotting did not extend to the movement over the stage platform and control of the actor's space, nor to the more subtle arrangement and deployment of scenes associated with Shakespeare.

Jonson is nevertheless to be given credit for successfully

applying certain features of important stagecraft. Resisting the tide of Elizabethan stage licence, in his time he was almost alone in pursuing the classical unities, and his concentration on a single location and a given span of time worked well for his comic structuring, and the pace and continuity of action he achieved made good use of the Elizabethan open platform. In matters of comic characterization, too, his example in the practice of the theory of humours remained high on the dramatic agenda for many years and continued to be remarkably workable in various ways. However, it cannot safely be claimed that character alone was the chief weapon in the successful skirmishes and encounters of his comic stage.

Recognition should go instead to the ease with which he assimilated the distinctive ambivalence of the Elizabethan stage and its ability to swing between the real and the illusory, with the consequent effect on actor and audience. For the actor a natural mode of disguising and role-playing while still being himself made such notable parts as Volpone and Mosca, Face and Subtle, Justice Overdo and Ursula the pig-woman in her transvestite role quite smooth and comfortable for an audience to accept and share. These characters have little to do with humours or any other rules of dramaturgy: they are all parts that exhibit a uniquely Jonsonian, histrionic sense – a joy in disguising and playing another role, or merely taking pleasure in the changing of a character's voice or costume. Ingenious comic plotting and preposterous conceptions of human character, salted with Jonson's sheer intoxication with language and his persistent thrust of satire, knew no equal in this period.

8

The Court masque

Four reigns and a new audience

Even though the masque is not wholly a dramatic form, indirectly its stage elements and procedures left an important legacy to the English drama that succeeded it, pointing to the way the scenic stage developed and how forms of ballet and opera came about. It is helpful to begin with a glance at its historical background.

The masque had no need for a dramatic shape or a narrative plotline. It was an aristocratic entertainment created in order to serve a private social occasion, and a sense of that occasion and its milieu is essential to an understanding of each masque: it gives it its meaning. In one sense, the masquers were intended to be its spectators, and the spectators its masquers, with its audience 'taken out' by the performers to join in the dance in order to generate an unusually participatory theatrical form: Allardyce Nicoll declared a masque to be 'an invitation to a dance'. Perhaps because anyone could play, professionals and amateurs, actors and courtly audience, as well as poets, dancers, singers and painters, Francis Bacon declared, 'These things are but toys'. The fact that at bottom the masque existed to be decorated in scene and costume, and choreographed to music, enhanced its impact as a spectacle, but limited its quality as literature. This was a toy whose few pages of text could take as many as three hours to present.

It survived through four reigns before its somewhat limited and precious achievement was swept away by the political tide of the Civil War. Along with his tilts and tourneys, Henry VIII (1509–47) took great pleasure in dancing and masquing, and it is from his Court in Westminster Hall on Twelfth Night of 1512 that we first hear of the English masque, in the words of Edward Hall 'a thing not seen afore in England'. In 1527 Henry built a 'House of Revels', a theatrical place where his mock castles and other scenic pieces could be set up. In 1545 he inaugurated a first 'Office of Revels', an institution that was for many years to bring strength and authority to each fragile art-work. Elizabeth I (1558–1603) was less inclined to dance than to make her magnificent royal 'progresses' round the country, but as gracious compliments to her distinguished visitors, the masque continued to flourish.

In the reigns of the Stuarts that followed more than a hundred masques, many of them now lost, were written and presented at the rate of one or two a year, costing more and more to mount as the years passed. In 1618 Ben Jonson's *Pleasure Reconciled to Virtue* cost £4,000; in 1634 James Shirley's *Triumph of Love* cost £21,000 – a shocking figure if translated into today's costs. The money lavished on these events had much to do with the royal prestige they upheld. With his wife Anne of Denmark, James I (1603–1625) revived the spirit of Henry's Court, and replaced Samuel Daniel with Ben Jonson as Court poet; the Queen immediately commanded him to write the Christmas masque of 1604 (*The Masque of Blackness*, below), and with Jonson and the architect and designer Inigo Jones (1573–1652) working well together the form reached new heights in poetry, design and music. With his wife Henrietta Maria of France, Charles I (1625–49) especially encouraged the visual development and stage presentation of the masque, but it was not long before Jonson and Jones fell out on matters of principle. James Shirley replaced Jonson as Court poet, and when in 1642 the King was deposed, his Court was dispersed, the theatres were closed and the masque had nothing to keep it alive as theatre. It had lost its performers and its audience at one blow, for they were virtually the same.

The elements of a non-dramatic form

Such elements were naturally elusive in the extreme, since however much planning went into the masque, the spirit of spontaneity had to be at the core of its participatory activity. Yet if its broad purpose lay in the pleasure of the impromptu, it nevertheless had to settle upon a 'fable' or theme (generally allegorical and moralistic, with the royal presence lending it a hint of the political), and determine the nature of its characters (generally the gods and goddesses or the shepherds and nymphs of classical myth and fable). At the centre of all is the awkward fact that the masque existed primarily for dancing and singing, and its pattern had to be essentially choreographic and operatic.

The masque commonly fell into three parts, made up of three dances and three songs – though this was by no means a rule. In 1604 Queen Anne fancied herself as a blackamoor and called upon Jones and Jonson to incorporate her whim in a suitable vehicle to celebrate the next Twelfth Night (1605). A look at their first successful collaboration, *The Masque of Blackness*, will indicate the way a masque was planned. Jonson turned his attention to Africa, and was pleased to learn that the African river Niger flowed into the Atlantic, thus providing the idea for the masque and two presenters, to be dressed by Inigo Jones: Oceanus, painted blue and dressed in sea-green, and Niger, black of skin and beard and decorated with pearls. Niger was to be blessed with twelve black daughters, so providing parts to accommodate the twelve ladies of the Court who were to dance in the masque either in blackface or in black masks. To supply a gracious theme that would touch the courtly audience, these dusky nymphs were supposed to have travelled the ocean in search of the new land of Britannia, where

> Their beauties shall be scorched no more;
> This sun is temperate, and refines
> All things on which his radiance shines.

(233–5)

Pretty compliments all round. However, the casting of parts was as nothing to the creative work yet to be undertaken.

The scene had to change from Africa to the Atlantic. From Jonson's notes we read,

> First, for the scene, was drawn a landtschap [landscape] consisting of small woods, and here and there a void place

filled with huntings [animals at prey]; which falling, an artificial sea was seen to shoot forth, as if it flowed to the land, raised with waves which seemed to move, and in some places the billow to break, as imitating that orderly disorder which is common in nature.

Here lay the major task assigned to Jones as architect and designer. The Old Banqueting House in Whitehall, where the masque was to be mounted, was not, as in former times, to be scattered about with houses or mansions and other scenic pieces dispersed around the acting area, but provided on a raised platform where stage machinery could be erected and concealed above and beneath the stage. Without diminishing the central space for the dancers, this encouraged the sort of perspective scene that Jones had observed during his Italian travels. Moreover, the quick transformation from land to sea was to be effected by dropping a front curtain on which the land was painted, ready to reveal a backcloth of sea against which waves could be moved by mechanical devices. The Office of the Revels had provided a hundred or so men to do this work at a cost of £3,000.

The nymphs, one of whom was the Queen herself, made their entrance inside a great mother-of-pearl shell that seemed to rise and fall with the water. Before them six tritons displayed themselves, behind them two sea-maids augmented the singing and beside them six sea-monsters carried on their backs the twelve Oceaniae as 'light-bearers' [torch-bearers often played by children]. With this extraordinary detail the masque opened to song, sung by one triton and the two sea-maids, all professional singers, while in a prologue Oceanus and Niger, soon joined by Aethiopia the moon, explained the meaning of what the spectator was to see. The tritons and nymphs, each carrying a fan painted with a symbolic emblem, then danced 'on shore' in what Jonson called 'their own single dance', one for which they had long rehearsed. So ended the 'entry' of the masque.

The second part of the event, which was the most important for the Court audience, was hardly scripted at all and could be of indefinite length. Upon the singing of another song, the nymphs were 'to make choice of their men' and dance 'several measures [slower dances] and corantos [tripping dances]'.

This was where the chosen spectators felt themselves a necessary part of the festivities, the spontaneous pivot of the evening. If the audience was not amazed and delighted by what had gone before, it was at least waiting for this, and it needed no rehearsal for the familiar dances.

A final song called the nymphs back to the sea, and for it Jonson wrote a delicate 'echo' song that carried a pleasing ambiguity:

> Daughters of the subtle flood,
>   Do not let earth longer entertain you;
> *1st Echo*. Let earth longer entertain you.
> *2nd Echo*.   Longer entertain you.

(279–83)

So was prepared the final or 'exit' dance to crown the festivities. The nymphs danced back into the sea, reassumed their places in their giant shell and the masque ended with a 'full song'.

This was the basic structure of the Stuart masque, its three parts rather loose and flexible, and its ingredients recognizable:

(1) Its *performers* were the convenient mixture of the occasion, courtiers of both sexes, perhaps with some children, but working in a framework of professional dancers, singers and musicians. This mixture of amateur and professional would have been socially unacceptable in the public playhouse.

(2) The *costumes* of the performers were ornate and expensive, suiting the splendour of the Court as well as the needs of the masque. They were colourful, frequently symbolic, but always fantastic, suggesting that the dancers enjoyed dressing up, as for a masked ball.

(3) The *settings* matched the appearance of the performers in inventiveness, and introduced elements of grandeur and pageantry chosen to flatter the Court and its visitors. Complicated machinery intended to change the scene and astonish the spectator developed rapidly at the hands of Inigo Jones, who spared no expense in researching bigger and better devices.

It fell to the poet and the designer to conceive a theme for their masque that embraced the needs of the occasion and satisfied the demands of such extravagant entertainment.

One other feature introduced by Ben Jonson that became indispensable was the *antimasque*. In *Lord Haddington's Masque*, devised for Viscount Haddington's marriage in 1608 and having the appropriate subject of Venus and Cupid, Jonson inserted 'twelve boys most anticly attired, that represented the sports and pretty lightnesses that accompany Love'. These boys were intended to make the audience laugh with a 'capricious dance to as odd a music', nod their 'antic faces' and make a 'variety of ridiculous gesture' (112). This interpolation, arranged as a foil to the main idea before the formal dancing began, was successful, and with his comic and satirical gifts Jonson was delighted to try it again.

In subsequent years the antimasque that preceded the main entertainment became even more grotesque, and could introduce beggars and fools, satyrs and animals, and all manner of bizarre creatures into this most rare and delicate of stage forms. Whimsical ear- and eye-catching variety rather than harmony of vision was the final target.

Inigo Jones and an alternative staging

Inigo Jones was a scenic designer *par excellence*, but it is also true that the English stage owes him a debt that, for good or ill, affected its drama – its playwriting – for the next three hundred years. As a man of the theatre, he combined his talents as architect and designer to good purpose. He studied Palladio's Teatro Olimpico in Vicenza in 1613, and visited the Medici Court entertainments in Florence two or three times, where he saw Sebastiano Serlio's perspective stage settings and Giulio Parigi's scenic devices in action. Thus armed, he was never lacking in ideas to meet the needs of the imaginative masques he was called upon to create.

After the unfocused use of the long, open banqueting hall with its simultaneous pieces set around the dancing and acting

space, Jones saw the advantage for scene and spectacle of a
raised stage within a proscenium arch. He introduced the
Serlian raked stage as early as 1605, so that the royal throne,
arranged on either side with tiers of seats for the Court and its
guests, was set well back from the stage, an arrangement
which greatly enhanced the stage illusion and its magical
effects. Inside the arch he arranged his painted backcloth,
setting it on either side with perspective wing pieces. This
encouraged a major tendency towards the pictorial in the
scenic arrangements of private theatres like the Blackfriars
during the period, and prepared the stage for the return of
a different kind of drama and theatre in 1660, when the
monarchy was restored.

The immediate effect of the change to a proscenium arch
theatre was to grant Jones his opportunity to design changeable scenery and create transformation scenes, with all the
spectacular delights and surprises these might entail. Machines
for moving waves and clouds were reasonably simple, but he
experimented throughout his career, and as early as 1605 he
used a stage on which were set scenic devices that could be
changed with surprising speed. For the *Hymenaei* [*The
Masque of Marriage*], his first wedding masque in 1606, he
used an early form of revolve, the *periaktoi* or *machina
versatilis* [turning machine], shown as a 'microcosm' or globe
in which eight dancers were to be discovered. With the help
of such a machine in *The Masque of Queens*, the scene
changed from Hell to the House of Fame to the figure of
Good Fame, all in white, and working as much on the vertical
axis as on the horizontal, suggesting that the best of the
masques were designed not as a series of stunning spectacles,
but more as an harmonious and unified effect. Nevertheless,
the impulse behind most of Jones's scenic design was speed
and surprise – the wave of the magic wand.

Jones had experimented with wing pieces on both sides of
the stage as early as 1608 in *The Hue and Cry after Cupid*:
drawn apart, the scene revealed another scene behind. In his
masque *Oberon* in 1611, he employed two such sets of wing
pieces that could be pulled apart in grooves to discover or
display three different scenes in all. The system of 'groove and
shutter' had arrived.

Jonson's descriptions indicate the intended effect. The masque began in rocky gloom:

> The first face of the scene appeared all obscure, and nothing perceived but a dark rock with trees beyond it and all wildness that could be presented.

Against this setting an antimasque was performed by a sinister group of ten satyrs who 'came running forth severally from divers parts of the rock, leaping and making antic action and gestures'. After this, a complete transformation in scene, light and style followed the cue line, 'See, the rock begins to ope!':

> There the whole scene opened, and within was discovered the frontispiece of a bright and glorious palace whose gates and walls were transparent.

From this evidence it seems that at this date Jones was making use of gauzes. The satyrs sang and danced again until a cock crowed and upon the cue 'See, the gates already spread!' the third scene was revealed:

> There the whole palace opened, and the nation of fays [fairies] was discovered, some with instruments, some bearing lights, others singing; and within, afar off in perspective, the knights masquers sitting in their several sieges. At the further end of all, Oberon, in a chariot, which to a loud triumphant music began to move forward, drawn by two white bears, and on either side guarded by three sylvans, with one going in front.

It is not known whether Oberon's bears were real, but Oberon was played by Prince Henry, in whose honour the masque had been written. The fays sang and danced, and finally Oberon and his knights began the dances of the masque with the 'beauties' in the audience, continuing until the morning came.

This use of grooves and shutters, the *'scena ductilis'* [tractable or drawn scene], brings dramatic properties to the masque, for with each change of setting it acquires a little more of the narrative ingredient. Visually, the audience is led deeper into the fairy world, and as the illusion increases in sight and sound, the rugged rocks are transformed into a civilized Italian palace, designed in splendid classical style to

7 Inigo Jones' *Oberon*, 1611. Oberon's palace in the rocks.

match the Banqueting House in Whitehall. Thus disorder is replaced by order, while the satyrs are taught how to behave more appropriately in the presence of the fairy King, and the knights advance from one palace to another equally magnificent in order to dance with their ladies. The production cost about £2,100, of which Jonson and Jones received £40 each as the 'inventors'.

Oberon was notable also for a distinct advance in *lighting effects*. Moving lights intended to dazzle the eyes had been used in Samuel Daniel's *Tethys' Festival* (1610), and Jones invented translucent scenes and 'sudden glories', and made use of candles with reflectors as well as 'divers diaphanal glasses filled with several waters that showed like so many stones of orient and transparent hues'. So *Oberon* enjoyed its 'bright and glorious palace' with the aid of transparent scrim and shifting lights and colours, all doubtless playing also on the glorious metallic and sequined costumes of the fairy court. Accounts for *The Temple of Jove* (1631) record that it used some twenty-three dozen torches and two hundred candles – extraordinary numbers – and Jones was pleased to observe, 'These shows are nothing else but pictures with light and motion.'

After *Oberon* we hear frequently of more and more elaborate scenic design, but based chiefly on shutters pulled and pushed in grooves in combination with ingenious machines. Yet increasingly is also heard a note of criticism. Thomas Campion's *Lords' Masque* of 1613, in the care of Inigo Jones, made a point of exhibiting much of the scenic machinery of the time, but in *The Golden Age Restored* (1615) John Chamberlain recorded 'no great commendation' of the production, 'save only for riches, their devices being long and tedious, and more like a play than a mask'. Here is evidence that the masque was ceasing to satisfy its expectations, and perhaps that the imbalance of poetry and spectacle was working to damage the form. Artistic imbalance, even the incongruity of its parts, evidently spoiled another, more famous, creation, *Pleasure Reconciled to Virtue*.

This masque employed and enjoyed special features, and we are lucky to have a fairly detailed description of the first performance in 1618 from a Venetian visitor, Orazio Busino, Chaplain to the London embassy. The Court was arranged for what appears to have been a proscenium performance:

> A large hall is fitted up like a theatre, with well secured boxes all round. The stage is at one end and His Majesty's chair in front under an ample canopy ... In the middle of the theatre there appeared a fine and spacious area carpeted all over with green cloth. In an instant a large curtain dropped, painted to represent a tent of gold cloth with a broad fringe; the background was of canvas painted blue, powdered all over with golden stars. This became the front arch of the stage, forming a drop scene.

> (*A Book of Masques* (1967), 232–3)

This is the first mention of a drop-curtain, and the development of the proscenium stage is foreshadowed in these words. In this instance it was there to conceal a fantastic set, that of

Mount Atlas, Jonson's symbol of wisdom, designed by Jones as the enormous head of an old man, as the directions indicate: 'His head and beard all hoary and frost, as if his shoulders were covered with snow.' The visitor reported that this head 'was alone visible up aloft under the very roof of the theatre' and that 'it rolled up its eyes and moved itself very cleverly'. This enormous object next opened to disclose Prince Charles and his masquers dressed in crimson hose and plaited white satin doublets trimmed with gold and silver lace; on their heads they wore long hair with crowns surmounted by tall white plumes, and their faces were covered with black masks. Jonson then opened the proceedings with two antimasques, one for dancers played by small boys as bottles and the other with more small boys as pigmies.

Pleasure Reconciled to Virtue was a failure. Not only were the antimasques not acceptable, prompting Nathaniel Brent to write that 'The poet is grown so dull that his device is not worthy the relating' and that 'divers think fit he should return to his old trade of bricklaying', and not only was the machinery no longer pleasing, prompting Edward Sherburne to write that 'It came far short of the expectation, and Master Inigo Jones hath lost in his reputation in regard to some extraordinary device was looked for (it being the Prince his first masque) and a poorer was never seen', but the King himself was bored enough to interrupt the show to complain that the dancing was inadequate. The visitor from Venice reported that he cried out, 'Why don't they dance? What did they make me come here for? Devil take you, dance.'

Ben Jonson and Inigo Jones were seeing the nature and purpose of the masque differently, with the result that the new art form was already showing signs of their breach. Both Ben Jonson and Inigo Jones were brilliant innovators and full of ideas, but the clash of two strong personalities undermined what was at bottom a shaky and uncertain framework for an art form. Jonson wrote his twenty-eight masques all in the belief that at their heart (he had earlier in *Hymenaei* written of their 'souls') lay an idealized poetry of dialogue and song conceived in and built firmly on classical myth: masques were to be 'the mirrors of man's life'. However, in spite of his broad experience in the public playhouse this was a literary judgment, perhaps one developed to counteract his sense that the masque, founded as it was on the dance as the mere expression of a social occasion, was too ephemeral an art form.

Set against this, Jonson saw the contribution of the arts of design in the masque merely as its 'body', with scene and costume and the invention of ingenious devices, its 'painting and carpentry', only as its external adornment. In 'An Expostulation with Inigo Jones' (1631) Jonson's frustration produced ironic lines painful to read:

> O shows! shows! mighty shows!
> The eloquence of masques! What need of prose,
> Or verse, or sense, t'express immortal you?

It was the poet who had the central and essential task of choosing the fable, and coordinating its elements of music, dance and poetry. So Jonson and Jones clashed, and the story of their falling out may be traced in the disputes about whose name should appear first on a title-page from *The Masque of Augurs* in 1622 to *Chloridia* in 1630 and *Love's Triumph through Callipolis* in 1631. It is not necessary to take sides: the contradictions are inherent in the form itself.

Such excesses on the stage were not seen again until the ingenious tranformation scenes of the Victorian popular theatre and the extravagant sets of today's million-dollar musicals. Altogether, in a period of strong non-illusionistic drama it seems natural that masque-like qualities of allegory and fantasy should order the stage and inform its performance without fuss. On such a stage, which was soon to pass to a much more pictorial condition, it follows that, even when the form of the masque served no further purpose, its powerful theatrical ingredients of music and dance would survive to emerge again as opera and ballet. The hidden snare in these developments is that the decorated scene depended increasingly upon an architectural stage, one dominated by the proscenium arch. For the proscenium arch was a feature which worked inexorably against that element in the drama that was in part its *raison d'être* and one of its fondest assets, the easy participation of the audience.

9

Jacobean experiment: exploring the form

'City' and other comedy

At the turn of the century many plays made the most of London as a rich source of material its audience could recognize, and the bustling activity of city life was often seen on the stage. The city offered a world of known streets and localities: in *The Shoemaker's Holiday* Dekker makes a point of running through a catalogue of familiar places when he has Simon Eyre speak of his fellow shoemakers as 'the flower of Saint Martin's, the mad knaves of Bedlam, Fleet Street, Tower Street and Whitechapel' (1, 223–5). Moreover, the London its audience knew was alive with a range of familiar types: courtier and gallant, merchant and tradesman, puritan and city wife; it also embraced the low life of tavern and brothel with their apprentices, rogues and swindlers, pimps and bawds. The panorama of London life lay spread before the eyes of the aspiring comic playwright: the places and the people, the rich and the poor, the high and the low.

The success of this 'city' or 'citizen' comedy is easy to understand: customary figures, common language and local references catch the attention of a local audience and for humorous or satirical purposes the comic stage offered limit-less perspectives on social class, human folly, greed and bigotry, or any other moral theme of its choosing. In Black-friars and Paul's the success of the children's companies at this time with this realism may be explained by the way their puppet-like, stylized performance appropriately lowered the spectator's defences, since some degree of stylish deceit and necessary teasing of the audience is evident in every city comedy. Jacobean city comedy has been elevated into a distinct dramatic genre.

The Elizabethan playhouse readily encompassed all of this, and also supplied an ideal medium for comic fantasy: it provided a home for *The Tempest* as well as *Bartholomew Fair*. Moreover, it could romp and frolic, and at the same time touch human feeling. As a result the comic stage in the early years of the seventeenth century offered a spectrum of dramatic forms, extending from cold satire to romantic tragicomedy, and covering a range of moods from the cynical to the sympathetic.

Thomas Dekker (*c.* 1572–1632) was a prolific playwright known to have written some forty-two plays. His best-known work, *The Shoemaker's Holiday* (1599), with its subtitle *A Pleasant Comedy of the Gentle Craft*, is a fair example of good-humoured, romantic comedy at the end of Elizabeth's reign. In its time it enjoyed a popular success when it was played at the Rose by the Admiral's Men, and afterwards at Court before the Queen on New Year's Day, 1600.

Some modern productions use *The Shoemaker's Holiday* to generate a hazy view of 'Merrie England', particularly since the play suggests its place in the long medieval tradition of drama. Reflecting the strong link between the medieval stage and the craft guilds, the play conveys a good sense of the corporate ceremonial created throughout the action by the shoemakers and their gentle craft. At the outset the audience is also reminded of the Lord Mayor of London's tradition of feasting (1.2), and this opening scene ends by presenting the Lord Mayor's procession complete with soldiers marching to a drummer, who *'pass over the stage'* – a common direction, not always for making use of the groundlings' yard as some have speculated, but for a wordless perambulation round the platform in a procession, often in a spectacular way. Dekker is always aware of the costume and personal decoration his actors must have, and the play ends on a similar note of celebration when Eyre, the new Lord Mayor, invites the company to his breakfast feast for the Shrove Tuesday holiday:

> ALL.   O brave shoemaker! O brave lord of incomprehensible good fellowship! Hoo, hark you, the pancake bell rings!

FIRK. Nay, more, my hearts, every Shrove Tuesday is our
year of jubilee ...

(18, 219–22)

Here the pancake bell rings, and the shoemakers '*cast up caps*'.
The whole play is punctuated by singing and dancing, and
suggestions of festivity are seen and heard throughout. Unusually, two 'three-man's songs' preface the text in a way that
suggests that they should be used, and repeated, at any
convenient point in the performance; in 1981 the National
Theatre used them to link its scenes.

The play shows no ambition as a piece of physical stagecraft.
It achieves a simple unity of place, the action being for the
most part inside or outside the house of its protagonist Simon
Eyre, but the setting is scanty. The stage affords an occasional
glimpse of humble working life: Jane in her 'sempster's shop'
(scene 12) and Hodge at his 'shop board' working with the
other shoemakers (scene 13), both conveniently managed,
probably, by the use of a door or the discovery-space. The
effective extent of Dekker's stage blocking is conveyed when
Jane is discovered at work by both the voyeuristic spectator
and her unwelcome lover Hammon, who is muffled and
spying on her, standing 'aloof' and 'at another door'. It is a
sinister moment, with Jane vulnerable now that her husband is
away, and Hammon confessing to the audience in tender
blank-verse soliloquy that he has eyed her like this before, and
wondering what to do next. There is strength in this simplicity, and in such a scene Victorian melodrama could well have
found a prototype.

Beyond any convention of place and space, however,
Dekker has structured his comedy in an unusual way, and it
has even been compared with the 'well-made play' of a later
century. The play not only smoothly weaves together three
separate plots, it simultaneously contrives to recognize and
comprehend three or four social ranks, inducing their interaction by the constant juxtaposition of their scenes.

At its centre the play is concerned to trace the rise of the
'madcap' shoemaker Simon Eyre in his progress from al-
derman and sheriff to become the Lord Mayor of London.
Moreover, this affable character, with his talkative wife

Margery and her little vanities, dominates the world of the play by his larger-than-life representation. When he leads Jane in crying and saying goodbye to her husband about to depart to the wars, he bursts upon the stage with a characteristic energy of speech:

> Leave whining, leave whining. Away with this whimpering, this puling, these blubbering tears, and these wet eyes! I'll get thy husband discharged, I warrant thee, sweet Jane. Go to!

(1.117–20)

This level of racy language is sustained throughout the play and his generous figure seems to embrace and colour all other performances. A second story recounts the romantic love of Rowland Lacy, nephew of the Earl of Lincoln, for a lady of a lower class in the face of parental opposition; this lady is Rose, the fair daughter of the former Lord Mayor, and to pursue her Lacy must disguise himself as a Dutch shoemaker. A third story concerns another romance, the love of the even more lowly Jane, the pretty wife of Ralph the shoemaker who has been impressed into the military. And these two stories are also complicated when a gentleman suitor, one Master Hammon, pays unwelcome court first to Rose and then to Jane.

Dekker keeps his biggest surprise for last. None other than the King of England makes his entrance at the end, a *deus ex machina*, no less. He moves graciously among his subjects, especially the apprentices, all 'friends of the Gentle Craft' (192), and while he is about it, meets his new Lord Mayor in his glorious robes and chain of office, grants the shoemakers the right to sell their shoes in Leadenhall, and, last but not least, settles the problem of the match of Rose and Lacy: 'Dost thou not know that love respects no blood?' (105), he asks. So ends this cheerful play on a note of happy resolution for all: 'Let's revel it at home' (194), the King cries – except that in his last line, with a final touch of reality, he also remembers that the war with France has still to be fought.

Francis Beaumont (1584–1616) was best known in his own time for the plays he wrote in collaboration with John Fletcher (1579–1625), sweeping, romantic tragi-comedies that now might be dismissed as melodrama. Yet he turned to such drama only after the failure of *The Knight of the Burning Pestle* (1607) when it was first played at the Blackfriars by the Children of the Queen's Revels in 1607. This burlesque comedy holds our attention today, perhaps for the reasons that it originally misfired.

Plays depicting the amazing adventures of a romantic hero had been popular not many years before – plays at the Globe like *Mucedorus* (1588) recounting the love of the Prince of Valencia for the Princess Amadine, and the prolific Thomas Heywood's *The Four Prentices of London* (*c.* 1600), which contrived to recount the heroic adventures of no less than four brothers played alongside one another. These plays themselves seem to border on self-parody, and were ripe for burlesque treatment. Nor was the Elizabethan stage a stranger to burlesque – we think of *The Old Wives' Tale* and *A Midsummer Night's Dream* with 'Pyramus and Thisbe', and the previous year Beaumont himself had written a mock-heroic comedy, *The Woman Hater*. So what went wrong with his *The Knight of the Burning Pestle*? Its dedicatory epistle offered two reasons: 'want of judgement, or not under-standing the privy mark of irony about it', that is, its satire on citizen playgoers and their silly tastes was either too offensive for a middle-class audience, or so subtle that those who frequented the private playhouse could not decode its meaning. Neither explanation is adequate, and a third possibi-lity must be entertained: that the unusual stagecraft, which distinguishes this from other mock-heroic plays, was too daring, even on a stage of non-illusion.

From the beginning Beaumont mounts an attack on play-house decorum, and boldly negates the proper distancing that comedy expects. In his Induction he has an apparent member of the audience, a 'Citizen' and a grocer by trade, climb on to the stage and confront the boy Prologue. The grocer objects to the play about to be presented, since its title, *The London Merchant*, appears to promise another attack on members of his guild. George the grocer is joined soon after by Nell his wife, who clambers awkwardly on to the stage with him – she needs help ('I'm something troublesome ... bear with me'). Beaumont's easy stagecraft makes free with place and time in the accustomed way, imagining locations in a dozen London sites from Aldgate and the Strand to Mile End and Waltham Forest, as well as places of fantasy like the cave for the giant Barbaroso or somewhere in Moldavia for the court of Princess Pompiona. It also makes free with the boundary between the real world of the audience and the illusory world of the stage, and does so physically. It is not surprising that performance produces teasing effects comparable with those in Pirandello's *Six Characters in Search of an Author*, and that when Beaumont's play was revived at the Aldwych in 1981, and the actor playing the grocer, Timothy Kightley, harangued the Prologue, a real member of the audience tried to intervene, stalking out when he saw that he had been tricked. However, the Aldwych was not the Blackfriars, and George and Nell's taste in plays scarcely corresponded with that of the Royal Shakespeare Company playgoer.

George and Nell interrupt the action throughout, and this activity is acceptable on a stage that, like that of *The Shoemaker's Holiday*, established the reality of the London scene and incorporated a merchant guild and the festivals associated with its members. The acts in *The Knight of the Burning Pestle* are also separated by 'interludes' consisting of songs and dances, so that they provide a continuity both of the action and in the spirit of the play, and help close the gap between actor and audience. Singing and dancing were well suited to the expertise of a children's company, and in all some forty or more moments of music and song punctuate the performance, removing any pathos latent in the story and reducing any threat felt to familiar make-believe.

The framing device created by this use of the grocer and his wife allowed three things to happen in performance:

(1) George and Nell seem to speak for the real audience and comment on the business of theatrical performance. Although they are in a select private theatre, they behave as though they are in a vulgar public one, speaking for an inferior audience. Nell in particular is highly opinionated, calling without hesitation for what she likes: a stage-fight, a love scene or a spectacular effect. Their interruptions are so constant that their commentary is like a thought-process or

a running critique. The device, nevertheless, is entertaining since they always manage to confuse drama with reality, as when Nell thinks she sees murder about to be done and calls upon her husband to fetch the law: 'Away, George, away, raise the watch at Ludgate ...' (3.92)

(2) This means that the original play, *The London Merchant*, now a play-within-a-play, is subjected to a bombardment of criticism and is awash in elements of parody from start to finish. A wealthy merchant, Venturewell, wants his daughter Luce to marry one Master Humphrey, a pompous Petrarchan lover who speaks only in terrible couplets and mixes his metaphors atrociously:

> love hath tossed me
> In furious blanket, like a tennis ball;
> And now I rise aloft, and now I fall.
>
> (1.164–6)

Jasper, the apprentice whom Luce really loves, makes an equally stuffy hero, however, and with his greedy mother would perhaps be intolerable if it were not for his jolly Falstaffian father, Old Merrythought, whose sole function in the play is to provide laughter and song.

(3) George and Nell complicate matters by demanding that their apprentice Rafe also climb on the stage to play the lead as knight-errant in an heroic adventure of their own choosing: Rafe will be 'The Knight of the Burning Pestle', and enact wild scenes of fearless chivalry. In this way the characters of the Induction also frame a second burlesque, a second play-within-a-play that runs parallel with the first. Since the second hero is as silly as the first, this doubling invites the real audience to compare one kind of romance with another and find them equally fatuous.

If Beaumont's play seems long and rambling and distractingly episodic, in performance the audience has a great deal to engage its attention as the action hops between one group of players and another. Its incidents grow increasingly wild as the dislocation between the real and the fantastic proceeds. The grocer and his wife are well pleased with their night's work and with Rafe's success as an actor. So they solemnly depart for home, unaware that they have confounded the dramatic law of gravity.

The failure of *The Knight of the Burning Pestle*, which was taken off after one performance, compelled Beaumont to change his approach to playwriting. He teamed up with John Fletcher, who had also been unsuccessful with *The Faithful Shepherdess* (1608), and their collaboration supplied the King's Men at the Blackfriars and the Globe with popular plays for the next few years. Fletcher's play had been a highly idealized pastoral, and its Arcadian lovers were a bit precious after the humours of the city comedies. However, in the Address to the Reader he excused what he had done by calling it 'pastoral tragi-comedy':

> A tragi-comedy is not so called in respect of mirth and killing, but in respect it wants deaths, which is enough to make it no tragedy, yet brings some near it, which is enough to make it no comedy, which must be a representation of familiar people, with such kind of trouble as no life be questioned.

Fletcher's was a formula for a different kind of play, and with Beaumont's skill in plot construction, it provided some ground rules for their successful collaboration in *Philaster, or, Love Lies a-Bleeding* in 1609.

It has been argued that this play was certainly a tragi-comedy because it could have ended either happily or unhappily. The basic story is of Philaster, who gives his page Bellario as a gift to Arethusa, the Princess he loves. *Ergo*, she is accused of lewd conduct with the boy, whom Philaster accordingly offers to kill. It eventually turns out that Bellario is really Euphrasia, a girl who dressed as a page only to be near her master. The twists in this tale are thus full of surprises – and of pathetic and titillating possibilities: in act 4 Philaster wounds each of the ladies when they are conveniently lost in a forest (needing no trees, the stage made a simple scene-change from the court), and in act 5 Bellario is threatened with being tortured and stripped before her true sex is revealed (the 1620 text has '*discovers her hair*', and the shaking loose of long tresses became a useful stage effect with which to expose a girl in disguise in Restoration comedy). The denouement is equally convenient: since Euphrasia vows never to marry, Philaster can have Arethusa and everyone can be friends.

After Jonson, the most arresting name for satirical city comedy in the period is that of Thomas Middleton (1580–1627), and his extraordinary range of workable styles from the farcical-satirical to the tragi-comic and tragic has placed him in the front rank of Jacobean dramatists. The first few years of the century had him writing several comedies for the children's companies in quick succession: *Michaelmas Term, A Mad World, My Masters, Your Five Gallants* and *A Trick to Catch the Old One* all fall between 1604 and 1606. Then, for the adult companies, he wrote *The Roaring Girl* with Dekker in 1608 and, on his own again, *A Chaste Maid in Cheapside* in 1611 – his best-known comedy because of its modern revivals.

None of these comedies displays a technical interest in the physical use of the new stages, and there are few stage directions indicating other than the purely conventional use of the two doors and an occasional 'above'. However, their introduction of shrewdly stylized moments of speech and characterization should not go unnoticed. As satirical comedies they are lighter in touch and tone than Jonson's, and Middleton's sly charm and gentle understatement may suggest, as they have to some, that he lacks much of a moral sense. But Jacobean 'realism' is an elusive quality. His topics are down-to-earth, usually those of money and avarice, and his characters are nearly always cheats and rogues. His scenes draw extensively upon the places a London audience would know well – Cheapside, Fleet Street, Highgate, all the familiar streets and places. To such an extent the plays seem to keep their feet realistically on the ground. The truth is that Middleton has his own comic fancy and writes his own sort of social critique for the stage, one that is perceptive in revealing human foibles and cunning in the traffic of the theatre.

Middleton's early comedy involves a favourite device that recurs exhaustively, that of deceit by disguise. In *Michaelmas Term* two apprentices, aptly named Shortyard and Falselight, repeatedly turn up in different disguises – to arrest the hero or lend him money on security of his estate, or something else. This comedy points to a rascally world of unexpected, if amusing, pretence and deception, until the usurer finally cheats himself. *A Mad World, My Masters* has young Richard Follywit and his friends outwitting his rich uncle Sir Bounteous Progress, again with multiple disguises: the plotters turn up first as a nobleman and his retinue, next as house guests and then as thieves, and Follywit even pretends to be Sir Bounteous's mistress.

Probably his best comedy, *A Trick to Catch the Old One*, played by Paul's boys for the private theatre, displays Middleton's special vitality. Its subjects are as usual greed and gullibility: with a little twist of earlier city plots, Witgood, the young prodigal from Leicestershire, comes to the city, his creditors baying at his heels, in order to cheat his miserly uncle Pecunius Lucre. Witgood opens the play with a disarming expostulation to the house: 'All's gone! still thou'rt a gentleman, that's all; but a poor one, that's nothing.' He intends to tempt his uncle by seeming to be a suitor to the imaginary Mrs Medler, a rich widow ('four hundred a year valiant [in worth]'), who is actually his courtesan mistress in disguise. In this way the comedy becomes one less of fortune-hunting than of widow-hunting, and before long a small crowd of characters show interest in her and her illusory wealth: not only old Lucre, but also his rival Walkadine Hoard, as well as Witgood's landlord, the two rivals for the hand of Hoard's niece and three comical creditors. They swarm like flies to the honeypot, and Middleton supplies them with clipped lines that suggest the nature of their ludicrous performance:

HOARD.	How? a rich country widow?
MONEYLOVE.	Four hundred a year landed ...
1 CREDITOR.	I am glad of this news.
2 CREDITOR.	So are we, by my faith.
3 CREDITOR.	Young Witgood will be a gallant again now ...

(2.2.13 ff.)

The complications escalate as the caterpillars proliferate.

Here it is possible to see some of the elements of stylization that belie any final realism in the London scene, with its whoring and swindling and lust after money. The principal characters are recognizably middle-class gentlemen and citizens, but they are all typed by name and to a man they are colourful rogues; moreover, there are altogether too many of them to present a realistic picture. If this arrangement seems mechanical and schematic, it is in keeping with the particular spirit of the action on stage. The text slows down with verse, but rushes forward with prose, and the playwright succeeds in setting a cracking pace as a norm of playing. Modern editors have seen fit to lard the original with directions like *Aside*, *Aloud* or *Takes him aside*, but the truth is that the lines are already alive with implicit asides and other hidden instructions for voice and movement. In the scene of Witgood and his creditors in 3.1, our hero is overwhelmed with gifts and spun about the stage, very much in the manner of the *commedia dell'arte*, and multiple asides add significantly to the effect of breakneck pace.

Sometimes a rapid sequence of entrances will do it, as in 3.3, and reminiscent of the Italian Pantalone, Middleton's old tyrants are probably expected to behave in the same way. In particular, with his abundant energy and high spirits, Hoard is a notable forerunner of Molière's doting miser Harpagon, with all his abrupt and rapid movements. In a characteristic soliloquy Hoard is animated by every fantasy:

> She's rich, she's young, she's fair, she's wise; when I wake, I think of her lands – that revives me; when I go to bed, I dream of her beauty – and that's enough for me; she's worth four hundred a year in her very smock, if a man knew how to use it ...
>
> (4.4.6–9)

Hoard's dream of married bliss is fraught with self-induced irony, and for the audience who knows the truth about the rich widow his mounting excitement is a joy. Middleton's world of cheats and gulls is as non-didactic as it is unsentimental, and the manipulation of rich old men and the pursuit of wealthy heiresses and widows for its own sake remained the stock-in-trade.

Philip Massinger (1583–1640), who wrote no less than thirty-seven plays of which nineteen are extant, was concerned to put London and its local colour back on stage, and took up his predecessor's ideas with more sentimentality. *A New Way to Pay Old Debts* (1621) echoes *A Trick to Catch the Old One*, with the prodigal Frank Wellborn trying to recover his lands. However, this comedy revels in the gargantuan villain Sir Giles Overreach, a monster of avarice in the tradition of Jonson's humours, a creature who spoke of himself as 'extortioner, tyrant, cormorant' (4.1). The part caught Garrick's eye in 1748 and has been a favourite with leading actors from Edmund Kean to Henry Irving and Donald Wolfit.

Massinger again managed to create a caricature of giant proportions in Lady Frugal, the vain and ostentatious matron of *The City Madam* (1632), a play which echoed *A Chaste Maid in Cheapside*. This lady makes her first magnificent entrance with her daughters Anne and Mary and their women: they have three looking-glasses between them and with this help they copy each other *'in several postures'* – 'I think I bear my years well', concludes Lady Frugal (1.1.79). With this play a theatrical style in which manners in themselves have become stagecraft is well advanced.

Domestic and revenge tragedy

Tragedy in the period was as prolific as comedy. Much of it resorted to the exotic Italy of the high Renaissance for its sensational materials of sex, murder and revenge, but it stayed fully within the English tradition of direct, non-illusionistic stagecraft, deploying and exploiting a maze of conventions of role-playing and disguise, masques and dumb shows and plays-within, asides and speech to the house. To enjoy the tragic or quasi-tragic drama of Marston and Tourneur, Webster and Middleton, is to discover a basic stagecraft that only incidentally has to do with verisimilitude and illusion: their tragic reality did not dress itself in realism, but was to be perceived well enough within the extravagances of performance.

The range of experiment in these years was wide, and tragedy did not follow narrow guidelines. A few plays that

have been named *domestic tragedy* or *bourgeois drama* span
the earlier years: some of the best-known are the anonymous
Arden of Faversham (1592), *A Warning for Fair Women*
(1599) and *A Yorkshire Tragedy* (1606), although the last has
also been attributed to Thomas Middleton. These are dramatic
equivalents of the popular ballad, since each retold a true
story of domestic murder familiar to the audience: in *Arden of
Faversham* the murder of her husband by an adulterous wife;
in *A Warning for Fair Women* the slaying of a London
merchant; and in *A Yorkshire Tragedy* the story of a brutal
husband who killed his children. Because of their bourgeois
topicality, these plays achieved a degree of domestic authenticity atypical of the Elizabethan stage. In particular, the
Epilogue to *Arden of Faversham* drew attention to what it
called its 'naked tragedy':

> Wherein no filed points [polished figures] are foisted in
> To make it gracious to the ear or eye;
> For simple truth is gracious enough
> And needs no other points of glozing [wordy] stuff.
>
> (15–18)

The audience is encouraged to look at *Arden of Faversham*
in this light. It is a play of direct emotions in eighteen scenes
and two or three simple locations – in the house, in the street,
on the London road. Alice Arden has taken a lover and wants
to be rid of her stupid husband; the action consists of her
repeated attempts to dispose of him with the help of her lover,
Mosby, and a pair of hired assassins, Black Will and Shakebag.
From the start Arden suspects his wife, and the sordid tale of
sex and violence is redeemed only by its carefully drawn-out
suspense and some well-placed moments of grim black
humour that arise each time the murderers fail to do their
work. A little sympathy for the victim and a suggestion of
conscience in the villain make a small contribution, but of
greatest interest are the household details that help familiarize
the scene – suspicion of the broth that Alice gives Arden for
his breakfast (scene 1), the game at tables [backgammon] that
provides the occasion for his murder (scene 14) as well as for
the play's famous frontispiece.

A Woman Killed with Kindness (1603) by Thomas

8   *Arden of Faversham*, anon., 1592: the frontispiece to the Quarto of
1633. The death of Master Arden at the 'game of tables' (scene 14).

Heywood (c. 1570–1641) also falls into this category of
middle-class domestic tragedy, except that it did not derive
from any newsletter of the day. It borrowed the plain-style of
Arden of Faversham, but it manipulated the revenge motif of
stories taken from the Italian. In its time it went into three
editions, a token of its success with the Queen's Men on the
stages of the Curtain and the Red Bull theatres. In 1971 it
enjoyed a notable revival by John Dexter at the Old Vic that
showed how moving it could still be. The main story is of the
seduction and adultery of Anne Frankford; betrayed by a
servant, she is discovered by her husband in bed with his
friend Wendoll. Instead of taking his revenge, Frankford
forgives her and sends her away; overcome with remorse, she
starves herself and dies in his arms – reminding the spectator
of the ironic 'kindness' of the title, which suggests the only
subtlety present in Frankford's stodgy character. Set in contrast, the play's sub-plot tells of this situation in reverse: after
a match at falconry, Sir Charles Mountford quarrels violently
with Anne's brother Sir Francis Acton, and in a debt of
honour sacrifices his virtuous sister Susan in marriage to this
man after she had previously run from him. Ignoring any
unity of time, these two plots are theatrically interwoven so
that they support each other's emotional impact right up to

the crisis. But it is not the plotting that accounts for the play's special qualities; rather, it is the unique ambience of provincial home-life with which the text is permeated.

The play begins with the wedding of the bride and groom to music, dancing and singing, and from the start Heywood has Frankford pronounce upon the joys of married life and a perfect wife. This sweet domestic picture is enhanced by a scene (scene 2) given over to a group of comic servants who catch the spirit of the occasion with a noisy dance in their clogs. The scene of Anne's seduction (scene 6) is delicately handled: Wendoll is not the complete villain when he calls on God to forgive him, and, alone on the open stage with him and with the tension of its space between them, Anne is not too quick to assent:

> What shall I say?
> My soul is wand'ring and hath lost her way.
>
> (150–1)

The audience is addressed and drawn into the scene, as it is when later it feels the pain that Frankford feels outside his bedchamber door at midnight – 'Once my terrestrial heaven, now my earth's hell' (13.15).

Scene 8 is rich in homely trivia – a supper table is cleared of food, cloth and napkins, and Frankford enters brushing the crumbs from his clothing. A carpet [table-cover] is spread, and stools, lights, cards *'and other necessaries'* (113) provided. He prepares to play an innocent game of cards with Anne and Wendoll, but their simple dialogue is heavy with *doubles entendres*:

> ANNE. Come, Master Frankford, who shall take my part?
> [be my partner]
> FRANKFORD. Marry, that will I, sweet wife.
> WENDOLL. No, by my faith, sir, when you are together I sit
> out; it must be Mistress Frankford and I, or else it is no
> match.
> FRANKFORD. I do not like that match.
>
> (124–9)

The innocent game becomes symbolic, and the domestic details assume pathetic proportions.

Heywood's pathos borders on moralistic sentimentality

towards the end of the play, but, at least in Anne's pining to death, it succeeds in securing some of that fatal inevitability which classical tragedy demands. First, Frankford's drawn sword threatens the *coup de grâce*, but a maidservant '*in her smock stays his hand*' (13.67) from a murderous revenge. Heywood actually has him thank her for stopping him. Next Frankford calls for his two children to be shown to their mother and then taken from her. Contrite and alone on the platform like a prisoner in the dock, Anne next offers herself as an example to all virtuous women in the audience (141), while from their beds to accuse her the stage fills with all the household servants; all in white smocks they create an impressionistic image of condemnation. The playwright adds a last master-touch in scene 14 when the loyal servant Nicholas spies Anne's lute 'flung in a corner' (12), a painful reminder of her former ways and a happier past. Timing the moment for maximum poignancy, Heywood in scene 16 has Anne play this instrument once more. So at the end the audience sees her, not as an adulteress, but intimately at home and graced by music. With her husband's last kiss on her lips, she dies, and his line is, 'With this kiss, I wed thee once again' (17.117) – the tragedy that began with a wedding thus ends with another, if a bitter one. It is tempting to recognize in this all the stratagems of a later melodrama.

Such pathos was not usual in the tragedy of this age. More often, the grisly horrors and disordered minds of Kyd's type of revenge play determined the style of performance. However, this did not mean that the macabre could not be edged with humour and the shocking made thought-provoking, all to create a drama of unusual interest. *Hamlet* (1600) was, after all, a revenge play.

The strangely ironic tactics of John Marston (1576–1634), with his self-conscious tone and stylistic tricks with language and performance, needed a specialized audience and the unorthodox playing his earlier plays received from St Paul's boys on the private stage. The enigmatic pair of plays *Antonio and Mellida* and *Antonio's Revenge* (1599) continues to puzzle directors and critics, but the consensus today seems to be that they belong to some category of theatre of the absurd or cruelty. When in *Antonio's Revenge*, for example, a gentle-man with the name Balurdo (which means 'fool') enters '*with a beard half off, half on*', telling the audience that 'the tiring man hath not glued on my beard half fast enough' (2.1.30–1), Marston is enjoying a metadramatic joke which undermines his play's seriousness as tragedy; at the same time, such strategy makes its horrors palatable as theatre. *Antonio and Mellida* begins with a Pirandellian induction in which the boy actors discuss their parts, and to a play that is more a burlesque than a romantic drama, Marston introduces one device after another. In particular he makes use of a cynical courtier, Feliche ['the happy one'], who remains outside the play as a commentator, not unlike Marston himself; in the sequel there may be a purpose in having him turn up as a blood-stained body.

This stagework strikes a note of high burlesque, but the spirit of the sequel, *Antonio's Revenge*, is different. After a warning of 'a sullen tragic scene' from the Prologue, the play opens with a startling change when Mellida's father Piero enters '*unbrac'd, his arms bare, smear'd in blood, a poniard in one hand, bloody, and a torch in the other, Strotzo following him with a cord*' – the image of the maniacal Jacobean stage villain. Notwithstanding that it is musical throughout, the second play proceeds to enact a series of gratuitous horrors, beginning with the sight of a character from the first play hanging in the discovery space and stabbed to death '*thick with wounds*'. A clock strikes the hour of midnight and appropriately a ghost arises from the trapdoor – it is the late Duke Andrugio declaring, 'I was empoison'd by Piero's hand' (3.1.35). At the instigation of the Ghost, who groans encoura-gingly beneath the stage, Antonio takes his revenge on Piero by stabbing his little boy to death and doing it with a kiss. The last act opens with a dumb show to prepare the audience for the obscenities to come, and at the end, in their disguises as masquers, his enemies tie up the monster Piero and '*pluck out his tongue and triumph over him*'. Then they offer him 'a dish to feast thy father's gorge' – it contains his son's severed limbs – before they run at him with their rapiers (5.5). To catch the ironic spirit of the occasion, we must imagine this macabre business executed in the light of the flickering candles in the private theatre, and then remember that the parts were played by boys: what larks!

Marston reiterated that a play to be understood should not be read but seen ('Remember the life of these things consists in action', he wrote in the letter to his 'Equal Reader' in *The Fawn*), and his *Antonio* plays suggest his complete confidence and proficiency as a tragic burlesquer. His text is alive with stage directions for procession and pageantry; he usually specifies the musical instruments he wants; and he makes clear when the actors are to use the different levels of the stage and whether their voices are to come from above or below. There are constant surprises, as when in 4.1 Antonio appears '*in fool's habit*' and begins to blow bubbles like a child, and when in 4.4. he lies on his back and performs a parody of grief.

His most admired play, *The Malcontent* (1604), is also difficult to identify by genre. It is set in exotic Genoa and works within a tragic revenge framework to deal with moral corruption and villainy in high society; yet Jonson would have seen it as a 'comicall satyre' and it was registered as a 'tragicomoedia.' It is another of Marston's experiments for the private theatre, performed in the Blackfriars with the company that became the Children of the Queen's Revels before the play was taken over, as the Induction tells us, by Burbage and the King's Men at the Globe. On this evidence, it must have been a success.

The unpredictable direction of this play is immediately conveyed by its curious exposition and a wildly absurdist battery of effects, including noise and smell, that assaulted and silenced its audience:

> *The vilest out-of-tune music being heard, enter* BILIOSO
> *and* PREPASSO.
> BILIOSO. [*Shouts to the upper level of the stage*] Why,
>   how now? are ye mad? or drunk? or both? or
>   what?
> PREPASSO. Are ye building Babylon there?

When the Duke of Genoa enters, the two officers of the court inform him that all the noise is coming from the malcontent Malevole's chamber, and the audience perceives the eponymous character first through the eyes of those he despises.

The 'ferret' Ferrado calls up to him and the noise stops, only to be replaced by the cacophony of abuse that pours from Malevole's mouth when he enters:

> Yaugh, god-a'-man, what dost thou there? Duke's Gany-mede, Juno's jealous of thy long stockings! shadow of a woman, what wouldst, weasel? thou lamb a' court, what dost thou bleat for? ah, you smooth-chinned catamite!
>
> (5–9)

So the audience meets the cynic Malevole, who is the deposed Duke Altofronto in disguise, a man of tortured mind whose role it is to observe society and its vices. He was also perhaps a misshapen mask for the playwright himself.

Malevole demonstrates as well as any character the concept of role-playing in Jacobean drama. In the Globe production's Induction, he first appears as Burbage in his own person. Next as Altofronto he wears his Malevole disguise within the story of the play in order to survive his enemies' wrath and endure the corruption of the Court around him. Throughout the play he also speaks for and to the audience by seeming to stand outside the action. He explains to the house:

> Well, this disguise doth yet afford me that
> Which Kings do seldom hear or great men use –
> Free speech.
>
> (1.3.161–3)

He repeatedly speaks in soliloquy and to his one friend Celso in a more sober verse style, and this perceptibly replaces the fractured prose of his disguise. On one notable occasion when he is speaking intimately to Celso, his enemy Bilioso makes an unexpected entrance, so that Malevole changes his voice in mid-flow, Marston inserting the unique direction, 'Bilioso *entering*, Malevole *shifts his speech*' (1.4.43). Finally, it is also possible to see Malevole as the 'presenter' or manager who is organizing the series of reversals that constitute the action of the play; this is especially obvious when he is hired by the treacherous Mendoza to murder the usurping Duke and instead decides to save him and make him a conspirator.

It cannot be said that the characters in *The Malcontent* are more than the two-dimensional creatures of the most lurid melodrama – the faithful Duchess and the lascivious Duchess, a pack of Court fools and minions and a cunning old bawd. Yet together they make up a wondrous picture of dark evil and smouldering depravity splashed across the canvas in a clash of repellent colours. With his characteristic tirades, Malevole manages to cross verbal swords and make witty passes at each fool or villain or bawd in turn, almost to the accompaniment of the music and song that is heard intermittently throughout the play. And this extraordinary piece concludes with a masque of four 'dukes' dressed all in white with weapons concealed under their robes; in the course of the dance, the masquers reveal their identities and force Mendoza to plead for mercy, which Malevole grants him before actually kicking him off the stage. Thus, to a flourish of cornets, the ceremonial of court life ends without ceremony, and so ends a provocative, if disorderly, excursion into new theatrical territory.

The Revenger's Tragedy (c. 1605) is usually attributed to Cyril Tourneur (c. 1580–1625), although some think it an early tragedy of Thomas Middleton. It demonstrates another principle, that appropriate stage business and stage conventions, if consistent and lurid enough, can sweep all before them. In this century, the play enjoyed college and university productions for many years before Trevor Nunn made his début with the Royal Shakespeare Company in 1966 by showing what an aptly flamboyant performance could bring to an antique text. Costumed in black and silver, stylized in acting, emphatically lit, this production was unforgettable – and Tourneur's play was also restored to the modern theatre.

To create a nightmare of man's evil and inhumanity, the play's elements and style of performance returned to the mythic Gothic horrors of Renaissance Italy, and painstakingly built up a brooding spirit of lust and corruption in an atmosphere of skulls and bones and guttering candles. At the beginning the revenger Vindice enters caressing the skull of his mistress Gloriana, poisoned nine years earlier by the lecherous old Duke because she would not submit to him. With the audience he watches those he hates pass over the stage in a torchlight procession like a dumb show: the

Duke ('grey-hair'd adultery'), his wife ('that foul incontinent duchess'), and their lustful sons Lussurioso and Spurio. When Vindice addresses the skull in his hand, he exhibits his *memento mori* of the night and talks of her beauty,

> Thou sallow picture of my poisoned love,
> My studies' ornament, thou shell of death,
> Once the bright face of my betrothed lady.

(1.1.14–16)

Meanwhile the audience contrasts the image of her loveliness with the hideous remains, and his moralizing reflects the long seething of his bile. Like the skull in *Hamlet*'s gravediggers' scene, Gloriana's skull takes on symbolic strength, and when the prop is seen again, it seems to come alive and requite all defiled women: in act 3 Vindice dresses the bone in a wig and the skeleton in fine clothes. Before it does its work of revenge, however, he addresses this gruesome image with a new revulsion, as if his venom now extends to all women: 'Does the silk-worm expend her yellow labours / For thee?' ... 'Surely we are all mad people, and they / Whom we think are, are not' (3.5.72–81). Finally he puts poison on its lips and a mask over the bony face and, having perfumed the air of an 'unsunned lodge' [a secluded summerhouse], where the Duchess and Spurio are to enjoy an incestuous encounter, he arranges for the Duke to take a mortal kiss from this grisly spectre in ghostly torchlight. Quaintly, the skull is 'a little bashful at first' (134).

The Italian characters of *The Revenger's Tragedy* are named like the vices of a morality play: Lussurioso stands for lechery, Spurio is bastardy, Ambitioso is ambition, Supervacuo is vanity, and all are members of the same odious family. They are flat characters, and, mechanically opposed by Gratiana [grace] and Castiza [chastity], the moral pattern is also flat. Yet, set against the more animated character of Vindice the revenger, their wooden qualities make of them an extraordinary *tableau vivant*, and it is he who manages them and their story, in order to display them to best advantage to the audience.

For most of the play this Vindice is in disguise, moving among his enemies, playing the part of the malcontent Piato and pandering to their depravity: it is this role that allows him to carry out his cold-blooded jest with the poisoned skull. He is another Jacobean role-player, a chorus figure, a commentator and a presenter, a scholar wit and a melancholy clown, as much as a mere character. In his repeated presence on the stage, he is always ready with a fierce soliloquy or a quick aside, and this constant habit of addressing the audience serves to remind it that the actor remains himself and that the play is only a play.

The final effect of this device is to thrust the action of the inner play back by degrees into a frenetic burlesque. In his own person in 4.2 Vindice is even commanded by Lussurioso to kill Piato, i.e., himself, and in 5.1 the Duke's corpse is dressed in his Piato disguise – until the spectator wonders who is the real Vindice, so ubiquitous and chameleon he seems. His roles grant the audience insights into, or impressions of, his full multifarious function, until at the end, following a further dumb show that discloses the new Duke at a banquet, he plays yet another part in his own 'masque of revengers' (5.3.39). In this masque, four dancers *'steal out their swords'* and kill four of those at table; whereupon another four dancers, a 'masque of intended murderers', enter as if prepared to do murder, but, thwarted, kill one another instead. In the general confusion some twelve bodies – including all the sons and stepsons of the ruling family – litter the stage in a macabre scene of death and futility. As for Vindice, he unwittingly condemns himself by boasting of his part in this carnage, and is marched off with his brother to be executed. The end is neat and suitable – he has become both the agent and the victim of the butchery.

The 1966 production treated this double masque as sickening black comedy. All its dancers and their victims at supper wore black cloaks topped by white death's heads, and danced a hideous saraband like a medieval *danse macabre*, a mad picture of death completing its inevitable mission. The dominant visual image of the play, the skull, was multiplied infinitely as the figures of doom moved unsmiling with their weapons of destruction against a black backdrop. It occurred to modern commentators that Antonin Artaud's theatre of cruelty and Samuel Beckett's theatre of the absurd well prepared the modern audience for the revival of Jacobean tragedy and its irrational assault on the senses. In his manifesto for the Théâtre Alfred Jarry in 1926, Artaud considered offering a production of Tourneur, arguing that the spectator 'will go to the theatre as he goes to the surgeon or the dentist ... knowing he will not come out unscathed'.

Webster and the macabre: *The White Devil, The Duchess of Malfi*

As a writer of revenge tragedies John Webster (*c.* 1580–*c.* 1625) readily adopted the regular catalogue of sensational devices, and took to formidable extremes the Renaissance notions of Italianate high society and its evil world of greed and intrigue, lust and corruption. To this he added his own brand of the theatrical macabre, sufficient for Shaw to dub him a 'Tussaud Laureate' and for others to find his imagination tortured: in his preface to *The White Devil* he wrote, 'I confess I do not write with a goose-quill winged with two feathers.' The poetry on Webster's stage is as sombre and unrelenting as the action it sustains, and when his plays are in performance, therefore, the actor is in danger of overkill and the audience of scepticism. This has been a risk run by a number of self-conscious modern productions, overplayed, overcoloured and overdressed in direst Gothic, whereas Webster's inflated dramaturgy calls for deflated playing.

Nevertheless, in marshalling and deploying the usual battery of skulls and graves, ghosts and madmen, Webster scores some remarkable triumphs. He shows a special skill in staging his images of sex and violence for maximum effect, and seems rapidly to have learned an effective stagecraft to support his poetry. He is comfortable using the familiar conventions of role-playing and disguise, as well as the expansive devices of choric speech, masque and dumb show. His reputation as the master of the macabre rests on two plays, *The White Devil* and *The Duchess of Malfi* (a third, *The Devil's Law-Case* (c. 1616), is a less characteristic satirical tragi-comedy), and for both he turned to true stories reported in recent newsletters. More importantly, to stand at the centre of his plays he rejected the revenging malcontents and choric commentators dear to Marston and Tourneur, and instead created in Vittoria Corombona and the Duchess of Malfi two major female parts, both subtly-shaded characters skilfully used to manipulate the sympathies of his audience. Further, Webster arranged his assortment of villains in such a way as to contrast their differences – their shades of evil and immorality, and their range of nervous sensibility to life and death – all to enhance and extend the response of his central characters to the fact of mortality.

The White Devil (?1612) was played by the Queen's Men at the Red Bull, a popular house designed like the Globe with a thrust stage, upstage doors and a balcony above. The play is one of heady atmosphere and intrigue: on the one hand, of whispers and asides, with the men and women of the Court spying on one another and eavesdropping to the point of voyeurism, and, on the other, of horrors, shocks and sensations. From the moment the adulterous lovers Vittoria and Brachiano are together in an embrace, they are watched in alarm by her mother Cornelia and with amusement by her pandering brother Flamineo and her Moorish maid Zanche; when they are together again in 4.2, Flamineo is even more of a facetious voyeur hovering about them. Vittoria loses no time in deviously encouraging Brachiano to murder his wife Isabella and her impotent old husband Camillo. This is done with the help of Flamineo and a Doctor, although the method of dispatch is anything but straightforward: Webster brings in a 'nigromancer' [a conjuror of black arts] to justify a pair of elaborate dumb shows played almost back-to-back. The first shows the Doctor poisoning a portrait of Brachiano, which Isabella *'in her nightgown as to bed-ward'* (2.2.23.7) then dutifully kisses as if in a nightly ritual. The second shows Flamineo and Camillo with a vaulting-horse, whereupon *'as* CAMILLO *is about to vault,* FLAMINEO *pitcheth him upon his neck, and with the help of the rest [handle], writhes his neck about, seems to see if it be broke, and lays him folded double as 'twere under the horse'* (2.2.37.6–9). The kind of acting appropriate to a dumb show lends these early murders a nightmarish quality, and the inappropriate laughter from the characters that precedes both of them contributes to their appalling irony.

Although the vile Flamineo seems to control the action, the focus increasingly shifts to the evil beauty Vittoria, 'the devil in crystal'. Her finest moment comes, as does that of the play, when she is put on trial for murder in a scene of Webster's own invention. Amazingly, the playwright contrives to elicit sympathy for her in her plight. He does this by showing the Court to be more corrupt than she is, and by endowing her with a dignity and a pride her accusers lack as she stands alone and vulnerable before them. At the start Webster lowers his audience's defences by the interpolation of a comic lawyer whose indigestible diction and legalistic language are as unacceptable to the spectator as they are to Vittoria. The Cardinal then arraigns her as a whore. He proceeds through a long speech, angrily building feeling in the Shakespearian manner by repeating his words – 'What are whores?' – 'What are whores?' – 'What's a whore?' – until she puts him down sharply with a short, dry retort: 'This character scapes me' (101). Comments aside by the English Ambassador ('The cardinal's too bitter' – 'She hath a brave spirit') help to guide the spectator's sympathetic response, and when she is sentenced to be imprisoned in 'a house of penitent whores', her rejoinder is admirable:

> My mind shall make it honester to me
> Than the Pope's palace, and more peaceable
> Than thy soul, though thou art a cardinal.
>
> (290–2)

The last act brings down the anticipated flood of fatalities. Good brother Marcello is run through by bad brother Flamineo, witnessed by their mother Cornelia who goes mad with grief (5.2); Lodovico poisons Brachiano's helmet so that he dies a lingering death until, disguised as Capuchin monks in their long cowls and seeming to perform the last rites, Lodovico and Gasparo torture and strangle him in front of Vittoria (5.3); she and Zanche shoot Flamineo with his pistols and *'tread on him'*, only to discover that he had taken the precaution of removing the bullets, whereupon Lodovico captures all three and dispatches them with blades before he is wounded himself (5.6). In 1969 Frank Dunlop saw Lodovico as a sexual sadist and had his assistants twist their daggers round and round 'to make Italian cutworks in their guts' as he had promised (1.1.52); and in 1991 Philip Prowse had Lodovico repeatedly thrust his dagger into Vittoria as if having sex, so prompting her line, ''Twas a manly blow' (232). However, with Flamineo as quasi-chorus, the last act is his, and he has almost the last word with his sardonic quip, that we 'cease to die by dying' (253).

The private theatre was more suitable for staging Webster's dumb shows, masques and tableau effects, and for any controlled use of light and darkness to create a macabre sensation. It is interesting to speculate, therefore, that although the stage of the Globe could also create imaginative impressions of theatrical chiaroscuro, the King's Men must have found their Blackfriars theatre more suitable for a production of *The Duchess of Malfi* (c. 1614), his next play. This revenge tragedy lacks a ghost, but it is replete with all the horrors of the genre, even going one better with wax figures of the dead, an antimasque of madmen and such ingenious devices as a dead hand and a poisoned Bible. This play is planned for shocks, and this may account for its subsequent revival in various shapes in every century. However, if this were all, the play would not be accounted the masterpiece it patently is.

The play's distinction turns on Webster's pursuit of variation and change in the nature and spirit of the action. The Duchess is not the merry widow of tradition, but in some ways a subtle and realistic portrait of a proud and sensitive woman who is something of a Christian martyr when faced with her tormentors. She appears even more human when set against the pair of fiends, her brothers: one is the psychotic tyrant Duke Ferdinand, abhorrent with hints of incestuous thoughts of his sister, and finally succumbing to gibbering lycanthropy; the other is the carnal Cardinal, whose mistress Julia's behaviour is in sharp contrast with that of the Duchess. Yet the creature who arrests most attention is the murderous ruffian Bosola, a man who, having served seven years in the galleys, is now charged with executing her: Webster makes him something of a philosopher (when he

played him in 1985, Ian McKellen on occasion wore spectacles), and by having him feel compassion, carefully modifies
the audience's impression of him and thereby shifts the whole
tone and mode of his theatre. When in act 4 Bosola and his
victim come together, the Jacobean stage witnesses one of its
greatest scenes.

For the period the plot is comparatively uncomplicated.
The Duchess chooses her steward Antonio for her second
husband, and since she must herself propose marriage indirectly, this affords an unusually tender scene between them.
But she knows that she is in danger if she remarries:

> I am going into a wilderness,
> Where I shall find nor path, nor friendly clew [thread]
> To be my guide.

> (1.1.359–61)

Webster virtually passes over their difference in rank as a
provocative theme, but the ill-fated marriage is unacceptable
to the brothers. Ferdinand therefore employs Bosola to spy
on his sister, so setting in train the ugly events of the play.
The audience is not to question how the Duchess has three
children before her secret marriage is discovered, but, in a
symbolic dumb show at the shrine of Our Lady of Loretto
where the Cardinal is installed as a warrior, the Duchess and
her family are banished (3.4). This is a preparatory device to
help the stage make an ingenious transition to a dreamlike
level. Next, Bosola, ominously masked in a ghostly vizard,
takes the Duchess and her two youngest children as prisoners
to Ferdinand, who, under the pretext of making reconciliation, prepares a diabolical revenge.

Ferdinand has vowed never to see his sister again, and uses
this as an excuse to visit her in darkness (Bosola tells her, 'He
comes i'th'night; / And prays you, gently, neither torch nor
taper / Shine in your chamber' (4.1.24–6)). Thus the Blackfriars audience only dimly perceived the hand that is offered
her to kiss as if it were Antonio's; when she finds it to be
cold to the touch of her lips, she realizes that it is a dead
hand detached from its body, and cries: 'Hah! lights! – O,
horrible!' (53); torches then reveal the hideous object to her
and to the house. Now it is Bosola's turn, and he discovers

'*behind a traverse*' – Webster makes easy use of the discovery-space for a special effect – the wax figures of Antonio
and the children as if they were dead. Again, the tableau
device helps create an illusion, here offering a premonition of
what is to come. For not only is the Duchess being put into a
trance, but as the action on stage shifts to the unreal and the
supernatural, so also is the audience. This trick with the wax
figures is balanced later by the unearthly effect of the echo
scene (5.3), in which Antonio seems to hear a voice from the
Duchess's grave. For the moment, she and the audience are
granted a short respite at the end of 4.1, when Bosola can ask
Ferdinand the question that is foremost in everyone's mind:
'Why do you do this?' Comes the cold answer, 'To bring her
to despair' (116).

From this time on, Bosola's pity for his victim grows
stronger, yet the nightmare is not yet at its blackest. No more
ironic convention existed in Renaissance stagecraft than the
antimasque of droll, lowlife dancers, and Webster conceived
the idea of filling the stage and surrounding the Duchess with
cavorting madmen, apparently released from 'the common
hospital' to her lodging. They dance in chains to music and
song that are no more than a 'hideous noise' (4.2.1), and
invoke a wild image of purgatory. However, on a fantasy
stage Bosola is another version of role-player, and for his final
torture he now abandons his persona as a malcontent philosopher to acquire that of a figure of death. He now plays an
ancient tomb-maker:

> BOSOLA.   I am come to make thy tomb.
> DUCHESS.   Hah, my tomb!
>   Thou speakst as if I lay upon my death-bed,
>   Gasping for breath: dost thou perceive me sick?
> BOSOLA.   Yes, and the more dangerously, since thy sick-
>   ness is insensible.
>
> (4.2.116–20)

The Duchess speaks for everyone in the theatre. Finally, when
Executioners enter with coffin, cords and bell, Bosola has a
last change of role: he becomes the common bellman 'that
usually is sent to condemn'd persons / The night before they
suffer' (173–4). As he tolls the bell, he intones,

Hark, now everything is still,
The screech-owl, and the whistler shrill
Call upon our dame, aloud,
And bid her quickly don her shroud.

                                                                    (178–81)

This constitutes a long preamble to the murders of the
Duchess, her maid Cariola and the two children that follow,
but for all this preparation the Duchess dies a full death, and
contributes to a rich part, as a string of modern actresses have
demonstrated – notably Peggy Ashcroft in 1945 and 1960,
and Judi Dench in 1971.

Webster concentrates the important action of the play in
this prison scene, and it is the test of any production. Played
on the bare and darkened stage, its action, like that of Lear on
the heath, is timeless and finally placeless, and the Jacobean
stage can be transfigured to help the spectator scale the
mountains of the mind. The staging of the macabre and
supernatural involves many aspects of performance, not least
those of style and pace, which affect the kind of music, speech
and movement. Webster especially deals in ritual and ceremony, finding it both in theatrical conventions like the dumb
show and the masque, and in such domestic functions as
weddings and funerals. Yet between these formal shows he
intersperses brilliant moments of intimacy and realism: for
example, from time to time the Duchess reveals her simple
dignity – 'I am Duchess of Malfi still' (4.2.142) – and at the
moment of her execution she thinks of her children in fetching
terms of the small details of their lives:

I pray thee, look thou giv'st my little boy
Some syrup for his cold, and let the girl
Say her prayers, ere she sleep.

                                                                    (4.2.203–5)

After she has been strangled, her unaffected resignation is so
contrasted with poor Cariola's sundry protests, including her
wails that she has not been to confession and is with child,
that the Duchess's dignity seems even more admirable. If the
modern theatre has difficulty in taking Webster's sensationalism seriously, as critics have suggested, he has more than

enough subtlety of thought and feeling, as well as variety of
pace and tone, to exercise its best talents.

Middleton, Ford and a psychological tragedy: *The Changeling, 'Tis Pity She's a Whore*

Una Ellis-Fermor called Thomas Middleton (1580–1627) the
Ibsen of the seventeenth century, and after a few of his
tragedies have been seen on the modern stage, he has risen in
the esteem of actors and playgoers. In the development from
innocence to depravity of Beatrice-Joanna, the central character in *The Changeling*, he created a extraordinarily pene-
trating study of female psychology, and today his wholly
unromantic treatment of women and marriage appears to suit
the times. *Women Beware Women*, written for the King's
Men in *c.* 1621, has been overshadowed by *The Changeling*,
written a year later in collaboration with the actor William
Rowley (*c.* 1585–*c.* 1625), but it remains a powerful picture of
the role of women in a society dominated by men, and for our
purposes it is particularly rich in exploratory stagecraft. Given
to a group of materialistic pretenders and deceivers, the lines
are noticeably thick with asides, if nothing else.

Again set in Italy, the play presents the cynical widow
Livia, who procures pretty Bianca, Leantio's wife aged
sixteen, for the Duke of Florence, and, under cover of her
marriage to a simpleton (the 'Ward'), gets her niece Isabella
for her brother Hippolito; meanwhile Livia wants Leantio for
herself. At the beginning, Middleton implies that Bianca is
perfectly artless and submissive by her long silence before she
asks a kiss of her husband, and in 1.3 he consigns her to the
safety of her mother-in-law and a balcony overlooking the
platform as if at a Florentine window, where the ladies may
observe the triumphal entry of the Duke. But the childlike
Bianca is excited: 'Did not the Duke look up? Methought he
saw us' (105). It is there *'above'* that in a chilling scene (2.2)
the Duke seduces the impressionable young girl with promises of wealth and luxury, a mere pawn to a black King,
while simultaneously on the platform below Livia plays at

chess with the Mother who should be protecting her. (Timothy O'Brien's design for Terry Hands's Royal Shakespeare Company production in 1969 paved Stratford's bare stage with a huge checker-board motif.) The physical distance between the two levels of action seems to set them in parallel and link them in irony. At the subsequent banquet of 3.3, Leantio's place as a cuckold wretched among the festive crowd is painful to watch.

Two plots are woven here. The second, that of Hippolito and Isabella, mirrors and echoes Bianca's, but on this level it is evident that the antics of the foolish Ward in his pursuit of a wife are intended to introduce farce into the tragedy, laughter in the dark. The Ward is endowed with comic characteristics: with his man Sordido he plays at 'trap-stick' [a game with a spinning stick] and shuttlecock and battledore, dances like a clown and constantly speaks with obscene innuendo; and his most explicit scene comes in 3.4 when he inspects the person of Isabella as for market, even to examining her teeth and legs. The acquisitive society shows its bestial side.

At the end (5.2), retribution descends almost perfunctorily in a bloody denouement of multiple and varied deaths – by fire ('*flaming gold*'), by falling through the trap, by asphyxiation (Livia is overcome by her own incense), by Cupid's arrows whose work is then completed with a sword and lastly by poison. This all takes place to the singing and dancing of a final masque, performed in the 1969 production on part of the stage raised to become a chessboard. Indeed, for all that domestic detail colours much of the action in *Women Beware Women*, its characteristic idiom is highly musical and theatrical, with scenes of banquet and masque taking on a ceremonial appearance. The whole mode of the tragedy thus assumes a curiously derisive duality.

The symmetry and formality of the chess game in this play may have given Middleton the idea for *A Game at Chess*, which the King's Men played for a record nine performances in 1624 before the Privy Council banned it. The political allegory of the (white) Court of James I of England in conflict with the (black) Court of Philip IV of Spain, with all the characters played like chess pieces, combined something of the medieval morality with a masque-like symbolism that was brilliant in conception, but while in its own day the protests of the Spanish ambassador caused the play to be taken off, in after years its topicality kept it from being put on.

The Changeling was produced by Lady Elizabeth's Men at the Phoenix and at Salisbury Court, both private theatres. The changeling of the title is one Antonio, a gallant who pretends to be an imbecile (another meaning of 'changeling') in order to pursue Isabella, the young wife of the keeper of a madhouse, all part of a comic sub-plot. However, the central tragedy divulges the way Beatrice-Joanna falls under the influence of her evil servant De Flores, suggesting another kind of changeling the Jacobean audience would understand and relish. The play's unusual study of the steamy sexual relationship between a beautiful woman and the ugly servant whom at first she loathes, has been the occasion of several amateurish psychological speculations about the sexual affinity between love and hate.

At the outset the pock-marked De Flores speaks in aside to reveal himself besotted with his mistress. Hovering in the shadows, he is shown to be haunting her every movement, and it is evident that this has been going on for some time. For her part, Beatrice was betrothed to the noble Alonzo de Piracquo five days before, although she already prefers another, Alsemero. Yet she cannot take her eyes off the servant she abhors, and line after line instructs both the boy-actor and the audience that this is so. At the end of the scene Beatrice's revulsion is confirmed when she drops her glove and De Flores picks it up: her violent reaction is, 'Who bade you stoop? They touch my hand no more' (228), and she throws *both* gloves down. Middleton's calculated restraint in his delicate handling of his principals and their interaction is apparent in their next encounter, in 2.1, which opens with two long soliloquies heard in parallel, speeches in which they both share their thoughts with the audience. Again, Beatrice cannot take her mind from De Flores, who increasingly appears to her like an omen and a threat:

> – This ominous ill-fac'd fellow more disturbs me
> Than all my other passions.

> (53–4)

I never see this fellow, but I think
Of some harm towards me.

(89–90)

The tragic snare is being set.

When Beatrice conceives the idea of using De Flores to dispose of her unwanted suitor, she sets about seducing him, despite her loathing. In 2.2 she calls him by name ('Ha, I shall run mad with joy' (70)), praises his looks and tells him to approach ('I'm up to the chin in heaven' (78)). The lines seem to tell the character what to do with her hands as she examines his skin and caresses his face (beginning with 'Her fingers touch'd me!' (81)), and they suggest exactly how long this fondling must continue. When between them they echo the *double entendre* of his 'service' to her (93, 96) and when she addresses him as 'Oh my De Flores!' (98), the audience may be excused for thinking that they are both already caught up by erotic appetite. Thus the contract for De Flores to murder Beatrice's betrothed is obliquely made in a cloud of ambiguous foreshadowing. It has been argued that Beatrice-Joanna's fickle personality is her downfall, but the complexity of her feelings makes the pressures upon her more enigmatic and pitiful than this suggests. Nevertheless, in true Jacobean style, in 3.4, it is not long before De Flores produces Alonzo's finger as proof of his death, and promptly demands his price.

> BEATRICE.   Thy language is so bold and vicious,
>   I cannot see which way I can forgive it
>   With any modesty.
> DE FLORES.   Push, you forget yourself!
>   A woman dipp'd in blood, and talk of
>   modesty?

(123–6)

When Beatrice realizes that she has no defence left, of neither her rank nor her sex, she is lost. 'Come, rise', he orders her, 'and shroud your blushes in my bosom' (167). She is now at last 'the deed's creature'.

Thereafter the play takes on the expected trappings of revenge tragedy. In particular, Beatrice's wedding to Alsemero is fashioned as a dumb show (4.1), and the Royal Shakespeare Company production of 1978 had De Flores raping Beatrice while upstage the tableau showed Alsemero marrying her in effigy. Also in the dumb show Alonzo's ghost appears to De Flores, showing him the hand with the missing finger. When Beatrice believes that her husband will submit her to a test of her virginity, in panic she has her maid Diaphanta take her place in her marriage bed. An edge of comedy is introduced, however, when it emerges that Diaphanta enjoys her task, and act 5 has Beatrice waiting impatiently (with the help of an off-stage clock counting the hours from one to three), fearful because the maid has not returned. De Flores conveniently expedites matters by setting fire to the house and burning Diaphanta to death. With the noise of bells and running servants, the fire precipitates an ending in which Alsemero finally learns the truth. He shuts Beatrice up with De Flores in a 'closet' where they are invited to 'rehearse again / Your scene of lust' (5.3.114–5). What occurs in the closet is for a while left to the lurid imagination of the audience, but De Flores also has a knife, and to forestall the torture that awaits them he stabs both Beatrice and himself to death.

Thus far *The Changeling* lacks that familar Jacobean ingredient of gruesome laughter, and this is supplied by the subplot otherwise introduced to comment on the main action. When Antonio pretends madness in order to seduce Isabella and cuckold the old doctor who keeps the madhouse, Isabella herself assumes madness, in 4.3, to deceive Antonio. Much of this is conventional farce, and in the seventeenth century it contributed to the continuing popularity of the play. A certain contrast is also intended between the faithful Isabella and the treacherous Beatrice. However, it is the proximity of the madhouse itself that is important to the general spirit of the play, and in 4.3 the stories are drawn together when a frenzied dance of madmen, something like an antimasque, spills over into the hectic scene of the fire (5.1), and completes the climax of Beatrice's nightmare of despair. A few years earlier madmen beset the Duchess of Malfi to accentuate her tragedy: in *The Changeling* their appearance is more frivolous, but they beset the audience just as effectively.

The three best-known revenge tragedies of John Ford (1586–

?1639) – *Love's Sacrifice*, *The Broken Heart* and *'Tis Pity
She's a Whore* – were all published in 1633, and probably
produced a year or two earlier; *Perkin Warbeck*, a chronicle
play, was published in 1634. Since Charles I came to the
throne in 1625, these are properly Caroline plays written for
the private theatres. Indeed, behind the customary, and sometimes derivative, patchwork of sensational forms and devices
of the genre, the stage boldly takes a different direction. The
expected sensations are still to be found – at the climax of
Love's Sacrifice Fernando rises from Bianca's tomb in a
winding-sheet; for all its pitiful lovers, *The Broken Heart* is as
blood-thirsty as ever, with Ithocles in a final scene trapped in
a mechanical chair bleeding to death; and in spite of its echoes
of *Romeo and Juliet*, *'Tis Pity She's a Whore* has Giovanni
skewering his sister's heart on a dagger. Yet within the
revenge framework, Ford introduces new attempts at structure and style, and especially a new emotionality, an engaging
sensitivity, that was much admired by Charles Lamb.

'Tis Pity She's a Whore was played by the Queen's
Company at the Phoenix in Drury Lane. It continued to
attract the interest of playgoers into the Restoration (although
Pepys did not enjoy it), and it has again found another
audience during the last hundred years. Ford returned his
scene to Italy, to Parma, and the play was again as different in
pace and feeling as in subject, the incestuous love of a brother
and sister, with the subsequent side-effects of adultery and
murder. To mark the new variation in pace, the spectator is
tossed precipitously into the situation, with Giovanni's obses-
sion and his predicament presented immediately in his confession to Friar Bonaventura, the representative figure of
morality and the Church. Soon after, his beautiful sister
Annabella is seen '*above*', where she and the audience watch
her crew of unattractive suitors quarrel over her, while her
physical separation reflects her isolation and defencelessness.
But she has eyes only for Giovanni and before the end of the
first act they are alone on the stage, with her brother swearing
his devotion and charging her to use his dagger in his heart:

> here's my breast, strike home!
> Rip up my bosom, there thou shalt behold

A heart in which is writ the truth I speak.
Why stand 'ee?

(1.2.209–12)

It is a gesture to remember later, but Annabella's general reticence is a sign of her attractive sensitivity, as well as her unwillingness to admit her own sinful feelings. Nevertheless, before the scene is over, the two are on their knees to one another sharing a vow and an embrace in a personal little ceremony which insinuates a strange wedge of ritualism into the realism.

After a brief but joyful encounter, in 2.1, following a night spent together, Annabella and Giovanni are never alone with one another again until almost the end of the play, a curious structural arrangement which has the effect of shifting the focus from a demonstration of incestuousness to the impact of the incest. In three or four scenes the obligatory comic distraction is provided by one of the suitors Bergetto and his servant Poggio, a pair of blockheads, and when, in 3.7, the buffoon is run through the midriff by mistake, the poor man must die a comic death. Two events are introduced, however, to trigger the tensions needed to raise the play to tragic intensity – Annabella's marriage and the revelation of her pregnancy. In 2.5, the Friar insists to Giovanni that the issue be resolved by Annabella's marriage to one of her suitors, and in Giovanni's presence, in 3.1, their father tells Annabella she must take the wealthy Soranzo as her husband. The scene in which the girl refuses him on the main stage while her brother eavesdrops from the balcony above shows Ford's comfortable use of simple platform patterns for maximum effect. Soranzo protests his love in chivalric platitudes, but Annabella ridicules him. The arrangement, with its asides on two levels, enables the audience to share three individual points of view, and appreciate the spatial reaction and interaction that make up the ironies of a delicate and intricate situation. Nevertheless, the scene ends on a more serious note when Annabella, now 'sick' in earnest, shows signs of being with child.

Ford next resorts to an extraordinary series of more conventionally theatrical tableaux and masques in order to build his situation to its culmination. The scene of Annabella's confession and repentance (3.6) was exactly imagined by the author, and it opens in the discovery-space like a dumb show:

> *Enter the* FRIAR *sitting in a chair,* ANNABELLA *kneeling and whispering to him: a table before them and wax-lights: she weeps and wrings her hands.*

The wedding of Soranzo and Annabella (4.1) is also enhanced by ceremonial toasting and feasting executed to the music of hautboys, so that Giovanni, in an aside, may lament his private loss only against a noisy and crowded celebration. This business soon changes to a masque of ladies, disguised in masks and clothed in white robes. They dance with garlands of willows, emblems of romantic grief, until one of the dancers, Soranzo's former mistress Hippolita, suddenly reveals herself. She seems to invite another toast to the married couple, but her true intention is to poison Soranzo. Unluckily for her, the treacherous servant Vasques has switched the cups and so she dies writhing in an ugly death herself.

Matters are now proceeding apace: Soranzo discovers Annabella's condition (4.3) and with the resounding line, 'Come, strumpet, famous whore', drags his new wife on to, and perhaps around, the stage in order to extract from her the name of the father of her child. But it is his servant Vasques who gets the truth from Putana, Annabella's nurse, and leaves orders for some murderous *banditi* to gag her and put out her eyes. Annabella manages to send Giovanni due warning that their secret is out in a letter written in her own blood (5.3), and Ford arranges another brief tableau in the discovery-space (5.5). In a scene reminiscent of the lovers on Juliet's tomb, Giovanni and Annabella are seen *'lying on a bed'* – by this time a truly symbolic property – and through tears they kiss one another repeatedly until Giovanni produces a dagger:

ANNABELLA.   What means this?
GIOVANNI. To save thy fame, and kill thee in a kiss.

(83–4)

For the climactic scene (5.6) Ford devised another sensational set piece. Soranzo has prepared a sumptuous banquet as the scene for his revenge, and into this a raging Giovanni bursts with Annabella's heart upon his dagger. The bleeding heart 'is proud in the spoil / Of love and vengeance' (11–12) and is intended to perform this double service in the eyes of the audience. The audience will have guessed what is happening – Giovanni had earlier offered his sister his own heart as a token – but it is all of a minute before he discloses whose heart it is. 'Be not amazed' (17) is Giovanni's cry, and this constitutes a hidden directive for the stage to remain frozen and the moment protracted. The bleeding heart acquires a symbolic function on the stage verbally and visually. When Giovanni recounts to Florio, his horrified father, the story of his children's incestuous love, the old man's heart breaks. At the last, Giovanni stabs Soranzo, and Vasques stabs Giovanni, so that the tragedy itself ends fittingly in a symbolic bloodbath in which all the principals have bled to death.

Arguably, the tragedy of this period pushed and probed further than the comedy. The so-called bourgeois tragedies made modest incursions into the possibilities of a more domestic drama and the speech and behaviour that went with it, but most tragedies in this period, especially with the increasing use of indoor theatres, made use of well-tried but apparently inexhaustible conventions of sensational disguise, dumb show and masque. Inside the parameters of revenge drama, with its expected tooth-dripping, crowd-pleasing sensations of blood and the supernatural, the tragedy of the early seventeenth century enjoyed to the maximum the illusionistic freedom of the playhouse it had inherited, both public and private. Because of the proximity of the house to the stage, the actors of the day were totally at home addressing and handling their audience in the moment by moment traffic of the asides and soliloquies that were the mainstay of the dialogue. However, this pales beside the ever-increasing demand for spectacle and sensation. There is a distinct sense that one playhouse was trying to outstrip another in 'special effects', as science fiction films tend to do today. Under these circumstances, the stage of Marston and Tourneur became the occasion for a spirited carnival of evil, and that of Webster and Middleton for excursions into the dark country of psychological chimera and nightmare.

10

The Restoration stage

Radical changes in the playhouse

The interregnum between the deposition of Charles I in 1642 and the restoration of Charles II in 1660 so accelerated the changes in the conditions of performance, some of which had been only hinted at before, that the next fifty years saw extraordinary innovation in almost all departments of the drama; in particular the audience and the playhouse changed completely. The reason is not far to seek: in 1642 Cromwell and his Puritan parliament passed an edict closing all of London's public and private theatres 'to appease and avert the wrath of God' and by 1649 had gutted and demolished them; the actors, meanwhile, were classed with rogues and vagabonds, risking their lives if they performed. The drama, however, is irrepressible, and during the Commonwealth period had not been wholly dormant. Private rooms, inns and even tennis courts had been pressed into service as playhouses; boys, as before, were used as actors; and new forms were devised to escape the law: 'drolls' like *Bottom the Weaver* were short farcical entertainments, and 'plays with music' were rudimentary operas imitating the Italian and drawing on the Court masque.

One such musical entertainment is the operatic *The Siege of Rhodes*. William Davenant (1606–68), who had followed Jonson as Court playwright, produced it in Rutland House, before a private, royalist audience in 1656, and again in 1658 in the Cockpit in Drury Lane. Of special importance, he had as his scene designer the man who had been Inigo Jones's assistant, John Webb (1611–72), and it is he who supplies the link between the scenic arrangements of the Jacobean masque and the changeable perspective scenery developed in the

Restoration playhouse. He adopted the Italian system of painted backgrounds and movable flats, making use of shutters set against fixed wings and borders to hide and frame them, and open or close on grooves. Designs for this musical drama have survived, and they show how on a tiny stage of 22 feet width and 18 feet depth, three sets of rocky wings passably suggested a spacious scene.

After Charles II returned from exile in France, fresh from experience of new theatrical developments on the Continent, he issued royal patents to Davenant and Thomas Killigrew (1612–83), loyal friends who were products of the pre-Commonwealth theatre, granting them a monopoly of the London stage for drama. It is a matter for debate whether this concentration of the drama was a good thing for the English stage, but at least the target audience was clearly identified, the changes were uncommonly rapid and they worked. For twenty-two years the two companies rivalled one another, until the Duke's Men took over the King's Men and played as the United Company for the next thirteen years.

Davenant assembled the Duke's Men, named for Charles's brother James, Duke of York, and Killigrew the King's Men. Desperately in need of a playhouse, both made temporary use of Tudor tennis courts for theatres: Killigrew working in Gibbons's Tennis Court in Vere Street (1660) and Davenant in Lisle's Tennis Court in Lincoln's Inn Fields (1661), which he opened with an expanded version of *The Siege of Rhodes*. A tennis court had a roof, a surrounding gallery, and had the same sort of intimate dimensions (about 75 by 30 feet overall) the private playhouses had previously enjoyed. If the area was divided at the line of the net, giving half the space to the actors and half to the audience, which would number about four hundred, something of the desirable intimacy of the actor–audience relationship was secured.

Presumably wanting to compete with Davenant's scenic effects, Killigrew soon adapted an old riding school in Bridges Street near Drury Lane as his Theatre Royal (1663), whereupon Davenant commissioned a new purpose-built theatre which became the Duke's Theatre in Dorset Garden, opening with Dryden's *Sir Martin Mar-All* in 1671. Then, following a fire in his Bridges Street theatre in 1672, Killigrew built a

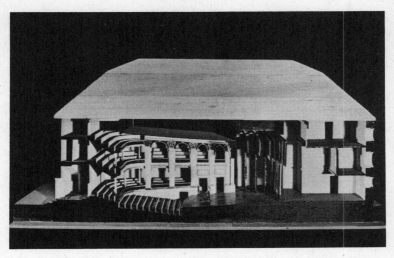

9 A Restoration playhouse, probably the Theatre Royal, Drury Lane as designed by Christopher Wren in 1674. (Model by Edward A. Langhans.)

scenic theatre in Drury Lane and moved there in 1674. This was the father of a line of Theatres Royal in Drury Lane, and it doubled the size of the house and the playing area without losing physical intimacy. Candle-lit overall, the spectator felt himself to be in the same room with the players, and so close to them that he caught their smallest expression of voice or gesture. In the picture is seen a raked stage facing ten benches in a raked pit. Of greatest importance, the stage itself consists of an apron that projects 17 feet in front of the proscenium, and allows for a depth of 15 more feet behind it to provide the space for four wings and three shutters in grooves.

The groove and shutter system of scene changing was as much concerned with enhancing the speed and continuity of the action as augmenting the spectacle. After the curtain had opened at the beginning of a performance, it stayed up and scenes were changed in full view of the audience. The doors, two or four of them, were always set in the proscenium and were the chief means of making an entrance and an exit, after which they became 'invisible' as on the non-illusory stage of the previous century until called into use again as a door or a hiding-place. When the shutters were slid apart at the start of a scene on certain occasions, an actor was '*discovered*', and when the shutters were closed at the end he would on a few occasions '*go within the scene*'.

The chief features of the Restoration stage may be summarized as follows:

- A *covered stage and auditorium* lit by windows above the stage, the light supplemented by candles. Light brackets and chandeliers illuminating the actors and spectators generally remained alight throughout, but, as in the masque, rare effects of light behind gauzes and transparencies were possible. The candles, made from mutton fat, added to the special atmosphere of the Restoration theatre – thick with the haze of the open flames, obnoxious with the smell of unwashed bodies and the latrines in the passageways.

- An *apron stage* that encouraged the actor to work in close proximity with the audience, rather than retreat into the dimly lit scenery of the upper area. As in earlier times, the apron remained unlocalized until a location was identified by an actor's lines or a scene change.

- The *proscenium arch* with *one or two doors* on each side. One of these doors sometimes provided a 'closet' to conceal an actor, but they chiefly served as entrances into the acting area. They were so situated that he entered immediately on to the apron and, as it were, into the house. The downstage position of the stage doors encouraged a downstage pattern of movement across the acting area, and explains the aside to the audience an actor commonly uttered on entrance.

- *Balconies* over the doors were made possible by their position in the proscenium arch and provided a second level, if a limited one compared with that of the Elizabethan playhouse. They served as a place for eavesdropping on the action taking place on the stage proper, and also as a chamber window for amorous scenes.

- A *music gallery* was provided above the proscenium for 'a consort of musicians' (usually a few strings and woodwinds) who always played in full view of the audience.

This feature indicates that music was usual in every kind of Restoration play.

Above all, the new stages established a system of *changeable scenery* that was to become a mainstay of the theatre for the future. At this time it was changed in full view of the audience and made no attempt at realistic illusion. In modern revivals of Restoration plays, a pretty pictorial setting like that of a toy theatre is sometimes to be seen graced with flunkeys carrying candelabras and striking attitudes, intended to evoke the spirit of Good King Charles's golden days.

It is easy to recognize how the conventions of Restoration drama emerged from these features. In spite of the new scenery and lighting, the playhouse was still one of non-illusion where prologue and epilogue, soliloquy and aside flourished, and the unities of place and time were disregarded. Actor and spectator were never more physically close, nor the drama more of a shared activity. Rarely had the house been more homogeneous, being made up of nobles and gentlemen of the Court and their ladies, together with some country gentry and their wives, a few civil officials like Samuel Pepys and some aspirant businessmen and professionals – altogether a narrow and sophisticated, if noisy, audience. It even found the playwrights from its own number and shared with them a common ground of privilege and social attitude. Intrusive playhouse humour was therefore legion, especially in the comedies. Only a Restoration actress like Elizabeth Barry (1658–1713), who probably played Mrs Loveit in Etherege's *The Man of Mode* (1676), could have accused her lover Dorimant of going behind the scenes and fawning upon 'those little insignificant creatures, the players' (2.2), when she herself was a player who had doubtlessly enjoyed similar attentions.

The players and the style of performance

Because of the King's approval and the Court's support, the actors eventually acquired new status and gained a small degree of respect – although the moral stigma of rascality and vagrancy remained until this century. With the establishment of regular companies again, and as the business of acting took on professional characteristics, individual players attracted admiration and gained a reputation for the stirring delivery of tragic verse or witty timing and comportment in comedy. Thomas Betterton (*c.* 1635–1710) was the leading actor in the Duke's company, and he is known to have taught his art in later years to others. A company numbered over twenty and performed six days a week every afternoon all year, except in the summer when audiences dwindled. A play did not expect to run for much above three days, so that repertories were large, and an actor was expected to recall his part with a quick rehearsal for up to a year. Each repertory was made up of plays new and old (Jonson, Beaumont and Fletcher were the popular choices from Jacobean times), as well as some pieces freely 'borrowed' and 'Englished' from France and Spain. When Lewis Hallam took a small company to America in 1752, his repertory consisted of no fewer than twenty-four plays 'and their attendant farces'. The players were always in the throes of learning and rehearsing when not on the stage, and probably had frequent recourse to making up their lines as they went along.

The actor's costume for tragedy did not aim at period authenticity – this was a development that took hold a century later. But the genre itself dictated that a tragic hero or heroine should be immediately recognizable, always by being dressed colourfully and especially by wearing heroic feathers. The Prologue to Sir John Vanbrugh's *The Mistake* (1705) reports,

> With audiences composed of belles and beaux,
> The first dramatic rule is, Have good clothes . . .
> In lace and feather tragedy's expressed,
> And heroes die unpitied, if ill-dressed.
>
> (*Revels History of Drama* (1976), p. 146)

And in *The Spectator* for 18 April 1711 we may read again that 'The ordinary method of making an hero, is to clap a huge plume of feathers upon his head.' The feathered head-dress persisted until Garrick's day.

M?SMITH *in the Character of* ALEXANDER.

When Glory like the dazling Eagle stood,
Perch'd on my Beaver in the Granick Flood.

10 William Smith as Alexander in Nathaniel Lee's *The Rival Queens* (1677) at Drury Lane in 1778: the tragic hero wore a mixture of eye-catching styles and an obligatory head-dress of feathers.

In comedy, stage costume was always 'modern dress', since the actor had to compete in appearance with the beaux in the audience, often wearing a patron's discarded clothes. His ability to wear his wardrobe well frequently became a source of humour in the lines, and was at the heart of the fop as a character. The principal item was a highly embroidered coat reaching to his knees, with noticeably wide cuffs and pockets low about his legs. Lace and ribbon trimmed his shirt and his shoes displayed a pair of high red heels. He wore or carried a plumed hat at all times, and his hair was as long as he could grow it – by the end of the century it was necessary to wear a full-bottomed wig that tumbled over his shoulders to provide the masses of curls deemed necessary. By that time cheeks of lacquered rouge punctuated with beauty spots were also the fashion for men as well as women. It follows that comedy made the most of 'smoking' [teasing and ridiculing] a country cousin like Sir Wilfull in Congreve's *The Way of the World* (1700), who enters a drawing-room in a dirty riding-habit and with mud on his boots. But the best of the jokes surrounded the indecorous behaviour of the beau who boasted French excesses and eccentricities. The Sir Foplings and the Lord Foppingtons carved a unique place for the fop on the English stage for the next two hundred years.

With such clothes and such particularity the Restoration beau's *levée* became a monstrous ritual, and in comedy the elaborate business of dressing for the day regularly presented opportunities for scenes of satirical laughter. The introduction of Lord Foppington in Vanbrugh's *The Relapse* (1696), 1.3, is an outstanding example of this ceremony, since in his outrageous vanity this creature first presents himself as if he is milord at an imaginary reception while he is still in a state of extreme and ludicrous *undress* – wearing nightcap, nightgown and bare or slippered feet. Thus the audience sees him as he is, and before he is reconstructed little by little to become a magnificent figure of arrogance and conceit. Here is altogether a brilliant and hilarious case of appearance contrasted with reality, and dramatized by slow degrees before the spectator's eyes.

The actor's props, like those of the beaux in the audience, were extensions of himself, effective instruments to display his behaviour in society. His hat and sword he wore indoors and out, and it was a test of his social aplomb for him to manage them so that they did not manage *him* – as when his hat disarranged his peruke or his sword plucked at a lady's skirts. He knew how to present himself well and make a conversational point by a graceful flick of his kerchief, or by taking an astute pinch of snuff. As the peruke grew bigger, so it acquired a life of its own: when Colley Cibber played Sir Novelty Fashion in his own comedy *Love's Last Shift* (1696), the audience applauded wildly when footmen carried his wig on stage in a sedan chair. It demanded the nice use of the comb on a curl, and the careful toss of the head to accompany a twist or a bow if the wearer were not to be blinded by his own hair. In Etherege's *She Would If She Could* (1668), 3.3, the pimp Rake-hell actually advises Sir Oliver Cockwood that a gentleman should never make love without wearing his wig, and the audience is left to imagine any problems that might arise.

King Charles II was also responsible for the appearance of *the actress* on the English stage. On his travels abroad he had enjoyed watching actresses perform, and now he cleverly found a reason that overcame the former objection to having the female sex exhibit itself in a play: was it not as offensive for the male sex to wear skirts? His patent of 1662 required women to play female parts, and they wasted no time in attracting audiences by their charm and appeal, not to mention the novelty of their presence. Thereafter a play could not risk its success without them, and theatrical history was never the same again.

Essentially, the Restoration actress brought sexuality to the theatre in a palpable, though not in any more realistic, way and the content of the drama suffered a calculated and a permanent change. Plays were now written which exploited the actress's sexuality, even to including scenes of flirtation and temptation, coquetry and seduction, and dressing and undressing (the '*toilette*'). As a convenient way of exhibiting those parts of the actress's anatomy that were normally concealed, the comedy developed the expedient of 'breeches scenes' which required her to wear male clothing for a good part of the play in order to exhibit her hips and legs, and place her in compromising situations. This had nothing in common with the theatrical tranvestism of the Elizabethan stage, where, of course, the female parts were played by the male sex.

Like the actor who had to rival the gentlemen in the audience, the actress had to compete in her costume and accoutrements to some degree with the ladies. Her dress constituted a riot of colour in a richly decorated *manteau* and train, and the petticoats that buoyed and buttressed them. *Décolletage* was lacy and low, and the bodice was stiff with vicious stays that shaped her appearance and controlled her every movement. Sitting was a critical matter of keeping bolt upright on the edge of the chair without missing it altogether, and walking and turning required the graceful government of her skirts and train.

Of the actress's many personal accessories in this period, two in particular served the comedies well and demanded her strictest attention: her vizard mask and her fan. The mask came into vogue early in the period and soon became the device by which a lady might appear incognito in public; as such it was indispensable, and she would not walk out without it, holding it ready to slip into place with pins; she could also hold it by a button caught between her teeth. The mask furnished the occasion for more flirtatious tricks played on the male sex, and in Thomas Shadwell's *A True Widow* (1678) the girls Isabella and Gartrude delight in visiting the playhouse in their masks in order to spy on their lovers. Sometimes, however, matters were complicated by the fact that prostitutes themselves wore masks when plying their trade in the playhouse or the street (they were, indeed, nicknamed 'vizards'). Naturally, when the mask was in use on the comic stage, the audience always had the pleasure of anticipating the moment when it would be removed.

A lady's use of the fan emerged later in the century, and became so important an extension of herself indoors and out that she would be considered to be 'undressed' if she forgot it. Edith Evans, perhaps the finest Millamant of modern times, believed that 'the only thing you can't do with a fan is fan yourself' (*Plays and Players* (December 1976), 39). At all times it visually signalled a lady's mood and could convey a whole vocabulary of silent commentary – pleasure or anger, consent or refusal. With its aid an aside could be delivered easily, and it was even possible to conduct an intrigue with two gentlemen at one time, the fan directing attention to one of them while simultaneously excluding the other. Probably because it was always in use, this accessory is rarely mentioned in stage directions, but when it is, the moment is sensational. Such a moment comes in Etherege's *The Man of Mode*, 2.2, when Mrs Loveit does the unthinkable and '*tears her fan in pieces*', signalling that the scene has reached a crisis and that her affair with Dorimant is at an impasse. However, when she has lost control of *herself*, the fan has also lost its magic properties.

As in good society, so on the stage, *the style of performance* was the passport to success and the *sine qua non*. The intimate conditions of the Restoration playhouse made all the more striking the ranting and canting of speech in tragedy and the kind of large, artificial gesture that was normal before Garrick. Betterton set the example, and when Edmund Curll published *The History of the English Stage* in 1741, he recorded the great actor's rules for dramatic speaking: for example, the actor expressed his love

> by a gay, soft, charming voice; his hate, by a sharp, sullen and severe one; his joy, by a full flowing and brisk voice; his grief, by a sad, dull and languishing tone; not without sometimes interrupting the continuity of the sound with a sigh or groan, drawn from the very inmost of the bosom.

Along with this kind of ranting went a host of appropriate gestures:

> You must lift up or cast down your eyes, according to the nature of the things you speak of; thus if of heaven, your eyes naturally are lifted up; if of earth, or hell, or anything terrestrial, they are naturally cast down ...
>
> You must never let either of your hands hang down, as if lame or dead; for that is very disagreeable to the eye, and argues no passion in the imagination ... I am of opinion that the hands in acting ought very seldom to be wholly quiescent.

(74–94)

J. H. Wilson put some of this together to provide an account of the totally conventional and unrealistic behaviour of the heroic lover:

> The posture of a dejected lover was like that of a man hanged, with his hands before him and his head on one side. Sometimes the unhappy lover wandered about the stage sighing, with his hand on his heart and his hat pulled down on his brows.
>
> He knelt to plead, stood erect to triumph, shook his fist in anger, beat his breast in sorrow, and flourished a handkerchief to mop up theatrical tears.
>
> (*A Preface to Restoration Drama* (1965), 24–5)

Far from eliciting laughter, the actor who was not master of all this posturing was unacceptable. As with ballet, there is pleasure to be had in witnessing the exquisite execution of movement and gesture, and even if the words were inaudible, the spectator had a fair idea of what was being said by watching these stage gyrations.

It was different in comedy, where prose speech and realistic behaviour perforce followed the norms established by the audience – except that the typical situations and characters of the plays were rather more spicy than real life. A Melantha and a Margery Pinchwife, a Millamant and a Mrs Sullen, were free spirits whose conduct was expected to go beyond the social sanctions of the time. The rakes Horner and Dorimant may have been modelled upon the Earl of Rochester and his like, but their conduct was nevertheless a glorious exaggeration of the truth, an audacious stretching of the possibilities.

Needless to say, the artificial gesticulating of the tragic stage, and its accompanying bombast, gave place in comedy to the range of pantomimic speech and behaviour that composed the 'manners' of social intercourse. In a notable passage in Etherege's *The Man of Mode* Harriet and Young Bellair teach one another how to convince their watching parents that they are courting:

> BELLAIR. Will you take your turn and be instructed?
> HARRIET. With all my heart!
> BELLAIR. At one motion play your fan, roll your eyes, and then settle a kind look upon me.
> HARRIET. So.

BELLAIR. Now spread your fan, look down upon it, and
tell the sticks with a finger.
HARRIET. Very modish!
BELLAIR. Clap your hand up to your bosom, hold down
your gown, shrug a little, draw up your breasts, and let 'em
fall again gently, with a sigh or two.

(3.1)

There is more, and these two exaggerate to emphasize every
point in front of their eavesdroppers, but it is clear that
Etherege enjoys taking inventory of social behaviour and
drawing attention to it. The provocations of the beau and the
teasing glances of the coquette were at the heart of Restoration
comic entertainment, and when in addition the actor displayed
his 'parts' and the actress her 'charms', drama had become a
positive exhibition.

Heroic drama and its conventions: *The Conquest of Granada, The Rehearsal*

There was almost no middle path between the dramatic genres
of the Restoration, which consisted of either light-hearted
comedy or the oppressively sober drama known as 'heroic'
(from the rhyming heroic verse in which it was composed).
Some early comedy chose to mix the slight and the serious,
but without producing the integrated tragi-comedy of the
Jacobean years. The Restoration heroic play – not to be called
a 'tragedy' because a happy end was *de rigueur* – was one of
the more short-lived forms in the history of the theatre,
lasting for ten or so years, and its popularity in its own time
remains something of a puzzle. However, it was born of a
troubled period of war and threats of war – at home the Civil
War itself and then Monmouth's rebellion, and abroad the
troubles in Ireland and the running maritime conflict with the
Dutch. In effect, the Restoration theatre had an audience of
self-consciously royalist cavaliers, the loyal 'Heroicks' of the
Civil War, and this may explain the general approval of the
heroic drama and its conspicuously ceremonial elements. The
spirit and style of opera was also carried over into the heroic

play in its glorious themes, inflated speech and rhyming couplets.

The heroic play has been charged with being based on theory and not practice. It was built very much to a formula and was conscious of its own decorum, deriving perhaps from the man who had been tutor to the King, Thomas Hobbes, and his thinking about heroic poetry, which was 'to raise admiration, principally for three virtues, valour, beauty, and love'. Decorum decreed that the feeling to inspire was that of admiration and wonder, which Aristotle had unaccountably neglected in his *Poetics*, emotions usually prompted by the presentation of a heroic figure making a noble choice between love and honour. He nourished an obligatory sense of poetic justice, justifying the axiom that 'None but the brave deserve the fair.' Nor did a hero have to die to be admired or a heroine be miserable to be virtuous. The same propriety required that Dryden in *All for Love* (1678) should see that Antony and Cleopatra were 'famous patterns of unlawful love, and their end accordingly was unfortunate' (the Preface, 9–11), and that in his *Troilus and Cressida* (1679) he should save Troilus from a final ambiguous exit by granting him a tragic death; and, in the most notorious example of all, that Nahum Tate (1652–1715) in his version of *King Lear* (1681) should reinstate Lear on his throne and marry Cordelia to Edgar.

This sort of justice savagely reduced the element of unpredictability in the drama, and when the Aristotelian tragic precepts of pity and fear again became the playwright's target, the heroic formula had nothing to offer and the vein ran dry. Nevertheless, the heroic stage followed its ideals. The characters – the hero a great soldier and lover, the heroine a paragon of purity – were superhuman in the way they thought, spoke and looked, and the events of the play were exalted and sublime. In his essay 'Of Heroic Plays' (1672) Dryden argued that the heroic poet was 'not tied to a bare representation of what is true, or exceeding probable'. To let go of reality gave him 'a freer scope for imagination' and by allowing him to manipulate his material, helped him 'to raise the imagination of the audience'. But in spite of the powerful example of the French neo-classical stage, Dryden in his *Essay of Dramatic Poesy* (1668) had already questioned the use of the Unities to create an illusion of reality, and it was not long before the popular tradition in English drama urged the return of disruptive, non-classical elements including violent action on stage, double plots, comedy and pathos.

The plotting of the heroic play engendered huge emotional conflicts, with the martial hero torn between his love and his duty to his country, and the virtuous heroine torn between her love and her duty to her father. Matters were often painfully complicated by the fact that the lady in question was the daughter of the hero's worst enemy, perhaps a villain who had usurped the throne or a despot of unspeakable evil. After such godlike characters and so sublime a theme, it is possible to identify the regularly supportive characteristics of the heroic drama:

- a romantic *setting* in a faraway country, like mysterious and exotic Spain, Mexico, India, Morocco and Peru.
- a spectacular stage of *painted scenes*: a splendid palace, a frightening forest, an ocean complete with shipping.
- the use of *machines* and sensational effects: thunder and lightning, gunpowder and explosion, ghosts and spirits from the trap or flown in the sky.
- *music and song*, left over from the opera, with drums and trumpets or singing and dancing, as appropriate.
- an elevated *diction* of extravagant, bombastic words, all rant and rave, spoken often in similes and usually in rhyming couplets.

One of the reasons why this genre produced no master-pieces was because of the unnatural style of speech, which consisted of such stilted couplets that no actor who spoke them could make them come alive. Yet the couplet was seen as integral to the form, and was given Dryden's formal blessing in *An Essay of Dramatic Poesy*, in which 'Neander' argues that a serious play is 'nature wrought up to an higher pitch' and heroic rhyme most suitable for tragedy 'as being the noblest kind of modern verse' (91). This essay is essential reading in the attempt to understand the thinking of Restoration heroic dramatists. The paradox is that the monotonous straitjacket of language, which so paralyzed the drama, was considered to be a kind of stagecraft in itself, an important part of the show. Perhaps it worked with some of the conventional musical function associated with opera. Nevertheless, when Nathaniel Lee (1653–92) decided to return to blank verse for *The Rival Queens* (1677), Dryden promptly followed suit in *All for Love*. This was his instinctive choice – blank verse had completely proved itself as a versatile vehicle for drama both high and low in the first part of the century.

John Dryden was the most prolific playwright of the age; he knew his audience well and his versatility enabled him to write with equal assurance both heroic plays of the artificial kind and witty social comedy in a more natural vein. He also chose to be at the centre of every critical issue, and after the *Essay of Dramatic Poesy*, his preface to *The Conquest of Granada* ('Of Heroic Plays', 1672) and his preface to *Troilus and Cressida* on neo-classical tragedy ('The Grounds of Criticism in Tragedy', 1679) help document the controversies of the day.

The *Conquest of Granada*, staged by the King's Company at the Theatre Royal, came in two parts and ten acts. Part I was produced in December 1670 and Part II in January 1671, and thereafter played to great applause on successive nights with the dashing Charles Hart as the magnificent Almanzor, and the inimitable Nell Gwyn as his noble Queen Almahide (acted against her natural bent for comedy). While this was not Dryden's best work, it exemplifies all the extravagant features of the heroic play, and to see it was to pass into the world of elegant fantasy its author wanted.

After its length, its excesses were seen in its lavish spectacle. The scene (painted by Robert Streeter) was elaborate and expensive, an image of sumptuous oriental luxury. The stage for the most part represented the red décor of the splendid Alhambra, the Moorish palace and fortress of Granada, the glorious images of *patio* and *sala* no doubt supplemented by the towers and ramparts of the citadels of Alcazaba and Albayzyn; the Vivarambla also appeared as if 'filled with spectators'. Every opportunity was taken to introduce exotic music and dance, like Almahide's Moorish festival of the Zambra in Part I, act 3. Almanzor kneels to his lady and declaims,

A happiness so high I cannot bear;
My love's too fierce, and you too killing fair.

(4.3.210–11)

The lines convey all the high-flown, knotted sentiments
heroic drama could desire, and in the mind's eye it is not
difficult to supply the appropriately colourful gestures of
tangled anguish to accompany them. The drama's content was
a model of heroic correctness, as John Evelyn's wife Mary
recorded in a letter: 'Since my last to you I have seen 'The
Siege of Granada', a play so full of ideas that the most refined
romance I ever read is not to compare with it; love is made so
pure and valour so nice that one would imagine it destined for
an Utopia rather than our stage' (J. H. Wilson, *A Preface to
Restoration Drama* (1965), 71).

As could be expected, a successful burlesque of the
heroic play appeared immediately after *The Conquest of
Granada*. This was *The Rehearsal* (1671) by George Villiers, Duke of Buckingham (1628–87), written some years
before, but delayed and awaiting a good target for its
attack. In this Buckingham caricatured Dryden as the poet
Bayes, and the story goes that he coached the comedian
John Lacy in the part, dressed him in Dryden's clothes, and
then took the poet to the playhouse to watch him squirm;
however, Bayes also represents any heroic playwright of
the day. The play's outstandingly useful device is to present
itself as a rehearsal, as a play-within-a-play, so that as the
action proceeds the author may solemnly explain his intentions to friends – and to the audience. Much of the fun
arises from the direct parody of lines from *The Conquest of
Granada*, but *The Rehearsal* provides an excellent compendium of the heroic conventions, each one of them ripe for
travesty.

The hero, now named Drawcansir, is unmistakably Almanzor: he is described by Bayes as 'a fierce hero, that frights
his mistress, snubs up kings, baffles armies, and does what he
will without regard to numbers, good manners, or justice'
(4.1), and when it comes to it he enters the battlefield '*and
kills them all on both sides*' (5.1). The exposition of what the
spectator needs to know is always a necessary convention,

and here it is mercilessly travestied when it is clumsily executed by underlings such as these:

> PHYSICIAN. Sir, by your habit, I should guess you to be the
>   Gentleman-Usher of this sumptuous palace.
> GENTLEMAN-USHER. And by your gait and fashion, I
>   should almost suspect you rule the healths of
>   both our noble Kings, under the notion of
>   Physician.
> PHYSICIAN. You hit my function right.
> GENGLEMAN-USHER. And you mine.
> PHYSICIAN. Then let's embrace.

(2.1)

Great armies wage war and are conveniently represented by eight soldiers with swords drawn, four at one door and four at another; to the sound of music the battle begins on the cry, 'Fall on!' and ends with *'They all kill one another'* (2.5); when the music strikes up again, the soldiers rise from the dead – to dance or kill again, as the case may be. The burlesque is rich in special effects, as when the two legitimate kings of the plot are to ascend their thrones, *'they descend in the clouds, singing, in white garments'* (5.1), and when the final battle *'is fought between foot and great hobby-horses'* (5.1) a stagey attempt at realism grotesquely miscarries.

This is a small sample of the host of theatrical jokes served up in the play, which set the guide-lines for many burlesques written in the next century. The formula of the 'rehearsal play' provided the perfect vehicle for the in-house humour of burlesque drama, because it set author, critic and audience on the same stage in order to subvert them all. In order to succeed, parody and burlesque need bad or overworked drama to begin with, as well as an audience familiar with it. There is always the difficulty that the drama to be sent up is *so bad* that it is already a parody of itself: there are limits to the ridiculous. In the case of Buckingham's play, the chief object of its ridicule, *The Conquest of Granada*, withstood the joke and continued to hold the stage for several years, but *The Rehearsal* itself remained popular in its own right throughout the next century, with its last professional production played as late as 1819.

The comedy of the sexes: *The Man of Mode, The Country Wife, The Way of the World, The Beaux' Stratagem*

The greatest achievement of the Restoration stage was to lay the foundations of a quintessentially English comic mode, and create a carefully cultivated vehicle of verbal wit intended to exhibit the battle of the sexes. The mode, in its many variations, may be traced through the comedy of Goldsmith and Sheridan, Pinero and Oscar Wilde, Shaw and Noel Coward, to the present day. In his *Lectures on the English Comic Writers* (1819), Hazlitt considered the years following the return of Charles II to be 'the golden period of our comedy' and his verdict, while addressed to a less robust age and somewhat apologetic, made its point:

> In turning over the pages of the best comedies, we are almost transported to another world, and escape from this dull age to one that was all life, and whim, and mirth, and humour ... We are admitted behind the scenes like spectators at court, on a levée or birthday.
>
> (70)

It was the comedy of a coterie and an intimate playhouse, and its audience enjoyed sharing the mocking perception of its own social and sexual behaviour with author and actor.

To some extent it may be claimed that in Restoration comedy 'realism' took the stage in earnest for the first time, and this is acceptable provided that it is recognized that it did not reflect the real world with any accuracy – this awaited the naturalistic movement inspired by the drama of Ibsen, Strindberg and Chekhov. Firstly, speech and behaviour on the comic stage of the Restoration was guided by a strongly satirical impulse and cast a necessarily distorting eye over what it saw. Secondly, for many years its subjects were limited to those affecting a homogeneous minority of the Court and the upper classes.

Nevertheless, the social decorum on the comic stage reflected that of the audience, and since speech and behaviour are indivisible and the players' lines must match their manners, Restoration comic stagecraft had much to do with

domestic and social conduct. If stage and conventional innovations were therefore few in the comedy of the period, novel
developments are found in the style of speech and performance. Points of growth may be identified:

(1) The Restoration stage invented a scintillating prose
    'reparty' [repartee] with its appropriate gesture and move-
    ment to suit the range of sexual situations and love-games
    newly open to it.
(2) In the traditional relationship of comedy the actors had
    the special task of satisfying a critical audience which was
    already intimately associated with the life-style it was
    witnessing on the stage.
(3) The presence of real women as actresses to replace the
    beardless boys of earlier years cried out for devices of
    plotting and performance to make the most of their
    physical presence.

The plays of the courtier and diplomat Sir George Etherege (c.
1634–91) set a standard of comic prose dialogue that was
elegantly witty and delicately civil. It was always a calculated
speech that was much more than any 'language really used by
men' such as Wordsworth wanted for his *Lyrical Ballads*.
According to Richard Steele in *The Spectator*, no. 65 of 1711,
it was the received opinion that Etherege's *The Man of Mode*
was 'the pattern of genteel comedy'. First produced in Dorset
Garden Theatre with the two best-known actors of the day,
Betterton as the rake Dorimant and Elizabeth Barry as the
original Mrs Loveit, this play was a firm success and continued so through most of the next century. After 1766 it was
not thought possible for so *risqué* a piece to find a new
audience, but in 1971 the Royal Shakespeare Company dar-
ingly up-dated it in jet-set style with Alan Howard as a new
version of the languid and carefree lecher.

If the play lacks much of the tension expected of drama,
from start to finish it persistently worked on the spectator's
non-dramatic interests. This began by modelling the manner
and style of Dorimant on London's most notorious profligate,
the Earl of Rochester – who no doubt was a happy member of
the audience himself. More importantly, the action, such as it

is, traces some four of Dorimant's amorous affairs, each differing from the last and presented almost like a guide to the range of possible amorous intrigues. The passionate but possessive Mrs Loveit and the complaisant and submissive Bellinda supply examples of how not to behave towards the opposite sex, and the innocent and virtuous Emilia and the shrewd and clever Harriet of how to outwit it. There are other women thrown in for good measure – Molly the whore, the superannuated Lady Woodvill, and other intrigues are glanced at in the elderly lust of Old Bellair and the sexual vanity of Sir Fopling, but each is marked by its emphasis on the etiquette and decorum called for by the occasion.

Key encounters therefore come across as exhibitions of polite speech and behaviour and Etherege seizes every opportunity to offer advice and make points to his self-interested audience. Act 1 is devoted to Dorimant's *levée* with much of the care appropriate to that of the fair sex. Then when the audience meets Mrs Loveit in act 2, she is already dressed, but still studying herself in a pocket glass with obsessive *amour propre*. When in act 3 the audience meets Harriet, however, and has a first sight of the one who is destined to master him, she is preparing to meet the day with a refreshing difference:

> BUSY.   Dear madam, let me set that curl in order.
> HARRIET. Let me alone, I will shake 'em all out of
>   order! ...
> BUSY.   Look, there's a knot falling off.
> HARRIET. Let it drop.

The demonstration complete, the explanation is not far to seek:

> BUSY.   Ah, the difference that is between you and my
>   Lady Dapper! How uneasy she is if the least
>   thing be amiss about her! ...
> HARRIET. Her powdering, painting, and her patching
>   never fail in public to draw the tongues and
>   eyes of all the men upon her.

This lady will evidently not be a slave to convention, or to the other sex, and the petulance in all those 'ps' immediately alerts the audience to the fact that to catch Harriet Dorimant will have to play his cards in some other way.

When the two confront each other at Lady Townley's salon in act 4, Etherege ironically plays off the visibly polite courtesies against their equivocally polite exchanges. There is more than a touch of mockery in both Dorimant's bow and Harriet's curtsy:

> DORIMANT. Where had you all that scorn and coldness in
>   your look?
> HARRIET. From nature, sir; pardon my want of art. I have
>   not learnt those softnesses and languishings
>   which now in faces are so much in fashion.

Their flirtation is a fencing-match in which two foils are probing for advantage; but neither party is giving ground and each is parrying with a thrust. The effect is all achieved with the words, which are rich in tone and alive with body language.

The Man of Mode is a rare compendium of sexual manners of coquettes and their beaux, but it also embodies an extraordinary guide to the fashions of the day. When Mrs Loveit is raging at Dorimant, his barb is cruelly aimed at the whole of the fair sex:

> What unlucky accident puts you out of humour – a point ill-washed, knots spoiled i' the making up, hair shaded awry, or some other little mistake in setting you in order?
>
> (2.2)

Dorimant is countering her attack in terms of a lady's *toilette*, almost as if her appearance and her temper were akin. When in scenes that are irrelevant to the trials of Dorimant, Sir Fopling Flutter comes 'piping hot from Paris', he and his infatuation with the latest French styles steal the show entirely. In 3.2, almost the middle of the play, he makes his first majestic entrance with a page to announce and attend him, and in all his new splendour he circles the stage saluting each astonished guest in turn. He then proceeds without much ado to display and comment on every detail of his dress, the catalogue growing faster and faster until he spins into an ecstatic dance. In 3.3, his second entrance in the Mall (at that date a walk in St James's Park) is embellished by a procession of six immaculate French footmen. For Lady Townley's ball in 4.1, he arrives magnificently masked (in

1971 John Wood as Sir Fopling was carried in as a caricature of the Sun King, no less) and believing himself incognito, although no one can mistake him.

This was an age of great stage fops – Mr Frenchlove in James Howard's *The English Monsieur* (1666), Monsieur de Paris in Wycherley's *The Gentleman Dancing-Master* (1672), the eponymous hero of John Crowne's *Sir Courtly Nice* (1685), Lord Foppington in Vanbrugh's *The Relapse* (1697) – but in Sir Fopling Etherege set the standard. Dryden saw him as the perfect fop and thought him calculated to hit a wide satirical target: 'Legion's his name, a people in a man' (the Epilogue); but Bonamy Dobrée's comment in *Restoration Comedy* (1924), 74, that 'Life would be the duller without him' suggests that satire was not uppermost in the author's mind when he created this fop: he seems to embody the joyful spirit of his play and his innocent vanity is infectious. He and his displays of dress and behaviour in park and drawing-room highlight the London world and its lotus life-style, and Etherege captures it all in his easy and cynical way. There is little criticism, less moralizing: neither Etherege nor his audience have any wish to mend their ways. The result is a delicate balance of humour and sympathy, related more to Chekhov than to Shaw.

What of stagecraft? In his previous play, *She Would If She Could* (1668), Etherege took a professional interest in making use of the stage he was presented with in Lincoln's Inn Fields. In act 2, he made exceptional use of the free space of the stage and its proscenium doors, in order to recreate a sense of the walks in Mulberry Garden and the pursuit by Courtall and Freeman of their willing prey, the girls Ariana and Gatty disguised with their vizards: he arranged the chase to run back and forth through all four entrances and across both upper and lower parts of the platform. In *The Man of Mode* there is none of this. In 2.1 the stage is Lady Townley's house, in 3.3 the Mall, and in each scene virtually all the characters circulate freely, only occasionally coming together in clusters. In this play location is less material, and Etherege successfully executes his design primarily by diverting sexual power-plays expressed in his polite exchanges of wit.

The novelty of seeing women on the stage for the first time prompted a new and unusual development in Restoration comic stagecraft, that of requiring the actress to wear male clothing and reveal more of her figure. Evidently as a stunt Thomas Killigrew put on his earlier *The Parson's Wedding* in 1664 cast only with women, and Beaumont and Fletcher's *Philaster* and Dryden's *Secret Love* also received this treatment. This play also permitted Nell Gwyn as Florimel to play a 'roaring girl' and swagger in breeches to mock the male sex. Here she is admiring herself in a mirror:

> Save you, Monsieur Florimel! Faith, methinks you are a very jaunty fellow, *poudré et adjusté* as well as the best of 'em. I can manage the little comb, set my hat, shake my garniture, toss about my empty noddle, walk with a courant slur, and at every step peck down my head.
>
> (5.1)

The 'breeches scenes', with women in men's clothing, were written for about a quarter of the comedies in the beginning, and plot after plot was devised to exploit the actress's sexuality and put her in titillating situations. These were parts that enabled an ambitious actress to better her lot, like Nell Gwyn and Elizabeth Barry, by finding a wealthy 'keeper' from the audience. Only after the appearance of actresses on the stage became more common and the theatre more respectable did the breeches convention disappear.

The Country Wife (1675) by William Wycherley (1640–1716) has one of the best examples of a well-integrated breeches plot. The play borrowed the rudimentary and infallible story of the old husband with a young wife from Molière's *L'Ecole des femmes* and then introduced the libertine Horner, played by the elegant Charles Hart, as the attractive male lead who thinks up the vicious ruse of pretending impotence (the idea possibly borrowed from Terence's *Eunuchus*) in order to outwit gullible husbands and gain access to compliant wives. Horner is soon encouraged to believe that the simple country girl whom jealous old Pinchwife has married has been disguised as her own brother to hide her from the depravity of the Town. The breeches scenes begin when Horner tries to unmask her.

However, the creation of Margery Pinchwife, the supreme achievement of this comedy, owes nothing to any borrowings. She was played by Elizabeth Boutell, and Betterton's *History of the English Stage* (1741) records that this actress 'was low of stature, had very agreeable features, a good complexion, but a childish look ... she generally acted the young innocent lady whom all the heroes are mad in love with' (21). Her three roles in the play – as the unsophisticated wife, as the pretended boy in breeches and peruke, and as herself, the knowing actress – emerge essentially as singular products of the Restoration comic stage. All the elements of a theatrical charade are present in her, and her contribution to the comedy is shot through with innuendo and ambiguity to bewitch her audience.

In 3.2 Horner descends upon Pinchwife and Margery in the New Exchange and '*takes hold*' of her:

> HORNER. ... Prithee, Pinchwife, who is this pretty young
> gentleman?
> PINCHWIFE. One to whom I'm a guardian. – (*Aside*.) I
> wish I could keep her out of your hands.
> HORNER. Who is he? I never saw anything so pretty in
> all my life.
> PINCHWIFE. Pshaw! do not look upon him so much; he's
> a poor bashful youth, you'll put him out of
> countenance. – Come away, brother.

Pinchwife is trying to pull his wife away and Horner to hold her, with Margery the unwilling and willing pawn between them. While this goes on, all three in rivalry appeal for the support of the house through aside or glance or innuendo. During the dispute between the men, Margery's ambivalence is wonderfully conveyed when her attempt to keep a sober expression on her face, and to move and behave like a man is repeatedly betrayed by her blushes and giggles and wriggles of pleasure. For his part Horner is determined to make her reveal her true sex and change back from boy to girl by handling her, flattering her with that reiterated epithet 'pretty' and, finally, making a blatant statement of his love. Meanwhile the furious Pinchwife has trapped himself by his own trickery, and tries not to repossess her lest he reveal her identity. In any case his protestations that she is 'a poor bashful youth' are utterly betrayed by her obvious eagerness to hear more. All the principals are playing a double game, with Horner increasingly tormenting Pinchwife, teasing Margery and gratifying himself at Pinchwife's expense. However, Margery herself enjoys her predicament every bit, and when in the end Horner and his friends kiss her one after the other, her disguise is forgotten, the truth about her identity is transparent and she is in a dizzy heaven of delight. As Margery moves away from her gaoler towards the friendly audience, it cannot be sure whether her vibrant voice is that of an innocent girl or a knowing actress.

Such pregnant situations are strongly devised for verbal innuendo and improvisational acting and conveyed in a dialogue that for the first time in this period allowed the audience to hear itself speaking. Nevertheless, the world of the play is peopled by Horners and Pinchwifes, Fidgets and Squeamishes, and the characters can only be taken as the caricatures their names suggest. For, unlike Etherege's, the play moves at a brisk pace on the level of farce, and its cool tone is wholly unsentimental. Horner's adultery is observed with a dry, comic eye, and when he is finally cornered by the women in the notorious 'china scene' (4.3), even he becomes an object of laughter. The technique of performance in this play is one of unemotional distancing, developing theatre as a social game in order to project a mad vision of wild and licentious sexuality.

In 1675 at Drury Lane *The Country Wife* took London by storm. The text was reprinted five times in twenty years, and the play remained popular on the stage well into the next century. Eventually its explicit subject-matter and outdated manners prompted a bland, expurgated version by David Garrick who renamed it *The Country Girl* (1766), but the evisceration proved to be its undoing. When Montague Summers revived the original to gasps of horror and dismay in 1924, it came up fresh as paint, and the modern London stage saw the first of a long line of modern Margerys played with every interpretation from country bumpkin to sly child bride, and it included some of the best comediennes of this century: Isabel Jeans, Ruth Gordon, Joan Plowright, Maggie Smith. It was also the start of the English stage's general rediscovery of the comic brilliance of the Restoration, a reassessment of its stageworthiness that has continued to this day with increasing admiration.

A note on the women playwrights: *The Rover*

It is a surprising consequence of the advent of women on the public stage in this period that a number of women also took to playwriting. Mary Cavendish, Duchess of Newcastle had published plays after 1662 with no intention of having them produced, and Katherine Philips had her tragedy *Pompey* produced in Dublin in 1663. It was altogether different with Aphra Behn (1640–89), who was 'forced to write for bread and not ashamed to own it', overcoming the immense social difficulties facing a woman writer. She wrote a prolific sixteen or eighteen plays (in 1677 no fewer than four comedies including *The Town-Fopp* and *The Rover*), boldly exploiting the new sexual licence, and before the end of the century her example had encouraged her more shadowy contemporaries Mary Pix, Mary De La Riviere Manley and Catherine Trotter to invade the stage chiefly with heroic tragedy. In the next century and contemporary with Farquhar, Susannah Centlivre (*A Bold Stroke for a Wife*, 1718) successfully continued the tradition in a less profane, sentimental style, and before the end of the century Elizabeth Inchbald (*Every One Has His Fault*, 1793) was writing a bitter-sweet comedy of domestic life. These writers brought with them a certain interest in familial issues and a more subtle psychological insight into married life.

Behn's themes are, however, of less interest than her craft. To draw an audience her comic situations were as bawdy as those of her male rivals. Her female characters were less passive and more witty, even more scandalous, than before, but she managed to bring a sly female perspective to the characterization of her men, whose sexual libidos usually revealed them as bullies, buffoons and foppish poseurs. In *The Rover*, the cavalier Willmore is 'the Rover' (first played by Betterton, possibly as a lusty travesty of the rakish Earl of

Rochester) who meets his match in verbal duels with Mrs Elizabeth Barry as the vivacious Hellena:

> WILLMORE. But hark'ee: the bargain is now made, but is
> it not fit we should know each other's names,
> that when we have reason to curse one another
> hereafter, and people ask me who 'tis I give to
> the devil, I may at least be able to tell what
> family you came of?
> HELLENA. Good reason, captain; and where I have cause,
> as I doubt not but I shall have plentiful, that I
> may know at whom to throw my – blessings, I
> beseech ye your name.
> WILLMORE. I am called Robert the Constant.
> HELLENA. A very fine name! Pray was it your faulkner
> [hawker] or butler that christened you? Do they
> not use to whistle when they call you?
> WILLMORE. I hope you have a better, that a man may
> name without crossing himself – you are so
> merry with mine.
> HELLENA. I am called Hellena the Inconstant.
>
> (act 5)

Such sparring of the sexes is in the impudent English tradition of Shakespeare's Beatrice and Benedick and Congreve's Mirabel and Millamant, and it here touches with its mockery, not only sex, but also society.

This is far from the 'woful' play expected of a woman: her scenes are spiced with wit and they sparkle with high-spirited slapstick and sword-play, as well as masquerades, disguises and breeches parts, for she is just as interested to expose the female anatomy to view as are her male counterparts, and to contrive immodest scenes that will ensure the success of her play. In one notorious scene (3.3) the 'jilting wench' Lucetta manages to have the puritanical Ned Blunt, a foolish country squire, strip to '*his shirt and drawers*' before he is unceremoniously dropped through a trap into a common 'shore' [sewer]. Florinda (played by Mary Betterton) is seen at night '*in an undress*', with a line to Willmore rich in its implicit direction, 'Wicked man, unhand me!' (3.5). In 4.2 the previously prospective nun Hellena pursues her man provocatively, if conventionally, dressed as a boy in breeches. In

4.5 Blunt is still in his drawers and offering Florinda violent rape:

> I will kiss and beat thee all over, kiss and see thee all over; thou shalt lie with me too, not that I care for the enjoyment, but to let thee see I have ta'en deliberate malice to thee, and will be revenged on one whore for the sins of another ...

In another audacious scene (act 5) which at first hints at the gang-rape of a well-born lady, the gentlemen draw swords to choose who shall have Florinda, at the time unknown to them because she is naughtily wearing the customary vizard-mask; however, the lucky man is none other than her brother Don Pedro, whose action when he gives chase thereby caps every-thing by suggesting the final outrage – incest.

It may be argued that Behn has appropriately placed her play and her predatory men in a world of Neapolitan carnival, one of courtesans and gipsies, masquing and dancing, but Linda LaBranche pointed out to me that the basic structure of the action in *The Rover*, for all its bristling intrigue and mistaken identity, has little to do with the subtlety of plotting and everything to do with a progressively physical 'towsing' of the actresses. The play advances from an anonymous, impersonal presentation of masked courtesans in the first act to the more particular and individualized licentiousness at the end – working out increasingly shocking scenes in which ladies of varying degrees of virtue are exposed to more and more sexual violence. Whether this is an instance of a certain shrewd feminism emerging on a militant Restoration stage is a question.

The comedy of the sexes tempered: *The Way of the World, The Beaux' Stratagem*

The 1690s were as theatrically animated, and as brazen, as the 1660s. The triplet of earlier comedies by William Congreve (1670–1729), *The Old Bachelor* (1693), *The Double Dealer*

(1694) and the lively *Love for Love* (1695), were written and well received in the best farcical and amoral spirit of the day, as were the racy and vivacious comedies of Thomas Shadwell (?1642–1692) with *The Squire of Alsatia* (1688) and *Bury Fair* (1689), and Sir John Vanbrugh (1664–1726) with *The Relapse* (1696) and *The Provoked Wife* (1697). However, it is thought that Congreve's next comedy, *The Way of the World* (1700), suffered at the box office because of the almost inevitable attack on the increasingly unbridled content of the London stage, although its failure in its own day may well have been due less to the new moralism than to its impossibly muddled plot. The attack came from the Rev. Jeremy Collier in his *Short View of the Immorality and Profaneness of the English Stage* (1698), and had the immediate effect of driving the Restoration jokes about sex and marriage into other channels.

Today, however, the reputation for being the most exquisite of all Restoration comedies and having the most subtle characterization rests with this same *The Way of the World*, which is nowadays often presented as something of a showpiece, a measure of an actor's accomplishment as a period stylist. It was played at Lincoln's Inn Fields with an all-star cast that included Elinor Leigh, an actress who delighted Colley Cibber with 'her very droll way of dressing the pretty foibles of superannuated beauties ... and modest stale maids that had missed their market' (*An Apology*, ch. 5); she had played the avid Lady Plyant in *The Double Dealer* and here she played her lusty successor, the doyenne Lady Wishfort. The cast also included the impeccable Anne Bracegirdle, who had inherited Elizabeth Boutell's parts and here played the radiant and sophisticated young Millamant. This comedy is a generation after *The Country Wife*, and Congreve is the contemporary of Addison and Steele, but it has the virtue of having notably re-created on stage a likeness of the way of life, if not of the way of the world, that its author perceived. He did it through a verbal control of tone and attitude, and the play provides a superb example of what a fastidious choice of words, a dancing style of speech and a confident pace and rhythm, could do to chisel out a character and animate it in performance.

11 William Congreve, *The Way of the World*, 1700. Mrs Pitt as
Lady Wishfort, act 3, in a print from Congreve's *Works*, 1776.

It is said that Congreve wrote the part of Millamant for Anne Bracegirdle (?1673–1748), whose admirer he was. If so, he flattered the character with lines that exhibit the actress's grace and charm, and direct her delicate coquetry, and some of her sparkle is captured in everything she says and does. Her first entrance in act 2 with the fop Witwoud in tow is announced unforgettably by her admirer Mirabell as if she were a ship at sea ('Here she comes, i'faith, full sail, with her fan spread and her streamers out, and a shoal of fools for tenders'), and when he asks why there is no 'flock of fine perukes' hovering round her, her languid dismissal of the question is heard in the brief witticism of 'Oh, I have denied myself airs today' as she slips away from him. Witwoud tries to get her attention with one or two quips, only to receive similar rebuffs: 'Dear Mr Witwoud, truce with your similitudes' and 'Mincing, stand between me and his wit', and again she spins away. When she finally accedes to Mincing's supposed reason for her tardiness, that she 'stayed to peruse a pecquet of letters', song and dance are in her celebrated lines:

> Oh, aye, letters; I had letters. I am persecuted with letters. I hate letters. Nobody knows how to write letters; and yet one has 'em, one does not know why. They serve one to pin up one's hair.

There is more here than the indifference of idleness. As she displays herself she finds time to change the subject twice, passing a comment on the epistolary art as well as putting down her questioner with the impertinent conceit of the throw-away coda. Such dialogue constitutes the notation for a ballet and is a stagecraft in itself.

Congreve's verbal wit and agility are used to mark the qualities in his comic characters in a variety of ways. In particular, his choice of words helps the actor to distinguish one character from another – a Witwoud, say, from a Mirabell:

> WITWOUD. My dear, I ask ten thousand pardons. Gad,
>   I have forgot what I was going to say to you!
> MIRABELL. I thank you heartily, heartily.

The decorum of speech is 'to frame each person so / That by his common talk you may his nature rightly know' (Richard Edwards, *Damon and Pithias*, (1571)). Congreve's choice of words permits his audience to anatomize a character and to know him by his speech.

The energy of wit also stoked the fire of innuendo and *double entendre*, the jokes and puns shared with the audience. They were always addressed to the house and thrived in the Restoration playhouse, since the intimate scale of performance and the homogeneity of speaker and spectator made such quips possible. It is not surprising, therefore, to find that the one convention of speech which especially flourished at this time was that of the *aside*. Since the actor entered downstage through a proscenium door, and played on the apron under chandeliers that also illuminated the audience, the aside, explicit and implicit (i.e., marked and unmarked), became ubiquitous, with some scenes alive with the consequent double-talk and the audience made forcibly aware of two views of the scene simultaneously.

Wycherley used the device more explicitly, and with particular gusto in contests between the Pinchwifes: 'O jeminy! Is this he that was in love with me?' – 'How she gazes on him! the devil!' Congreve's *The Way of the World*, by contrast, bristles with more implicit asides, especially in scenes in which the audience is to perceive the ironic levels of comedy more slyly. When, for example, Lady Wishfort prepares to meet her supposed lover Sir Rowland, she practises her postures and attitudes, explaining that 'A little scorn is alluring', her woman Foible's smooth response is, 'A little scorn becomes your ladyship' (act 3).

The new element emerging strongly in Congreve is one of *verbal humour*, in which wit results because of a discrepancy between a character's situation and what he says, the incongruity producing laughter. This effect upon an audience in the theatre has recently been named 'discrepant awareness'. In the mock courtship of Lady Wishfort and Sir Rowland, for example, the hoax forces a spirit of parody, verging on burlesque, upon the performance and colours everything said

by the two of them, so that the audience is acutely conscious
of their hypocrisy:

> LADY WISHFORT. If you think the least scruple of carnality
> was an ingredient –
> WAITWELL. Dear madam, no. You are all camphire and
> frankincense, all chastity and odour.

It is possible that a witty obliqueness was prompted by the
need to evade Collier's censoriousness. In any event, this style
of parody and verbal humour becomes a powerful tool in the
comedy of Farquhar.

George Farquhar (1678–1707) was among the first of the
Restoration comedians who were 'professionals'. He had had
some experience as an actor in Dublin's Smock Alley Theatre
and had there found a friend in the outstanding actor Robert
Wilks (1665–1732). All this was before Farquhar wrote a
series of effective comedies for the London stage; these
included *Sir Harry Wildair* (1701), which compromised with
Collier by making its hero a rake when he was drunk and a
moralist when he was sober. His last two comedies broke
with the urban tradition and were set in the country. *The
Recruiting Officer* (1706) profited from Farquhar's short
experience of a commission in the army, and had Shrewsbury
as its setting. Its hero, the recruiting officer, was Captain
Plume (played by Wilks), who did his recruiting in the
bedroom, and it invented a brilliant variation on the fop in the
regimental and uniformed Captain Brazen (played by Colley
Cibber (1671–1757), an actor who had a gift for playing fops:
Sir Novelty Fashion in his own *Love's Last Shift* (1696), and
Lord Foppington in Vanbrugh's *The Relapse*, among others).
Farquhar's play also created an exceptional breeches part for
his heroine, Silvia (Anne Oldfield): she joined the army as an
ensign to follow her lover and consequently found herself the
victim of some strange military rites of passage. It can be said
that in plotting, at least, Farquhar had a good sense of the
stage.

The Beaux' Stratagem (1707), played at the Haymarket,
was again set in the country, this time in Lichfield. The

provincial life it depicted was full of characters who suggest the wider range of interest in the play: a French prisoner of war and an Irish priest, an innkeeper and his daughter (Cherry the barmaid), a familiar country lady of good works and a highwayman – something of the Hogarthian world view is here, and the play smacks of the alehouse more than the boudoir. The young male lead has been multiplied to become Aimwell and Archer, a pair of rakes with their eye to the main chance, the first more principled than the second – retaining the best of both worlds, but essentially making another concession to the new morality. Their female objects of interest are two inviting prospects trapped in the country and observed with some sympathy: the young heiress Dorinda and the beautiful young wife of the repulsive Squire Sullen. The comedy consists in the efforts of the men to gain access to these ladies.

Farquhar's style of writing, however, is yet another kind of stagecraft. It has been characterized by some critics as romantic and sentimental, but in performance its parodistic language comes across with burlesque exuberance. Even the thinking about marital problems and divorce that surprisingly occurs in the last act is expressed with playful nonchalance. This verbal technique keeps reality at arm's length, diminishes an audience's resistance and ensures its freedom to laugh. The function is seen most clearly in the scenes of Archer's seduction of Mrs Sullen, where the sexuality is strong and the comic tension high; but it is all a trick.

Archer sees her portrait and promptly '*looks at the picture and Mrs Sullen three or four times, by turns*'.

> ARCHER. Pray, madam, who drew it?
> MRS SULLEN. A famous hand, sir.
> ARCHER. A famous hand, madam! Your eyes, indeed, are
> featured there, but where's the sparkling
> moisture, shining fluid, in which they swim?
> The picture indeed has your dimples, but
> where's the swarm of killing Cupids that should
> ambush there? ...

(4.1)

With the clever rake's repeated pausing, turning and staring at Mrs Sullen, his acting is marvellously overdone, like his words. The speech continues in this style of saccharine parody to a point of disbelief – at least for the audience, if not for the lady. Besides, in act 1 he had spoken to Cherry in much the same way. The next time Archer meets Mrs Sullen, the scene is her bedchamber, no less; provocatively, she is *'undressed'*, a bed has been pushed out and Archer is hiding in a 'closet', i.e., behind one of the proscenium doors. He leaps out and *'takes her hand'*.

> MRS SULLEN. What, sir, do you intend to be rude?
> ARCHER. Yes, madam, if you please.
> MRS SULLEN. In the name of wonder, whence came ye?
> ARCHER. From the skies, madam. I'm a Jupiter in love,
>   and you shall be my Alcmena.
>
> (5.2)

The rhythms and allusions are more ridiculous than ever. Archer is quickly on his knees to her and Mrs Sullen is soon running from him with a shriek that is too faint to be believed. The chase that ensues is round the formidable object that is her bed, until consummation is interrupted by the comic entrance of the servant Scrub *'in his breeches, and one shoe'*. The audience may decide whether this is romantic love or all an entertaining sham; at all events, Restoration comic form is bursting at the seams.

The last decades of the seventeenth century saw extreme differences of stage practice. If it is a matter for wonder that the wildly polarized genres since known as the heroic drama and the comedy of manners could share the same stage, it is no less strange that extremes of difference in stage setting and acting style could go with them. However, the solemn plays died and left only their structural engineering behind, whereas the conventions of the comedy lived on as an indestructible dramatic force. The former perpetuated a proscenium arch which could magically conceal a new spectacle that flourished and developed and became part of the concept of 'theatre' a wider public understood. The latter used the proscenium frame as a mirror to reflect a common humanity. Restoration comedy, whatever the moral verdict upon it, supported an enduring satire, a comfortable humour and a technique of sexual comedy that provided the basis for English drawing-room comedy to this day.

11

The Georgian theatre

Stage developments

The accession of George I to the British throne in 1714 offers a new point of departure in the story of the English playhouse and its stagecraft. The Georgian theatre confidently developed the system of scenic wings and shutters set in perspective and sliding in grooves – a system less common on the Continent – and this arrangement persisted to Irving's time. In eighteenth-century London the important changes came with the increasing size of the audience and the number of *the playhouses and their capacity*.

In 1660 Charles II licensed only two companies, and at the end of the century London had only three playhouses – Drury Lane, Lincoln's Inn Fields and Dorset Garden. By 1732, and in spite of the licensing restrictions, London's bigger and socially wider audience enjoyed five playhouses:

(1) The *Theatre Royal, Drury Lane*, which had followed the contentious management of Christopher Rich (from 1693 to his death in 1714) with a management by a 'Triumvirate' of veteran actors: Colley Cibber, Robert Wilks and Thomas Doggett (replaced afterwards by Barton Booth). Drury Lane supplied the model for the general design of the Georgian theatre, not the *Dorset Garden Theatre* with its 36-foot deep auditorium like an elongated tube. Dorset Garden declined and was not heard of after 1706.

(2) *Lincoln's Inn Fields*, which had been managed by Christopher Rich's son John (1692–1761). This was replaced in 1732 by the sumptuous new *Theatre Royal, Covent Garden* and occupied by the former company. On opening, Covent Garden held 1,400 people, but by

1792 it had expanded to hold some 3,000. In 1732 it had an auditorium of 86 feet from proscenium to back-of-house (Drury Lane at the time had an auditorium of 48 feet), and this, with its deeper galleries, introduced new problems for the actor to be seen and heard.

(3) The *Queen's Theatre* (later the *King's*), Haymarket, designed as an opera house by Sir John Vanbrugh in 1705 and also known as the Opera House. This was a palatial edifice inside and out, with an arched proscenium with three Greek columns a side and a domed Palladian ceiling and roof.

(4) The *Little Haymarket Theatre* (not to be confused with 3) had been built in 1720 by John Potter, who speculated on the growing market with a small, unlicensed house. After 1730 this playhouse became Henry Fielding's scene of operations. It played without a licence until 1766, when it was enlarged.

(5) *Goodman's Fields*, also unlicensed, had opened under Thomas Odell in 1729, and continued under Henry Giffard in 1732.

The *Sadler's Wells* 'music house' followed in 1765 and the *Royalty* in 1785. By the end of the century the playhouses, music houses and aquatic and equestrian amphitheatres had proliferated, and their increasing number in the capital is not only an indication of bigger and different audiences, but also of a wider range of theatrical entertainment. The stage and the drama was finding a new place in society.

The larger size of the playhouses and the consequent change in their stage features shows itself in the few plans and drawings that survive. The history of the Theatre Royal, Drury Lane offers an example. The theatre of Wren's design in 1674 would have held about five hundred persons, altogether a comfortable size for actor and spectator. By deepening the galleries, reducing the apron and having single proscenium doors, the design by the Adams brothers in 1775 multiplied the capacity three or four times to over 2,000. Not long after, the design by Henry Holland in 1794 went still further. It enlarged the pit, had five galleries and was reputed to hold as many as 3,611 people. (Holland had also

12 The stage of the Theatre Royal, Covent Garden (1732) as seen at the time of the Fitzgiggo price riot during Thomas Arne's opera *Artaxerxes* in 1763. The playhouse is bigger, but the doors and boxes still face an apron stage, with more chandeliers hanging over it.

tried to eliminate the proscenium doors altogether, but this was resisted.)

The effects on the plays and the performance of so large an auditorium can readily be imagined. Wren's proscenium opening of 31 feet had expanded to 43 feet, but as the audience grew bigger, the apron grew smaller and the distance of the stage from the spectators greater. As a result, the drama grew more detached and remote. This was a matter of importance for the players, and Cibber was quick to point out the differences when he compared what he had known before:

> By this original form, the usual station of the actors, in almost every scene, was advanced at least ten foot nearer to the audience, than they now can be; because, not only from the stage's being shortened, in front, but likewise from the additional interposition of those stage-boxes, the actors (in respect to the spectators, that fill them) are kept so much more backward from the main audience, than they used to be: but when the actors were in possession of that for-warder space, to advance upon, the voice was then more in the centre of the house, so that the most distant ear had scarce the least doubt, or difficulty in hearing what fell from the weakest utterance . . .
>
> (*An Apology* (1740), 225)

Cibber's whole regretful piece is worth reading. Happily not all Georgian theatres assumed such gargantuan proportions as Drury Lane and Covent Garden, and the surviving play-houses from the period at Bristol, Richmond and Bury St Edmunds strike a better balance between capacity and size.

Nevertheless, it was inevitable that new demands for spectacle on the stage brought about rapid physical changes in the shape and size of the playhouse. In particular, the English stage sought to emulate the success on the Continent of the scenery used in French and Italian opera and ballet. In particular, the period saw the increasing development of *perspective scenery*, by which the painted pieces set on the stage appeared to diminish to a distant point of infinity. Such scene design sought to deceive the eye of the beholder and suggest a more realistic and extensive space within the constricted proscenium arch, although this effect also risked distorting the height of the actor as he moved among the set pieces.

This was one development in scene setting. To meet the growing variety of scenic needs over the years, the number of painted scenes held in stock increased: palace or temple, church or tomb, forest or garden and many more, each with its appropriate properties. In addition, the single set of painted back shutters found in the Restoration period multiplied in the latter part of the eighteenth century in order to vary the distant scenic picture accordingly.

To meet the demand, the better houses began to employ their own scene painters (who were to all intents and purposes the 'scene designers' of the day). In 1747 John Rich set the pace at Covent Garden by hiring Giovanni Servandoni (1695–1766) of the Paris Opéra to design the scenes for his productions, including the harlequinades in which Rich himself played Harlequin under the stage name of 'Lun'. To satisfy the taste for scenic spectacle and surprising stage devices, the great actor and the manager at Drury Lane David Garrick (1717–79) made the notable appointment from Paris in 1772 of Philip de Loutherbourg (1740–1812), who designed some thirty productions. De Loutherbourg's work went beyond painted scenery, and as well as shutters and flats he built ramps and levels, achieving a vertical dimension within the acting area. He also developed transparent scenery for such effects as those of flames or moonlight, and invented the lighting to go with them. As a result, Drury Lane led the way in a new style of flexible staging. By the end of the century, the pictorial stage had usurped the literary theatre, and Shakespeare had begun his long struggle with the painter's art.

The *stage lighting* was still the overall illumination of the Restoration playhouse. It was made up of brackets and hoops of candles which lit both the actor and the audience. By comparison with the electric light of today they lent a uniquely dim, yellow, flickering and shadowy appearance to the scene. 'Floats', or candles floating in troughs at the foot of the apron, had been developed after 1673, and threw light unnaturally upwards on the faces of the actors. But in the eighteenth century the use of the proscenium little by little invited concealed lighting, and again the actor was encouraged to retreat into the scenic area of the stage. When Garrick visited the Opéra Comique in 1771, he was impressed by de Loutherbourg's lamps hidden behind the side wings, and other of his special effects. In Garrick's production of *A Christmas Tale* at Drury Lane in 1773 only de Loutherbourg's scenic effects received any praise, but at least they saved the production. In the play's garden scene (3.1) the heroine Camilla has a rhapsodic speech to her lover:

> My fancy teems with a thousand apprehensions, all my senses are in disorder. I heard or thought I heard strange noises in the air, even now my eyes are deceived, or this garden, the trees, the flowers, the heavens change their colours to my sight, and seem to say something mysterious which is not in my heart to expound.
>
> *(The objects in the garden vary their colours.)*

De Loutherbourg contrived to satisfy the requirements implied in these lines and the correspondent for *The London Chronicle* of 25–8 December 1773 reported with astonishment that 'the trees change colour alternating from green to red, resembling fire'. This effect was achieved by turning coloured silks on a pivot in front of the lights in the wings, and the audience was as enchanted as Camilla. In 1782 de Loutherbourg went on to bewitch London in the Spring Gardens with the exhibition of his 'Eidophusikon', a miniature theatre capable of producing spectacular scenic effects of light and colour.

The actors' *costumes* continued throughout the century for the most part as contemporary dress, and prints of familiar scenes from Shakespeare regularly have the gentleman in tricorne hat, knee breeches and full-bottomed coat, and the lady in powdered wig, tight bodice and full-skirted gown.

The biggest effect of the scenic stage and the larger auditorium was to force the actor to change his *style of acting*. As long as there was overall illumination, the actor still appeared to be in the same room as the spectator and continued to play to the house in that particular way that suggested the audience was in collaboration with him. However, the new audience now embraced 'box, pit and gallery' and the different parts of the auditorium marked a cross-section of the people of London, as the actor knew well: the upper classes and the *beau monde* in the boxes, the middle and professional classes and their wives in the pit and the servants and journeymen in the galleries.

The greater scale of performance called for massive movement and gesture and a 'ranting' voice. In *A General View of the Stage* (1730) Wilks describes how an actor might assume different emotions gracefully. 'Admiration', for example, had

> the eyes fixed upon the object; the right-hand naturally extends itself with the palm turned outwards; and the left-hand will share in the action, though so as scarcely to be perceived, not venturing far from the body; but when this surprise reaches the superlative degree, which I take to be astonishment, the whole body is actuated: it is thrown back, with one leg set before the other, both hands elevated, the eyes larger than usual, the brows drawn up, and the mouth not quite shut.
>
> (118)

Aaron Hill's important *Essay on the Art of Acting* (1779) attempted systematically to categorize the passions and divide them into ten – joy, sorrow, fear, scorn and so on – indicating for each the requisite gesture and tone.

All things conspired to produce the first age of great exhibitionistic actors and actresses, each of whom imposed some feature of his or her work upon the art of acting and the interpretation of a particular part. However, the middle of the century was especially the age of Garrick, whose 'natural and easy' performances as Richard III, Macbeth and Lear in tragedy, and as Abel Drugger and Sir John Brute in comedy, set new standards. His was very different from the statuesque style of the French classical theatre of the time: his sudden shifts of feeling and mood, his variety of speech and gesture, sometimes quick, sometimes slow, had his audiences in thrall.

The 'sentimental' convention

One consequence of the change from an aristocratic audience to a bigger, broader public composed more of middle-class merchants, professional men and their families was to curtail the bawdy content of the drama, and the moralistic shift in taste governed everything on the stage for many years to come. In his *Short View* of 1698 Collier assumed he was taking the side of the ladies in criticizing what he called 'the language of the stews' and 'scenes of brutishness' when he wrote, 'He that treats the ladies with such discourse, must conclude either that they like it, or they do not.' The impact was immediate – thus in his preface to *The Constant Couple* (1699) Farquhar wrote,

> I have not displeased the ladies, nor offended the clergy; both which are now pleased to say, that a comedy may be diverting without smut and profaneness.

In his Prologue to the play he reinforced the point:

> The ladies safe may smile: for here's no slander,
> No smut, no lewd-tongued beau, no double entendre.

Then in 1704 Queen Anne endorsed Collier when she ordered her Lord Chamberlain 'not to license anything that is not strictly agreeable to religion and good manners' (Public Records Office: L. C. 5–153), so that in effect a big step was taken towards imposing a new censorship of taste on the theatre and turning the stage into a pulpit.

The upshot was a marked shift to a sentimental mode of playwriting, although, since feeling is no stranger to the drama at any time, and since there were signs of change some years earlier, literary history has found the change difficult to date. Thomas Otway (1652–85) called up pathos in his tragedies *The Orphan* (1680) and *Venice Preserved* (1682), and in an odd mixture of melodrama and comedy the tragedy *Oroonoko* (1695) by Thomas Southerne (1660–1746) worked up an emotional response to the story of an African prince and his wife sold into slavery in Surinam. With an eye to business in 1696 Colley Cibber wrote a comedy of great popularity, the first of some thirty plays of his, *Love's Last Shift*, which moved its audience to sympathy and actual tears because Amanda remained loyal to her husband when she was tempted and the rake Loveless experienced a fifth-act reformation.

If the beginning of sentimentality was uncertain, its definition was more so. Emotional moralizing embodies both positive and negative traits: on the one hand a positive, humanitarian warmth and on the other an unctuous pity that smacks of self-esteem – an ugly and unChristian quality that Goldsmith noticed in 1773 when he suggested that the new comedies pardoned instead of ridiculing our faults and so had their success from 'flattering every man in his favourite foible'. Sentimentality is a disposition balanced delicately between hypocrisy and sincerity, at best defined, like any theory, by its practice.

The genre of *tragedy* found a major author in the fashionable essayist Joseph Addison (1672–1719). In the event, he wrote the inflexible blank verse *Cato* (1713), stiff with the classical unities. According to decorum the audience is not permitted to see Cato fall on his sword, and the stage direction for 5.1 is deemed to be enough:

> CATO solus, *sitting in a thoughtful posture: in his hand* PLATO's *book on the Immortality of the Soul. A drawn sword on the table by him.*

These words sum up the static stylistic characteristics of the performance. Nicholas Rowe (1674–1718) enjoyed a popular following with *Jane Shore* (1714), whose central character aroused pity for her relentless repentance and whose unendingly pitiful speeches must certainly have appealed to Collier's ladies.

The best that can be said for the new 'genteel' *comedy* was that it had acquired a social consciousness, the worst that it was merely Restoration comedy eviscerated. Cibber's *The Careless Husband* (1704) contains the familiar characters of the rake and the coquette, and has a superlative fop in Lord Foppington, but the scene (5.5) in which Lady Easy discovers her husband Sir Charles asleep *'without his periwig'* in a chair beside Edging, her maid, would have been unthinkable at an earlier date:

> Enter LADY EASY, *who starts and trembles some time, unable to speak.*
> Ha! bareheaded, and in so sound a sleep!
> Who knows, while thus exposed to th' unwholesome air,
> But heav'n, offended, may o'ertake his crime ...

And, believe it, she *'takes a steinkerk [scarf] off her neck, and lays it gently on his head'*.

The extraordinary popularity of *The Conscious Lovers* (1722) by Richard Steele (1672–1729) established the pattern for a reformed comedy. The play stayed in the repertory for forty years, inspiring 491 performances and forty-seven editions before the century was over. In his preface he defended the play's pathetic story by arguing that it introduced 'a joy too exquisite for laughter' and that tears which 'flowed from reason and good sense' were appropriate in comedy – farther than this any theory of *la comédie larmoyante* could not go. The distress of Indiana, the penniless orphan, drew tears on all sides, and in Fielding's satirical novel *Joseph Andrews* (1742) Parson Adams praised the play because it contained 'some things almost solemn enough for a sermon'.

The behaviour of the 'conscious' [sensitive] couples is exemplary: they are restrained, they hesitate and blush, they speak lines that are morally impeccable. In the following exchange the hero Bevil has risked telling Indiana that he 'esteems' her, and she is pleased:

> INDIANA. Esteem is the result of reason, and to deserve it from good sense, the height of human glory. Nay, I had rather a man of honour should pay me that than all the homage of a sincere and humble love.
> BEVIL JUNIOR. You certainly distinguish right, madam; love often kindles from external merit only –
> INDIANA. But esteem arises from a higher source, the merit of the soul –
> BEVIL JUNIOR. True. And great souls only can deserve it.
> *Bowing respectfully.*
>
> (2.2)

The scenes shuttle back and forth between house and lodgings, his and hers respectively, and there are no advances in staging worth recording.

The formula for a sentimental comedy was straightforward. The former Restoration rake had to become, or see the possibility of becoming, a clean-living 'man of sense', if only by a last-act stroke of reformation; his female counterpart, the witty coquette of earlier times, must become a sober and virtuous lady. All their dramatic values now resided in their sense of social propriety and inherent honour, and providence, no matter how mechanical, would always be there to reward virtue with a happy ending. Smother the mixture in moral aphorisms and the recipe was complete. The sentimental mode in one shape or another is still alive and well.

The burlesque mode: *The Beggar's Opera*

In a context of sober comedy and somber tragedy, the Georgian stage was not all tears: that most frivolous of dramatic forms, *burlesque,* was one of its outstanding contributions. If the purpose of parody is to ridicule literature by imitation, the special province of burlesque is to mock forms of drama and theatre, everything from play and performance to acting and the actors themselves. In *The Burlesque Tradition* (1952) V. C. Clinton-Baddeley offers an illuminating comparison with satire:

> Satire [is] violent and angry: but burlesque is never angry, because its criticism is directed not against faults of virtue, but against faults of style and humour. It wants to destroy nothing – not even sententiousness, its dearest enemy: for if sententiousness were dead there would be one less joke in the world to laugh at ... Satire must laugh not to weep. Burlesque must laugh not to burst.
>
> (1–2)

The burlesque method is straightforward: exaggeration to the point of incongruity and absurdity – if the heroine is distressed, she must go mad; if she goes mad, so must her confidante, on the principle that an audience can never have enough of a good thing. The major houses began regularly to present a burlesque *afterpiece,* a brief, usually one-act, entertainment, to complement the main play. Eventually, in order to complete the double-bill, the 'whole show' of the evening, performances were forced to begin at 5.00 pm in order to close by about 9.00 pm.

With the accustomed variety of stage activity, the afterpiece took a number of forms, and burlesque assumed several guises:

pantomime [in the eighteenth century meaning 'a dumb show', often with music] and, later, *pantomime-ballet*: inspired by the Italian *commedia dell'arte*, English versions of Arlecchino and the French Pierrot performed laughable skits and magic tricks, usually without words: *Harlequin Sorcerer* appeared in 1717 and *Harlequin Dr Faustus* in 1723.

farce [the French source of the word meant 'stuffing']: a quick, light treatment of a humorous situation, with spoken lines. David Garrick wrote thirty or forty popular farces for Drury Lane, mostly adapted from the French; popular titles were *The Lying Valet* (1741), *Miss in Her Teens* (1747) and, adapted from Shakespeare, *Catherine and Petruchio* (1756).

burletta ['a little joke' from the Italian *burla*]: a skit with words and music, again inspired by *commedia dell'arte* performance. Its music and songs were important as a way by which the minor theatres evaded the licensing laws. The burletta developed into the *extravaganza* of the next century.

ballad-opera [an early form of *comic opera* and *operetta*]: a musical afterpiece which was encouraged by the success of Gay's full-length production, *The Beggar's Opera*.

In many ways *The Beggar's Opera* (1728) by John Gay (1685–1732) was the most extraordinary theatrical event of the Georgian period. His burlesque of tragedy, the rehearsal-play *The What D'Ye Call It* (1715) that he ironically identified as 'tragi-comi-pastoral farce', had been performed with fair success at Drury Lane, but thirteen years later Cibber did not risk putting on *The Beggar's Opera*. However, with unexpected foresight John Rich accepted it at Lincoln's Inn Fields and, in the event, as the audience realized it was watching a clever satire, the play was received with wild enthusiasm. It had a record first run of sixty-two performances, and it counted over 1,000 before the end of the century. Yet the reason for this success is still something of a puzzle. The play uniquely mixed drama and popular song to produce one of the first and finest examples of 'ballad-opera'. It also uniquely combined a burlesque of a quasi-tragic romance with social and political satire, an incendiary mixture. Somewhere in the fusion of all these ingredients lies both the reason for its success and also the failure of the many attempts made to imitate it (twelve new ballad-operas appeared within a year, twenty-two more within five years). No typical conclusions can be drawn from it.

Gay's targets in his play are kaleidoscopic. In terms of political satire the squalid underworld of Newgate prison and its environs represents Sir Robert Walpole's government, and at the same time manages to include many of the politicians, lawyers and businessmen in London. In *The Intelligencer* (no. 3, 25 May 1728) Swift put the matter succinctly:

> The author takes the occasion of comparing those common robbers of the public, and their several stratagems of betraying, undermining and hanging each other, to the several acts of politicians in times of corruption.

In particular, Walpole is represented as Peachum [to 'peach' is to inform], a rogue who organizes a gang of thieves and pickpockets, pimps and whores; he claims to be as 'honest' a businessman as anybody, although at his own convenience he informs on others for his own profit. High-level ministerial quarrels are therefore seen as quarrels among thieves, and on the first night the squabble between Peachum and Lockit the gaoler (2.10) was taken to be that between Walpole and Lord Townshend, his brother-in-law and Foreign Minister. William Cooke records that the house was 'in convulsions of applause' and it is not surprising that the Lord Chamberlain did not permit production of Gay's sequel, *Polly* (1729), which had to wait until 1777 for a production by George Colman the elder.

The picture of corruption in *The Beggar's Opera* is extended to include all of society when it touches such matters as choosing a husband. In act 1 Polly Peachum confesses that she has married the highwayman Captain Macheath for love and her mother is appalled at her stupidity:

> POLLY. I did not marry him (as 'tis the fashion) coolly and deliberately for honour or money. But I love him.

MRS PEACHUM. Love him! Worse and worse! I thought the
girl had been better bred. Oh husband, husband! Her
folly makes me mad! My head swims! I'm distracted! I
can't support myself. – Oh! (*Faints.*)

(1.7)

Mrs Peachum is quickly revived with a glass of cordial, and it
turns out that all is not lost, since Peachum has the idea that
Macheath could be 'peached' at the next sessions – 'The
comfortable estate of widowhood is the only hope that keeps
up a wife's spirits' (1.10).

The workings of Gay's burlesque are especially challenging.
They are more complicated than is usual in burlesque because
he chose a musical form to control the manner of performance
and the response of his audience. The conventions of opera
were comparatively new to London: two Italian operas had
been performed in 1705, largely in English, *Arsinoe* at Drury
Lane and *Camilla* at the Haymarket. They were written and
played in a novel artificial style that stylized their material
attractively, although their Italian origin provoked a degree of
national prejudice that Gay turned to good account by his
prolific use of well-known English songs. He garnered some
sixty-nine tunes that were largely remembered for their edge of
bawdy wit, wrote graceful new lyrics to suit the situations in
his play and had them orchestrated by J. C. Pepusch, the
musical director at Lincoln's Inn Fields. In this way the tone of
the play automatically achieved a dual level of irony and
allusion, the discrepancies between sweet words and a pregnant
situation being both amusing and cutting, the stylizing placing
the performance just beyond reproach. Moreover, the large
number of songs ensured that they held the key to the
playing, not only telling the story for the audience, but setting
the pace and spirit of the piece for the actors. The play used
no operatic recitative, but it had no trouble in balancing the
songs and the dialogue. By conforming to a few operatic
conventions – providing the arias, two or three choruses for
the gang (their drinking song, in 2.1, and their exit song, in
2.2, for example) and several duets (between Macheath and
Polly, and Polly and Lucy), the songs introduced a semblance
of formal operatic practice; they also managed to introduce

one or two dances – a cotillion and chorus for Macheath's ladies, in 2.4, and even a bizarre 'dance of prisoners in chains', in 3.12.

The target for the burlesque, nevertheless, was not only opera, but also heroic tragedy. If there was no operatic recitative, there was also no heroic verse. After the impudent title and the short framing scene played between a Beggar, the apparent composer of the opera, and an equally disreputable Player, an actor/musician there to serve the 'Muses', the play went straight to its objective. Peachum counts his gains as he sings lines that are the immediate guide to the play's satirical inversion, concluding:

> And the statesman, because he's so great,
> Thinks his trade as honest as mine.

(1.1.7–8)

Instead of some stately palace, the scene is one of tavern and prison, with an atmosphere of poverty and crime, peopled by such 'low' characters as Mrs Coaxer the bawd, Molly Brazen and Betty Doxy the prostitutes, Jemmy Twitcher the pickpocket and Harry Paddington the 'pad' [highwayman]. The hero Macheath is also of course a criminal, a highwayman who is betrayed and imprisoned, who escapes and is recaptured, and who, finally, is condemned to be hanged; in prison the daughters of his enemies fight over him, and when four more of his innumerable 'wives' seek him out, each bearing a child, he gladly welcomes his execution:

> What – four wives more! This is too much. – Here – tell the Sheriff's officers I am ready.

(3.15)

However, romantic convention called for a happy ending and the Beggar/author reluctantly agrees to a reprieve. Thus the play ends with a jolly dance by the assembled company.

Every mistreatment of heroic decorum is a deliberate effrontery, and none more so than the sentimental moments that Gay introduces to ensure that his 'Newgate pastoral' concoction is completely distracting and misleading. Polly's solos are pathetically justified by her idealistic resistance to her parents' treachery and by her honest love for her condemned husband. In their moving duets at the end of the first act, the feelings associated with her are extended to include Macheath himself, and by the time of the obligatory scene in the condemned cell, which finds Macheath drunkenly singing a bitter sequence of ten little airs, the villain/hero has won the sympathy of the audience (3.13). The mixture works: music blends with drama, sentiment with satire, comedy with realism. The rich wit and the glorious sense of humour that lie behind Gay's conception provide the bonding for the performance and enable the burlesque to aim in several different directions.

In spite of its farcical ingredients, any performance of *The Beggar's Opera* has to put a limit on the realism of the scene; indeed, it is conceivable that the beggars should behave like gentry and the songs be rendered as formally as possible, although no formula will be definitive. Yet the play is securely in the repertory and to this day has not wanted successful revivals following Nigel Playfair's audacious production in 1920.

For Drury Lane in 1779 Richard Brinsley Sheridan (1751–1816) wrote the best of all English burlesques, *The Critic; or, A Tragedy Rehearsed*. Direct political allusion was much reduced (Lord Burleigh is a caricature of the flaccid Prime Minister, Lord North), with the advantage that this piece is conceivably a rare example of a timeless burlesque, one unaffected by the limited knowledge of the audience. The vain Sir Fretful Plagiary is a caricature of the playwright Richard Cumberland, but this in no way limits the witty treatment Sheridan here accords all authors. The play depends hardly at all on the verbal parody of other, contemporary texts. What in effect Sheridan did was to marshal and concentrate in one play-within-a-play almost all the heroic conventions the English stage had ever employed, and then ridicule them one after another by ludicrous demonstration before subjecting them to the critical questioning of an on-stage audience.

Dramatic conventions are shown for the unbelievable stage tricks they really are. Thus, how preposterous it is for one character to tell another what he already knows in order to provide an exposition:

> DANGLE. Mr Puff, as he *knows* all this, why does Sir Walter
> go on telling him?
> PUFF.   But the audience are not supposed to know any-
> thing of the matter, are they?

(2.2)

Addison had written in *The Spectator*, no. 44, 20 April 1711,
'For the moving of pity our principal machine is the handkerchief ... A tragedy could not subsist without it', and the
joke is unmistakable when grief requires the heroine to run
mad with a white handkerchief, and is coupled with a
confidante to echo her every feeling and gesture like a
shadow. The irony is immediately clear when a soliloquy is
performed that puts the realistic idea of wordless thought into
practice and delivers the speech in complete silence, like that
of Lord Burleigh when he *'goes slowly to a chair and sits'* and
then *'comes foward, shakes his head and exit'*:

> DANGLE. What, isn't he to speak at all?
> PUFF.   Egad, I thought you'd ask me that – yes, it is a
> very likely thing that a minister in his situation,
> with the whole affairs of the nation, should have
> time to talk!

(3.1)

Sheridan makes generous use of the comic principle of
'proliferation' to farcical effect. Nothing is more ridiculous
than when actors speak only in asides, and have so many that
the dialogue does not permit them to address one another.

Goldsmith's comedy: *She Stoops to Conquer*

The best of Georgian drama was yet to come, and it was an
achievement in comedy. At the time when George Colman
(1732–94) was managing Covent Garden, David Garrick
managing and acting at Drury Lane and Samuel Foote (1720–
77) appearing in his own comedies at the Haymarket, the
contest for the taste of the audience that had been smouldering
for years flared up in theory and practice. 'Genteel' or sentimental comedy offered the spectator a moralistic experience
that was immensely popular, the comfortable outcome of a

play indicating its path to virtue and happiness; 'laughing' or satirical comedy sought to entertain the spectator with a more rugged, Jonsonian comedy of humours that did not hesitate to make fun of contemporary behaviour with the help of a range of eccentric characters. Garrick favoured the former, and at Drury Lane in 1768 produced with great success Hugh Kelly's *False Delicacy*, in which various lovers are too sensitive to explain their misunderstandings and true feelings. In 5.2 a character speaks for the author: 'The stage should be a school of morality; and the noblest of all lessons is the forgiveness of injuries.' Even more popular in 1771 was *The West Indian* by Richard Cumberland (1732–1811). Here the hero enjoys a sensibility too nice to seduce the heroine; so he reforms and decides to marry her instead, and is properly rewarded by finding that she is an heiress.

To such maudlin material it fell to Oliver Goldsmith (1728–74) to offer a challenge in his first play, *The Good-Natured Man* (1768). This Coleman presented at Covent Garden only six days after Kelly's triumph – a mistake, as it turned out, since the audience was not ready to be affronted by Goldsmith's innovative and antisentimental tactics. On the first night Goldsmith also dared to include an hilarious scene in which his impecunious hero Honeywell is besieged by the Dickensian Timothy Twitch the bailiff and his 'follower' [assistant] little Flannigan, characterized as having 'a wife and four children'. The sentimentalists in the audience no doubt took offence at hearing Twitch speak for them:

> I love to see a gentleman with a tender heart. I don't know, but I think I have a tender heart myself ... Humanity, sir, is a jewel. It's better than gold. I love humanity.

> (act 3)

When Honeywell's beloved, Miss Richland, enters, the bailiffs are caught on stage, and to deceive her they must behave like gentlemen and offer polite conversation, which they do not hesitate to do:

> BAILIFF (*after a pause*). Pretty weather, very pretty weather for the time of year, madam.
> FOLLOWER. Very good circuit weather in the country.

> (act 3)

Goldsmith's humour is here instinctive, but the scene was hissed on the first night and, so he reported in his preface, it was 'retrenched in the representation'. It must be said, however, that Honeywell is relentlessly 'good-natured' and he is as reformed as if he were in any moralistic comedy of the day.

Goldsmith's assault on tearful comedy was not over, and soon after Covent Garden was to produce his masterpiece, *She Stoops to Conquer* (1773). This played eighty-three times before the century was over, and has been in the classical repertory ever since. Notwithstanding Horace Walpole's verdict that Goldsmith had written nothing but a low farce whose drift tended to 'no moral, no edification of any kind', Dr Johnson in his customarily blunt way considered, according to Boswell's report, that the play had achieved 'the great end of comedy – making an audience merry'. The short theoretical tract Goldsmith published a few weeks before the play opened, *An Essay on the Theatre; or, A Comparison between Laughing and Sentimental Comedy*, also suggests that he had given his previous failure some thought. In this essay he leaned towards 'that natural portrait of human folly and frailty, of which all are judges, because all have sat for the picture' and invoked what he took to be Aristotle's concept of comedy as 'a picture of the frailties of the lower part of mankind'. Above all, he returned to the attack on sentimental comedy, considering it to be 'flattering every man in his favourite foible' and too facile in the writing. Goldsmith concluded:

> It is not easy to recover an art when once lost; and it would be but a just punishment that when, by our being too fastidious, we have banished humour from the stage, we should ourselves be deprived of the art of laughing.

The play is accordingly replete with ironic hits at moralistic comedy and is sprinkled with superb samples of 'low' characterization, from Tony Lumpkin and his drunken companions in The Three Jolly Pigeons to Diggory of the barn and Roger of the plough whom Hardcastle provocatively promotes to be footmen at table. Above all, nothing was more ignoble than the idea at the heart of the plot, that to win her lover a heroine could behave like a barmaid. Nevertheless, in his renewed attack Goldsmith had struck a balance between the demands of broad comic characterization working in specific scene patterns and a generous sense of natural human comedy.

Scene changes were still accomplished with painted wings and shutters changed *a vista* [in full view of the audience], but the stage now carried suggestively realistic props like ale-mugs and a punch-bowl, pipes and a fire-screen: Goldsmith was already using the stage setting for its contribution to his comic situation. Most of the action is set in, and keeps returning to, the 'old-fashioned' country house of the old-fashioned Hardcastle, a house which, his wife is pleased to point out, is 'an old rumbling mansion, that looks for all the world like an inn'. The error the heroes Marlow and Hastings make in taking Hardcastle's house for The Buck's Head is perpetuated by Kate and is elaborated throughout the play. It will provide a constant source of comic scenes, many achieving something of a *coup de théâtre*, like Tony's deception in act 1, the behaviour of the visitors in Hardcastle's house and the interview between Marlow and Kate in act 2, the theft of the jewels and the barmaid scene in act 3 and the scene of the imaginary Crackskull Common in act 5.

All this is set up visually from the beginning *in the scenery and décor*. In fact, Goldsmith's plot is remarkably self-generating, so that in the best tradition of modern farce a single mistake at the inn snowballs into 'The Mistakes of a Night', the play's subtitle. The action holds out the more beguiling pleasure of expectation rather than that of surprise: since the joke of the inn itself does not occur until well into act 2, much of the spirit of act 1 therefore lies in preparing the audience for what is to come. Not only does Hardcastle 'love everything that's old' (including old campaign stories of the Duke of Marlborough and Prince Eugène, as well as a daughter who dresses like a simple country housewife), but conversely Mrs Hardcastle is the new-fangled, pretentious wife, thereby setting up a host of 'country' jokes to please a town audience – when the satirical barbs do not turn back on them. It also follows that the fashionable mother is blessed with a country-bred son to plague her, so that in the best Shakespearian tradition Goldsmith has leave to create Tony

Lumpkin. This irresistible character was promptly recognized as mixing the elements of fool and wit – an overgrown boy to laugh *at* and a rascal able to trick the fine gentlemen to laugh *with*.

In this Goldsmith manages a smooth synthesis of critical laughter and affectionate feeling, and human comedy underlies even his most burlesque and satirical moments. The Hardcastles open the play with a delightful travesty of country life, but at the same time this picture is cast in a kindly light. Even the mockery of Kate's first painful interview with Marlow, a parody full of sentimental moral aphorisms, comes across as shared human comedy:

> MISS HARDCASTLE. You were going to observe, sir –
> MARLOW.   I was observing, madam – I protest,
>   madam, I forget what I was going to
>   observe.
> MISS HARDCASTLE (*aside*). I vow and so do I. (*To him*) You
>   were observing, sir, that in this age of
>   hypocrisy – something about hypoc-
>   risy, sir.

> (act 2)

The interview reflects every stiff encounter between young people, and the audience is embarrassed for *both of them*. Moreover, Kate's reiteration of the word 'hypocrisy' constitutes a wickedly implicit aside to the house.

Goldsmith's command of a range of comic skills is visible in his writing. Even in the brief extract above, he is to be seen exploiting all shades of the aside, from the sort engendered by the machinery of the plot to that signifying a broader rapport with the audience. The proximity of actor and spectator was still such as to encourage a wealth of innuendo and indirect address, and major scenes like that of Hardcastle's reception of Marlow and the sentimental interview between Marlow and Kate are dependent upon the convention; in the first, both parties are perplexed and in the second, both are exasperated. Moreover, these asides not only insist that the actors share their feelings with the house, but they also ensure that the pace of the scene is fast and the irony sharp: the social forms played slowly at one pace and the reality of the criticisms coming quickly on their heels. Other functions of the aside are fundamental to the success of act 3, first in the scene of the loss of the jewels in which Tony torments his mother with the refrain, 'I can bear witness to that', pronounced in tones that mean one thing to her and another to the audience, and then in the scene of Kate's masquerade as a barmaid, in which both she and Marlow are able to reveal another side of their natures:

> MARLOW. Suppose I should call for a taste, just by way of trial, of the nectar of your lips; perhaps I might be disappointed in that, too!
>
> MISS HARDCASTLE. Nectar! nectar! that's a liquor there's no call for in these parts. French I suppose ...
>
> (act 3)

Their amorous encounter is conducted as a physical chase and retreat, and simultaneously as a witty verbal thrust and parry.

Some of our sense of a character's animation also derives from the role-playing that is woven into the structure of the comedy. Kate in particular enjoys several layers of persona: she must play the honest daughter to her father, the demure young lady who greets Marlow politely, the maidservant who impersonates Farquhar's vivacious Cherry from *The Beaux' Stratagem* and the Kate who charms the audience by confiding in it as her own self – each role clearly heard in the idiom and rhythm of her speech. English comedy had seen no such versatile heroine since Rosalind in *As You Like It*.

The play ends with the happy union of Kate and Marlow, but even here any sentimentality in their relationship is undercut by carefully arranged detail. When Marlow feels the first touches of true affection for Kate in act 4 and pronounces the aside, 'By heaven, she weeps!', she is only *'pretending to cry'* and probably peeping through her fingers as she assesses his qualities. When in act 5 he falls on his knees to her, he does so before an on-stage audience of eavesdropping parents, so that his performance remains comically distanced. When at the last he learns the truth, all Kate does by way of forgiveness is to taunt him according to the inexorable stage direction,

'*They retire, she tormenting him to the back scene.*' Kate and Tony Lumpkin are the spectator's constant representatives on the stage in *She Stoops to Conquer*, so that the 'love scenes' are played in the vein of burlesque and at the end the Georgian audience is left with an irresistible Lumpkin view of society.

Sheridan's comedy: *The School for Scandal*

That the comedies of Richard Brinsley Sheridan completed the attack on sentimental moralism is questionable, but there is no doubt that his particular skills as a dramatist – his witty dialogue, his preparation and construction of a comic scene and his sense of comic balance – place him in the front rank.

His first comedy, *The Rivals* (1775), made a poor start and was taken off after its first night at Covent Garden. It had been miscast and was too long, so Sheridan cut and rewrote it in ten days, making the hero less of a fortune-hunter and the characters of the irate father Sir Anthony Absolute and the stage Irishman Sir Lucius O'Trigger less coarse. The result was a success: the play had 106 performances before the end of the century and has continued in popularity to this day. Although the play reveals its weaknesses in its uncertain satire and mixture of styles, without any theoretical preamble Sheridan had tackled the sentimentalists head on. It opens with its chief target, the romantic young lady and wealthy heiress Lydia Languish, seen in 1.1 reclining on a sofa and reviewing the latest fashionable novels she has been brought from the circulating libraries of Bath. It emerges that she has carried her romantic feelings into real life by desiring only to marry into poverty, although this is the extent of her somewhat limited role as a comic character. The play's sub-plot has another young lady of quality, Julia, in difficulties with her melancholy lover, Faulkland, because he is troubled by too nice a sensibility – he is always jealous; however, this character-istic, presumably intended for laughter as a Jonsonian humour, in fact went down rather well with a Georgian audience accustomed in the theatre to approve fine feelings and their sentimental expression in words.

Sheridan doubly ensured the successful working of his comedy by furnishing it with a gallery of stock types, farcical eccentrics who have down the years guaranteed great comic performances. The inimitable Mrs Malaprop is devoted to Lydia's upbringing and education (''Tis safest in matrimony to begin with a little aversion'). Sir Anthony is at the centre of a classic scene of disagreement and misunderstanding between father and son (2.1), a scene whose rhythms are exquisitely calculated to end in the explosion of Sir Anthony's temper. And the fiery Sir Lucius takes it upon himself to teach the country squire, the would-be gentleman Bob Acres, how to challenge his rival in an hilarious scene of a mock duel (5.3). And some of the play's success, both in its own time and today, must be due to its author's personal acquaintance with Beau Nash's city of Bath, whose world of gossip and fashion, of Pump Room and Assembly Room, supplies a recognizable setting better than any painted scenery. In all this the attack on the sentimentalists seems of less account.

His masterpiece *The School for Scandal* appeared two years later in 1777, produced at Drury Lane when he was manager. This time he wrote the play with more care and limited its mistakes: it ran for seventy-five nights and played for 261 more before the century was over; it has hardly been off the boards since. Its plot and style reveal shades of Molière (*L'Ecole des femmes*, *Tartuffe*), Wycherley (*The Country Wife*) and Congreve (*The Way of the World*), but the whole is firmly under the confident control of its author. Although sentimentality is targeted in the character of Joseph Surface and his moralizing sentiments, with Joseph and his brother Charles cast as a kind of Master Blifil and Tom Jones, a hypocrite and a man of feeling, the old struggle with sentimentalism is dying, and, notwithstanding the moralizing of Joseph, is forgotten as the play gets under way.

The comic action rests on three strong pillars of interest held in particular equilibrium. Each is graced with the glitter and crackle of Sheridan's witty dialogue and each is tightly crafted for the desired response of the audience. The three centres of interest consist of:

- Three 'scandal' scenes (1.1, 2.2 and 5.2), which almost frame the story of Joseph's attempted intrigue with Lady Teazle and generally supply a background of satirical frivolity to the comedy.

- Two scenes which embody the amusing quarrels between the old husband Sir Peter and his young country wife Lady Teazle (2.1 and 3.1).

- Two major discovery scenes, 'the auction scene' (4.1, which reveals Charles drinking with his friends) and 'the screen scene' (4.3, which finds Joseph in his library), the two scenes designed to expose their characters and resolve their stories.

The scandal scenes seem to be written in another style and to belong in another play; Joseph's hypocrisy is too grotesque and Charles's generosity too gratuitous.

The scandal-mongers are treated as a good joke and their gossip does not bear on the main action of the play, but they exhibit Sheridan's command of dialogue as personal weaponry and put on display a range of pretentious social caricatures – the vindictive Lady Sneerwell, the silken slanderer Mrs Candour, the narcissistic Sir Benjamin Backbite and his vain uncle Crabtree. 'Needs there a school this modish art to teach you?' asks Garrick in his Prologue, but only a playwright with a meticulous sense of visual and aural performance could compose the controlled ebb and flow of these poisonous rhythms:

> MRS CANDOUR. She has a charming fresh colour.
> LADY TEAZLE. Yes, when it is fresh put on.
> MRS CANDOUR. Oh, fie! I'll swear her colour is natural. I have seen it come and go.
> LADY TEAZLE. I dare swear you have, ma'am: it goes off at night and comes again in the morning.
> SIR BENJAMIN. True, Lady Teazle, it not only comes and goes, but, what's more, egad – her maid can fetch and carry it.
>
> (2.3)

Each line is shaped for a partial retreat and a studied pause in order to renew the attack, the assembled company balletically twisting and craning and rocking in unison to catch each quip, the laughter swelling to a climax before the next sally is begun, the next victim abused.

The Teazle scenes of domestic quarrelling have a rhythm of their own, one which requires Lady Teazle to give her dour husband as good as she gets, and better. For this reason alone Sheridan abandoned the idea of reproducing the less sophisticated, rustic ways of a Margery Pinchwife or a Kate Hardcastle. The quarrels are structured like musical movements, each with a pace and tone of voice to match a pattern of gesture, each new development ending on a scorching witticism:

> SIR PETER. You forget what your situation was when I married you.
>
> LADY TEAZLE. No, no, I don't; 'twas a very disagreeable one, or I should never have married you.
>
> LADY TEAZLE. There is but one thing more you can make me to add to the obligation – and that is –
>
> SIR PETER. My widow, I suppose?
>
> LADY TEAZLE. I should think you would like to have your wife thought a woman of taste.
>
> SIR PETER. Aye – there again – taste! Zounds! madam, you had no taste when you married me.
>
> (2.1)

For all this needling Sheridan is careful to allow a little affection to show through. In Sir Peter, Molière's clown Arnolphe and Wycherley's cuckold Pinchwife have given place to a more sympathetic character ('With what a charming air she contradicts everything I say'), and this scene concludes with a telling glimpse of another side of him.

The auction scene and the screen scene both carry the stamp of comic inevitability. In particular, with the full knowledge of the audience the perfectly oiled machinery of the screen scene drives to an inexorable climax. The famous picture in the Garrick Club points to the formal symmetry and simplicity of the two proscenium doors and the single screen carefully placed centre stage in front of the back shutters that depict Joseph's library.

With increasing embarrassment to Joseph the neat plotting

13 Richard Brinsley Sheridan, *The School for Scandal*, 1777: the screen scene (4.3) at Drury Lane: the apron is still prominent and the shadows suggest new lighting.

adds one character after another to the scene – first Lady Teazle, then Sir Peter, then Charles – each requiring a new hiding place from the limited supply. With a sense of impending disaster the action builds its tension with more and more asides, faster and faster pace, up to the last moment when the screen is thrown down. At the crisis the stage is all but frozen in a tableau:

CHARLES.	Lady Teazle – by all that's wonderful!
SIR PETER.	Lady Teazle, by all that's damnable!
CHARLES.	Sir Peter, this is one of the smartest French milliners I ever saw. Egad, you seem all to have been diverting yourselves here at hide and seek – and I don't see who is out of the secret. Shall I beg your ladyship to inform me? Not a word! Brother, will you be pleased to explain this matter? What! Is morality dumb too? Sir Peter, though I *found* you in the dark, perhaps you are not so now? All mute ...

(4.3)

As Charles proceeds quizzically round the stage, the audience relishes each character's situation in turn.

Nevertheless building blocks alone do not make a good play, and the triumph of *The School for Scandal* comes of Sheridan's having blended Jonsonian characterization and Restoration wit with a dash of Georgian sensibility. If Charles is still the prodigal nephew, in his role as the antithesis of his brother and catalyst to the main plot he reserves a little of the audience's laughter to himself. If the Teazles enact the familiar situation of the old cuckold and the young wife, in the eyes of the audience Sir Peter's return to marital bliss and his lady's recovery of a little wisdom and virtue do not come amiss. Without some degree of charity the part of Sir Peter Teazle would not have provided the challenge taken up by a roll-call of great actors.

The drama's drift towards a natural balance of thought and feeling acknowledges that theatre is an affective art and that sympathy is a useful, if not an essential, ingredient in a richer aesthetic response. The Georgian theatre saw the beginning of the picture-stage, but even though the demands of paint and light were increasingly felt, with no way to dim the lights, with no magic to change the scene, it was still constrained by non-illusion. It therefore demanded neither what was real nor what was unreal, and the balance of fiction and verisimilitude resulted in the frank interaction between text and actor, and between actor and audience, that produced great creative artists like David Garrick and Sarah Siddons, and encouraged the first great revival and rediscovery of Shakespeare on the stage. This easy balance between two worlds had much to do with the fact that the Georgian theatre increasingly encouraged large new audiences for the future.

12

The Victorian theatre

A century of theatrical discovery and evaluation

The literary reputation of the bulk of nineteenth-century English drama is low; yet it is of little use to ask why no dramatic masterpieces were written until nearly the end of the period. It is more to the point to recognize that this was a time when a variety of new forms of dramatic activity were tried and tested, and large new audiences were in the making. The result was that many new theatres were opened, an astonishing number of new plays were written (some 20,000 between 1850 and 1900, ten times as many as between 1700 and 1750) and a host of effective conventions were put into play. Above all, a major theatrical genre evolved: this was the *melodrama*, a name coloured by its unfortunate reputation. However, if we accept that drama is the supremely reactive art, in melodrama it found a formula for seizing and holding the attention of a wide audience. Its impact was such that it grew to be as much a style as a genre and embraced many forms that could touch either tragedy or comedy. In power and appeal it still constitutes, with modifications, the dominant mode of the twentieth century. On the lucid, if unsophisticated, Victorian stage were born most of the techniques of today.

The mainstream of Victorian drama followed a frankly 'presentational' mode, exulting in its make-believe as 'illegitimate' theatre, that is, drama presented with varying degrees of music and dance in order to evade the law that restricted 'straight' plays to the patent houses. Before the century was over it had accommodated itself to the more realistic style of society drama and the so-called problem play, and successfully tempted the upper- and middle-class audience back into the theatre.

In order to supply excitement and spectacle, and comedy and tears, to new audiences made up from the lower and lower-middle classes, the melodrama grew up in a hard school of pragmatic theatre. In this process it absorbed and devoured material from any source it fancied. The form had flourished in late eighteenth-century France, and after the success in London of Thomas Holcroft's *A Tale of Mystery* (1802), freely adapted from the romantic *Coelina* of Guilbert de Pixérécourt (1773–1844), many Parisian *boulevard mélodrames* found their way on to the London stage. In later years hungry theatre managers continued to look abroad for new material, and regularly crossed the Channel to Paris to check the romantic stage successes of the prolific Eugène Scribe (1791–1861). Scribe was himself responsible for more than 400 plays, and was skilled in constructing an exciting drama that was theatrically effective, but too often written to the shallow, mechanical formula of *la pièce bien faite* [the well-made play]. His natural successor was Victorien Sardou (1831–1908), who wrote almost as many plays, but who is today remembered only for the coinage G. B. Shaw used to describe Sardou's theatre: 'Sardoodledom'.

In the early years English melodrama also turned to the contemporary cult of the Gothic horror story, particularly following the wild success of 'Monk' Lewis's *The Castle Spectre* at Covent Garden in 1797. It found that the popular stage could readily assimilate and domesticate the simple formula of (1) a vulnerable heroine (2) trapped in a gloomy medieval castle and (3) threatened by a brooding villain until (4) the hero saved her. This sort of romantic thriller reached its height of popularity with Charles Maturin's *Bertram; or, The Castle of St Aldobrand*, as played furiously by Edmund Kean at Drury Lane in 1816: when Bertram is shipwrecked on the rocks of the priory of St Anselm, he discovers that his beloved Imogine is married to his enemy Aldobrand; as a consequence Bertram murders his rival, kills himself and with a confident finality leaves Imogine to run mad with despair. Early melodrama was also delighted to adapt the romantic and sentimental novels of popular writers like Scott and Dickens. Scott's pageantry lent itself to a spectacular stage-craft, and his strong central characters (Richard the Lionheart,

Mary Queen of Scots and others) invited popular casting. As a result, Scott had nineteen of his novels dramatized. In the case of Dickens, his practice of writing his novels episodically in powerfully conceived and highly emotional scenes also encouraged the legion of adaptors, and some eighteen of his novels and stories reached the stage.

Many would-be poetic playwrights slavishly imitated the Greek or Elizabethan tragedy they knew, but few were prepared to submit their work to the discipline of the stage or its conventions. Understandably, the pseudo-classicism of the remote past failed to reflect the live audience, and the often unmotivated, introspective heroes of the romantic poets did not enlighten it. In complete contrast to the work of the poets, most Victorian melodramas sought their themes prosaically in English social and domestic life, and this subject may be said to have occupied the chief attention of the popular stage. It was a scene peopled, not by great and heroic men and women, but by sailors and farmers, landlords and bankers; its stories told, not of great exploits and famous victories, but of poverty and wealth, work and the factory, drunkenness and gambling, homelessness and even slavery.

The Victorian playhouse

The vigorous growth of the population of London (quadrupling from 959,310 in 1800 to 4,536,267 in 1900) coincided with an increase in the number of playhouses. In 1832 Parliament instituted an inquiry into the royal patents and the causes of the decline of the drama, and in 1843 finally passed a Regulation Act for the theatre which ended the monopoly of the patent houses. The outcome was an unusual increase in theatre building in the latter half of the century. By 1850 London had more than twenty theatres, and by 1900 more than sixty, of which thirty-eight were in the West End, together with some forty music halls close by. The provinces eventually acquired some twenty royal patents. Most of these houses also shared the rapid development at this time of scenic machinery and the technical crafts of the stage. Such was the success of the minor houses, the patent theatres found themselves having to compete with them.

One feature shared by the major and many of the minor theatres was a characteristic growth in their *size and scale*, a feature that drastically affected both play and performance. After being consumed by fire, Covent Garden was rebuilt in 1809 to a design by Robert Smirke and had a proscenium opening 42 feet wide and a stage 68 feet deep; the length of the house from the footlights to the back of the boxes was some 70 feet, and its capacity was about 3,000. After another fire, Drury Lane was rebuilt in 1812 to a design by Benjamin Wyatt, and had a proscenium opening 33 feet wide and a stage 96 feet deep; the length of the house from front of stage to the back was 86 feet, and its capacity was upwards of 3,000. Such big audiences became normal.

The word that recurs in contemporary descriptions of these new theatres is 'cavernous' and in her time the great tragic actress Sarah Siddons called Drury Lane 'the tomb of the drama' because to be heard she had to howl and bellow. The participation of the spectator was still eminently desirable, but increasingly the stage saw the development of a 'consumer's' art in which the theatre became a factory and the drama the product of mechanical engineering.

As the theatre grew larger, significant changes occurred in the standard Georgian *auditorium* of box, pit and gallery, an arrangement that had served to separate and distinguish the social classes of its audience. As the 'orchestra stalls' became more socially desirable, patrons of the former pit found themselves in the rear, until in some theatres it disappeared altogether; the fashionable boxes that surrounded the former pit multiplied until they were transformed into one, two or even three balconies built out over the house by the structural principle of the cantilever. With the poorer patrons retiring to the back of the stalls and the highest galleries becoming 'the gods', in the 1840s the stalls exchanged their backless benches for seats that were more like chairs and could be reserved by the purchase of a ticket.

At the beginning of the century both acting area and auditorium were lit overall by candles and oil-lamps, *sources of light* that were difficult or impossible to manipulate during

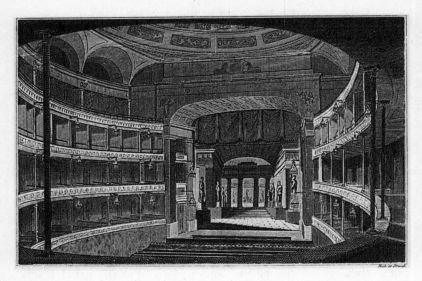

14 The interior of the Theatre Royal, Covent Garden in 1810:
stage doors remain, but the picture-frame proscenium has arrived.

the performance. *Gaslight* was first introduced in 1817,
although the disagreeable smell of its flares and the regular
danger of asphyxiation or fire introduced new problems.
Nevertheless, spectacular effects of light were attempted, like
the storm scenes in Macready's *King Lear* at Covent Garden
in 1838, as described by the correspondent to *John Bull*, 25
January:

> Forked lightnings now vividly illume the broad horizon,
> now faintly coruscating in small and serpent folds, play in
> the distance; the sheeted element sweeps over the fore-
> ground and then leaves it in pitchy darkness ...

It was in the age of gaslight, reportedly in 1849, that it became
possible to darken the auditorium, a momentous development
that facilitated a theatre of visual illusions, especially under
Irving.

Limelight replaced gaslight and was regularly employed by
Charles Kean at Covent Garden after 1855. The limited
control of the focus of the new lighting naturally dictated the
limited choice of the actor's position on the stage, and it

became *de rigueur* for key lines to be delivered downstage centre: not that this mattered much, since on the English stage at this time the realistic blocking [grouping] of two or more actors was virtually unknown. Nevertheless, with the help of gauzes and transparencies and coloured flares, the theatre began to create beautiful effects of chiaroscuro and moonlight, and offer wonderful exhibitions of fireworks and magic. *Electricity* was finally introduced for the first time at the Savoy Theatre when D'Oyly Carte opened it with Gilbert and Sullivan's *Patience* in 1881, and a theatre of illusions had at last arrived.

In 1800 the stage itself, with its proscenium doors, stage boxes and fashionable spectators prominently to either side, was still very much an apron, or 'thrust' stage, and the actors perforce played chiefly on the forestage among their audience. *Scenery* was still painted on wing pieces and shutters that had to be pushed or rolled on grooves in front of a back-cloth. The proscenium curtain was raised at the beginning of the play, and scene changes were made in full view of the audience until the curtain was lowered at the end of the last act. Flats that closed nearer the audience permitted a 'front scene', also called a 'carpenters' scene' because it concealed the noisy work of the scene changers busy building a 'full scene' behind it. Stock scenery – forest, mountain, palace – was ready to hand, and this was increasingly built in three dimensions. Later, when curtains could be dropped more easily, scenes were changed out of sight more readily. Acts and scenes were written or arranged to 'alternate' so that more elaborate scenery could be put in place behind a front curtain that was itself the backing for a simpler one. Naturally, as the stage became more concerned with scenic and other visual illusion, the actor withdrew to give way to the machinery of spectacle and the apron receded.

The theatre eventually became the repository for many scientific wonders of Victorian *stage machinery*. A moving 'diorama' changed the stage picture by rolling a painted canvas up or down, or on or off. Aquatic effects were possible, and waterfalls were particularly popular. Sadler's Wells, famous for its nautical dramas, had a great tank of water 90 feet long and 5 feet deep raised mechanically for sea-battles and shipwrecks and storms at sea. The 'flying ballet' made use of a scenic tower, and with the help of traps and lights startling effects of the supernatural were magically created.

The drive towards realistic illusion was unstoppable. In 1841 Madame Vestris and Charles Mathews tried out the idea of a 'box set', and when in 1880 Squire Bancroft turned the proscenium opening at the Haymarket into a picture-frame, the apron had finally gone. He proudly advised the public that

> a rich and elaborate gold border, about two feet broad, after the pattern of a picture-frame, is continued all round the proscenium, and carried even below the actors' feet. There can be no doubt the sense of illusion is increased.

The proscenium doors were removed at last, and realistic doors were now set inside a room with three walls and a cloth for a ceiling – only 'the fourth wall' was missing. Theatre became a grand peep-show, with the spectator staring through the empty side. Alas, performances within the picture-frame seemed two-dimensional and frieze-like, at least until the dramaturgy was developed which drew him into the action. When that happened, audiences felt that the fourth wall was behind it, not in front.

Nevertheless, the development of a realistic setting already contained the seeds of its own destruction. Theatrical illusion and the spectacular stage arose at the expense of a natural intimacy between actor and audience, and encouraged stage speech reduced to declamatory rant, larded with comic or melodramatic asides to the audience and fragmented by clap-trap pauses for effect. It also promoted an histrionic move-ment and gesture that for many years was artificially stylized to a code established by a few giants of the stage and embellished with 'points' [bits of business invented by the actor in order to emphasize his character or crucial moments in the action]. However, well before the end of the century the impulse of the stage to reunite actor and audience took a realistic direction. It remained only to ensure that conven-tional stage speech was tamed and delivered in an unaffected, conversational and natural voice, and that the style of acting matched a more naturalistic dialogue.

More natural speaking and acting seemed close to revolutionary when Tom Robertson made his modest attempts at writing in a more everyday vein, but it was encouraged by the development of a more sophisticated social problem play at the hands of Henry Arthur Jones, Oscar Wilde and Arthur Wing Pinero. The process was completed by the subversive invasion of the world's stages by the realistic thinking and practice of Henrik Ibsen. By the time of Queen Victoria's death in 1901, another philosophy of drama, that associated in Britain with the name George Bernard Shaw, demanded to be heard.

The profession and the star system

The state of the profession in the nineteenth century partly explains the constraints and freedoms working upon the drama. The burgeoning Victorian theatre was one of great actors and great managers, and their power and authority determined not only what plays were chosen, but also the way in which they were performed. The so-called 'star system' had its rise in this century, and it sanctioned and safeguarded the stock companies which supported it. The nature and experience of Victorian drama is inextricably tied up with the financial and artistic paternalism inherent in the system, and individual actor-managers and entrepreneurs gained an ever-tighter grip on its whole business of playwriting, acting and production. The following short check-list of outstanding names suggests a century of intense theatrical activity:

- *John Philip Kemble* (1757–1823), a great, if formal, tragedian of 'statue-like appearance' (Hazlitt, *The Times*, 25 June 1817), who set a strong example of graceful acting of the 'teapot' school of gesture. He made his début as Hamlet in 1783 and gave his farewell as Coriolanus in 1817, also managing Drury Lane and (after 1803) Covent Garden during difficult years of transition.

- *Robert Elliston* (1774–1831), actor, managed the Surrey

Theatre in 1809 and the Olympic in 1813. Presenting burletta, and in the Surrey even mixing Shakespeare and ballet, he developed these theatres into leading houses in London for the new 'Melo-Drama'.

– *Edmund Kean* (1787–1833), a tragedian of genius, made his début as Shylock at Drury Lane in 1814 and probably saved that theatre from bankruptcy. His natural brilliance as an actor resulted in an incomparable Othello, and this and other Shakespearian roles helped establish the classical repertory.

– *William Charles Macready* (1793–1873), actor-manager at both Drury Lane and Covent Garden, was one of the few romantic tragedians who could rival Kean. A man of culture, he helped reform the actor's text of Shakespeare's plays. In rehearsal it was usual for the leading actor merely to give his cast the cues, but Macready resolved 'to rehearse with the same earnestness as I should act'. On this evidence he may claim to be the first director.

– *Madame Vestris* (1797–1856), opera singer, became London's first woman manager when she took over the Olympic in 1831, producing many celebrated spectacles, as well as the extravaganzas of J. R. Planché. With her should be associated her husband, *Charles Mathews* the younger (1803–78).

– *Samuel Phelps* (1804–78), actor-manager. After the monopoly of the patent theatres had been removed in 1843, he transformed Sadler's Wells Theatre and ran it as a first-rate Shakespeare house for nearly twenty years.

– *Charles Kean* (1811–68), son of Edmund, was actor-manager at the Princess's Theatre and something of an antiquarian scholar whose work in the production of Shakespeare was commended for the historical accuracy of its scenery and costume.

– *Edwin Booth* (1833–93), Shakespeare tragedian. He was one of the first great American actors to win a reputation in London and Europe. In New York he ran the Winter

Garden Theatre, and in London he alternated the parts of Othello and Iago with Henry Irving at the Lyceum.

– *Henry Irving* (1838–1905) was an actor-manager who earned a reputation for performances of intense feeling and vivid movement. At the Lyceum Theatre, where his best work was done, he created a spectacular stage in which he paid careful attention to detail. He worked with *Ellen Terry* (1847–1928), and between them they dominated the theatre of the last years of Victoria's reign.

– *Squire Bancroft* (1841–1926), actor-manager. With his wife *Marie (née Wilton* (1839–1921)), he ran the Prince of Wales's Theatre (now the Scala) and then the Haymarket. Together they also promoted the plays of Tom Robertson and a more realistic drawing-room comedy.

– *Herbert Beerbohm Tree* (1853–1917), an actor-manager who played romantic and character parts, especially in Shakespeare. He was associated with the Haymarket and built Her Majesty's Theatre, notable for its rich and elaborately realistic sets.

– *George Alexander* (1858–1918) was actor-manager at the St James's Theatre and a performer of immense style in drawing-room comedy. His *fin-de-siècle* theatre encouraged new English playwrights, notably Arthur Wing Pinero and Oscar Wilde.

The star system flourished into the twentieth century and began to fade during the First World War. Seen in perspective, it brought with it as many blights as blessings. It contributed to the vigorous growth and economic survival of the Victorian theatre, but one disadvantage of the system, especially when irradiated by such stars as these, was that the new audiences were often more interested in the actors than the plays they performed, and the intense competitiveness and showmanship of the Victorian stage did nothing to discourage this. With such performers, the system certainly raised the standard of acting and built up strong companies and worthy repertories, but the dominance of the star was in the last analysis the ruthless force that determined and constrained the conduct of the Victorian stage and limited its range of plays.

One result of the system was to strengthen the long tradition of the 'stock company'. The 'stock' referred originally to the repertory of plays the company called upon for a nightly change of bill, or at short notice for any reason, but it also implied the necessary complement of actors and actresses, usually about ten or twelve in number, who supplied the character 'types' needed for the repertory. Naturally, the range of types varied from one company to another, and the needs of a company that was resident might be different from those of one that was touring, but it is possible to identify certain recurring roles and the particular kinds of actor who played them over the years:

The Leading Man, normally the star, was an actor capable of playing the central parts in Shakespeare's tragedies. He was complemented by *The Leading Lady*. *The Heavy*, usually the villain of melodrama, was often complemented by *The Female Heavy*. *The Old Man* played the father or the old husband, and was the reason why these two were always elderly and grey haired. He was usually complemented by *The Old Woman*. *The Juvenile Lead* was the young lover, who might or might not also serve as *The Light Comedian*. He was complemented by *The Second Lady*, or *Ingénue* [the *Soubrette* of today]. *The Low Comedian* played strong, central, 'character' roles in broad comedy and farce. Subsidiary parts were given to *The Walking Gentleman*, *The Walking Lady*, *The General Utility* of both sexes, who had to be prepared to step into any part, and *Supers* [supernumeraries]. There might also be a *Principal Dancer* and a *Vocalist*.

The system provided an apprenticeship for aspiring actors, and even encouraged the ensemble acting that was a feature of the best theatre in the next century. However, the arrangement of the stock company also suggests that any play with a large cast, for example, some of Shakespeare's, was likely to suffer doubling and cutting. It also suggests that any business-like playwright made sure that he tailored his play to the company he knew. This system contributed to the uniformity of the Victorian play and the inflexibility of the repertory.

The decline in the system was brought about by the same economic necessity that accounted for its rise. Commercial constraints hit hard, and idle hands on the stock company's payroll, rising rents and increasing costs for the elaborate costumes and scenic spectacles left little room for failures at the box office. In the twentieth century the long run of a play that was better suited to a company's economic size and need prevailed over the repertory of the stock company and finally hastened the demise of the actor-manager.

The melodrama: *Black-Eyed Susan*

The unprecedented rate of growth in the population of London was the immediate cause of a cultural revolution in the English theatre. The formerly upper- and middle-class audience was replaced by a new middle and lower-middle class, whose numbers were steadily swollen from the growing mass of urban workers, widely different in background and taste. Not since Elizabethan times had the common people gone to the theatre in such numbers, and in early Victorian times they were hardly more literate than they had been two hundred years before. However, the new audience was conscious of its position in society, as contemporary ballad and newssheet record, and as the aspirations of the Chartists indicate after 1838. And the new audience was as tyrannical a patron as ever an audience was. In 1809 the O. P. [Old Prices] riots occurred when John Philip Kemble tried to raise the cost of entrance and reduce the number of cheap seats at Covent Garden, and this event was a sure sign that the new audience had found a voice.

Every branch of the popular entertainment industry was quick to respond to the new market. Hundreds of 'penny gaffs' and 'blood-tubs' sprang up, places of entertainment of questionable legality that had as their target younger working-class people, to whom they offered a never-ending array of crude shockers and sensational playlets. By the middle of the century all the minor houses were presenting mostly unsophisticated melodramas guaranteed to be robust in plot and character, and always endowed with a happy ending and a moral precept. The storyline of these popular pieces was judiciously enlivened with a touch of violence and a breath of furtive sexuality, as a sample of titles conveys:

H. J. Byron   *The Lancashire Lass; or, Tempted, Tried and True*, 1867
C. H. Hazlewood *Pure as Driven Snow; or, Tempted in Vain*, 1869
W. H. Abel   *Faith under Peril; or, A Father's Dishonour and A Daughter's Shame*, 1873

The eloquent subtitles had the force of spelling out what the audience wanted to know. However, by the turn of the century the rowdy playgoers of earlier years, if not banished to the balconies of the big new theatres, had increasing recourse to the boisterous music halls and popular working-class houses like the Surrey, the Royal Victoria, the Britannia, the Pavilion and others of coarser taste. It comes as a surprise to realize that by this time (1879) Ibsen had long since published *A Doll's House*.

The widespread and immediate effectiveness of the melo-drama was in great measure due to its strict code of conventional signals, whose simplicity enabled the action to proceed with sure footing at breakneck speed.

The *characters* were stereotyped for instant recognition of their virtues and vices. The cast always included a heroine, a girl of impeccable purity, who was often the hapless source of conflict between the hero, who might be a young farm labourer or a simple-hearted desk clerk, and the villain, who was usually from the moneyed class and might be a squire or landowner or a ruthless employer.

The characters were identified by their *costumes* and associated *colours*. The heroine always wore white, the traditional symbol of innocence and purity. She also wore a pretty straw bonnet, which at times of stress slipped from her head and was held by a ribbon; if through adversity she found herself in a snowstorm, the bonnet was conspicuously missing. A sailor's hat and pigtail signalled a Jolly Jack Tar and usually a hero, but a redcoat [soldier] was likely to be treacherous and a seducer. The aristocratic 'toff' ['swell' or 'nob'] was identified by his fashionable topper and frock coat, but if a gentleman's clothes were out at knees and elbows, misfortune had befallen him and he 'had seen better times'. If the heroine entered in rags, it was certain that she had suffered some form of moral degradation. The villain wore black and sported a black cloak, an opera hat, a cane and a black moustache, while his opposite number, the villainess (if there was one) might reveal black hair and a swarthy complexion, her dress and ribbons often of the colour appropriate to a scarlet woman.

In those huge playhouses, and to counteract the distortions of the footlights from below and the floodlights from above, the Victorian theatre made big advances in *make-up*, and greasepaint itself arrived from the Continent in 1877. Contemporary handbooks and photographs indicate that painting one's face was also done according to stereotype: a ruddy complexion signified hearty youth and was associated either with sailors or with young men in love; blue shadows suggested the unshaven cheeks of a low comedy character; a white face indicated sickness and imminent death.

Many books offered to instruct the actor in how to make the correct *gesture* for each occasion, and in 1822 one text of choice was Henry Siddons's *Practical Illustrations of Rhetorical Gesture and Action Adapted to the English Drama*, which recognized no fewer than sixty-nine standard postures. From a survey of 'the passions' in a magazine series from Edinburgh, *The Way to the Stage, or How to Become an Actor and Get an Engagement* (1852), a single sample suggests the rest:

> *Dotage, Infirm or Old Age* shows itself by hollowness of eyes and cheeks, dimness of sight, deafness and tremor of voice, hams weak, knees tottering, hands or head paralytic, hollow coughing, frequent expectoration, breathless wheezing, occasional groaning, and the body stooping under an insupportable load of years.

The acting approach in each case was clearly thoroughgoing, and 'love', 'anger', 'grief', 'despair', 'wonder' and many other emotions were treated in similar detail. Special attention was paid to the more symbolic gestures, like wiping the eye with a handkerchief for grief, wringing the hands for despair and dropping to the knees as suppliant or suitor. The more important the role, the more there was for the actor to do: a villain strutted about on the stage, swaggered his shoulders in his vanity and brandished his legs as a threat. These histrionics were not without their critics, and the young William Poel wrote in 1874, 'A man, when he tells his friends he hopes to go to heaven, does not point towards the sky to demonstrate his meaning. Why, then, should it be done on the stage?' (Robert Speaight, *William Poel and the Elizabethan Revival* (1954), 25).

On occasion the whole cast froze, each player adopting his or her typical gesture. This formed what was known as a '*picture*' or '*tableau*', which like an engraved illustration in a Victorian novel might sum up the moral point of a crucial situation, and often created a thoughtful breathing space at an emotional climax, or justified a significant scene change or the momentous fall of a curtain.

The stage *setting* was especially meaningful. A city street was a natural harbour for villainy and crime, and a tavern was expected to encourage drunkenness. A country cottage, however lowly, was a haven of virtue and domestic bliss, whereas a wealthy ancestral home signified luxury and idleness, and was the likely abode of sinners. Attempts were usually made on the heroine's virtue or the hero's life in dreadful weather: the thunder and lightning that has presaged the wrath of the gods since ancient times, with the liberal addition of realistic rain and snow, no less foretold peril for the characters of melodrama. Agnes, the heroine of W. T. Moncrieff's *The Lear of Private Life* (1820), made sure the point was not missed when she pressed her hand to her heart and said, 'What is this storm that rages now without to that which rages here?'

On the aural side, declamation rather than conversation was the order of the day, a mode of *delivery* that was cultivated only with the help of a deliberate style of rhythmical prose or verse in the dialogue. The villain's 'tragedy oaths' still enjoy an immortality in modern pantomime: 'Distraction!' – 'Blood and thunder!' – 'Hell and confusion!' However, it is not to be supposed that when in J. E. Carpenter's *Love and Honour* (1855) Captain Melville tapped on Jessie Gray's window after dark with the intention of abducting her, any young woman would actually say, 'Why do you seek me at this untimely

hour?' nor that her seducer would reply, 'Resistance is vain; –
you must comply with my desires.' Or that even a jolly sailor
like Philip in J. B. Buckstone's *Luke the Labourer* (1826)
would say on entering, 'Anybody ahoy?' and have at his
command an endless stream of nautical turns of phrase: 'I'll
pitch you to Davy Jones in the twinkling of a handspike' –
'Shiver my topmast' – 'Handspikes and buntlines, but I'll
know who are', and so on. In this unreal context the Victorian
playwright did not hesitate to strew his dialogue with *soliloquies* and *asides*, rhetorical devices that persisted to the end of
the century.

Possibly the strongest aural element was the *music*, which
had in the beginning provided the legal excuse for performing
melodrama in the minor theatres. Musical cues punctuated the
text of the play from start to finish and expressed the mood of
every scene; they also covered the scene changes, and introduced and defined each character's role on entrance and
helped him off-stage too; they underscored the moments of
tension and excitement, and accompanied each tableau; they
enhanced scenes of violence and matched every fight blow for
blow. The piano accompaniment of the silent cinema copied
the example of the old melodrama, and even in talking
pictures the persistence of background music suggests that it
has not lost its power to manipulate an audience's reactions.
At the same time music can cover up any number of weaknesses in a story – just as it does in grand opera or musical
comedy. In the Victorian melodrama songs and dances were
also freely sprinkled through the play, and any character
might burst into song: since in the first place his lines inclined
to the condition of music, this was a convention that was
hardly incongruous.

In the world of melodrama the values were as simplified as
these perceived signals. The signals the audience perceived in
the play were therefore often profoundly unreal. The conflict
at the heart of each melodrama was a black-and-white confrontation between the forces of good and evil, set up without
ambivalence and instantly recognizable. Moreover, vice was
always punished and virtue always rewarded, like the debit
and credit of a balance sheet – even the direst suffering was a

pleasure to watch if the audience knew there would be some compensation. This tidy result was often accomplished by the intervention of providence, which sometimes turned up in the last act as a complete surprise – a lost relative, a missing treasure, even a total stranger. The obligatory ingredient at all costs was divine justice.

This powerful strategy was so transparently didactic in intent that it could be applied to a wide category of plays. Especially in demand on both sides of the Atlantic were 'gambling' and 'temperance' plays: not only did these dramas offer a rousing story, but no leading actor was likely to refuse the histrionic opportunity of a slow descent into starvation or *delerium tremens*. Nevertheless, the range of subjects suitable for moral object lessons was wide: the depravity of city life, the neglect of work or family, the consequences of failing to pay the rent, the usurer's greed and above all the ever-present temptation to sexual immorality. The single formula of the melodrama fitted every sin or transgression.

Black-Eyed Susan, which played at the Surrey in 1829 under R. W. Elliston's management, displays all the ingredients for success and from many hundreds of melodramas provides a good example. It was a first nautical drama by Douglas Jerrold (1803–57), who had served in the Navy during the recent war with Napoleon, and was larded with naval airs supplied by Charles Dibdin the younger. The hero was played by the popular actor T. P. Cooke, who had himself been a sailor, and London rejoiced. The production proved to be a milestone, engendering other nautical plays and encouraging the odd practice of writing sailors into plays that had nothing whatever to do with the Navy. It remained in the repertory until 1897, appearing under a number of different titles and as both an opera and a burlesque. The royalty system had not then been introduced, and it is sad to report that Jerrold was paid a simple lump sum of £60 for his work.

In its nautical and patriotic spirit the play in its day made an unmistakable appeal. Dickens wrote to the author after the first night, 'It was so fresh and vigorous, so manly and gallant, that I felt as if it splashed against my theatre-heated face along with the spray of the breezy sea.' In *Blood and Thunder* (1949) M. Willson Disher wrote,

No drama was ever more nautical; no other seamen so redolent of tar, so virtuous compared with landsmen, so full of sea-faring oaths, exclamations, similes and metaphors – salt water is rarely out of their mouths and often fills their eyes.

The plot, however, barely merits consideration: it turns on a story of a vicious landlord who threatens to evict a poor widow and her daughter unless the rent is paid, and its ingredients for success come from elsewhere. To begin with, the play's simplicity is a powerful element. In its action it gets straight to the point, and the exposition of the plot is heard in the first few lines. Gnatbrain is an honest countryman who promptly accuses the villain Doggrass of having got rid of the hero William to the Navy:

> GNATBRAIN. ... Didn't you make him turn a sailor, and leave his young wife, the little, delicate black-eyed Susan, that pretty piece of soft-speaking womanhood, your niece? Now say, haven't you qualms? On a winter's night, now, when the snow is drifting at your door, what do you do?
>
> DOGGRASS. Shut it.
>
> (1.1)

This villain is a man of few words, but before the exposition is over, the good Gnatbrain addresses the house in order to emphasize all it needs to know about him: 'That rascal has no more heart than a bagpipe!' Such direct statements from stage to auditorium are mandatory markers along the narrative path.

With Jacob Twig the bailiff at her heels, Susan is the widow's daughter who could be shut out in the threatened snow, and her problems do not come singly. She is also besieged by suitors for her hand in the shape of two ancillary villains, Captains Hatchet and Crosstree, both of them (to the disquiet of the audience) naval *officers*. Hatchet puts it out that Susan's husband William is dead, as much to bring an affecting grief to the heroine as to justify his attentions to her. The widow is never seen and the husband is absent, but Susan has Gnatbrain to defend her. This he manages to do when Jacob is taking inventory by knocking him down with a rolling-pin (Gnatbrain triumphantly '*stands in attitude*') and then locking him out (Gnatbrain comments, 'A bailiff, like a snowstorm, is always best on the outside').

To turn the mood of the play around, 1.4 offers '*A view of the Downs*' and calls for a sight of '*The fleet at anchor*' – an important moment of painterly spectacle. This is lustily reinforced by loud music and shouts off-stage: '*three cheers*' twice go up, and a troupe of Jolly Jack Tars enters singing and dancing. They constitute a prelude to the entrance of William, who is back from the wars and full of life:

> Huzza! huzza! my noble fellows, my heart jumps like a dolphin – my head turns round like a capstern; I feel as if I were driving before the gale of pleasure for the haven of joy.

So William and his sailors make a boisterous musical entrance, and when a happy gaggle of girls joins them laughing and singing, the stage is full and colourful. William is simple, honest, sentimental – and patriotic to the point of jingoism. Beyond his flood of nautical expressions, he actually does not have a lot to say, but at least he is there to save black-eyed Susan from her seducers. Unfortunately, the nautical celebration of coming ashore is short-lived, and Jerrold changes the mood again – first when Hatchet enters to do his worst, and then again when Crosstree enters to do his. Thus in two separate scenes in the first act, William is compelled to strike a blow for virtue, and each occasion is strongly marked with a significant tableau.

Alas, these sober tableaux and the change of musical tempo from quick to slow give everyone due warning: William has made the mistake of striking a superior officer – a capital offence, and distinction of rank must be preserved. So the last act centres on a court martial in which William is tried for drawing a weapon on Captain Crosstree – one of the many predictable trial scenes that has satisfied the melodramatic taste of much modern theatre. Here in the setting of 2.2 Jerrold presents another kind of stageworthy spectacle: an Admiral at the head of the table, three guns on each side and the Union Jack above, with six captains and sundry mariners and marines formally disposed at and around the table. With this impressive ceremonial and plenty of music William is sentenced to death, the Admiral shaking his hand and the prisoner dropping to one knee in a noble act of submission. A good deal of time is then allowed for pathetic farewells, with William singing 'Black-Eyed Susan' and Susan in tears. Yet! – at the last moment Crosstree reveals that William has already received his discharge, so that he cannot in fact have committed the crime of which he stands accused. All in a moment the mood of the play changes again, now from the depth of despair to the height of joy. William is reprieved, the music swells and the cheers of the sailors echo round the house at the fall of the curtain.

With all the elements of drama working together, such sudden extremes of feeling, however predictable, characterized this popular form, and it did not seem to matter that the sensational manipulation of the audience, visually and aurally, was unashamedly contrived.

Working on both sides of the Atlantic, the Irish actor Dion Boucicault (?1820–90) wrote more than a hundred plays – someone said of him that he wrote plays 'as a hen lays eggs' – and developed an innovative style of Irish melodrama with *The Colleen Bawn* (which opened in New York in 1860 before going to London), *Arrah-Na-Pogue* (opening in Dublin, 1864) and *The Shaughraun* (New York, 1874). He was most admired for his clever exploitation of the new mechanics of the stage, and to his ingenuity the beginnings of the Victorian 'sensation drama' may be attributed. M. Willson Disher considered that Boucicault's achievement arose from his method of 'borrowing a plot from one source and a scenic device from another, and then adding a newly invented apparatus which would remind an audience of its modern life'. For *The Colleen Bawn*, for example, Boucicault borrowed the sad little story of Eily O'Connor, who was drowned by her husband Danny so that he could make a wealthier marriage. In the play the 'sensation' focused on tossing Eily into a water-cave, specially built on the stage with transparent water made of blue gauze with small boys concealed beneath it to make the waves stormy. In Boucicault's version Danny is shot at from the shore and Eily (played by his wife Agnes Robertson) is saved from the water by a death-defying leap executed by the author himself playing the singing part of a comic Irish poacher, Myles-na-Coppaleen.

A rainbow of comic styles: *The Importance of Being Earnest*

Just as it welcomed every form of melodrama, the theatre of the period was open to all manner of comic expression. T. J. Dibdin's *Don Giovanni; or, A Spectre on Horseback!* (1817) was advertised with a fine disregard for the proprieties as 'A comic, heroic, operatic, tragic, pantomimic, burletta-spectacular extravaganza': the comic impulse was experimental or merely running riot. At all events, the comic mode gathered a large variety of labels:

Pantomime, which had originated with the Italian *commedia dell'arte*, emerged again during the Regency period (1811–20) as a *harlequinade* without dialogue. In *The Examiner* Leigh Hunt was delighted with it: 'The stage is never empty or still; either Pantaloon is hobbling about, or somebody is falling flat, or somebody else is receiving an ingenious thump on the face, or the Clown is jolting himself with jaunty dislocations, or Colombine is skimming across like a frightened pigeon, or Harlequin is quivering hither and thither' (26 January 1817). Pantomime took another form as a Christmas entertainment before the end of the century.

Burletta freely mixed all the comic genres in practice, but in law defeated definition: on one occasion the Lord Chamberlain's office ruled that it should contain 'not less than five pieces of vocal music in each act', and on another described it as 'a short comic piece, consisting of recitative and singing, wholly accompanied, more or less [*sic*], by the orchestra'. It was associated with the Adelphi and also the Olympic, where under Madame Vestris's management the theatre was saved in 1831 by the popular *Olympic Revels*, the first of a series of burlettas by J. R. Planché (1796–1880). In his hands the burletta was blended with the extravaganza.

15 Dion Boucicault, *The Colleen Bawn*, the Adelphi Theatre, 1860: on the rock Danny is shot, while in the water Eily is drowning.

The extravaganza was a dramatic revue, defined by Planché himself as 'a whimsical treatment of a poetical subject'. In practice it was an elegant and charming fairy or folk fantasy with much singing and dancing. It also made satirical reference to contemporary operas or anything it chose. Under Vestris it was enhanced with an ingenious 'transformation scene' or some other form of scenic magic.

Burlesque knew no rules: the actors exhibited, according to an observer, 'a frantic outburst of irrepressible animal spirits'. In particular, it was inevitable that the bubble of po-faced melodrama should be pricked, and it fell to the burlesque style of comic opera invented by Gilbert and Sullivan to complete the work, beginning with the gentle satire of *HMS Pinafore* (1878).

Farce, a play in one or two acts which upset reality by concocting absurd situations performed at a furious pace. It abounded in coincidence, mistaken identities and ridiculous encounters: it was the French *farceur* Georges Feydeau's rule that if certain characters should on no account meet, they must soon do so – often in a bedroom. Earlier farce was played in the *commedia dell'arte* style with rapid asides to the house and a great deal of slapstick, but under the influence of Scribe's French farce, its visual buffoonery acquired some of the discipline of the well-made play, as in the familiar *Charley's Aunt* (1892) by Brandon Thomas (1849–1914) and *The Gay Lord Quex* (1899) by Arthur W. Pinero (1855–1934).

High comedy, a play usually in three acts, did not evolve as a distinctive form in the Victorian period. It was either derivative from the comedy of manners of the previous century, or conditioned by the pressures of melodrama, farce or burlesque. Even the best of the Victorian comedies, Oscar Wilde's *The Importance of Being Earnest* is in debt to the mechanics of farce and the burlesque of W. S. Gilbert (1836–1911).

In this mode of farcical comedy all examples in English are outclassed by one of the best constructed plays, *The Importance of Being Earnest* (1895) by Oscar Wilde (1856–1900). This play has often been seen as a satirical commentary on contemporary *mores* – such Victorian ceremonies as taking tea, courtship and marriage, and so on – but Wilde gives it the subtitle 'A trivial comedy for serious people', and it is exactly what it says. While it may well turn its audience's expectations upside down, it is not, thankfully, either important or earnest in its social criticism. As stagecraft, however, it has a perfection that marks the end of a long process in the history of the English comedy of manners, and its greatest virtue lies in its unusual consistency in tone and style – in itself a devastating weapon of dramatic satire.

It was produced by George Alexander for the patrons who went to the fashionable St James's Theatre, a smaller house with a capacity of 1,200. According to Hesketh Pearson, Alexander catered for the tastes of society like the manager of the Savoy Hotel and 'seldom deviated one hair's breadth from the safe path of correct riskiness'. It is a play of immense wit, and deceptively so. If the irreverent little maxims offered in almost every line lightly touch issues of the family, society and even art ('In married life, three is company and two is none' – 'Divorces are made in Heaven' – 'The good ended happily, and the bad unhappily. That is what Fiction means', etc.), by such persistent inversions they take the play in performance on to an unexpected level of impropriety. The simple plotting itself, of what happens if you show a respectable face in town and practise 'bunburying' [being yourself] in the country, or if your happiness turns preposterously on being christened Ernest, must be played out with the deadly seriousness required by farce. John Gielgud, who has directed the play several times, indicates that the young men, for example, must conduct themselves with an 'irreproachable exactitude',

> hitching their trousers before they sit down, stripping off their gloves, shooting their cuffs. Their hats are worn at exactly the right angle, their canes carried with an air of studied negligence. They have never been seen in Bond Street or Piccadilly without top-hats and frock-coats.
>
> (*Stage Directions* (1963), 80)

In performance the comedy works as mockery through the

puppet-like tone and style of the playing, by which the St James's audience is disarmed and invited to view itself.

The play is built of encounters, usually of two characters at a time, and episode after episode demonstrates the automatic side of human behaviour, as between the sexes, the social classes or the generations. The seriousness of social propriety is conveyed by the stiff dignity of the characters and marked by a perfect balance, and sometimes even symmetry, of voice, gesture and blocking, so that the action is repeatedly cast into comic perspective. The term 'artificial comedy' was never more appropriate than when this play is performed with stylized precision. It is, incidentally, this quality that has encouraged the amusing modern tradition of dressing and designing it like a colourful fantasy, unlike the more realistic décor of the first production.

The gentle but consistent pressure of exaggeration in each character's lines at the first encounter between Jack and Gwendolen in act 1 exactly captures the *principle* of the relationship between male and female at the time of a proposal of marriage:

> JACK.   I would like to be allowed to take advantage of Lady Bracknell's temporary absence –
>
> GWENDOLEN. I would certainly advise you to do so. Mamma has a way of coming back suddenly into a room that I have often had to speak to her about.
>
> JACK (*nervously*). Miss Fairfax, ever since I met you I have admired you more than any girl – I have ever met since – I met you.

In her position of power Gwendolen is sitting (as Alexander's directions confirm) with a supreme confidence, while Jack, the suppliant, is on his feet. She is relaxed and still and coolly looking askance, while he is tense and restless as he searches for a way to broach the subject. Her speech is clipped and authoritative, while his is rambling and hesitant (Wilde added the nervous pauses later, but they are implicit in the writing). All these details add up: theirs is the intimacy of the snake and the rabbit.

When Jack enters slowly from upstage in act 2, he is '*in deepest mourning*'. His frock-coat is complemented by black gloves, black cane, black hat, black crape hatband and (playing Jack himself) Alexander sported even a black-bordered pocket handkerchief. The audience has been forewarned of Jack's plan to allow his brother 'Ernest' to die of a chill in Paris, but nevertheless this incongruous image, that of a figure of mortality caught against the sunny garden setting and about to announce the death of someone who ironically at this moment is flirting with Cecily off-stage, comes as a surprise to everyone. The production arranged that the audience caught sight of Jack before those on stage, and William Archer described the original effect:

> The audience does not instantly awaken to the meaning of his inky suit, but even as he marches solemnly down the stage, and before a word is spoken, you can feel the idea kindling from row to row, until a 'sudden glory' of laughter fills the theatre.
>
> (*The World*, 20 February 1895)

Only then, when the audience is itself aware of the comic values in the scene, does Wilde allow the other characters an appropriate response:

CHASUBLE. Dear Mr Worthing, I trust this garb of woe does not betoken some terrible calamity?
JACK. My brother.
MISS PRISM. More shameful debts and extravagance?
CHASUBLE. Still leading his life of pleasure?
JACK (*shaking his head*). Dead!
CHASUBLE. Your brother Ernest dead?
JACK. Quite dead.
MISS PRISM. What a lesson for him! I trust he will profit by it.

The sanctimonious reactions of Chasuble and Prism are thoroughly in keeping with the way the play has projected these two, and as Jack goes on to embroider his story, the pieties the audience expected from them are confirmed. Meanwhile the happy entrance of Algernon as 'Ernest', back from the dead and dressed in one of his most colourful 'Bunbury suits', is every moment anticipated.

This remarkable play also generates a method of controlling the strings of its marionettes by duplicating their speech,

movement, gesture, pace and tone. When Cecily and Gwendolen meet in act 2, each suspicious of the other's motives,
their quarrel goes back and forth like a rally in tennis. Each
one's speech and gesture are echoes of the other's; their voices
are equally polite or equally icy; they sit down together, rise
together and speak their asides like echoes. In adversity they
cling together, and on reconciliation in act 3 they defend
themselves against the two men like mirror images of one
another, even, finally, to speaking a crucial line in unison:
'Your Christian names are an insuperable barrier. That is all!'
The picture is of two girls who are intrinsically alike and
motivated by the same set of attitudes, thus representing the
rest of their sex.

As for the men, their moment of greatest idiocy is also
projected by mirroring. At the end of act 2 their quarrel again
makes use of the echo device:

> JACK.   I wanted to be engaged to Gwendolen, that is
>   all. I love her.
> ALGERNON. Well, I simply wanted to be engaged to
>   Cecily. I adore her ...

The possibilities of moving the puppets to match these
fatuous lines are endless, and as the two men play face to face
with voice and gesture balanced, their childishness is cleverly
illuminated. This trick works even better when the squabble
develops into a tug-of-war about what they are eating, and
when the weapon, like the cucumber sandwiches of act 1, is a
plate of muffins. If this is social satire, its mode is deceptively
farcical and flawlessly exhibitionistic.

The advent of realism: *Caste, The Second Mrs Tanqueray*

High comedy or low melodrama is, like any drama, a distor-
tion of actuality, but already in the 1860s there were signs of
'reform' and a degree of new realism. Stage scenery tried to be
more accurate in representing streets and buildings; stage
lighting for exteriors and interiors, and for night and day, was
more sensitive; the box set looked like an actual room with

real doors and constituted a planned acting area; and authors searched for subjects that would reflect the world of the popular audience. Working together, these factors encouraged a steady change to a more discriminating style of staging and acting.

In earlier plays there were many realistic moments, and *The Ticket-of-Leave Man* by Tom Taylor (1817–80), produced at the Olympic in 1863, already hinted at the social problems that captured the interest of the new audience. Reform of the style of performance is especially recognizable in the work of the actor-playwright Tom Robertson (1829–71), especially in the sequence of plays *Society* (1865), *Ours* (about the Crimean War, 1866), *Caste* (on class differences, 1867), *Play* (on gambling, 1868), *School* (1869) and *M.P.* (on electioneering, 1870), written for the Bancrofts at the Prince of Wales's Theatre. This theatre was smaller and its middle-class audience more homogeneous, and in this situation both playwright and managers were determined to produce a play with more subtlety. Robertson rehearsed the actors in a more natural and less rhetorical manner of playing, and, using the whole stage, achieved something like ensemble performance, with no actor trying to eclipse his fellows. Box sets were planned with attention to the detail indicating the class and income of the occupants. Doors and windows were expected to work, and small hand-props like pipes and umbrellas, or cups and saucers, were introduced to increase the natural behaviour of the characters and often became part of the 'business' of a scene. Robertson's drama, therefore, was not inappropriately labelled 'cup and saucer comedy'.

The stiff, synthetic mechanism of *Caste* is characteristic of the early well-made play. It is a comedy in three acts which changes its set in acts 1 and 2 in order to convey the contrasting life-styles of the two classes of people in the play. One set depicts a simple, somewhat shabby, lower-class room in the imaginary London suburb of 'Stangate' and the other a well-to-do appartment in Mayfair; act 3 returns to the scene of act 1 with the addition of key details that indicate the passage of time and the change of circumstances. Each act carries the audience through a phase in the development of the play's theme, one clearly expressed at the opening of the play

by the Dragoon officer Captain Hawtree when he is asked
why his friend the Hon. George D'Alroy should not marry
the ballet-dancer Esther Eccles whom he loves:

> Caste! – the inexorable law of caste. The social law, so
> becoming and so good, that commands like to mate with
> like, and forbids a giraffe to fall in love with a squirrel.

The result is that George marries Esther against the wishes of
his formidable mother, the Marquise de St Maur, the stereotype of an inflexible dragon, and is then ordered to India on
active service. The actress playing Esther is required to run
the gamut of emotions when in act 3 she learns that her
husband has been killed.

Esther's baby boy dominates and determines the structure
of the action in act 3, being present on stage throughout, like
an invisible prop in a cradle. At the outset her lively sister
Polly draws attention to the baby by speaking to him in
soliloquy, as indeed does their drunken father Eccles, who
puffs smoke in the baby's face, envies him his milk and finally
steals the coral from around his neck. This child also brings
the Marquise back into the action in search of her grandson,
and when, finally, George returns from India alive after all, it
is the child who reunites the family: for the tableau curtain she
is seen bending over the cradle. The repeated aphorism is
'True hearts are more than coronets.'

Structurally, the play is under a rigorous discipline, and
Robertson's sense of a new and realistic stagecraft is apparent.
There is a moment near the end of act 1 when two centres of
interest are working simultaneously on stage, their counterpoint creating a theatrical statement that is more at the heart
of the play than any thematic protestation about caste. The
idealized couple of George and Esther are amorously tête-a-
tête by the fire while the less complicated Polly and her
sweetheart Sam Gerridge are in the middle of a lovers'
quarrel:

> GEORGE. I never really think of anything else but you.
> ESTHER. Really?
> SAM (goes to *bureau, misses cap, looks around, sees it on
> floor, picks it up angrily, and comes to Polly, who*

> *is sitting by the table*). I won't stay here to be
> insulted. (*Putting on cap*).
> POLLY.   Nobody wants you to stay. Go! Go! Go!
> ESTHER.   And shall you always love me as you do now?
> GEORGE. More.

The quarrel develops as Polly changes her mind and locks the
door (a working door) to stop Sam's going, so that he must
climb out of the window (to everyone's surprise, a working
window). Sam is the sort who whistles and tosses his cap
across a room, and believes that 'people should stick to their
own class'; the animated Polly was thought by Dickens to be
'a one-girl imitation of the Christy minstrels' – she sings and
dances and at one point prances up and down like a soldier on
horseback, using her parasol as a lance. Not only do the pairs
of lovers effectively comment on one another, showing two
aspects of the loving relationship as well as two sorts of social
behaviour, but by a touch of low comedy the author manages
to undercut the maudlin lines of the leading characters and
understate the depth of their devotion, a double-focus stagecraft not unworthy of Chekhov.

By using the detail of real life to manipulate an audience,
late Victorian drama was able to introduce a new range of
subjects, where causes were more attractive to the box-office
than effects, where characters could be ambiguous and not
simply good or evil, where the formula did not always require
a moral ending and happiness was not the only reward. But
problematic themes that did not admit easy answers could not
be expressed in stereotyped situations with two-dimensional
characters. A socially honest drama had also to be theatrically
realistic: the external trappings of stagecraft had still to point
to what was intrinsically internal and subtextual.

The growth of the social problem play (sometimes named
'society drama') coincided with the techniques of *la pièce bien
faite* [the well-made play], although the practice of many
post-Brechtian playwrights indicates that there is no necessary
connection between a realistic subject and a realistic style. On
the Victorian stage, however, the example of Scribe and
Sardou in Paris imposed a certain law of logical dramaturgy
upon the writing of a social play and its performance. When
the mechanism of the well-made play did not creak, its

discipline in fact served a good deal of modern drama well. Its object was to ensure that the spectator was on the edge of his seat at all times. To effect this, the story of the play began, like Greek and neo-classical tragedy, at the crisis, so that the audience was plunged quickly into the predicament of the hero or heroine. The method called for more exposition of past events than usual, but it permitted no irrelevance. By a series of revelations, turns and reversals, the situation grew increasingly tense until it was insupportable, and at this point the play supplied the *scène à faire* [obligatory scene] in which what was hidden is revealed. It is said that Sardou wrote this scene first and worked backwards from it.

Oscar Wilde wrote three problem plays by this procedure: *Lady Windermere's Fan* (for Alexander at the St James's, 1892), *A Woman of No Importance* (at the Haymarket, 1893) and *An Ideal Husband* (at the Haymarket, 1895). He was able to write about exclusively upper-class characters for a society audience, and rather indulged himself in writing a dialogue of epigrammatic wit. He created a world of glittering drawing-rooms and incriminating letters, handsome bachelor quarters and lovely ladies hiding behind curtains. Each play focused on a scandalous secret, usually connected with a woman: in the case of *An Ideal Husband*, the focus is perversely on Sir Robert Chiltern, for once a *man* 'with a past'. In *Lady Windermere's Fan* the ostracized Mrs Erlynne wishes to recover her place in society, but when her daughter Lady Windermere is nearly discovered in Lord Darlington's rooms, she protects her daughter's reputation at the expense of her own, an ending of somewhat ambiguous morality. In fact the working title of the play had been *A Good Woman*, and its ironic subtitle remained *A Play about a Good Woman*. Wilde was not the amoralist he was taken to be, but had a moral purpose of his own.

It is hard not to admire the way the play is constructed. In performance the audience is not troubled by the contrivances of an improbable plot. Rather, it is soon caught in the grip of a four-act structure in which each scene takes a step towards an inevitable end. In the inception of the play, George Alexander, the producer who also played the part of Lord Windermere, recognized that at some point the audience had to learn of Mrs

Erlynne's identity, and he correctly argued that this should occur early on so that the spectator might share with the author every ironic development of the action. In the event, however, the audience learns the truth only after it has had a chance to share Lady Windermere's agony of mind.

Against the polite background of the Windermere home, act I reveals the principals in an increasingly tortured square dance of sophisticated lovers. It also introduces the lady's fan, a hand prop that begins as a simple birthday present from husband to wife and grows in theatrical importance in every scene as it binds the story together. Above all, act I establishes the fact that the appalled Lady Windermere believes Mrs Erlynne to be her husband's mistress. Her first soliloquy ends 'How horrible!' and the curtain falls on Lord Windermere's dilemma:

> My God! What shall I do? I dare not tell her who this woman really is. The shame would kill her. (*Sinks down into a chair and buries his face in his hands.*)

At this point the audience has a first hint of the hidden relationship.

Against the lighter comedy of the ball in act 2, where the Duchess of Berwick demonstrates how to ensnare a wealthy Australian as a husband for her colourless daughter, the audience learns of the potentially adulterous relationship between Lady Windermere and Lord Darlington, but it is not until the end of this act, when Mrs Erlynne has a helpful soliloquy, that it can be sure that Lady Windermere is her daughter.

Act 3 brings the *scène à faire*. Provoked into leaving her husband, Lady Windermere waits alone in Darlington's rooms, and it is there that Mrs Erlynne confronts her:

> Back to your house, Lady Windermere – your husband loves you! He has never swerved for a moment from the love he bears you. But even if he had a thousand loves, you must stay with your child.

At this critical moment most of the gentlemen of the play enter in high spirits. The ladies must hide, and Lady Windermere inadvertently leaves her fan on the sofa. Now the author painfully suspends the action, so that the audience cannot forget the fan. With strong dramatic irony, the conversation is of women and moral behaviour – until at last the fan is spotted. The pace speeds up when Windermere challenges Darlington, until unexpectedly, in a true *coup de théâtre*, Mrs Erlynne steps forward to claim the offending object.

> MRS ERLYNNE.   I am afraid I took your wife's fan in
>   mistake for my own, when I was leaving
>   your house tonight. I am so sorry.
> *Takes fan from him.* LORD WINDERMERE *looks at her in contempt.* LORD DARLINGTON *in mingled astonishment and anger.* LORD AUGUSTUS *turns away. The other men smile at each other.*

The curtain falls on a tableau of facial expressions, leaving the audience to savour the complexity of the moment and the significance of Mrs Erlynne's sacrifice. Act 4 brings the ship safely back to harbour: Lady Windermere has returned to her husband and child, but never learns who her mother is.

The actor-dramatist Arthur Wing Pinero (1855–1934) was the author of fifty-five plays, and several of his early farces have been successfully revived, especially *The Magistrate* (1885, adapted as *Little Lies* and revived as recently as 1983), *The Schoolmistress* (1886) and *Dandy Dick* (1887). However, he shared an ideal of realism with Henry Arthur Jones, who wrote in 1895 of his intention 'to treat the great realities of our modern life upon our stage'. Pinero's particular interest in a realistic tradition on the English stage is confirmed by his late tribute to Tom Robertson when he created the character of Tom Wrench in *Trelawney of the 'Wells'* (1898) and set much of the action in a theatrical lodging-house of the 1860s, offering a host of insights into 'the profession' of the day, especially the changes in its style of acting. It is really a play about the theatre and has been a favourite since it was written: London actually saw two productions in 1992 and 1993. In act 1 the leading actress complains that Tom wrote speeches that 'were so short and had such ordinary words in them' that they did not give her the opportunity a professional actor needs. His reply is historically memorable:

> M'yes. I strive to make my people talk and behave like live people, don't I – ? ... To fashion heroes out of actual, dull, everyday men – the sort of men you see smoking cheroots in the club windows in St James's Street; and heroines from simple maidens in muslin frocks. Naturally, the managers won't stand that.

For although, like Wilde, Pinero wrote chiefly about upper-class society, he eschewed the artificiality of Wilde's problem play characters, and wrote a more natural dialogue. Pinero had tried his hand at realism in *The Money-Spinner* (1881), a satirical treatment of gambling, and had attacked the double standard of sexual morality in *The Profligate* and *Lady Bountiful* (both 1891), but it was not until *The Second Mrs Tanqueray* was produced at the St James's Theatre in 1893 with particularly sensitive performances by Mrs Patrick Campbell as Paula and George Alexander as Aubrey, that everything fell into place. This play took London by storm: it was praised as an example of excellent stagecraft and was held by some to be great literature and by others to be a touchstone for the new drama.

The play was none of these things, but it has certain virtues. Its theme is again the double standard, posed as a test on family life when Paula Tanqueray, formerly of questionable class and 'a woman of easy virtue', tries to sustain a marriage in good society. In spite of his love for her, her husband Aubrey cannot forget the past when he discovers that she was once the mistress of the man whom his 'iceberg' daughter Ellean wants to marry, and Paula kills herself. This story has been criticized because it suggests that the play asserts the conventional moral lesson of melodrama, that a fallen woman must pay for her sins. But Paula's character is drawn so warmly that an audience cannot help feeling sympathy with her in her predicament; for her part, the convent-bred Ellean is so righteous that her censure becomes self-criticism; and for all that the 'other man' is a brave and charming army officer, the audience is less ready to forgive the excuse of his having been 'a bit wild at one time' and having lived 'a man's life'. The bitter ending is logical, but its moral reflects less on the woman than on society. This is reinforced at the end by

Aubrey himself, who guides the audience to a thinking and feeling response:

> Curse him! (*Hurling his book to the floor.*) Curse him! Yes, I do curse him – him and his class! Perhaps I curse myself too in doing it. He has only led 'a man's life' – just as I, how many of us, have done!

His curtain line is, 'If I had only been merciful!'

Yet none of this would work if Pinero had not first exercised a degree of skill as a realistic playwright. The lengthy exposition of act 1 has what the audience needs to know conveyed by Cayley Drummle while Aubrey is writing a letter, and Drummle is used as an all-too-convenient confidant, but in performance this is done unobtrusively and with lifelike ease. Soliloquies and asides have gone, and although incriminating letters turn up relentlessly, riveting incidents accumulate irresistibly. Pinero also hits upon the useful device of staging a comic parallel to the case of Paula and Aubrey in the less troubling persons of Sir George and Lady Orreyed (happily named 'Dodo' and 'Birdie') who have made an accommodation with society.

The outstanding contribution to making the play credible arises from Paula's characterization. She is a creature of mixed and varied feelings, sufficiently human to show bitterness and ill temper, and subtly observed. Pinero also has the gift of bringing the character to life in a variety of situations. For example, the truth comes out in the *scène à faire* of the last act, but Paula's sense of the animosity between herself and her step-daughter inhibits her speech and it is Ellean who has the burden of *guessing* the truth:

> ELLEAN. Why, after all, what can you know! You can only speak from gossip, report, hearsay! How is it possible that you – ! (*She stops abruptly. The two women stand staring at each other for a moment; then* ELLEAN *backs away from* PAULA *slowly.*) Paula!
> PAULA. What – what's the matter?
> ELLEAN. You – you knew Captain Ardale in London!
> PAULA. Why – what do you mean?
> ELLEAN. Oh! (*She makes for the door ...*)

The moment is partly understated and surprisingly under control, extending an invitation, as it were, to the actress to make her own contribution in the pauses. Paula Tanqueray was a part that made Mrs Campbell a leading actress, and graced the careers of Madge Kendal, Eleonora Duse and Gladys Cooper. The demands of the professional stage and of the new realism had found a compromise.

The nineteenth century saw fundamental changes in the English stage and its stagecraft. At the end of Victoria's reign the new playhouses were being purpose-built for particular kinds of drama and different kinds of audiences. Granted a handful of knighthoods, the profession of acting had acquired respectability, and with it the playwrights also gained in status. Comedy that was little more than a clown show at the beginning of the century became a source of wit and satire. With the discipline of the well-made play crude melodrama was refined to craftsmanship, and in the so-called problem plays it learned to manage its subject-matter and manipulate its audience with some subtlety. If the English stage had yet to recognize the nature and extent of the revolution taking place on the Continent, guided by Ibsen, Strindberg, Hauptmann and Chekhov, it at least anticipated the new century not without a degree of readiness.

13

Bernard Shaw and his stage practice

Shaw the Ibsenite: *Mrs Warren's Profession*

The workings of a Shavian play still surprise and tease the critics and scholars. On the English stage, the Irishman George Bernard Shaw (1856–1950) was the major innovator of modern times in managing the actor and his audience, effectively breaking general resistance to the reform of the drama and enabling the new century to explore its stagecraft freely. Within a few years he had taken bold steps away from any contemporary ideals of realism in performance and towards a more urgent realism in purpose. In his day he fluttered the critics by flouting convention and constraint, and by developing his sense of a play as a discussion with the audience. Shaw despised the careful carpentry of the well-made play: in his review of Pinero's *The Second Mrs Tanqueray* he was scathing about the 'dead machinery' and the 'lay figures' the author had substituted for 'vital action' and 'real characters' (*Our Theatres in the Nineties*, vol 1, 46), and although Shaw could construct a play of social realism with the best of them, and did so, he increasingly used the medium of the theatre to find other ways of reaching an audience.

At this time the well-made play was espoused by many critics, including Shaw's friend, the young Scottish critic William Archer (1856–1924). Ironically, it was Archer who started Shaw on the road to playwriting, even though Archer advised him to give up writing plays because he thought he had no obvious talent for the stage. (Before Shaw finished, he

(References are to the Standard Edition of *The Works of Bernard Shaw* (1931–1950))

had written several masterpieces – and altogether fifty-two plays and one-acts.) The relationship between Shaw and Archer begins with the story of the tortured composition of *Widowers' Houses* (1892), which recalls the debt they owed to Ibsen.

Ibsenism proper arrived in London through Archer's articles and translations, and a single matinee performance in 1880 of *The Pillars of Society* under the Robertsonian title *Quicksands*. The production caused scarcely a ripple, but, upon the call for author, Archer took his bow and thereafter became Ibsen's translator and self-appointed guardian in English. This event led next year to a meeting with Shaw in the Reading Room of the British Library, where Archer found him 'alternately, if not simultaneously' poring over *Das Kapital* in French and the score of *Tristan und Isolde*: these two men, both aged twenty-nine, shared their common enthusiasm for Ibsen. In 1884 Henry Arthur Jones emasculated *A Doll's House* under the title *Breaking a Butterfly*, reducing the original to an English setting in which Humphrey and Flossie (Torvald and Nora) are, according to conservative convention, tearfully *reconciled* at the curtain. The preface to *Plays Unpleasant* tells how the next year Shaw and Archer decided to collaborate in the writing of an Ibsenite comedy in English on the topic of slum landlords, with Shaw agreeing to supply the dialogue to Archer's plot. At this time Archer believed that the essence of good drama was the well-made structure of exposition, conflict and resolution, and it was this meticulous plotting he passed to Shaw. The Irishman had no use for any of this and soon told his partner, 'Look here, I have written half the first act of that comedy, and I've used up all your plot. Now I want some more to go on with' (*Prefaces* (1934)). The collaboration came to a quick end.

In 1889 Archer's translation of *A Doll's House* received a respectable production at the Novelty Theatre with Charles Charrington and his wife Janet Achurch. In 1891 the enterprising director J. T. Grein (1862–1935) inaugurated the Independent Theatre Society with an epoch-making production of Ibsen's *Ghosts*, and now looked about for a native play in the same vein. Shaw patched together the fragments of his play about landlords, added a last act, called it *Widowers' Houses* and volunteered the rather muddled result. The play had a contentious production in 1892 at the Royalty Theatre, where it was received in pandemonium. Upon the call for author, Shaw, nothing loath, jumped on the stage to deliver a lecture on socialism, delighted that he had made a reputation at a stroke: in his words, 'I had not achieved a success; but I had provoked an uproar; and the sensation was so agreeable that I resolved to try again' (Preface, xi).

Although the public was far from approving the new realism, Ibsen's influence came to be felt nevertheless, since playgoers began to expect a challenge to their assumptions from every new play. The process was slow, even misleading. Shaw insisted that all great drama was didactic, and he understandably made his supporters uneasy. *The Quintessence of Ibsenism* (1891) began life as a political lecture to the Fabian Society, which may explain its provocative tone, but it tells more about the visionary new playwright Bernard Shaw than about Ibsen's own intentions. Shaw's next attempt at an Ibsenite comedy, *The Philanderer* (1893), deliberately set Ibsenite against non-Ibsenite in a discussion of 'the new woman' (an imagined development from the Nora who leaves her family in *A Doll's House*). It was not surprising that the play could not find a producer, so Shaw quickly decided to return to the spirit of his first play and for *Mrs Warren's Profession* (1893) chose the subject of organized prostitution, one designed to shock.

The design of the well-made play provided a powerful way of exploring and revealing the truth about the marriages of characters like Nora in *A Doll's House* and Mrs Alving in *Ghosts*, but Ibsen broke with the mechanics of the Scribean formula by insisting that the interrelationships of the characters and the interweaving of their memories provide an authentic ground for realistic action. Shaw has little of this in *Mrs Warren's Profession*. To be sure, the events of the past operate on those of the present, and the drama explodes in act 4 in a grand *scène à faire* between Mrs Warren and her daughter. Yet, in spite of the assertions of his interest in the motives of real people, his concern is with the hypocrisy of society, not of people. For Shaw, realism meant the revision of social history. But he keeps his eye on the audience, and his play emerges in successive scenes of confrontation – not so much between one character and another as between the actor and his audience. Behind Shaw looms the momentous shadow of Brecht. Shaw published his first three plays under the title *Plays Unpleasant* and made it clear that his intention was 'to force the spectator to face unpleasant facts' (preface, xxii) and to compel him to take a fresh look at his own assumptions.

Mrs Warren's Profession was rejected by the Lord Chamberlain's office and was performed privately by the Stage Society in 1902. The police closed it in New Haven and New York in 1905, and it did not receive its first public performance in England until 1925. Yet it has survived vigorously with all its passionate indignation at the humbug in society's views on women and marriage, especially after the resurgence of interest in the feminist cause in recent years. That a woman's worth is to be assessed by her sexuality is an idea that Shaw expands by inventing Kitty Warren, who secretly runs a chain of elegant brothels to support herself and her daughter Vivie – as well as fund an investor, the English gentleman Sir George Crofts. Thus far the story follows the melodramatic pattern of the lady with a murky past, whose dark secrets are revealed as the action proceeds.

Yet the play is mostly light in tone and rich in quintessentially Shavian tricks. It begins, for example, with a pretty girl lying in a hammock set in an idyllic scene:

> *Summer afternoon in a cottage garden on the eastern slope of a hill a little south of Haslemere in Surrey. Looking up the hill, the cottage is seen in the left hand corner of the garden, with its thatched roof and porch, and a large latticed window to the left of the porch ...*

After a little the audience begins to notice subversive details: '*a lady's bicycle*' is propped against the wall, '*a pile of serious-looking books*' are on a kitchen chair; the girl wears '*a plain business-like dress*' with a pen and a paperknife at her belt; and she shakes hands with '*a hearty grip*' and manhandles furniture vigorously. It emerges that she is reading mathematics at Cambridge with the intention of practising actuarial work, conveyancing and law, 'with one eye on the Stock Exchange', and that after work she likes 'a cigar, a little whisky, and a novel with a good detective story in it'. No romantic heroine here – this is Vivie Warren, a Shavian new woman, and this pretty scene is the perverse setting for a play about the white slave trade.

Like the ghosts in Ibsen's play, Mrs Warren's business is never explicitly mentioned, but it persists as a disquieting shadow in the background. In act 2 Shaw tricks his audience, as Mrs Warren first tricks her daughter, by justifying her actions with an account of her previous poverty and gently widening the concept of selling oneself:

> What is any respectable girl brought up to do but to catch some rich man's fancy and get the benefit of his money by marrying him? – as if a marriage ceremony could make any difference in the right or wrong of the thing! Oh, the hypocrisy of the world makes me sick!

The act ends almost in a tableau with an embrace of mutual understanding between mother and child, the mother '*instinctively looking upward for divine sanction*'.

In act 3 Shaw has Sir George propose to Vivie, and on her refusal of the man she calls a scoundrel to his face, he informs her, and the audience, that the 'hotel' business is thriving and is in fact the source of her scholarship money at Cambridge. Vivie, along with the audience, is made to feel an accomplice in crime. The emotional crux of act 4 is alive with the spirit of melodrama, but it is used to convey a particularly ambivalent message. Vivie the new woman rejects both her mother and a life as a respectably married woman, wife to Frank Gardner, a charming if vacuous young man. The conventional appeal of the mother is heard: 'Who is to care for me when I'm old? ... You've no right to turn on me now and refuse to do your duty as a daughter.' To which Vivie is '*jarred and antagonized by the echo of the slums in her mother's voice*' and which she answers with a quiet deliberation that itself echoes Nora at the end of *A Doll's House*:

> My duty as a daughter! I thought we should come to that presently. Now once for all, mother, you want a daughter and Frank wants a wife. I don't want a mother and I don't want a husband.

She has defied every temptation and at the curtain is seen plunging into her work. She is indeed her mother's daughter, and the truth has set her free.

The uses of comedy: *Arms and the Man*

In these early 'realistic' plays the basis of Shavian stagecraft was already laid. Building on the well-made formula, setting character against character as in a comedy of manners, spicing the dialogue with sudden touches of wit and the action with visual surprises, Shaw was writing a realistic parable strongly didactic in intention but seasoned with laughter, a modern morality play with a difference. He believed that he was writing social problem plays of the kind Ibsen had invented, as appears when he wrote in *The Quintessence of Ibsenism* (1891),

> Ibsen substituted a terrible art of sharpshooting at the audience, trapping them, fencing with them, aiming always at the sorest spot in their consciences. Never mislead an audience, was an old rule. But the new school will trick the spectator into forming a meanly false judgment, and then convict him of it in the next act, often to his grievous mortification.

> (145)

Nevertheless, as a reformer Shaw was getting nowhere. Whether it was his tendency to preach, whether it was his impulse to shock, the realism he offered was not enough. The mixed reception with which *Widowers' Houses* was greeted, and the disastrous clash with the censor over *Mrs Warren*, brought him to the view that he must practise to deceive.

He began to cast about in the Victorian repertory for acceptable genres that might serve him: romantic melodrama or farce, comic opera or satirical fantasy – or jolly mixtures of any of these. He chose to draw on any convention, any device, any genre he pleased, and above all he recognized that the lighter spirit of comedy would best disarm his audience. When it came to publication, he decided to call his next group of plays *Plays Pleasant*: *Arms and the Man* (1894), *Candida*

(1895), *The Man of Destiny* (1895) and *You Never Can Tell* (1899). Sugaring the pill worked well, and these are among the most successful of his plays today.

Arms and the Man has been repeatedly revived, and comes up freshly every time, which in part speaks to the permanent aspect of its antimilitary topic. Shaw directed this play himself at the Avenue Theatre in 1894, and at the first of fifty performances there was but a single 'boo' (the familiar story has it that at the curtain Shaw replied, 'My dear fellow, I quite agree with you; but who are we against so many?') However, also in the audience that night was the Prince of Wales, who is reported to have said, 'The author is, of course, mad.' This reaction was not his alone, and in a revival at the Duke of York's Theatre just after the First World War officers in uniform got up and walked out. The idea that a professional soldier would conduct himself unlike a gentleman in front of a young lady, let alone substitute chocolate creams for ammunition, was unthinkable.

The play's plot is intentionally romantic and mawkish, telling of a heroic cavalry captain in the Serbo-Bulgarian War of 1885, the adoring young lady he leaves behind and the dirty enemy soldier who bursts into her bedroom. This story abounds in dramatic clichés such as no comedian could resist deflating, and it is immediately apparent that Shaw's approach is one of burlesque. Raina on the balcony when the curtain rises is '*intensely conscious of the romantic beauty of the night*' and '*gazing at the snowy Balkans*'. The lines call for a broader acting and speaking style, making the stage picture larger than life, as when Raina's mother describes the cavalry charge at the Battle of Slivnitza:

> Can't you see it, Raina: our gallant splendid Bulgarians with their swords and eyes flashing, thundering down like an avalanche and scattering the wretched Serbs and their dandified Austrian officers like chaff. And you! you kept Sergius waiting a year before you would be betrothed to him. Oh, if you have a drop of Bulgarian blood in your veins, you will worship him when he comes back.

Here Shaw is planting images that will be taken up later in the play when another view of the battle is offered and when it is known that the battle was won because the leader could not stop his horse running away with him; but the spirit of worship and adulation pervades the action for the first two acts. Moreover, with the help of such inflated speech Shaw could amplify and vary his characters vividly. Desmond MacCarthy, the leading Shavian critic in his day, concluded that 'as a dramatist Mr Shaw's gift for caricature is a perpetual temptation to him' (*Shaw* (1951), 86), and this at least acknowledges that Shaw's comic method was frequently one of glorious exaggeration.

In this play Shaw's comic impulse includes the burlesque of conventional heroics and teasing the audience by upsetting expectations. The colourful costumes and exotic settings are those of the romantic operetta that remained popular well into the twentieth century, but the attitudinizing of the heroic lovers is witnessed only *after* the audience knows some of the truth about Raina:

> RAINA.   (*placing her hands on his shoulders as she looks up at him with admiration and worship*). My hero! My king!
> SERGIUS. My queen! (*He kisses her on the forehead*) ...
>
>   (act 2)

As for the teasing, it begins from the first act, when the muddy and bedraggled enemy soldier enters the young lady's bedchamber at night, and eventually sits on her bed and finally falls asleep on it. This soldier is too tired to be interested in sex and the highly pregnant situation is rendered totally chaste.

Behind these devices lies a dialectic intention of greater importance. Shaw's audience undergoes a process of re-education as the minds of the major characters are deliberately stripped and shown in a new light. After his bout of heroic love, Sergius is shown in a coarse flirtation with Louka the pretty maidservant, who readily chooses a fool of Sergius's class as a way of advancing her station. Bluntschli, the enemy soldier who has no illusions about war, and who behaves like a cool businessman whether he is provisioning the army or running a string of hotels, nevertheless falls in love with Raina and confesses that he has 'an incurably romantic disposition'.

Above all, Raina turns out to be a Shavian woman whose romantic posturing is soon deflated by Bluntschli in act 3:

> RAINA.   (*staring haughtily at him*). Do you know, sir, that you are insulting me?
> BLUNTSCHLI. I can't help it. When you strike that noble attitude and speak in that thrilling voice, I admire you; but I find it impossible to believe a single word you say.

In this way heroism is dissociated from romantic love and in an overwhelming *anti*climax at the end of the play Raina accepts the marriage proposal of her chocolate-cream soldier, now revealed as a Swiss mercenary and the owner of innumerable horses and carriages, houses and hotels. It is clear that the idealistic heroine also has a purely mercenary soul.

Shavian discussion drama: *Major Barbara*

The extraordinary run of new plays and experimental productions for the Stage Society, 1904–7, provided Shaw with a liberating experience as writer and director. This notable development took place at the old Royal Court Theatre, Sloane Square, under the enlightened management of J. E. Vedrenne (1867–1930) and Harley Granville Barker (1877–1946), then a young actor-director of twenty-seven. The brave seasons at the Royal Court marked a turning-point in the English theatre. The actors approached each production as a dedicated team: they were paid little, minor parts were given the same attention as major, and ensemble performance became a feature of production. They also managed to establish the first repertory theatre in England. Needless to say, all this went some way to undermine the star system that still dominated the London stage. After 1919, moreover, this enterprise had a close parallel in the Theatre Guild of New York, which went on to produce nearly all of Shaw's plays. The capacity of the Royal Court was small (614) and Shaw and his players knew their highly selective audience well: he claimed that the patrons were 'not an audience but a congregation'. Plays by Barker himself, Galsworthy, St John

Hankin, Masefield and Yeats were staged at the Royal Court, but by far the largest number of performances (701 of 988) were Shaw's. The Royal Court was his nursery.

These three years were also a turning point in Shaw's career as a playwright. The conditions enabled him to experiment with a feature of his drama that had already appeared in his earlier plays, especially the *Plays Unpleasant*. This was the element of dramatized discussion, which took on formidable importance in the middle plays, especially *Man and Superman* (1903), *John Bull's Other Island* (1904), *Major Barbara* (1905) and *Getting Married* (1908). In *The Quintessence of Ibsenism* Shaw had said he believed that Ibsen had replaced the well-made structure of exposition-situation-unravelling with a new pattern: that of exposition-situation-discussion (135). Pursuing this argument, he insisted that in Ibsen's theatre 'we are not flattered spectators killing an idle hour', but 'guilty creatures sitting at a play', involved like the King and Queen in *Hamlet*. He concluded,

> The technical novelties of the Ibsen and post-Ibsen plays are then: first, the introduction of the discussion and its development until it so overspreads and interpenetrates the action that it finally assimilates it, making play and discussion practically identical; and, second, as a consequence of making the spectators themselves the persons of the drama ... the substitution of a forensic technique of recrimination, disillusion, and penetration through ideals to the truth.
>
> (146)

This describes the scheme that Shaw had in mind for himself, particularly since the concept of interpenetrating the action with discussion suited the less mechanical arrangements he preferred in the composition of a play.

The discussion plays have been unfairly called 'thesis plays', but plays like *Man and Superman*, *John Bull's Other Island* and *Major Barbara* do not preach. They are not plays *about* an argument, but plays *of* argument, and Shaw does not supply the answers to his problems nor deal in simple solutions. They come near to being *dialectical* plays, suggesting that Shaw was a forerunner of Brechtian drama. At such moments of address the drama can be alive in the audience, just as a physically static stage can be intensely disturbing in the mind. In *Pygmalion* (1912) Profesor Higgins turns Eliza Doolittle, a Covent Garden flower-girl, into a duchess; but the crisis comes later, when the experiment in social engineering is over, the fine gentlemen are weary of it and the excitement has died down. 'What's to become of me?' cries Eliza in despair, and at that point the real play begins for her and for the audience.

To enable the discussion to work on an audience, the methods of comedy nevertheless called for strong reinforcement, and it is possible to recognize what happened to characterization and plot structure.

(1) *Characterization*. To show the unromantic and pragmatic side of his characters became an imperative: in *Pygmalion* Eliza astounds the audience when she leaves Higgins because of his limitations as a man; in *The Devil's Disciple* (1897) Judith, the wife of the minister no less, falls in love with Dick Dudgeon the Devil's disciple himself. To equalize debate Shaw allowed no villains and no heroes, insisting that 'the conflict is not between clear right and wrong' (*The Quintessence of Ibsenism*, 139): Sartorius, the callous landlord of *Widowers' Houses*, was also a fond father; Morell, the dull husband in *Candida*, was also a good clergyman. Contrasts in character embodied conflicts between attitudes, not morals, often between the idealist and the realist: in *Arms and the Man* Raina and Bluntschli hold romantic and practical views, but they reverse their positions in the course of the action; in *Man and Superman* John Tanner is the idealistic intellectual when it comes to revolutions, but Ann Whitefield is the ruthless realist when it comes to marriage.

(2) *Plotting*. As Shaw's character surprises become more outrageous, so the structure of a play suffers a reversal. In *Pygmalion* Eliza ought to be pleased to be a lady, but she is not and the action takes on a second climax to put Higgins down; in *Man and Superman* Ann Whitefield ought to behave like a lady and not pursue the man she wants as a husband, but she does what she wants to do and Tanner who was the hero finally capitulates. The

impulse of paradox is strong in these instances. Shaw arranges events to reveal how they relate to one another. In his preface to *Major Barbara*, for example, he points out that the Salvation Army refuses Bill Walker's conscience money for hitting Jenny Hill, but cannot afford to refuse that of Bodger the distiller: the dramatist shows the connection between things that seem unrelated, and by juxtaposing these two incidents is able to create a dramatic explosion.

Man and Superman offers an example of an unconventional dramatic structure for a Shavian discussion play. The critic A. B. Walkley suggested Shaw write a Don Juan play about 'the duel of sex', and in his 'Epistle Dedicatory' Shaw outlined his story as 'the tragi-comic love chase of the man by the woman', adding that 'my Don Juan is the quarry instead of the huntsman' (xviii). Paradox is already present, and on one level Shaw uses his plot to advance his notions about the Life Force [Creative Evolution], in which the female is the predator concerned with the future of the family and the race, while the male is allowed to believe that 'no female of any womanliness or delicacy would initiate any effort in that direction'. Then, 'when the terrible moment of birth arrives ... he slinks out of the way of the humblest petticoat', until he eventually 'drivels into erotic poetry or sentimental uxoriousness' (xix).

In the the early scenes of the play the inverted chase and the inevitable duel of sex affords much of the initial comedy in a drawing-room setting. The words echo, dance and sparkle off the tongue, and some of Shaw's best comic rhetoric is generated by the contest between John Tanner (originally played by Granville Barker made up as the young, auburn-haired and bearded Shaw) and his 'boa constrictor' partner Ann (played by the beautiful Lillah McCarthy), who indeed wears a feather boa and at one point slips it round his neck. There is more than a touch of burlesque in the lines, and with their satire of Victorian ideals of femininity and romance, the audience, not thinking it is required to believe its implications, is inclined to laugh even when Tanner offers a serious argument.

To this extent *Man and Superman* works and plays like any comedy, but Shaw gave his third act over to an arresting change in tone and style, a flight into fantasy. The 1905 production at the Royal Court excluded the central scene in hell (3.2), and in 1907 act 3 received a separate production; the whole play was not played until 1915 in Edinburgh and 1925 in London. Ann's sinister intentions of marriage drive Tanner to escape to the Continent by car, and in the Sierra Nevada he is captured by one Mendoza and his band of brigands. It is then that Tanner dreams he is Don Juan and in hell. From the tradition of Tirso de Molina, Molière and Mozart, Shaw has Don Juan meet Doña Ana (Ann), the Statue who is her father the Commander (Ramsden) and the Devil (Mendoza). Ann and Tanner are in hell and wish to be in heaven; Ramsden was in heaven, is bored with it and wishes to be in hell, so that it is in hell that this quartet comes together to discuss the purpose of life. The scene constitutes a lengthy one-act play that became known as *Don Juan in Hell*.

The sudden switch to allegory in comic-opera fantasy form in act 3 is useful in several ways:

- It permits a restatement of the ideas from the society comedy of acts 1 and 2, suggesting that life in hell is a comedy of manners, and vice versa. At the same time it reveals hell and its implications to the audience bit by bit, and does so with a degree of comedy through Doña Ana's eyes: 'I in hell! How dare you? ... I might have been so much wickeder! All my good deeds wasted! It is unjust.' (85–6)
- At this time Shaw had a liking for simple, abstract design (Gordon Craig's work was becoming known, and *The Art of the Theatre* was published in 1905) and admired the bare platform of William Poel's Elizabethan revivals. Shaw therefore presents the scene in hell on an empty stage without representation of sky or stars or scenic effects of any kind. He called for *'omnipresent nothing'* and *'utter void'* (83), thus distancing the audience by visual remoteness and allowing it to see the reality of the sex war in act 1 as if for the first time. In some productions the lines of this scene are *read* from lecterns placed

in fixed positions on the stage, distancing the scene even more.
– It frees the discussion for exaggerated flights of the imagination that border on mystery and vision, for example:

> (Juan) 'Have I not told you that the truly damned are those who are happy in hell?'
>
> (87)

> (The Devil) 'In the arts of life man invents nothing; but in the arts of death he outdoes Nature herself.'
>
> (102)

> (Juan) 'To be in hell is to drift: to be in heaven is to steer.'
>
> (128)

Shaw took every advantage of the dream to expand his theory of the Life Force by discourse and not by demonstration.

Nevertheless, brilliant as it is, the scene is so external to the main action that it stops the play. There are visible links between Acts 2 and 3 in doubling, characterization, dialogue and subject-matter, but with Tanner now the winner and not the loser, the content has changed and the drama is fractured. *Don Juan in Hell*, unlike the Murder of Gonzago in *Hamlet*, is not integrated with the main action and is not justified as a play-within-a-play. Moreover, in saying that it could be played separately, Shaw acknowledged the play's uncomfortable structural defect, and the only other time he wrote anything like this was *Fanny's First Play* (1911), a three–act comedy simply framed between a prologue and an epilogue. In *Major Barbara* two years later Shaw experimented again with a new pattern for a discussion play and created a structure that better followed the actual process of an audience's dramatic perception.

Major Barbara proposes a dialectic on the role of religion in society, and in three acts, each of a different style, it shows its audience three social groups, three economic conditions and three perspectives. Within the acts the characters are chosen to offer conflicts of thought and feeling, and the changes of location and style themselves invite and enact a debate.

Act 1 sets the scene in an upper-class house in 'Wilton Crescent', where wealth and comfort abound and Lady Britomart rules her domain; in particular she presides over her son Stephen and two daughters, Sarah, a bored, fashionably dressed young lady, and Barbara, who is in the Salvation Army and wears its severe uniform. The act is played in high comic style, at times echoing Oscar Wilde ('Really, Barbara, you go on as if religion were a pleasant subject. Do have some sense of propriety'), and performance reaches a degree of comic tension before the arrival of their long absent father, Andrew Undershaft, a tycoon who manufactures armaments. Since Barbara's passion is to save men's souls, and Undershaft's is to sell arms, father and daughter make a compact that proposes the itinerary for the rest of the play as well as the basis for its dialectic. The lines represent a characteristic exchange of Shavian balance and polish:

> UNDERSHAFT. Well, I will make a bargain with you. If I go to see you tomorrow in your Salvation Shelter, will you come the day after to see me in my cannon works?
> BARBARA. Take care. It may end in your giving up the cannons for the sake of the Salvation Army.
> UNDERSHAFT. Are you sure it will not end in your giving up the Salvation Army for the sake of the cannons?

> (262–3)

Act 2 puts the play into a scene of Dickensian realism and well-made playwriting. In the West Ham shelter on a cold January morning the audience is to see Major Barbara at work. By reasoning she single-handedly subdues the 'rough customer' Bill Walker, who has assaulted two of the women. He offers a sovereign as compensation, but Barbara will have none of it. The audience sees through his eyes when Bill remains on stage to hear Mrs Baines the Commissioner joyfully announce that Lord Saxmundham the distiller has offered £5,000 if someone else will give another £5,000. Undershaft also sees all this, and enjoys writing a cheque in order to compel Barbara to choose between her beliefs and his blood money. The crisis creates an Ibsenesque sensation that the 1950s would have called 'existential', both for

Barbara and her audience. In her anguish she leaves the Army.

After a brief return to Wilton Crescent where Barbara is seen without her uniform, act 3 shifts the location and the style a third time. The scene is at the foundry, but touches abstract symbolism in its design. The view is of a smokeless town of beautiful white walls, coloured tiles and slender factory chimneys, yet in the foreground the stage itself is a gun emplacement that mounts a huge cannon pointing at the town, and it is also decorated with one or two large ugly shells and scattered about with several mutilated dummy soldiers showing straw protruding grotesquely from their gashes (Shaw later had them dressed as even more obvious Victorian redcoats with epaulets and cockades). Visually the stage is a cosmic Utopia ironically menaced by the destructive source of its own wealth.

Barbara and the rest find everything in Perivale St Andrews to be socially and aesthetically perfect, and Undershaft the realist begins his temptation of Barbara the idealist. The scene becomes one of a debate about spiritual honesty which cannot fail to involve the spectator, and Shaw sustains to the end the dialectical device of its ambiguity. For if the audience thinks that both Undershaft and Barbara have won their arguments, the compromise still forces it to choose, and the play passes Barbara's anxiety on to the spectator. Shaw's own comment was that 'the play was a success, but the audience was a failure'.

The play was remarkably successful in its game with dramatic form and its areas of dramatic innovation: the ascent from light comedy to abstract discussion, the balancing of attitudes and ideas, and the emergence of an increasingly exquisite ambiguity in the substance of the play. If in *Major Barbara* the audience has the sense that the author himself is playing the devil's advocate, it may be that in this play Shaw at last found a non-naturalistic plane on which to write his kind of modern morality.

Visionary departures: *Heartbreak House,*
Saint Joan

It has been said that all art aspires to the condition of music. Shaw's life-long interest in opera, that most abstract of forms, found its way into his dramatic work in odd ways. He wrote by ear, speaking the lines as he wrote and afterwards declaiming them to friends. In rehearsal he repeatedly told the players to 'get the music right' or 'sing the words, don't say them'. Sybil Thorndike reported that he treated his dialogue almost as a musical score, and Granville Barker, faced with Shaw's long speeches, called the plays 'Italian opera'. It is possible to argue the case that a whole play, *Heartbreak House* (1919), was composed like a piece of music. For the leader of the new English realism, these signs suggest a curious paradox in the direction Shaw took after the First World War.

Another characteristic akin to this is often present in Shaw's later drama: a shift into a dreamlike mode with pronounced symbolic overtones. The first act of *Caesar and Cleopatra* has the girl Cleopatra asleep between the great paws of the Sphinx on a heap of red poppies in the moonlight, while the strange music of *'the windswept harp of Memnon'* plays over her. The dream sequence of *Man and Superman* all but overwhelms the rest of the comedy. The last act of *Major Barbara* assumes a fantastic idiom mixed of beauty and horror, a symbolic ambiguity. Each part of *Back to Methuselah* (completed 1920) invites an impressionistic treatment. *Heartbreak House*, begun in the terrible year of the Somme, moves steadily towards a shocking apocalyptic vision of the state of England. It may be that Shaw was aware of the expressionistic changes overtaking the Continental theatre during the war years.

At all events, the mixing of dramatic genres and the shifting of mood and atmosphere occur noticeably in *Heartbreak House*. The bulk of the play is a witty social comedy satirizing the upper classes, but its last act borders on allegory and symbolism: the ship of state is adrift and plunging towards chaos, the setting calling for the stage to look like the poop of a ship. For the play's first production, presented by the

Theatre Guild in New York, Lee Simonson designed a set with high galleon windows running the breadth of the stage. Into this situation wanders Ellie Dunn, an innocent among a group of sophisticates, and it is her increasing disillusion that strings together the parts of the play. Her education begins when she meets Captain Shotover, an old sea dog with '*an immense white beard*', which is sometimes used to make the actor up to look like Shaw himself as an old man. Shotover is massively disillusioned himself, a Lear who assumes the air of a philosopher and a mystic.

The haunting last act is the most remarkable in the play. It was prompted by a Zeppelin raid in 1916, and it consists of a series of theatrical sensations culminating in one huge explosion when a bomb drops on the house. The group, lit by an electric lamp, is in the garden by a flagstaff on a moonless night. First there is 'a sort of splendid drumming in the sky' and this becomes a succession of dull explosions in the distance, mingled with orchestral music by Beethoven. Through all this the characters behave like lunatics: the cultivated Randall Utterword plays his flute while his wife Ariadne lolls voluptuously in a hammock; the businessman Mangan starts to strip off his clothes and Ellie announces that in spirit she is now Shotover's wife; Hector Hushabye runs to switch on all the lights and his wife Hesione and Ellie '*throw themselves into one another's arms in wild excitement*'. When '*a terrific explosion shakes the earth*' and the glass is shattered in the windows, the curtain dialogue is heard like lines from a black comedy:

> MRS HUSHABYE. What a glorious experience! I hope they'll come again tomorrow night.
> ELLIE (*radiant at the prospect*). Oh, I hope so.
> *Randall at last succeeds in keeping the home fires burning on his flute.*

Ellie had earlier spoken of 'this silly house, this strangely happy house, this agonizing house, this house without foundations. I shall call it Heartbreak House.' Shaw had found his way into the theatre of the absurd.

From the beginning the critical verdict on *Saint Joan* (1923) was in dispute, even when the play was widely accounted

Shaw's masterpiece. It is an exercise in transposing the genres, and this alone upset some critics. It offers to be a medieval history play based on the actual trial of Joan of Arc, and yet it persists in teaching its audience lessons in modern political science. It establishes its heroine in witty scenes of comic brilliance, and yet hits a note of tragedy before she dies. At its centre are lengthy discussions that halt the action in the way audiences have come to expect, and its great trial scene sets the stage for Shaw's most determined debate. The play concludes with an epilogue many think superfluous and destructive.

Yet from another point of view, *Saint Joan*'s spectrum of styles makes it the most ambitious of Shaw's experiments in stagecraft. For his chronicle play Shaw was resolved not to allow Joan to seem a sentimental English witch or a pretty French saint, but with a sensational climax that involved burning at the stake took the risk of making it an out-and-out melodrama. In his preface he explained, 'I have taken care to let the medieval atmosphere blow through my play freely' (49), although Desmond MacCarthy found that it was full of spiritual anachronisms, from Joan's belief that God spoke through her imagination to the idea that she was an early Protestant. At the same time he acknowledged that Shaw wanted to suggest a certain continuity in the idea of history and promote a philosophy of his own.

Shaw was also anxious to captivate his audience by traditional comic methods, and in three brisk initial scenes he sweeps the spectator into an entertaining, if preposterous, world of medieval superstition. First, he presents the apparent miracle of making hens lay eggs, and then of having a slip of a peasant girl, all breathless confidence, take the wind out of pompous squire Robert de Baudricourt:

> Captain: you are to give me a horse and armour and some soldiers, and send me to the Dauphin. Those are your orders from my Lord.

> (scene 1)

Shaw next introduces the amazing story of Foul Mouthed Frank, drowned for swearing, to complement Joan's chilling reception in Chinon. He promptly turns this into an example of her ability to enjoy a joke ('Coom, Bluebeard! Thou canst

not fool me. Where be Dauphin?') and spot the Dauphin in
the crowd:

> Gentle little Dauphin, I am sent to you to drive the English
> away from Orleans and from France, and to crown you
> King in the cathedral at Rheims, where all true kings of
> France are crowned.
>
> (scene 2)

Finally, Shaw writes an almost lyrical scene 3 in which
Dunois the French commander waits for Joan on the bank of
the Loire, hoping the wind will change in order that the
French may raise the siege of Orleans. No sooner has she left
than the pennon streams in the wind.

In a daring scene 4 the action of the play is halted, and the
mode switches boldly to discussion in order to focus on the
theme. In the English camp the Earl of Warwick, his chaplain
de Stogumber and Bishop Peter Cauchon are characters
chosen and drawn to represent whole national and religious
organizations and attitudes. Shaw is dealing in something
more than stereotypes, as he suggests in his preface when he
frankly asserts that the spectators 'will have before them not
only the visible and human puppets, but the Church, the
Inquisition, the Feudal System, with divine inspiration always
beating against their too inelastic limits' (49). This mode of
writing is continued into Joan's trial (scene 6), depicting Joan
herself as a Shavian individualist. She is almost another new
woman, almost another superman, as she resists the forces of
religion and society arrayed against her. It is here that Shaw
implants the anachronistic ideas of modern protestantism and
nationalism that have offended the purists, but captivated his
audiences.

Joan's character itself is sufficiently particularized for an
audience to be untroubled by philosophical diversions. Shaw
drew her as a simple country girl with a natural wit: in
performance in the twenties and thirties Sybil Thorndike
endowed her with a 'Loamshire' accent, and in 1954 Siobhan
McKenna granted her a winning Irish lilt. Shaw had placed
her in one compelling situation after another, and it was this
quality of tension and conflict in the drama that illuminated
his creation most. In her trial scene her situation as a lone

female on an all-male stage, a victim of the huge forces of Church and state and a martyr to her beliefs, inevitably elevates her to a mystical role. When she refuses to sign the recantation that implies her lifelong incarceration, her lines soar to a level of rhetorical poetry:

> I could do without my warhorse; I could drag about in a skirt; I could let the banners and the trumpets and the knights and soldiers pass me and leave me behind as they leave the other women, if only I could still hear the wind in the trees, the larks in the sunshine, the young lambs crying through the healthy frost, and the blessed blessed church bells that send my angel voices floating to me on the wind. But without these things I cannot live ...
>
> (142–3)

In 1924 Desmond MacCarthy considered that Thorndike could not bring out Joan's sweet and angelic side because, dreading the sentimental, Shaw had made the beauty of her character too ascetic. In 1954, however, Harold Hobson thought that McKenna played Joan 'as a girl who has veritably seen God'.

The fantasy of the epilogue seems self-defeating, but this scene is nevertheless Shaw's important flight into fantasy, designed expressionistically to ensure the timelessness of his subject. He had taken the well-made formula at its crisis and produced a sustained demonstration of outstanding discussion drama, one that offered no answers, but achieved a dry-eyed tragedy. Yet even then he deemed it necessary to add an epilogue intended to modify or suppress any residual feeling for Joan. In the preface he had written of 'the romance of her rise, the tragedy of her execution, and the comedy of the attempts of posterity to make amends for that execution' (45): at the last he is still concerned to upset any complacency. It is a windy night twenty-five years later, and the scene is in the bedchamber of the Dauphin, now Charles the Victorious. Shaw proceeds to show the result of burning Joan in terms of clowning comedy, and with a final dialectical undercutting, one by one he brings on-stage the principal characters for a broad reprise of the play. When everyone is kneeling to the newly canonized saint, Shaw relishes one last jest: what if Joan were to return?

> JOAN.   And now tell me: shall I rise from the dead,
> and come back to you a living woman?
> *A sudden darkness blots out the walls of the room as they all spring to their feet in consternation.*

Everyone on stage recoils from her in alarm and dismay, and in a striking lighting effect after the Continental fashion, the characters are silhouetted as they steal away, until the solitary figure of Joan herself is picked out in the white radiance of a spotlight.

Like no other, the Shavian drama lifted the English stage from the doldrums of the Victorian age and inspired new departures in twentieth-century theatre. Shaw believed that good theatre, like all good art, is built on reason, and with determination promoted the Shavian law that the quality of a play is the quality of its thinking. If occasionally Shaw's people sound like recorded ideas, the surprising thing is that his ideas so often behave like people.

14

Twentieth-century developments and variations

A wealth of resources

In the history of the English stage the twentieth century is by far the richest in new plays, and those selected for notice in this chapter, without pretending to be comprehensive, are the mile-posts, some of which pointed the drama in a fresh direction. The formula for realistic drama, with its idea of 'a slice of life' trapped in a box set, persisted in varying degrees for many years, but the stage never restrained its urge to be representative and symbolic, and to take advantage of the imaginative and unreal properties of the medium. Bernard Shaw helped take the lid off a Pandora's box, and his work marks the English resuscitation of the drama as a trail-blazing art form: after Shaw no good playwright was unaware of his responsibilities to the dramatic form as a social artist.

Throughout the period the stage became ever more aware of international developments. In the early years the impressive use made of Dublin's pioneering Abbey Theatre could not be ignored. Nor did the French stage, which dominated Western drama in the nineteenth century, relax its grip when realism was replaced by a fashionable symbolism in the twenties and thirties. German drama also made its contribution in the twentieth century: during the First World War Berlin pursued a youthful rebellion through expressionistic theatre, and was subsequently swept along by the new thinking of the socially oriented 'epic theatre' of Piscator and Brecht. Throughout these years the innovative conventions of film, radio and television dramaturgy encouraged a liberating stagecraft of quick scene changes and flexible story-telling.

As for the physical apparatus of the theatre, at first sight the Victorian playhouse seemed to have evolved the right working conditions for the English drama and could create almost any realistic picture required. The actors had become accustomed to pulling back into the scenic area and felt free to behave as if there were no audience present. In sum, the concept of 'dramatic illusion' was paramount and any earlier convention that tended to disturb it – a soliloquy, for example – could be accommodated by the actor's pretending to talk to himself or the furniture. The naturalistic acting and ensemble performance of what was later known as the 'Stanislavky' school were understandably happy on this stage.

Nevertheless, other theatrical forces arose to shatter the settled conventions of proscenium arch production following the movement for an Elizabethan revival and the work of William Poel (1852–1934), which rejuvenated the medieval and Tudor impulse towards open staging and a closer actor–audience relationship. Open staging with a scenic area at the rear became the natural development in the second half of the century because of its flexibility: this arrangement permitted the range of drama from plays that required full scenic staging to plays that called for a complete freedom from realistic illusion. On the one hand, experiments with theatre-in-the-round proved that even the intensely realistic plays of Ibsen and Chekhov might be comfortable in it. On the other, open staging naturally accommodated the 'portable' [travelling] companies that proliferated after 1968: these were smaller, semi-professional groups working in pubs and halls, on lorries and trucks and in the open air. Tyrone Guthrie insisted that the theatre was not a peep-show, and that it had 'more important things to do than to bamboozle the public into thinking that fictions are reality'.

Discussion of creative innovation by the modern stage artist in the twentieth century, by the costume designer, the set designer, the lighting designer and especially the director, all imaginative contributors in their own right, is unfortunately beyond the scope of this study. It must be said, however, that an individual vision is often compelling enough to find and establish a convention, a poetics, for a particular play or production, as has been the case during and after the Second World War in the work of Guthrie and Peter Brook. Both Guthrie and Brook have gone beyond the requirements of a

textual interpreter to generate fresh modes of theatre which
have been assimilated into general theatre practice.

Edwardian social realism: *Strife*

In the early years of the twentieth century the search for a
new direction in English playwriting after Ibsen continued
fitfully. The Vedrenne–Barker years at the Royal Court
represented the Edwardian consciousness on the stage, but
there never was an English Ibsen. Nevertheless, the Court
experiment did turn up, other than Shaw, two or three
dramatists who may be seen as social and political realists.
They wrote 'thoughtful' problem plays mostly in the well-
made tradition, but with little humour and less poetry, and
their endeavour soon sputtered out.

It has been a puzzle that Harley Granville Barker's gifts as
an actor and director did not extend to his playwriting. As an
actor for Poel and Shaw, he was clear about the leaden
qualities of the Victorian theatre he wanted to avoid. If his
plays are of interest today, it is because his realistic studies of
Edwardian England, while loquacious, were more understated
than those of his contemporaries. The play that made his
reputation at the Court was *The Voysey Inheritance* (1905), a
drama, like his others, of middle-class family life made up of
many characters revealed slyly to the audience through quasi-
Chekhovian small talk. The story is of the tragic education of
Edward Voysey, who inherits money that has been made by
fraud and finds himself trapped into continuing the business
by similar methods. The Barker touch is felt when he refuses
his audience any pontificating trial scene or other striking
scène à faire that might resolve the problem, and it is never
known whether or not Edward is prosecuted.

Considered by some to be Barker's most incisive piece of
playwriting, *Waste* (1907) risked reflecting the activities of
living politicians, mixing sex and politics even to the point of
touching on the subject of abortion, illegal at that time;
needless to say, the play was promptly banned. It had a
private reading by the Stage Society, but sadly was not given a

public production until 1936. In this play Barker made determined use of a brilliantly dry, cultivated conversation exchanged in realistically solid, period sets in order to fill out a fastidious picture of the ruling political circle. At a typical house party, the career parliamentarian Henry Trebell, author of a bill for the disestablishment of the Church, no less, commits the indiscretion of having an affair with a married woman. The lady finds herself pregnant and dies having an abortion; Trebell, his life ruined by the scandal, shoots himself: altogether a grim social image of tragic 'waste' and a study in Edwardian realism at its most urgent.

The Madras House, produced at the Duke of York's Theatre in 1910, also has a notable originality. It is a rambling comedy of many characters (there are seventeen women in the cast) that deals wittily with female repression in Edwardian society. Henry Huxtable is a well-to-do draper running a Bond Street fashion-house, a man, however, who is blessed with six unmarried and frustrated daughters. In act 1 the audience learns of their pathetic lives at home in Denmark Hill:

> Some time ago a gentleman proposed to Jane. And mother said it would have been more honourable if he had spoken to father first, and that Jane was the youngest and too young anyhow to know her own mind. Well, you know she's twenty-six...

In act 2 the daughters are cleverly mirrored by a seraglio of sales girls who must 'live in', according to the practice of the day, on the premises of the dress shop, to be as rigidly supervised as slaves. In act 3 they are also likened to the fashion models who are paraded seductively in the exotic emporium in order to sell their wares. Meanwhile, in the real world outside, the realities of male-dominated marriage close in remorselessly, and the virginal middle-age of the spinster daughters grows ever nearer.

Barker's virtue was that he did not follow the conventional rules for fashioning a realistic play; the plays of John Galsworthy (1867–1933) suffered because he followed them too closely. He was the best of the English well-made playwrights and he worked to rule, selecting a solid social problem (usually directly identitified by a Robertsonian title, *Strife*, *Justice*, *Loyalties* and the like) and tackling it with a well-built, muscular plot. He was less interested than Barker in studying human nature, and his characters tended to be created merely in order to activate the plot. With little humour and less lyricism, he pressed his subject home with studied impartiality, and usually ended his play with a tableau curtain that represented a dramatic question-mark, so passing the ball to his audience. Nothing he could do prevented his theatre from coming across as wooden and didactic, yet in his day he was immensely popular. When in *The Silver Box* at the Royal Court in 1906, a down-and-out steals a silver cigarette box and gets hard labour, in contrast with a wealthy young socialite who steals a girl's purse and is discharged, this representation of the double standard for the rich and the poor made Galsworthy's reputation. When the prisoner Falder jumps to his death at the end of *Justice* (1910), it brought the audience to its feet, and the Home Secretary, Winston Churchill, felt impelled to change the law on solitary confinement. The friction between Galsworthy's lively social topics and his lifeless method of presenting them must account for the verdict that his plays have dated.

The play that has been most revived is *Strife* (1909), which takes as its subject the struggle between capital and labour during a strike at a tin-plate foundry. The detail of Barker's careful style of direction at the Duke of York's Theatre where the play opened added to its strength, and the fashionable, well-dressed audiences who had come to see so unusual a subject made the occasion something of an historic event: the play may be given the credit of being an early form of documentary drama. Yet no director could conceal the mechanics of the stagecraft, the action alternating automatically between the two factions in the dispute. The first act is set in the fine dining room of the Manager's house, used as a boardroom presided over by the Chairman old John Anthony, a big man with thick white hair and sharp eyes; then the second act is set in the squalid cottage kitchen of Roberts, the workers' leader, a lean man with a slight stoop and hollow cheeks. The wooden signals of Victorian melodramatic scene and character are inescapable.

The plot is presented as a battle of iron wills between these two stalwarts, but human character is of little account, even when, to raise the emotional temperature, Roberts's starving and consumptive wife Annie dies in pitiful circumstances. At the end Roberts loses his control over the men and Anthony resigns his position on the Board. Before the fall of the curtain the two enemies stare at one another in respect and silence, leaving the Secretary to the Board and the Union representative to have the last words:

> TENCH. D'you know, sir – these terms, they're the *very same* we drew up together, you and I, and put to both sides before the fight began? All this – all this – and – and what for?
> HARNESS (*in a slow, grim voice*). That's where the fun comes in!

The Dublin initiative: *The Playboy of the Western World, The Plough and the Stars*

At the turn of the century a different set of forces were building a native drama in Ireland, one that outshone anything London had to show. The Irish dramatic movement was essentially amateur in the best sense – luminous and exhilarating because it was using the stage to conduct a dialogue that mattered to its community audience. In so doing it incidentally engineered a revolt against the commercial diet from London of Victorian melodrama, problem play and musical comedy, and substituted a simple, popular drama that is as fresh today as it was then. It may or may not have been a good thing that it was associated with the nationalist aspirations of the day; suffice it to say that at this time the Dublin stage managed to embrace both poet and politician, and helped further the cause of Home Rule as well as rekindle the fires of Ireland's legendary past.

The movement began in a literary way, with the poet W. B. Yeats (1865–1939) founding the Irish Literary Society first in London in 1891 and the next year in Dublin as the National Literary Society; when in 1899 he joined Edward Martyn,

George Moore and Lady Gregory, all of whom had written plays, together they started the Irish Literary Theatre, and in 1902 this became the Irish National Theatre Society. The early statements of the movement's intentions are therefore those of poets, not actors, and far removed from Ibsenism and the naturalistic thinking of the Continent, of which Yeats in any case disapproved. He called instead for what he believed was a 'popular' theatre, one in which the sources of art lay in 'the vitality of the Irish legends', 'the simple emotions that make all men kin' and 'the living imagination' that survived in the peasants. It was unlucky that the urban Dubliners who saw his early plays knew little of the Irish legends and had long dissociated themselves from the peasantry.

Nevertheless, Yeats was a power to be reckoned with, and his ideas about a new theatre were inspirational. In October 1903 he wrote in the Society's journal, *Samhain*,

> I think the theatre must be reformed in its plays, its speaking, its acting, and its scenery. That is to say, I think there is nothing good about it at present.
>
> *First.* We have to write or find plays that will make the theatre a place of intellectual excitement – a place where the mind goes to be liberated...
>
> *Second.* If we are to restore words to their sovereignty we must make speech even more important than gesture upon the stage...
>
> *Third.* We must simplify acting, especially in poetical drama, and in prose drama that is remote from real life...
>
> *Fourth.* Just as it is necessary to simplify gesture that it may accompany speech without being its rival, it is necessary to simplify the form and colour of scenery and costume.

Here was a prescription for a poetic theatre that could generate a mystical world, and these criteria in due time highlighted his own experiments in verse drama. For the present, however, the primary concern was the practical business of getting a play produced, and the fact was that they had no Irish actors and no Irish playhouse.

The Irish Dramatic Movement is almost totally the work of the Abbey Theatre, and is not to be understood without it. However, the details of this romantic enterprise are quite unromantic. The Abbey was actually the disused Mechanics' Institute in Abbey Street, and had at one time been the city morgue. It was bought by the tea heiress Annie Horniman, an Englishwoman who had little sympathy with Home Rule and who insisted that an Englishman be hired as director – Ben Iden Payne. The theatre was tiny, with a capacity of 562 and a proscenium opening of 21 feet, a height of 14 feet and a depth of 16 feet, a space so restricted that an actor who wanted to enter from another side had to use the lane behind the building. This was the stage that conditioned the form and style of the great plays of the first generation of Irish playwrights. If it made no difference to Yeats's verse dramas, its scale was just right for the peasant cottages and tenement rooms depicted by Lady Gregory (1882–1932), J. M. Synge (1871–1909) and Sean O'Casey (1880–1964) and their brand of poetic realism.

Yeats himself was loyal to his own tenets even if his verse plays were never in the mainstream of Abbey productions. As early as 1892 he had written a small masterpiece of Irish drama in *The Countess Cathleen*, produced in 1899 and revised several times over a period of twenty-four years as he became more familiar with the theatre. Owing something to the symbolism of Maeterlinck, it is a dreamlike play about rural life and its poverty, and to redeem the peasants the mystical Countess Cathleen, who stands for holy Ireland, is paradoxically willing to sell her soul. This was the first of many short verse plays in a lyrical vein. *On Baile's Strand* (1904) was the first of a cycle of five telling of King Cuchulain, Ireland's legendary hero, and when in 1916 Yeats wrote *At the Hawk's Well*, the first of his *Four Plays for Dancers* (1921), he turned for the conventions of his new symbolic style to the *Noh* drama of Japan. Thereby hangs a tale.

He spent his years as a playwright evolving a special philosophy for poetic drama, determined from the beginning to keep it 'at a distance from life' and to reserve its non-naturalistic qualities, because he wished to portray, not external reality, but the reality of the soul. Part of the work of abstraction therefore involved eliminating 'character', until the figures on the stage were seen, not as people, but as symbols representing states of mind. It followed that his strength lay, not in the customary elements of drama – these he dangerously ignored – but in his poetry and the way the lines were spoken. These principles radically affected his requirements for performance, and in *Samhain* (1904) and his notes to *Four Plays for Dancers* he rehearsed his ideas about the new theatre:

(1) *Acting style.* 'The actors must move, for the most part, slowly and quietly, and not very much, and there should be something in their movements decorative and rhythmical as if they were paintings in a frieze.' Later: 'We must get rid of everything that is restless, everything that draws attention away from the sound of the voice.'

(2) *Character and mask.* There was to be no realistic intrusion of the actor, who was to wear a mask to make him abstract and impersonal. 'The face of the speaker should be as much a work of art as the lines that he speaks or the costume that he wears, that all may be as artificial as possible.' Yeats's plays become increasingly cold and hard.

(3) *Setting.* Poetic drama 'should have no realistic, or elaborate, but only a symbolic and decorative, setting. A forest, for instance, should be represented by a forest pattern and not by a forest painting.' Yeats was attracted to the simplifying designs of Edward Gordon Craig (1872–1966), who designed the stylized setting of rocks and trees for *The Hour-Glass*, produced in 1912.

This style of performance was extreme, and someone was quick to coin the term 'Cuchulainoid' to describe it.

At the Hawk's Well (1916) was first performed in the *Noh* manner in Lady Cunard's drawing-room in London. It tells a piece of the Cuchulain story in which the hero King meets Old Age at the Well of wisdom and immortality. The play begins when three Musicians enter with faces made up to resemble masks, and their singing accompanies the ritualistic unfolding of a black cloth bearing the pattern of a golden hawk; thereafter they accompany the movements of the actors with gong or drum or zither. The Well is represented by a square of blue cloth, and its female Guardian crouches under

a black cloak. A masked Old Man approaches for nourishment, but every movement is made to the tap of a drum, so
that he seems to be only a puppet. When the young Cuchulain, also in a mask, approaches the Well, the Guardian throws
off her cloak to reveal a dress suggesting a hawk and its wings,
and after a hawklike dance leads him wordlessly away to do
battle.

In a note to the first performance Yeats wrote, 'My theatre
must be the ancient theatre that can be made by unrolling a
carpet, or marking out a place with a stick, or setting a screen
against the wall.' (*Plays and Controversies* (1923), 416). The
problem was that while Yeats's writing grew more abstract,
the acting at the Abbey grew more realistic, and his principles
applied hardly at all to the work of his fellow playwrights and
not at all to the audiences they were cultivating.

Synge, an Anglo-Irish Protestant of the land-owning class,
had to learn about the peasantry of Yeats's vision, but he did
so as a playwright who saw his countrymen with the eyes of a
realist. Writing only in prose, he developed an artificial, but
inimitable, style of lyrical Anglo-Irish that was graced with
Gaelic cadences, and his gifts as a playwright overwhelmed all
Yeats's theories and took the new drama along lines its
founders had not anticipated. To top this, he had a comedian's
talent for tickling and inflaming his audiences, bringing the
Irish National Theatre the attention – and the money – it
needed. His first one-act, *The Shadow of the Glen* (1903),
used the simple situation of countless French farces, that of
the old husband pretending to be dead in order to spy on his
young wife. Yet this little comedy was indicted for having
'attacked the sanctity of marriage' and for suggesting that an
Irish girl could be unfaithful to her husband. A farcical
marriage has no place in political sentiment and the patent for
the theatre was withheld. When *The Playboy of the Western
World* was produced in three acts in 1907, its audiences broke
into riot and the police were on the scene for a week, but the
fame of the Abbey Theatre was ensured.

Christy Mahon is the callow farm lad on the Mayo coast
who runs away thinking he has killed his father with a loy
[spade]. Arriving at a village shebeen [pub], his tale makes him

16   W. B. Yeats, *At the Hawk's Well*, 1916: costume design for the
Guardian of the Well by Edmund Dulac.

a hero, especially in the eyes of Pegeen and the girls, but when his father turns up, alive after all, he is a hero no longer. So simple a story comes from the same gentle stable as the comedies of Lady Gregory, but it is astonishing what biting humour Synge can derive from its unsophisticated outlines. Audiences were indignant at his 'blasphemy', less provoked by the admiration accorded a parricide than by the idea that an unmarried Irish girl would hide a bachelor under her roof. Thereafter they found all manner of details offensive, down to the mention of Pegeen's 'shift' [petticoat] and the names of the saints which decorate the dialogue throughout. They failed to see the preposterous irony in Christy's new-found glory: 'Wasn't I a foolish fellow not to kill my father in the years gone by?'

In every scene Synge's comic construction works to manipulate the response of the spectator. In act 1, much of the action reveals the slow change of mind among the regulars in the shebeen, from suspicion of the stranger in their midst, to their mixed fear and respect, and finally to their ludicrous obsequiousness on hearing that Christy had killed his father ('That'd be a lad with the sense of Solomon to have for a pot-boy, Michael James'). In act 2, when Christy's inflated story is still growing with his confidence, the scene of the village girls' adulation of him, partly teasing, partly fawning, together with the designs of the formidable Widow Quin, widens the comic reference to include community and matrimonial implications. To this point each development is balanced against the pathetic image of Christy's immaturity, and in the classical way the audience is in a conspiracy with the author and remains happily omniscient. In act 3 Synge brings his surprises: when the community discovers that it has been deceived, irony follows irony to develop a cynical 'black' comedy intended to stagger the mind of the spectator.

The appearance of Old Mahon, as if risen from the dead to take revenge on his son, precipitates the unexpected. First Christy actually attacks his father with a loy; next the crowd in the shebeen turn on Christy and drops an actual rope around his arms and offers to take him to the police; then Pegeen takes a glowing sod from the fire and actually burns him on the leg. The reality of this ugly business finally dispels any romanticizing about Christy that Pegeen and the patrons of the shebeen, or the audience, had enjoyed:

> MEN (*to* PEGEEN). Bring the sod, will you?
> PEGEEN (*coming over*). God help him so. (*Burns his leg.*)
> CHRISTY (*kicking and screaming*). Oh, glory be to God!

The burning, like a shot from a gun, is received as hard reality by the audience, an unfunny effect with no trace of fantasy: reality is no joke. The play proceeds on a new level, so that when Old Mahon returns to claim his son, Christy surprises everyone by going off with him. When Pegeen's stuffy fiancé Shawn suggests that now Father Reilly can marry them, she boxes his ear, pulls her shawl over her head and breaks into '*wild lamentations*', crying, 'Oh, my grief, I've lost him surely. I've lost the only Playboy of the Western World.' In those pathetic lines Synge lets us hear at the last a note of tragedy.

The Abbey Theatre became a forum for the cultural aspirations of an emerging nation. After the establishment of the Irish Free State (1922), the Irish stage acquired new strength and in Sean O'Casey found its greatest playwright, one who developed both a more vigorous and aggressive realism and in the end a more expressive poetic drama. Born into an urban slum, O'Casey knew about the life of the poor, and there was nothing mythical or mystical about the back streets of Dublin. He was also a pacificist by persuasion and following the Troubles of the Easter Rebellion of 1916 and the Civil War of 1922, his antimilitaristic plays, *The Shadow of a Gunman* (1923), *Juno and the Paycock* (1924) and *The Plough and the Stars* (1926), again roused the wrath of the passionate Dublin audience. For O'Casey offered them a degree of realism the Abbey had not known, mixing elements of tragedy with humour in a way that at times attained a Chekhovian objectivity. He knew little of Synge and the National Theatre: if he had a model, it was that of Dion Boucicault whose Irish melodramas he saw in his youth, and whose pathos and sentimentality he introduced from time to time into his own work.

Juno and the Paycock is the most erratically sentimental of the early plays, but with Sara Allgood and Barry Fitzgerald in the title parts of Juno and 'Captain' Jack Boyle, and the Irish comedian F. J. McCormick as his crony Joxer Daly, it was the most successful in the history of the Abbey and has continued to be popular ever since. Juno is the long-suffering wife and the Paycock [peacock] is her voluble drunkard of a husband, both stereotypes from temperance melodrama. Their son Johnny is wounded in the civil fighting and executed for desertion by his former comrades, while their daughter Mary is made pregnant by a villain of an Englishman. With its plot lurching from disaster to disaster as Boyle and Joxer grow drunker, the play might have sunk into its own sea of soap; but O'Casey visits Juno's lines with a poetry of his own, turns his Paycock into a masterly comedian and unpredictably deflects his emotional moments with a tough, irreverent humour. O'Casey saved the Abbey from bankruptcy and became a force to be reckoned with.

With the same explosive mixture of pathos and cynicism, O'Casey's greatest play, *The Plough and the Stars*, dared to tackle the most sensitive area of recent Irish history, the Easter Rebellion of 1916. He saw fit to mock unsparingly religion, sex and patriotism, 'the trinity of Irish taboos' (David Krause, *Sean O'Casey* (1960), 39), and when the famous patriot Joseph Plunkett stepped from the rebel head-quarters of the General Post Office to read the Proclamation of the Irish Republic, O'Casey contrived to make the spectator see him through the eyes of a whore waiting for customers inside a public house. Like *The Playboy of the Western World* nearly twenty years before, this was an occasion for rioting: Ria Mooney, who played the prostitute Rosie Redmond, was told her career was finished, and the spectators fought with the actors on the stage and tried to set fire to the curtain. Yeats rebuked the audience with the immortal words, 'You have disgraced yourselves again', but the Irish movement naturally proceeded on its lusty way.

Strong objectivity or cynicism, however it is seen, was essential to distance the subject of *The Plough and the Stars*, and combinations of such contraries as pathos and clowning, and realism and heroics, are woven through the action. The personal tragedy of Nora Clitheroe and her husband Jack, a commandant in the Irish Citizen Army, is set among a lively bunch of relatives and neighbours in a Dublin tenement who represent a cross-section of the community: Peter Flynn is a belligerent old soldier reliving his past glories, the Covey is a dedicated young Communist (O'Casey mocking himself), Bessie Burgess is a Protestant Orangewoman from Ulster, Mrs Gogan is a Catholic from the South, and Fluther Good, an almost choric figure originally played by Barry Fitzgerald, holds the centre and says whatever suits the occasion. Through the agency of the stage O'Casey orchestrates deliberate incongruities among this assortment of characters, and finally dares to bring on British Tommies to balance the Irish irregulars.

The incongruities reach a crescendo in the public house during the scene of the Uprising in act 2. The set is arranged in such a way that the Barman and Rosie are in the foreground and the figure of a man addressing the noisy crowd outside is silhouetted from time to time against a back window. As the pub is empty, the two inside have nothing to do except prepare for business, the Barman wiping the counter and Rosie toying with a glass of whisky.

> BARMAN (*wiping counter*). Nothin' much doin' in your line to-night, Rosie?
> ROSIE.   Curse o' God on th' haporth, hardly, Tom. There isn't much notice taken of a pretty petticoat of a night like this...They're all in a holy mood...

Against this tone of dry detachment the audience heard the stirring words it knew well, those of Padraig Pearse, the republican leader:

> It is a glorious thing to see arms in the hands of Irishmen. We must accustom ourselves to the thought of arms, we must accustom ourselves to the sight of arms, we must accustom ourselves to the use of arms... Bloodshed is a cleansing and sanctifying thing...

The words echo the Eucharist and the 'holy mood' of Peter and Fluther was reflected in the Dublin audience, so that when this pair '*enter tumultuously*' calling for drink ('A meetin' like this always makes me feel as if I could dhrink

Loch Erinn dhry!'), it is not hard to understand the outrage of those who again failed to see the joke.

The mixing of religious and political attitudes and the weaving of tragic and farcical tones builds up to the end, and act 4 brings together a chaos of disparate effects: fighting outside in the street, the body of Mrs Gogan's consumptive child in a coffin, a huddle of Irishmen playing cards, news of Clitheroe's death, the crazed singing of a traumatized Nora, a dying Bessie Burgess caught in a sniper's fire and singing a hymn to Jesus as she dies, two Cockney soldiers drinking the tea Nora had prepared for her husband and a chorus of 'Keep the home fires burning' to match the rattle of machine-gun fire and the boom of artillery off-stage. This was a new kind of poetry of the theatre.

Such stagecraft already suggests that even O'Casey's ugly realism was not enough for him, and that he was looking for a form of expressionism. Indeed, after he left Ireland following the stormy reception of *The Plough and the Stars*, in England he wrote the first of an experimental series of plays that aimed to integrate realistic and expressionistic modes of playwriting. *The Silver Tassie* (1928) has a second act set in the trenches of the First World War in which '*every feature of the scene seems a little distorted from its original appearance*', the realistic characters of act 1 become abstract, and the soldiers speak their lines rhythmically. Yeats could not understand why O'Casey had turned from his Irish realism to a German way of writing, and the upshot was that he rejected the play; it was an inestimable loss to the native theatre that O'Casey remained in exile. The *Observer* published St John Ervine's letter to O'Casey on this occasion: 'I do not object to Yeats regarding himself as the Holy Ghost, but I complain that he is sometimes inclined to regard himself as the entire Trinity' (3 June 1928).

O'Casey's particular conjunction of farcical tragedy and the colourful Anglo-Irish dialogue he favoured were suited to his irregular experiments in expressionism. With impersonalized characters, dreamlike episodes and unlocalized, symbolic settings he enjoyed a freedom from the realistic imperative that his predecessors had not known. Unfortunately, lacking the constraints of the Abbey stage and audience, the plays of his later years were also uncertain successes. Of these the wartime *Purple Dust* (1940), a comedy of Anglo-Irish relationships set in a Tudor mansion in modern-day Ireland, and *Cock-a-Doodle Dandy* (1949), a moral fantasy and a paean to life, are the most esteemed.

After O'Casey the Irish stage continued to offer plays of universal appeal, if of less individuality, and in the latter half of the twentieth century certain theatrical talents have been worthy of the Abbey at its best. Unluckily, the work of Tom Murphy (1935–) has scarcely been seen outside Dublin, but that of Brian Friel (1929–) has found a wide acceptance, and his delicate humour and sensitive studies of Irish life have invited experiments in poetic styles of production. *Philadelphia, Here I Come!* (1964) and *Faith Healer* (1979) achieved an international success, and their ease and spontaneity have been matched by subsequent plays like *Dancing in Lughnasa* (1990) with its moving impression of family memories in County Donegal set against its harvest festival. Apart from uncharacteristic excursions into political theatre and the occasional use of Brechtian devices – dividing the stage, splitting characters and interjecting extended monologue and direct address to the audience – Friel has not lost his gift for creating perceptive lyrical pictures of the domestic Ireland he knows. Early comparisons made with the gentle compassion and subtle intensity of Chekhov's naturalism have endured.

Towards a drama in verse: *Murder in the Cathedral*

Yeats's all too private experiments had no successors and, written for an exclusive audience, his plays became increasingly subjective – the last quality the stage can accept. In any case, attention was redirected between the Wars to the attempt to create a new verse drama by another poet working outside the orthodox London theatre. T. S. Eliot (1888–1965), an even more private poet and one inclined towards the style of French symbolist poetry, came to the drama with an unlikely mission: to discover what made the Elizabethan poetic stage workable and how to recreate in verse a moral or religious drama for a modern audience.

Eliot's arguments for verse drama after three hundred years of virtual silence were persuasive and they caught the literary imagination, but in the end all his theory proved to be academic. Always searching for the ways verse could be justified as a stageworthy medium, several of his early essays shrewdly analyzed some of the major Elizabethan playwrights, and in his discussions of poetic drama he posed these basic questions:

(1) How can the complex thoughts and feelings of a poet be conveyed through *characters in action*? In a later lecture, *The Three Voices of Poetry* (1953), Eliot distinguishes the first voice as the one a poet uses when talking to himself, the second as the one he uses when speaking to his reader, and it is the third which communicates through dramatic characters. In each character the poet must put 'some bit of himself', which 'may be the germ from which the life of the character starts'.

(2) Given that poetry is a better vehicle than prose to guide and intensify the feelings, what *kind of poetry*, what idiom, would be understood by a twentieth-century audience? Or, put another way, 'How would people today speak if they could speak in poetry?' (Eliot's Introduction to S. L. Bethell, *Shakespeare and the Popular Dramatic Tradition* (1944), ix)

(3) If the drama were to escape from the surface of life, what *dramatic conventions*, i.e. unreal devices, are allowable in order to free the stage and its drama from the grip of realism, from what the director Michel St Denis called the mud of naturalism?

(4) What changes of *form and structure* should be expected in the play as a whole? In a broadcast Eliot asserted that 'To work out a play in verse...is to see the thing as a whole musical pattern...which intensifies our excitement by reinforcing it with feeling from a deeper and less articulate level.' (*The Listener*, 25 November 1936)

Eliot wanted a poetic drama that was more than a drama in

verse, and in his essay on John Marston he argued for 'a kind of doubleness in the action, as if it took place on two planes at once'. The audience was to perceive 'a pattern behind the pattern'. (*Selected Essays* (1932), 229, 232)

Eliot was not entirely the theorist, and it is to his credit that his sense of experiment never died, each play taking a new direction. He had written poems that resembled dramatic monologues, like 'The Love Song of J. Alfred Prufrock' (1917), 'Gerontion' (1920) and parts of 'The Waste Land' (1922); or else that embodied a dramatic situation, as in 'Portrait of a Lady' (1917) and the 'Sweeney Agonistes' fragments (1926). His first play came about in response to a specific request from Bishop George Bell, then Dean of Canterbury, who had in 1929 founded the Religious Drama Society and needed new plays for its annual Canterbury Festival. Eliot obliged with a play about the martyrdom of Thomas à Becket and named it *Murder in the Cathedral* (1935). To his self-imposed criteria, he now added the challenge of having to win over a festival audience with a religious play. In the event, the eight hundred performances of its first two or three years made it a landmark in the history of modern English drama.

The fact that the scene was to represent Canterbury Cathedral dictated the physical conditions of playwriting and performance. That it was also an historical subject determined its costume and décor, and raised expectations of authenticity and atmosphere that always attach to period drama. That it told a familiar story from the history of the Church under festival conditions meant that its audience was already partial and also decided the writer's perspective. As for the language and conventions of the play, these too were governed by the unusual context of a church performance. So Eliot did not have his troubles to seek, and whatever the play achieved could not really count towards a modern revival of verse drama. Nevertheless, he proved that the bold use of conventions could shake the drama free from realism.

The writing had to conjure up the twelfth-century cathedral and at the same time meet the actual needs of the Chapter House where it was to be performed. This had been furnished with an awkward end-platform 36 feet wide and a narrow

9 feet deep, on which were placed a number of low screens as wing-pieces. Luckily the physical features of a church are essentially those of an open stage, and an open stage is suitable for the rituals and liturgies of the Church. In addition, a pulpit served for a sermon-soliloquy, the nave [aisle] for the entrance of Thomas's assassins, and so on. The spectators also found themselves seated like a congregation, and, following the Greek tragic convention, a Chorus of the Women of Canterbury mediated between the Archbishop and his flock, the actor and his audience.

Eliot's Chorus does everything its Greek model would be expected to do: interpret the past, intensify the present and anticipate the future, and in addition it represents the secular world and the common people, keeping the play human in the awesome presence of a martyr and a saint. The Chorus also shapes the pattern of the play as it speaks a series of incantatory speeches designed to catch the feeling of the action and encourage the intended response as it changes from foreboding and fear to terror and horror. The lines of the Chorus also signal the mood in voice and movement, from the hesitation of the entrance lines,

> Here let us stand, close by the cathedral. Here let us wait.
> Are we drawn by danger? Is it the knowledge of safety,
>   that draws our feet
> Towards the cathedral?...

to the unease in the macabre images intoned just before the killing:

> I have smelt them, the death-bringers, senses are quickened
> By subtile forebodings; I have heard
> Fluting in the night-time, fluting and owls, have seen at
>   noon
> Scaly wings slanting over, huge and ridiculous...

These speeches are made up of a spoken stressed verse, faintly reminiscent of the alliterative verse of the medieval plays, and although it can hardly be considered the natural example for a modern verse speech, such verse is efficient, as here, in carrying soprano and contralto voices in contrasting tones, as well as variations in tempo and gesture.

The basic Aristotelian requirements of plot and character

did not work so well. Martyrdom focused nearly all the interest on a single character, encouraging the poet to speak in the first or second voice, and limiting dramatic values. Nor could this one-character limitation be minimized by the four morality play Tempters who weaken Thomas's resolution with temptations of pleasure, power and pride, nor by the four Knights who kill Thomas solely out of duty to their King. The Tempters lacked individuality because their temptations were contrived and without hope of success, and the Knights lacked depth because what they did was a foregone conclusion. In fact, Eliot's text had to face all the problems of dramatizing a moral history without the possibility of surprise or tragedy.

Certain devices worked well in performance. Because of the limited number of good amateur players, the first producer, E. Martin Browne, doubled the Tempters with the Knights and so by serendipity suggested that the enemies Becket was fighting within himself were in parallel with those without, a tactic adopted by other directors since. In a production for the Royal Shakespeare Company at the Swan Theatre in 1993, Steven Pimlott ingeniously had the Fourth Tempter act as a mirror-image of the Archbishop, so that Thomas saw a distorted reflection of his own pride. One original device was unique in charging the imagination of the audience: after Thomas is ritualistically killed before the altar and the Chorus has filled the air with a poetry of shrieking and horror, the Knights, suddenly sober, *'advance to the front of the stage and address the audience'* in order to excuse what they have done. In effect, posing as comic upper-class Englishmen and speaking in modern prose, they break out of the dramatic frame of religious history. The place in the action, the switch in the convention of speech, the shift in the level of response, the shock of a new perspective, all contribute to a startling alienation-effect as good as any in Brecht.

Of Eliot's later plays, *The Family Reunion* (1939) and *The Cocktail Party* (1949) warrant attention because they pursued other routes to a successful verse drama. Both of these plays carefully chose a contemporary situation, and were written as drawing-room drama, thus avoiding the period stamp with which unnatural speech might be associated. Christian themes were still present, but no longer in the context of the Church: it was to be a religious theatre without God. For this Eliot developed a conversational verse form that slipped readily from prose to poetry and back again – in *The Cocktail Party* even to the point where a spectator who had not seen the text might wonder whether it was written in verse at all.

In both, however, he aimed at the two levels of action that would enable the audience to perceive a submerged meaning. Both plays used elements of Greek tragedy to lend universality and timelessness to the plot, *The Family Reunion* telling the story of a curse on an ancient house, albeit a somewhat unChristian concept, and seeing life through the eyes of a modern Orestes, the unhappy Harry, Lord Monchensey. In this play Eliot also created the effect of a chorus, whereby from time to time Harry's family of aunts and uncles unexpectedly turned their faces to the audience and spoke their lines in unison. The audience was not so much alarmed by this as by another element from Aeschylus's *Oresteia*, that of the Furies of retribution. Before they could be propitiated, however, they had somehow to be accommodated in the family drawing-room, and in his lecture *Poetry and Drama* (1951) Eliot admitted that sometimes they looked like uninvited guests from a fancy-dress ball, or else appeared to be swarming across the stage like a football team.

The Cocktail Party was a success in ways that its predecessor was not. It had the shadow of another Greek tragedy behind it – the *Alcestis* of Euripides, with Heracles as the equivalent of the 'unidentified guest', Sir Henry Harcourt-Reilly (played originally by Alec Guiness as a radical psychiatrist with bristling hair). Nevertheless, the play is announced as a comedy, and, using the same chatty three-stressed line as before, develops deceptively from frivolous gossip to become a drawing-room comedy about marital shenanigans. Before it is done, however, Eliot sneaks in another Christian martyrdom, that of the society girl Celia Coplestone, who becomes a missionary. Spiritual matters emerge from mundane reality rather clumsily, and it is alarming when three of the characters call themselves 'The Guardians' and intermittently drink either a toast or a libation, shattering the realistic frame as much as any Furies.

This device of shifting from one kind of play to another was a principle Eliot had suggested in *Poetry and Drama* (1957):

> The audience should find, at the moment of awareness that it is hearing poetry, that it is saying to itself: '*I* could talk in poetry too!' Then we should not be transported into an artificial world; on the contrary, our own sordid, dreary daily world would be suddenly illuminated and transfigured.
>
> (27)

It is part of the author's attraction that he so often announces what he intends, that his reader is inclined to believe he has actually done it. The press believed that a new verse drama had arrived, but it reckoned without the powerful Continental influences of surrealism and expressionism, the absurd and the epic theatre, which Eliot, like Yeats before him, seemed determined to eschew.

W. H. Auden (1907–73), in collaboration with Christopher Isherwood (1904–89), toyed with an expressionistic charade in *The Ascent of F6* (1936), and in 1937 it achieved a production under Ashley Dukes at his non-commercial little Mercury Theatre at Notting Hill Gate, with incidental music by the young Benjamin Britten. The enterprising Mercury Theatre also brought to public attention the talents of Christopher Fry (1907–), a juggler of jewelled words and phrases. Eliot once remarked of Fry, 'If that young man wants to write poetic plays, he must first learn to be less poetic.' (George Jean Nathan, *The Theatre Book of 1950–51*.)

From the point of view of stage experiment, his technically most accomplished play was written for the Festival of Britain and for performance in a church. *A Sleep of Prisoners* (1951) was produced in St Thomas's, off Regent Street, and, like *Murder in the Cathedral* before it, the physical acting area, an open stage and bare arena, was itself a theatrical opportunity, its features in Fry's play supplying a jungle, a mountain, a tower, a furnace and a tree. As befits a more sober subject, the language is more spare, although this did little to resolve the complexity of a plot interwoven in an episodic cat's-cradle of stories. Four prisoners of war, each a different type, spend a night locked up in a church, where in a fit of temper a fight breaks out. As a consequence each man re-enacts a dream of violence in a story taken from the Old Testament, and each man plays in his own and in another's dream, revealing his own personality and what the others think of him. All this embodies the point of the play, that conflict arises when mankind cannot see the truth about itself.

Michael MacOwan, the play's first director, reported that it seemed to stage itself, and that every move and piece of business was almost inevitable, 'so vivid had been the picture in Christopher Fry's mind while he wrote it'. Here was a skill and an economy that suggested a strong future for the author, but with the other verse playwrights the world passed him by in favour of Beckett and Brecht.

The surreal and the absurd: *Waiting for Godot, Travesties*

Against theatrical logic, the English stage had a brief flirtation immediately after the Second World War with French surrealistic theatre, the first of two strong mid-century liberating forces. After the Holocaust and Hiroshima there is no need to justify the appeal of a theatre of the absurd, which echoed some of the negativism and despair implicit in those events. Nothing of this mood in itself makes for good theatre, but the techniques and devices, the self-conscious theatricality, introduced to make it digestible, are special. Laughter seems indispensable to the success of this drama, triggered by a few characteristic elements: ridiculous and unpredictable plotting; time and space, and cause and effect, that are illogical; characters who are eccentric, often motiveless; a pace that can be farcically fast or tragically slow, unrelated to content. Absurdism constitutes a blasphemy against the feelings, and the final perception is one of farce or tragedy, but when it works well, its impact is unforgettable.

The Irishman Samuel Beckett (1906–89), writing first for the Paris, then the London stage, exercised a surprising influence on Western theatre, if only because the conventions he employed were startlingly extreme, reducing theatre to primary images. His themes were also radical, exhibiting life and death, and time and eternity, in a hostile and Godless world. The play that shook the established theatre was *Waiting for Godot* (written in 1948, first produced in Paris in 1953). The plot that is no plot tells of two men, Vladimir and Estragon [Didi and Gogo], who live in fruitless expectation of the arrival of Godot, a mysterious being who sends messages that he is delayed, but who never comes. For two acts they pass their time in mere existence, twice meeting two other human beings, Pozzo and Lucky, who eventually also leave them 'waiting'.

Beckett dismissed 'plot' as of no account in order to emphasize not what happens, but how it happens. Since the story does not develop, information is at a premium, and metaphors and symbols at a discount. The setting is of a drab, empty stage representing '*a country road*', although one bare tree represents a specific place; when this grows a few leaves, they signify that time has passed. The characters are also derisory: Didi and Gogo may be tramps, since they exist at a level of destitution, troubled by feet or bladder, eating a carrot; but they look and behave like clowns. They also quarrel constantly, Didi arguing spiritually, Gogo earthly, so that they are less like two individuals than a relationship. The intruders Pozzo and Lucky are also mutually reflexive, depending upon one another like master and servant, bound together in mutual hate and fear. All dialogue is crosstalk, the topics trivial, the manner generally that of the music-hall stage:

> VLADIMIR. Ah yes, the two thieves. Do you remember the story?
> ESTRAGON. No.
> VLADIMIR. Shall I tell it to you?
> ESTRAGON. No.
> VLADIMIR. It'll pass the time. (*Pause.*) It was two thieves, crucified at the same time as our Saviour.
>   One –
> ESTRAGON. Our what?

(act 1)

This discussion of a sacred subject like the Crucifixion is treated as a comic exchange. The surface of such dialogue is pure frivolity, but all beneath is grim anxiety. At the end of the play the two attempt to hang themselves from the tree with the cord that holds up Gogo's trousers, which therefore fall about his ankles. The audience laughs, seeming to ridicule suicide, and Didi decides they should postpone the hanging till the next day.

The text, even in this serious context, is full of the comic business appropriate to clowns, whether from the Italian *commedia dell'arte* or the English and Continental circus. In later years Beckett himself directed some of his plays in Germany, beginning with *Endgame* in 1967 and including *Waiting for Godot* in 1975. Not only did he show himself to be a meticulous director, but demonstrated that every line was exactly right kinaesthetically, embodying the movement, gesture and business he visualized when he wrote it. In spite of his apparently uninhibited stage, he believed in the finality of the text and not in the improvised contribution of the actor, whose personality he wished to exclude.

This goes some way to explaining the sense of reductive theatre in his stagecraft. In *Endgame* (1956), his next play, his principal character, Hamm, is blind, confined to a wheelchair and initially '*covered with an old sheet*', and two others, his parents Nagg and Nell, are confined in ashbins. The '*bare interior*' of the set has '*high up, two small windows, curtains drawn*' in a '*grey light*', an image of prison or purgatory. Hamm's servant, Clov, is instructed to move with a '*stiff, staggering walk*' like a robot, and everything he does is mechanical. But Hamm, his tyrant of a master, is also a creature of habit, as if programmed for his end, and between them they symbolize a life that proceeds from one hollow moment to the next. Such a moment occurs when Clov discovers a flea in his trousers:

> CLOV (*anguished, scratching himself*). I have a flea!
> HAMM. A flea! Are there still fleas?

Shakespeare anticipated this touch of the absurd when in *King Lear*, Edgar as his madman Poor Tom, links what is

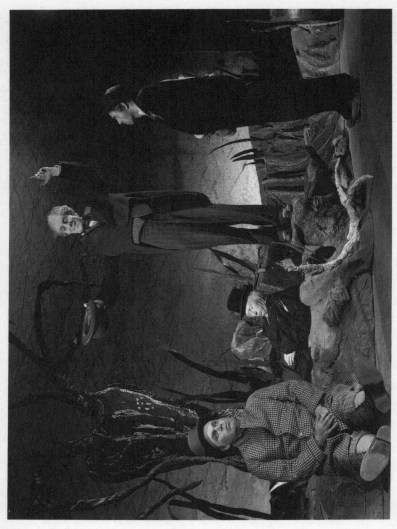

17 Samuel Beckett, *Waiting for Godot*, 1953; the first English production directed by Peter Hall at the Arts Theatre in 1955.

momentous with what is insignificant in life – 'to prevent the fiend, and to kill vermin' (3.4.163).

Beckett's theatricality, from the beginning a mechanistic parody of normal stagecraft, proceeded from 'reductionism' to 'minimalism' (putting criticism at a loss for words). In the best classical tradition of farce, characters were puppets, clockwork creatures moving like Clov or the actor in the desert in *Act without Words, I* (1956) who is spurred into life by a whistle from the wings. In *Krapp's Last Tape* (1958) one player talks to himself on a tape-recorder, and in *Happy Days* (1961) Winnie is buried first to her waist, then to her neck, in a mound of earth. *Play* (1962) has three nameless characters whose heads protrude from '*three identical grey urns*' and whose words are prompted by the flashing of individual spotlights. *Come and Go* (1965) has three women sitting stiffly on a bench, linked only by their memories of the past. *Not I* (1973) stages merely the lips and teeth of a talking mouth '*about 8 feet above stage level, faintly lit from close-up and below*'. *That Time* (1974) has an '*old white face, long flaring white hair as if seen from above outspread*' and set '*about 10 feet above stage level*'; this face does not speak itself, but listens to three disembodied voices. The physical requirements of these directions alone anticipate a tiny audience if any facial details are to be seen, and at the end Beckett denied the theatre its legitimate working elements and the actor his traditional command of his audience. With austerity on-stage and despair off-stage, Beckett's symbolic drama had the distinction of being at once the height of academic fashion and a theatrical *reductio ad absurdum*.

The academic symbol-chase continued with Harold Pinter (1930–), who was one among many new dramatists who found Beckett's inroads into the realistic theatre illuminating and inviting. Beckett was inimitable, but in an interview in 1960 Pinter was happy to acknowledge his influence. It was therefore more an accident of history that Pinter was associated with the theatre of the absurd, since it soon became apparent that he was not a private playwright. He showed no interest in the metaphysical nature of man, but rather more in his psychological needs: more like Kafka than Beckett. Nor was he at all interested in a symbolic theatre, as he repeatedly insisted: 'I start off with people, who come into a particular situation. I certainly don't write from any kind of abstract idea. And I wouldn't know a symbol if I saw one' ('Writing for Myself', *Twentieth Century* (February 1961), 168). Pinter is a domesticated, and a more human, Beckett.

He served his apprenticeship as a repertory actor in the traditional proscenium theatre, and apart from his familiarity with the episodic qualities of a television script, he was not concerned with unconventional staging. His dramaturgy is nevertheless highly original, specifically in areas of illogical plotting, elusive characterization and an exceptionally colloquial dialogue. In Pinter's hands these three elements make a formidable combination:

(1) *Plot.* He starts with an uncomplicated, even commonplace, situation: 'All I try to do is describe some particular thing, a particular occurrence in a particular context.' Two people live in reasonable security in a room; but the room has a door and they are afraid of what is outside, who can come in, what may threaten their safety (*The Room*, 1957). Two contract gunmen in a basement await their orders to kill, with only a dumb waiter to give them instructions (*The Dumb Waiter*, 1957). A man hiding in a boarding-house is terrorized by two intruders who soon reduce him to imbecility and lead him away, presumably to an asylum (*The Birthday Party*, 1958). A son brings his new wife home to meet his family, all men, whom she has no trouble in dominating as wife, mother or mistress (*The Homecoming*, 1965). However simple, Pinter's plots are not 'well-made': things can happen illogically and remain unexplained; they do not 'develop' laterally, rather, they penetrate vertically.

(2) *Character.* Pinter displaces the comfortable concept of a sympathetic 'hero' by one of an 'antihero'. This character is divested of all the trappings of realistic information about his history and background, his personality and motivation. In practice, the author refuses himself any more knowledge of his characters than he allows his audience, and then only as they are identified in the

course of the performance. The silence – and inscrut-
ability – of a harmless old matchseller completely changes
the behaviour of a well-to-do, middle-class couple (*A
Slight Ache*, 1959). A woman, possibly only in the
imagination, visits her old room-mate and her husband
after twenty years, and her presence is enough to evoke
ambiguous memories that undermine their married relationship (*Old Times*, 1971). In a programme note to the
production of *The Room* and *The Dumb Waiter* at the
Royal Court in 1960, Pinter defined the surrealistic world
of his characters:

> There are no hard distinctions between what is real and
> what is unreal, nor between what is true and what is false.
> The thing is not necessarily either true or false; it can be
> both true and false...A character on the stage who can
> present no convincing argument or information as to his
> past experience, his present behaviour or his aspirations,
> nor give a comprehensive analysis of his motives is as
> legitimate and as worthy of attention as one who, alar-
> mingly, can do all these things.

(3) *Dialogue*. Pinter has the sharp ear of an actor and writes
in an idiom so colloquial that his lines frequently evoke
laughter in themselves: the term 'Pinteresque' was soon
coined to describe his style. When spoken by an actor the
rhythms of the lines are repetitive and inconsequential, so
that the words seem to be extemporary, and the pauses
and silences, like Chekhov's, are often more articulate
than the words themselves. Like Beckett's, his working
method is constantly to simplify, 'to pare away', as he has
said. There is wit in his ability to reproduce the exact
tones and hesitations of human speech, and this serves his
exploration of the human personality well.

Pinter's work developed steadily in theme and style over
the years. His early black comedies, once called 'comedies of
menace', were essentially light in spirit. Of these *The Birthday
Party*, initially misunderstood, has since been repeatedly
revived and exemplifies Pinter's early manner. Its first act goes
to extremes to establish a picture of realistic life. Stanley is

'*unshaven, in his pyjama jacket and wears glasses*', and is first
seen at breakfast:

> STANLEY. What's this?
> PETEY.   Fried bread.
> MEG (*entering*).   Well, I bet you don't know what it is.
> STANLEY. Oh yes I do.
> MEG.   What?
> STANLEY. Fried bread.
> MEG.   He knew.

This exposition of simple-minded, even subnormal, living
lowers the audience's defences against the 'menace' to come.
Yet it is never known whether Stanley is lying about his past
as a persecuted pianist, and in so ludicrous a context his true
character remains obscure. The act ends when the ingratiating,
sinister pair Goldberg and McCann arrive with their suitcases
intending to stay, and they offer to throw a party for Stanley's
birthday.

Much of act 2 is given over to a terrifying, Kafkaesque
interrogation of Stanley; it begins quietly and turns into a
nonsensical nightmare of brainwashing. The victim sits in a
chair with his back to the house so that his inquisitors seem to
address the audience too:

> GOLDBERG. Why did the chicken cross the road?
> STANLEY.   He wanted...
> MCCANN.   He doesn't know. He doesn't know which
>   came first!
> GOLDBERG. Which came first?
> MCCANN.   Chicken? Egg? Which came first?
> GOLDBERG and MCCANN.   Which came first? Which came
>   first? Which came first?
> STANLEY *screams.*

Stanley is reduced to gibbering speechlessness by the irrational, staccato questioning, and remains inarticulate
throughout the wild birthday party that follows. Next day, in
act 3, Stanley is taken away, now shaved and dressed in the
clothes of a city gentleman: '*striped trousers, black jacket, and
white collar...a bowler hat in one hand*'. Whatever uncertain
identity he may have had has now been lost in this conformity,
and the stage reverts to the silly small-talk with which it began.

What critics thought obscure in 1958 today seems, as

Waiting for Godot now does, a straightforward allegory presented as a surrealistic horror story. What distinguished the approach was Pinter's sense of fun: 'I like comedy', he said in an interview with William Tennyson for the BBC in 1960; 'I enjoy amusing myself when I write and it's nice to know I amuse others.' However, it was this sense of humour that gave his plays their acutely painful edge.

The ironic quality persisted through the earlier plays, but declined as their farcical element diminished. Black comedy gave way to psychological studies like *No Man's Land* (1975), in which two poets, one a literary lion (originally played by Ralph Richardson) and the other a seedy hanger-on (played by John Gielgud), meet again in a haze of shadowy memory and literary allusion. This play, with *Old Times* and the memory studies *Landscape* (1968) and *Silence* (1969), in which characters who are isolated on the stage speak more in monologue than dialogue and seem to live in separate worlds, have been grouped together as 'memory plays'. They are notably static, but *Betrayal* (1978) also qualifies as a memory play in which the circumstances of adultery are more stage-worthily played in nine scenes seen in reverse time. Pinter acknowledges that 'the mistiness of the past' (*New York Times*, 5 December 1971) is of great interest to him, and he makes a point of employing this as a way of manipulating character and its shifting identity. In recent years, more politically orientated plays, *One for the Road* (1984), *Mountain Language* (1988) and *The New World Order* (1991), involve intimidation and mental torture as a chilling metaphor for the instability of the personality.

The scatter-effect following the disintegration of the naturalistic convention resulted in a handful of iconoclastic playwrights bent on exploiting the new quasi-absurdist licence. Joe Orton (1933–67) invented a unique style of fast-paced, lunatic farce aimed candidly at exposing social and sexual hypocrisy. The recurring pattern was one of parody, provocatively offering an outrageous idea couched in a speech and manner that was smooth and composed, even serene and genteel. When the trick worked, as it usually did, an audience was convulsed, and so disarmed, by laughter.

Orton came to attention with *Entertaining Mr Sloane* (1964), which was touched with Pinteresque menace and the cut and thrust of a meticulous dialogue. The play introduces a repulsive young man, 'Mr Sloane', who is willing to accept a bisexual role in a preposterous *ménage à trois* with an older couple, the brother and sister Ed and Kath. This ugly pair turns out to be sexually rapacious and Mr Sloane turns out to be a murderer – although with this sort of plotting, it is the game played, not on the stage, but with the audience, that demands evaluation. In an even more zany spirit, the juxtaposition of irreconcilable opposites also works wonderfully well in *Loot* (1966), a parody of a whodunnit thriller. This caper centres on Fay, a nurse, whose dead patient, Mrs McLeavy, lies on stage in her coffin. When her son needs to hide a cache of stolen money, Mrs McLeavy is unceremoniously tipped into a wardrobe so that bundles of bank-notes may be stuffed in her place. Set in a psychiatrist's consulting-room, the sexually explicit *What the Butler Saw* (1968) both in its title and its action seems to parody itself. In a wildly provocative travesty of human carnal excesses, the target for mockery is again the moral inhibitions of the audience.

Boos were regularly heard from parts of that audience on the first night of an Orton production, as perhaps befits what John Lahr has called the work of an 'outrageous and violent prankster's spirit of comedy'. He immediately qualified this by saying that it was this spirit that created 'the purest (and rarest) of drama's by-products: joy' (Introduction to Joe Orton, *The Complete Plays* (1977) 27–8).

In the savage imagination of Peter Barnes (1931–) absurdism, like its cousin expressionism, manifested itself as an inky black comedy, mixing Antonin Artaud's theatre of cruelty and its shocking visuals with Peter Handke's notion of *Publikumsbeschimpfung*, designed to affront the audience. In his programme note to *The Ruling Class* (1968), the play that brought him to theatrical attention, he wrote,

> The aim is to create, by means of soliloquy, rhetoric, formalized ritual, slapstick, songs, and dances, a comic theatre of contrasting moods and opposites, where everything is simultaneously tragic and ridiculous. And we hope

never to consent to the deadly servitude of naturalism or lose our hunger for true size, weight, and texture.

Barnes identified *The Ruling Class* as 'a baroque comedy', by this evidently meaning a wickedly extravagant satire on the aristocracy and its abuse of power. In it we meet the insane line of the unconscionable Earl of Gurney, the last member of which is a Franciscan friar who believes he is Christ. In *Leonardo's Last Supper* (1969) Barnes offered a one-act fantasy in which the great painter wakes in a charnel-house with a vision of Hell, thinking he is dead. When the undertaker's family sees that Leonardo is still alive, it cares not a whit for the glories of the Renaissance, but, drowning him in a bucket of excrement, prefers to make a profit from selling his body-parts.

The Bewitched (1974) also dips into history for a further attack on the class system: in a fast-paced farce a repulsive spastic image of the epileptic Carlos II of Spain is set against the horrors of the Inquisition he incites. *Laughter!* (1978) again finds an historical monster in Ivan the Terrible who in Part I demonstrates an obscene abuse of his power. This, however, is nothing to Part II, in which the inhuman managers of Auschwitz's gas-chambers strip their dead victims of their valuables. This nightmare of a play dares to end in carefully shocking taste with the jokes of two stand-up Jewish comics who invite the audience to join them in singing to the brotherhood of man.

If offending the audience was Barnes's intention, the audience has regularly recognized as much by rejecting his overtures, and it took Trevor Griffiths (1935–) with his more calculated and gentle play *Comedians* (1975) to suggest that only the better forms of humour can be truly subversive.

With the production at the 1966 Edinburgh Festival of the ingenious one-act *Rosencrantz and Guildenstern Are Dead*, lengthened for the National Theatre in 1967, the name of Tom Stoppard (1937–) was immediately associated with the new wave of absurdist drama. Ros and Guil, the two characters of the title, are comically trapped in Hamlet's play, unable to control events right up to the fatal end. They echo Didi and

Gogo from Beckett's play and are equally at a loss, but the interweaving of Shakespeare's plot, which they do not understand, and their desire for an independence they cannot have, hints also at Pirandello's illusion of frightening reality. If it was more intellectual than profound, Stoppard's highly original theatricality was a welcome development on the comic stage.

Stoppard's next play, *The Real Inspector Hound* (1968), is an amusing burlesque of the conventional whodunnit: '*A tennis ball bounces through the french windows, closely followed by Felicity*' is one stage direction. The story is presented as a play-within-a-play that goes one step further when the critics Birdboot and Moon, assigned to review the new play, become involved with the mystery. Soon after '*the phone starts to ring on the empty stage*' and Moon steps on to the stage to answer it, turning to Birdboot to say, 'It's for you.' Following this, Birdboot discovers that the body on the stage is that of Moon's superior, so that Moon becomes the detective in lieu of Inspector Hound, who sits in the stalls in his place. In this way the real and the fictional worlds are thoroughly confused, and John Russell Taylor commented that 'It all fits together with a sort of demented clockwork precision' (*The Second Wave* (1971), 104).

Thereafter Stoppard's theatrical inventiveness took a philosophical turn with *Jumpers* (1972), which was given a virtuoso performance at the National Theatre by Michael Hordern in the central part of George Moore, a professor of Moral Philosophy. The play is itself an example of theatrical dialectics, balancing a philosophical argument about the existence of God and morality with the physical gymnastics of a company of eight acrobats, and so teasing the audience with an incongruity of mind and eye. Stoppard's ingenuity in juxtaposing apparently unrelated matters reflects the sparkle of his stagecraft, but introduces the doubt that he may be simply playing a game.

To date his most accomplished comedy of ideas is *Travesties* (1974), a concoction of amazing coincidences and juxtapositions, some factual, some fantastic. In early 1918, when the First World War was still at its bloodiest, it happened that three young revolutionaries in art and politics were living in neutral Zurich: the Irish avant-garde novelist James Joyce, the Rumanian Dada poet Tristan Tzara and the Russian political leader Lenin. To these Stoppard added an unknown official from the British consulate, Henry Carr, wounded in the trenches and recently a prisoner of war, whose uncertain memory and '*his various prejudices and delusions*' provide a flashback structure for the action as he reminisces. Stoppard also discovered that, after Lenin had left, Joyce produced Wilde's *The Importance of Being Earnest* with the English-speaking community in Zurich, and this prompted him to double some of his characters with those in Wilde's play and parody some of his episodes and lines when he felt like it. *Travesties* was therefore completely receptive to what Stoppard called 'time slips'. Michael Billington found irresistible a surrealistic mixture that combined 'Wildean pastiche, political history, artistic debate, spoof-reminiscence and song-and-dance in marvellously judicious proportions. The text itself ...radiates sheer intellectual *joie de vivre*' (*Guardian*, 11 June 1974).

This freedom of convention is supported from the start by the way the stage is set. Its two locations, Henry Carr's drawing-room and the Zurich public library, are both only what Carr remembers, and since he may have been '*immobile on the stage from the beginning, an old man remembering*', the locations merge, as they did in the first production. The play begins with a Prologue in the library, where Tzara, Joyce and Lenin are all three at work. Tzara is composing a poem by cutting up words written on a piece of paper and then reading the result, Joyce is dictating another unintelligible muddle of English, Latin and German, and Lenin is talking to his wife in Russian. The scene proceeds with two girl assistants jumbling up the coloured folders in which Joyce and Lenin have placed their notes, and with Joyce discarding and picking up scraps of paper from the floor, one of which turns out to be Lenin's. This lunatic prologue cleverly prepares the audience for the hesitation and faltering of Carr's memory.

The theatrical licence and dizzy invention suggested by the unusual opening never slackens. Imperceptibly the text slides in and out of Wilde's highly artificial style some six or eight times, and seems to lift the action again and again on to the level of the ridiculous. For an example, Gwendolen's parody of her namesake's dialogue addresses Tzara as if he were Jack Worthing and enables Stoppard to make one of a hundred mischievous comments on the newfangled in the arts:

> GWEN.   Alas, a fashionable girl in society receives few
>   opportunities for intellectual connections. When
>   Henry told me he had a friend who edited a
>   magazine of all that is newest and best in literature,
>   I knew I was destined to love you.
> TZARA (*amazed*).   Do you really love me, Gwendolen?
> GWEN.   Passionately!

(55)

Travesties is either a brilliant theatrical review of the avant-garde in art or a vastly amusing image of triviality, more concerned with puzzles than people.

Technically speaking, English stage surrealism has come a long way since Beckett (if of course it has not arrived at Beckett's starting point). *Arcadia* (1993) continues Stoppard's teasing approach to playmaking by not only chopping between topics like landscaping and algorithms, but also between centuries, a process which challenges an audience, if not also a comfortable dramatization. In *Indian Ink* (1995) he compounds two countries, India and England, and two generations, of the 1920s and the 1980s, to make a more lyrical and digestible repast.

Social realism in the wake of Brecht: *Serjeant Musgrave's Dance, A Map of the World*

The post-war revival of the English theatre is associated with the enterprise of George Devine (1910–66) and his revival of the English Stage Company at the Royal Court Theatre after 1956. The arts constantly renew themselves by rebellion, and the realistic theatre of the well-made play was ripe for rehabilitation, ready for a return to nature. Where the plays offered by London's West End committed the ultimate sin of following, not leading, taste, the English Stage Company, with a policy of finding room in economical productions for as many new writers as possible, made English drama a subject for debate as it had not been since the advent of Ibsen. After six years nearly a hundred new plays had been tried out, if only in readings, and such names as John Osborne (1929–94), Arnold Wesker (1932–) and John Arden (1930–) had come to the surface, their plays often of working-class life and resolutely 'kitchen-sink'. The system at the Royal Court may be faulted in that it missed the opportunity to establish an acting ensemble that would have given a stronger stamp to lesser plays, and in that it failed to set up a repertory that would nurse along a play attempting innovative stagecraft, but in the circumstances it was lucky to have an early success in Osborne's *Look Back in Anger* (1956), which gave the Company the financial support it needed to survive.

Osborne's play struck a note of controversy and dissension that shot the English Stage Company into public notice. Jimmy Porter, its unlovely hero ('*a disconcerting mixture of sincerity and cheerful malice, of tenderness and freebooting cruelty; restless, importunate, full of pride, a combination which alienates the sensitive and insensitive alike...*'), had a line of vituperative dialogue that struck the ear with a new quality of realistic speech, a dialogue that was in itself an attack on the complacency of the middle-class audience. He was an antihero, a split-minded misfit in a play whose plot was almost entirely one of discord and conflict. Its spirit caught the imagination of the fifties by pitting one generation against another, and the unromantic misalliance at the centre of the play, the marriage of working-class Jimmy to middle-class Alison, was sufficient to divide the audience against itself. Jimmy was the prototypical 'angry young man', a violent figure of love and hate, self-laceration and self-pity.

The play's reputation for social iconoclasm, however, concealed its conformist limitations. The 'kitchen-sink' setting was daring: an attic room in a Midlands city like Birmingham alien to the West End stage, and with its sloping ceiling and two small windows almost symbolic of social malaise in itself; otherwise the action remained firmly within the proscenium arch and in 1961 Osborne himself considered it was 'rather old-fashioned'. The content raised class consciousness, but in form and style the play follows the pattern of the well-made drama of pre-war days, full of retrospective detail of character and event. It is also at bottom a 'family' play, and discussion about it was for the most part an analysis of Jimmy's neuroses and his unhappy marriage, as if it were any soap opera. In fact, its plot is coherent and its logic simple: the ill-matched couple fight, and then may, or may not, come together again, although it hardly matters which. Nevertheless, in the years that followed echoes of Jimmy Porter were heard in several Royal Court plays, and if *Look Back in Anger* has not dated, it is because its central character is still hypnotic and his voice is still urgent.

However, in 1956 another major event occurred that was to change the direction of English drama even more radically in the remaining years of the twentieth century. This was the London visit of the Berliner Ensemble, which for many offered a first sight of the drama of Bertolt Brecht (1898–1956) and its special style of aggressive performance.

Brecht's drama and his stagecraft supplied at a stroke a host of practical examples of antinaturalistic theatre, together with its theoretical rationale and its Marxist underpinning of the social relevance of good theatre. *Encore* was the London periodical that supported the new British drama, and *The Encore Reader* reported candidly,

> In Brecht, the English dramatist found a writer who combined commitment with poetry; aesthetic discipline with dialectical rigour. To be 'Brechtian', then, was to be politically concerned, theatrically bold and artistically disciplined. It is little wonder he became the national paragon.
>
> (*The Encore Reader* (1965), 135)

Under Brecht's aegis, acting and directing were political acts, and the result was a new theatre of ideas. Nevertheless, it was a lot to swallow all at once.

The elements of Brecht's theatre, which he developed and modified over a lifetime, were endlessly deliberated by his devotees:

(1) *The stage and its setting.* To achieve a condition of non-illusion, Brecht aimed at a simplified, even bare, stage, and insisted that all its secrets be seen, including the rail that

supported the curtain and the hand that drew it. The props and scenery used were only those that were necessary to make a scene work. Lighting was bright and white, without atmospheric effect, and its electrical source had also to be seen. Film projections and written placards supplied direct information as to the location, the context and the purpose of a scene, thus removing some of the subterfuges of exposition usual in conventional dramaturgy and dialogue.

(2) *The plot and structure.* Brecht abandoned the three or four act ordering of the action and the careful building of conflict and emotion characteristic of the well-made play. This was replaced by a sequence of short scenes, preferably juxtaposed with one another in such a way as to make ironic statements. According to George Devine, this plan served 'to break up the normal involvement of the audience, to discourage the kind of hypnosis that is accepted as normal by us' (*Encore*, April 1956). In the Germany of the twenties, episodic structure had been known since the work of Erwin Piscator (1893–1966) at the Berlin Volksbühne as 'epic' [i.e., narrative] theatre.

(3) *Musical interpolation.* The use of music and song, often introduced by Brecht into a story as a form of commentary external to the plot, was another device to break up the hypnotic flow of the action. Music was never used to accompany a text in order to heighten it, but rather to sharpen its impact and to contradict the speaker. Naturally, any musicians and their instruments were visible to the audience.

(4) *The acting.* The style of acting was to be 'presentational', not naturalistic or representational. The actor's task was to demonstrate the position or attitude [*Gestus*] of a character, and this might require the wearing of a mask, so fixing his role or character. In *The Messingkauf Dialogues* Brecht said of the actor: 'He must give up his *complete conversion* into the stage character. He *shows* the character, he *quotes* his lines, he *repeats* a real-life incident...The incidents are *historicized*' (Brecht's italics, trans. John Willett).

(5) *The performance.* The total effect was to be one of non-

illusion, with the actor on occasion directly addressing the audience and, as it were, reaching out to it through the proscenium arch. The effect of this approach was to 'distance' the audience from the story and create a *Verfremdungseffekt* [alienation effect], which 'reverses the tendency of the actor to impress or hypnotize the audience with his versatility or his personality' (Devine, *The Encore Reader* (1965), 16). The 'magic' of the theatre of illusion was not for Brecht, it was wrongly assumed, for his was a drama, not of feeling, but of reason.

(6) *The audience.* When all the tactics and stratagems of writing and performance were working according to plan, the effect was intended to deflate the Aristotelian notions of sharing feeling [empathy] with the characters and counteract any emotional crisis [catharsis] in the spectator. Rather, the object was to undermine his assurance and leave him in a thoughtful and critical state of mind. If this was audience participation, it carried no sense of subservience.

Brechtian theory is by no means at odds with English stage tradition. The Shakespearian experience itself shows that it is possible to suffer with Hamlet and be critical of him too. For Brecht certainly did not always suppress an audience's need to share a character's feelings, which would have undermined the nature of any dramatic activity, nor in his best plays is there an absence of emotional excitement – far from it.

The German influence was felt in all departments of English stagecraft, and it was especially potent among directors and writers, who found that epic theatre had more to offer than symbolist drama or theatre of the absurd.

John Osborne also changed tack. His next play, *The Entertainer* (1957), was written soon after the miscalculation of the Suez War, and concerned itself with nostalgia for the days of Empire and the sense of national futility which followed the débâcle. In order to undercut any naturalistic approach, the play adopted a music-hall framework with a faint Brechtian air of German *Kabarett*. In a note to the text Osborne explained:

I have not used some of the techniques of the music hall in order to exploit an effective trick, but because I believe that these can solve some of the eternal problems of time and space that face the dramatist, and, also, it has been relevant to the story and setting. Not only has this technique its own traditions, its own convention and symbol, its own mystique, it cuts right across the restrictions of the so-called naturalistic stage. Its contact is immediate, vital, and direct.

The seedy provincial hall, complete with bored dancing girls and a symbolic Britannia posing in the nude as a centrepiece, was in fact a dying phenomenon at that date, and provided a perfect metaphor for the condition of the nation. In this setting the unfunny comedian, the 'entertainer' Archie Rice (first played by Laurence Olivier), strove to eke out a living with blue jokes, so dividing the audience against itself, some of whom laughed and some of whom did not. The music-hall treatment framed Archie's story like a play-within-a-play and lent the stage a strong satirical bite, but it could not conceal the traditionally realistic story-telling of the domestic plot, in which the Rices lose a son in the fighting and their marriage collapses. Nevertheless, the alternation of scenes, jumping between the appearances of Archie before the footlights and his exhausted return to his lodging, 'dead behind the eyes', is effective, and in many respects the hollow man Archie Rice is a more powerful symbol of post-war Britain than Jimmy Porter.

Mixing verse and prose, deploying ballads and direct address, the work of the social realist John Arden was more directly modelled on that of Brecht, but his deliberate cultivation of ambiguity in order to divide an audience and make it think has cost him a wide following. *Serjeant Musgrave's Dance* (1960) is an antiwar play that was a commercial failure, but it has been played all over the world and can claim to be the most Brechtian play of the post-war English stage. Subtitled 'An Un-historical Parable' in the best epic tradition, it throws obstacles and distractions in the way, so that the position of the playwright – and the audience – remains elusive to the end.

To begin, the period and place are unconventionally trans-

posed to those of a Victorian mining town in the north of
England, caught in midwinter and in midstrike. Deserting the
British Army from some colonial campaign, a serjeant and
three soldiers appear to be either strike-breakers or a recruiting team for Her Majesty's forces, when in truth their
mission is a religious one: led by the fanatical serjeant Black
Jack Musgrave, they plan to frighten the townspeople with
the horror of war. At first the town dignitaries, the Mayor
(who is also the owner of the mine), the Parson (who is also a
magistrate) and the Constable, are seen as the hypocritical
representatives of the government, the Church and the law,
supporting the soldiers to distract the colliers. However, as in
a detective story, the truth emerges slowly and is not known
until act 3, when everyone is thrown into confusion – the
spectators included – by unpredictable developments.

In the early morning in the town's market square the
soldiers hold their recruiting meeting. Everyone is dressed in
colourful official regalia and one of the soldiers beats his
drum; *'the stage is filled with noise and movement'* and a
supply of beer is arranged. The Mayor makes a parody of
a speech to the Queen, and the Parson gives the parody of a
blessing. It is at this point that the ironies begin to flow and
tension to mount. On a plinth draped with bunting Musgrave
takes a rifle from a box and begins to demonstrate how it
works.

> This – (*he indicates the trigger*) – you should know what
> *this* is, you should know what it does...Well, the rifle's a
> good weapon, it's new, quick, accurate. This is the bayonet
> – (*he fixes his bayonet*) – it kills men smart, it's good and
> it's beautiful. But I've more to show than a rifle. Open it
> up!...This is the newest, this is the smartest, call it the most
> beautiful. It's a Gatling gun, this. Watch how it works!

His urgency increases as, haranguing the audience, he makes
threatening rattles like the machine gun, and one of the
soldiers swivels it to face directly at the audience – both
the imaginary one in the market square and the real one in the
theatre. The drum rolls again and again as Musgrave calls for
the flag to be hoisted, whereupon a rope is pulled up to the
cross-bar of a lamp-post on the plinth. However, instead of

the Union Jack, a skeleton dressed in soldier's uniform dangles there as if on some kind of grotesque gallows or crucifix – a true *danse macabre*. This *coup de théâtre* is capped by Musgrave himself, who dances beneath the gruesome figure, waving his rifle, *'his face contorted with demoniac fury'* and sings,

> Up he goes and no one knows
> How to bring him downwards.

He goes on to report that the dead soldier was a comrade killed on duty, and also that he was one Billy Hicks, 'late of this parish'. They have shot five hostages for him, and now the intention is to fulfill the 'Logic of God' and kill twenty-five of the townspeople.

Musgrave is either a pacificist preaching at gunpoint or a madman crazed by violence, and the play comes close to the notion of a Theatre of Cruelty as initiated by Artaud. With its mixed elements of ritual and farce (the colliers are drilled like Fred Karno's army in 2.2), its unlovable characters, its structural dialectic and its refusal of any comfortable solution to the issue raised, the play is an outstanding example of 'insulting the audience'. It is arguably more Brechtian than Brecht.

The English stage today is wealthy beyond belief in its supply of playwrights, able to draw upon a pool of some three or four dozen good or promising younger writers. The new director-dramatists who have taken to the free stage are often those who have worked under the haphazard conditions of road-show, portable or trucking theatre, who have set up in clubs and pubs, streets or school halls, and those who have inhabited the 'fringe' of arts festivals like that in Edinburgh. They have sometimes collaborated and sometimes directed each other's work, thus associating themselves with the philosophical or political causes espoused – nuclear disarmament, antiapartheid, feminist and others – and seeing drama as a necessary part of a semi-documentary, mostly satirical, counter-culture.

The theatrical heresies of Edward Bond (1935–) made his the extraordinary case of a younger playwright who graduated from the Royal Court to the National Theatre, where he directed several of his own plays in a range of non-illusionistic styles. He usually called for a bare stage and little or no scenery, in this way putting all the weight on his actors, their vivid and often shocking activity and his heightened language, although his audacious subjects have often obscured his craftsmanship. His plays are parables of man as a creature of brutality, which alone places his work beyond the purely political. At the Royal Court an early play of ugly urban realism, *Saved* (1965), focused on a scene in which a child in a pram is mindlessly stoned to death, which troubled everyone from the critics to the Lord Chamberlain. Also at the Royal Court, *Lear* (1971) was a sensational *reprise* of Shakespeare's tragedy, presenting the King as a despot who does not divide his kingdom, but with forced labour builds a wall around it and himself. In full view of the audience, his sadistic daughters devise gruesome tortures and themselves die violent deaths. In the end it is Lear, not Gloucester, who is strapped to a chair and blinded. *Bingo* (1973) visits Shakespeare in his retirement in Stratford, where he is consumed with self-loathing in a world of greedy land-enclosure and starvation. This play ends when Shakespeare poisons himself.

Bond's determined break with theatrical conservatism had everything to do with the abolition of stage censorship. The battle had been simmering since the time of G. B. Shaw and Granville Barker at the beginning of the century (*Mrs Warren's Profession* had been banned in 1893 for its theme of prostitution, and *Waste* in 1907 for touching on abortion). Now the permissiveness of the 1960s and the ban put on Bond's *Saved* for its ugly scenes of physical violence (although in fact intended as a fierce dramatic statement about contemporary society) and on his *Early Morning* (1968) in which Queen Victoria is seen in a lesbian relationship with Florence Nightingale, precipitated the Theatre Act of 1968 and the closing of the Lord Chamberlain's office. This in turn made available a wide range of brisk new material to the more abrasive new playwrights: the careful nudity of the musical *Hair* in 1968, implicit sexuality as in Peter Shaffer's *Equus* (1973), the representation on stage of God and Jesus, the defamation of royalty and living political figures, all, subject to the laws of libel, were now possible. The coarser language of common life could at last be spoken on stage for the first time, and for a while it was *de rigueur* to include a little sex and profanity in every new play. This cheap practice soon grew tedious, but Christopher Innes has pointed out in *Modern British Drama* (1992) that the removal of the constant need to defer to the censor has permitted changes to be made in the course of production as often as occasion demands.

To select one representative of the new heretics, the prolific David Hare (1947–) is both politically engaged and technically inventive. He takes every advantage of the self-conscious theatre of non-illusion: he asks for a minimum of scenery and writes a play of many changing scenes and acrobatic time; he doubles parts (*Fanshen*, 1975, has thirty parts played by nine actors); and he does not hesitate to address the audience through the proscenium arch and play havoc with illusion. *Brassneck* (1973), written in collaboration with Howard Brenton (1942–), uses projected scenery throughout and opens with a huge photograph of Churchill and the Royal Family on VE Day, thus injecting a documentary quality into a play intended to satirize corruption in national and local politics after the Second World War. *Knuckle* (1974), written in the style of a Mickey Spillane thriller, trails its gun-running private eye, Curly Delafield, through sixteen scenes of money speculators and bankers, crooks and hustlers – in, of all places, suburban Guildford. *Teeth 'n' Smiles* (1975) ends with a derelict rock group playing 'Last Orders on the Titanic', symbolically suggesting a sinking British ship of state. *Plenty* (1982) tells the tale, partly in flashbacks, of Susan Traherne (first played by Kate Nelligan at the National Theatre), an Englishwoman who helped the French Resistance during the War and returns home to the disillusion of a world of greed and corruption.

Hare's work is nothing if not ambitious, and his plays have embraced both the national political scene and immense global issues, always aiming to make a manageable theatrical occasion out of seemingly intractable material. In the international arena, the aptly named *A Map of the World* (1982) may claim to be his most ingenious mixture of political debate and practical theatre to date. The subject is the relationship between Europe and the Third World, and the play focuses on a UNESCO conference on world poverty and injustice held in Bombay. There an Anglo-Indian novelist, Victor Mehta, is brought into conflict with a British newspaperman, Stephen Andrews. Mehta is politically right-wing and lives in Shropshire (recalling V. S. Naipaul), and as a writer he is fastidiously correct in his pursuit of the truth ('often from the best of intentions we tell ourselves lies', act 2); Andrews is young, white and passionately left-wing. Both – rather super-fluously – are also attracted to an American actress whose sexual favours appear to be the prize awaiting the winner of the argument.

The impact of all this, however, is doubled and redoubled because of the inventive dramatic framework within which Hare has placed his story. The play the audience watches in the theatre turns out to be a film being produced in a film studio, and in turn this film is seen to be based on the fiction of Mehta's novel, although in reality and in real time the people in the play are the characters in the film. In *A Map of the World*, therefore, Hare's stage manipulates a Pirandellian illusion which is deliberately made to trivialize and distort the tremendous subject of human suffering, while at the same time it compels the audience constantly to reassess its values. Hare's reality, his truth, is sharply recognizable because the audience is compelled to see the issues from first one view-point and then another, repeatedly re-evaluating what is being debated. In an interview the play's first designer, Hayden Griffin, indicated that the comparatively bare stage made possible its quick scene changes, which had the virtue of inducing the spectator's maximum participation:

> You're saying to the audience...you're watching a real scene, it's modern stage design, so you could be in a number of places, not obviously a film studio, and then we suddenly move everything, and they realise. One technical thing is that we make the audience pan the shot: they are made to feel that they're the cameraman. We use about five different moving elements, including lights tracking – and the actors, as they play, are moving on a revolve.
>
> (*Plays and Players*, February 1983, 13).

Hare's experiments with an unconfined and non-realistic stage space have continued energetically, especially in his recent trilogy on the Anglican clergy, British law and party politics in *Racing Demon* (1990), *Murmuring Judges* (1991) and *The Absence of War* (1993), all produced at the National Theatre.

Women playwrights in the later twentieth century: *Cloud Nine*

Since Shaw the new winds of a political stage have been blowing ever stronger, with the increasing participation of women as directors and playwrights. There had been individual and exceptional female excursions, like that of Lady Gregory in the early development of the Irish theatre or Elizabeth Robins's suffragette play *Votes for Women!* in 1906; in the middle of the century Dorothy Sayers (*The Zeal of Thy House*, 1937 for the Canterbury Festival) and Anne Ridler (*The Shadow Factory*, 1945 for the Mercury Theatre) contributed verse plays to the religious drama movement; soon after the Second World War, Joan Littlewood's work with her Theatre Workshop promoted Shelagh Delaney's acerbic view of working-class life through the comic-pathetic eyes of the pregnant girl Jo in *A Taste of Honey* (1958) and Ann Jellicoe brought a sense of zany sexual liberation to the stage with *The Knack* (1961). Meanwhile women novelists increasingly wrote or adapted their work for the stage (Enid Bagnold, Doris Lessing, Iris Murdoch, Bridget Boland, Dodie Smith, Muriel Spark), although circumstances, chiefly social and domestic, continued to determine that it was the novel to which women naturally turned for literary expression.

However, with the liberating influence of the Second World War, the advent of Brechtian theatre and the abolition of stage censorship in 1968, women were encouraged to turn to the stage in order to raise public consciousness about feminist issues. In particular, the uninhibited and non-illusionary stagecraft of the 'fringe' or 'alternative' theatre [i.e., theatre dissociated from established methods of production] was well suited to provide a subversive dramatic idiom for the new sexual politics and issues of gender discrimination. Besides the fringe theatres, all three of the subsidized theatres in London, the Royal Court, the Royal Shakespeare Company and the Royal National Theatre, saw it as their responsibility to give space to the new plays, and in addition several women's companies were formed: the Monstrous Regiment, Mrs Worthington's Daughters, The Women's Theatre Company, The Women's Theatre Group among others. In this way the English stage mustered a remarkable number of new women playwrights who quickly exploited the new territory, often elaborating and refining their material in actors' workshops over a period of time before it was performed. Pam Gems (1925–) and Caryl Churchill (1938–) are two pioneers who have experimented boldly with innovative stage conventions.

From *Queen Christina* (1977) to *The Blue Angel* (1991) Pam Gems carefully juxtaposed the received romantic ideas about famous women of history, legend or fiction with a coldly conflicting realism, and first worked out what shock tactics the feminist stage could bear in the way of surprises and reversals. Her drama developed from a more naturalistic treatment to a sensational assault on the audience, setting a romanticized and sentimental subject against a harsher, more realistic picture by a free juxtaposition of scene and style that served to undermine the spectator's comfortable picture and detonate her theme with great effect. *Queen Christina* makes full use of the technique of reversal when, shattering her image of Greta Garbo and beauty, Christina is reared as a man and looks like a man; moreover, her plain appearance and icy intelligence repel the opposite sex, which predictably prefers 'a womanly woman'. When she abdicates the throne, tragically it is too late for her to assume the stereotypical feminine role, and the crucial choice between motherhood and sexual independence is – like medieval casuistry – accentuated as theatre. *Piaf* (1978) takes the idea of the well-known cabaret singer, and between her familiar moments of Parisian singing, interjects hard, realistic scenes of her drug-addiction, alcoholism, whoring and violence. *Camille* (1984) subverts the tender story of the consumptive courtesan from Dumas and

Verdi by emphasizing from *Mrs Warren's Profession* the Shavian conception of female exploitation, presenting the rather more melodramatic picture of a woman forced to sell herself to maintain her independence. There is a fierce didacticism behind the implicit questions to society posed by such plays as these.

Caryl Churchill was first associated with the Joint Stock Company under Max Stafford-Clark's direction, then with the Royal Court Upstairs and the National Theatre, and she has worked up a highly original style of parody, often using song and dance, and sometimes outrageously cross-casting and cross-dressing her characters to make points about gender and race. Her work exemplifies the extremes of non-naturalistic convention-bending that a free and vigorous stage can attempt in the pursuit of her causes: to criticize the oppression of women, the injustices of colonialism and the evils of apartheid and racism. Her theatre offers a compendium of dramatic devices open to new writers who wish to shock the spectator into attention:

- with her early experience of writing for radio, and following Brechtian and epic theatre initiatives, her *structure of scenes* is often episodic, even cinematic, permitting a fluid treatment of place and time. Leaping temporal barriers has become a hallmark of her work.
- a parodistic approach to *characterization* is apparent in her effects of cross-dressing (man as woman, woman as man), age reversal (adult as child, child as adult) and racial cross-casting (black played by white). A mischievous comic style, an antic theatricality, is brought to the stage by such a stratagem, although it must be said that as a regular convention this has a limited future.
- physical elements of *music and dance*, together with stylized movement, are liberally introduced to undercut any psychological realism in the style of performance and to extend the fantasy of the action. The level of farce and parody achieved makes possible scenes that are explicitly sexual and would otherwise be offensive.
- the dissipation of realism gives the *dialogue* the freedom to follow patterns of its own, orchestrated sometimes in

staccato exchanges, sometimes as monologue, sometimes dropping into rhyming couplets. Writing for radio also encouraged experiment with the effect of overlapping lines and simultaneous speech. Here Churchill was using words and speech, not as conversation or dialogue, but essentially as a musical instrument.

Cloud Nine (1979) heaped one new convention upon another in its attack upon sexual oppression and Victorian colonialism, and contrived to find a parallel between them. In her introduction to the play, Churchill explains,

> The first act of *Cloud Nine* takes place in Victorian Africa, where Clive, the white man, imposes his ideals on his family and the natives. Betty, Clive's wife, is played by a man because she wants to be what men want her to be, and, in the same way, Joshua, the black servant, is played by a white man because he wants to be what whites want him to be. Betty does not value herself as a woman, nor does Joshua value himself as a black. Edward, Clive's son, is played by a woman for a different reason – partly to do with the stage convention of having boys played by women (Peter Pan, radio plays, etc.) and partly with highlighting the way Clive tries to impose traditional male behaviour on him.

And the roles are cemented by little jingles, such as:

CLIVE.   My wife is all I dreamt a wife should be,
          And everything she is she owes to me.
BETTY.   I live for Clive. The whole aim of my life
          Is to be what he looks for in a wife.
CLIVE.   My boy's a jewel. Really has the knack.
          You'd hardly notice that the fellow's black.
JOSHUA.   My skin is black but oh my soul is white.
          I hate my tribe. My master is my light.

In addition, Vicky, Edward's little daughter, is played by a dummy. The theatrical role reversals made for a stage full of unpredictable surprises, curiously accentuating gender and race. Churchill commented, 'We were initially taken with how funny the first act was and then by the painfulness of the relationships' (Prefatory note, 1983).

In act 1 British social values in the nineteenth century are

totally exploded by the casting, which also inhibits any reflex
reaction to the subject:

> BETTY.   You must never let the boys at school know you
> like dolls. Never, never. No one will talk to you,
> you won't be on the cricket team, you won't
> grow up to be a man like your papa.
> EDWARD.   I don't want to be like papa. I hate papa.

Edward is duly slapped, and when we see him again he is duly
contrite:

> EDWARD.   I said I didn't want to be like you and I said I
> hated you. And it's not true and I'm sorry, I'm
> sorry and please beat me and forgive me.
> CLIVE.   Well there's a brave boy to own up. You should
> always respect and love me, Edward, not for
> myself, I may not deserve it, but as I respected
> and loved my own father, because he was my
> father. Through our father we love our Queen
> and our God, Edward. Do you understand? It is
> something men understand.
> EDWARD. Yes papa.   (1.3)

The satirical points plod a bit, but the pace of events is lively
and the comic action is consistently challenging. The author
takes a pleasure in setting up a jolting blackout curtain, and
this act ends with Joshua about to shoot his master Clive,
with Edward looking on and doing nothing about it.

A change of location in act 2 gives Churchill the opportunity to make a bold experiment with stage time. The scene is
now a London park in 1979, a hundred years later, so that the
audience expects the Victorian values to be totally superseded,
but in order to make sure the great changes of attitude to sex
and marriage are theatrically emphatic, the characters of act 1
are played as if only twenty-five years older: in this way
everyone, character and spectator alike, is self-consciously
aware of the enormous social and domestic revolution that
has taken place. If the audience is made to feel a little giddy,
the trick works.

Some of the cross-gendering continues: Betty is now more
realistically played by a woman, the actress who played her
son in the first act, and the actor who played Betty is now her
son Edward. The more the characters are played according to

their correct sexes, so it is perceived that they are more complete as human beings. Only a little girl of five (played at the Royal Court by Anthony Sher), is played by a man, partly to reverse the image of Edward as a woman, partly to lend a man's weight to what Churchill writes of as 'the emotional force of young children' and partly to show how a girl is still expected to behave. Now the play is free to introduce shocks and sensations, shattering one received social convention after another:

> LIN.   You're gay, aren't you?
> EDWARD. I beg your pardon?
> LIN.   I really fancy your sister. I thought you'd under-
>   stand.
>
>   (2.1)

Accordingly Victoria leaves her husband for Lin, her female friend, wondering whether going with a woman counts as adultery. Edward is now a homosexual who joins his sister in their hatred of men, announcing at the curtain of 2.2 that he thinks he's a lesbian. When towards the end of the play the characters from act 1, Edward, Clive and Betty, enter as a reminder of how things used to be, the spectator may be forgiven for feeling a little bewildered.

The implicit and ancient notion that a stage convention is something assumed and then forgotten is clearly not part of Churchill's strategy, and in subsequent plays her tactical manipulation of stage and audience has continued confidently. *Top Girls* (1982) is an all-female play, presenting a group of famous women who represent different historical periods and geographical places and mix fact and fiction; but together they symbolize the exploitation of women: a Victorian lady explorer and a Japanese Buddhist nun, Dull Gret from a Brueghel painting, Pope Joan and Patient Griselda. The dramatic innovation in this play is a careful overlapping or simultanous utterance of speech (a technique also pursued in later plays), chiefly to suggest how frighteningly alike are these vastly different characters, each of whom suffers in spite of her achievement, each dominated by some man, whether a father, a lover or a husband.

The domestic and sexual role of women repeats itself and

remains a persistent theme for the feminist stage, but after *Serious Money* (1987), which attacks the stock market, Churchill's more recent plays have broadened to include more general social and political targets, offering opportunities to mix documentary material in the manner of Brecht with a verse drama of fantasy and symbol. At another extreme *The Skriker* (1994) has been described as 'a fairy tale for the 1990s' and it slips between reality and magic, its tiny cast performing by gesture, speech and dance to a torrent of Joycean words that are alive with rhymes and puns, sense and nonsense. While still touching reality in an imaginative *mélange*, language has been fractured to serve the needs of a grotesque stage game.

At the end of the twentieth century an audience's expectations of an evening at the play are not as before. It no longer demands and anticipates a magic show of breath-taking sensations, a pageant of colour and costume, a ritual of surprises – all these things can be had at a price from the musical spectacles associated with Andrew Lloyd Webber, or created with greater success in the cinema of such producers as Steven Spielberg. Today's playgoers are not looking for illusion: they are content to be aware that they are in a theatre and expect the play to remind them from time to time that this is so. This stage flirts with any genre, often in the same play, and passes deftly, and sometimes recklessly, from scenes of documentary realism or sophisticated drawing-room comedy to those of stylized ritual or knockabout farce.

The actors need no longer pretend that the audience is not there, but may frequently address the house, or even dance or sing, freely breaking out of the frame of the fiction. The new drama is uninhibited by the presence of a proscenium arch, and it is perfectly at home on an open stage. It draws surrealistically upon any trick of film, radio or television editing, secure in the knowledge that the spectator will make the adjustment. When a change of location is called for, no curtain need fall, no lights be dimmed, and the audience is not surprised to see the actors themselves come to the aid of the stage hands when they are required to carry props or furniture, or move simple flats or screens. The action of the play proceeds, not in heavily representational, marked-off acts and scenes that convey well-defined locations and slices of time, but in episodes of any length that create a rhythm of their own.

The degree of 'audience participation' has thereby increased significantly, not necessarily in any physical way, but in the sense of having shared with the playwright and the players the pleasure of generating and realizing the play event. A David Hare or a Caryl Churchill are today the pioneers, and twenty or thirty years after the heyday of the Royal Court the English stage proposes and accepts political and non-commercial topics without the distrust that was the case before the Second World War. In one important sense the radical English stage we see at the end of the twentieth century is returning to the simplicity it knew in its beginnings.

Index

Abbey Theatre, 360, 366ff
Abel, W. H., 314
'above', 119, 127, 131, 134, 228, 233
absurd, theatre of the, 128, 161, 214, 220, 355, 383ff, 400
Achurch, Janet, 339
actor, acting, xiii, xiv, 1, 29–30, 90, 164, 168, 241ff, 279ff, 306, 312, 344, 361, 368, 369, 399
actress, 169, 245ff, 256ff, 260
Adams brothers, 275
Addison, Joseph, 266, 290
address to the audience, 56, 66, 71, 74, 95, 102, 121, 151ff, 210, 236, 400, 413
Adelphi Theatre, 322, 323
Admiral's Men, 93, 118, 123, 200
Aeschylus, *Oresteia*, 318
Aesop, 174
afterpiece, 284
Agate, James, 97–8
Aldwych Theatre, 128, 204
Alexander, Sir George, 311, 325ff, 332ff
alienation effect, 400
allegory, 41, 47ff, 73, 102, 103, 106, 111, 154, 159, 174, 189, 198, 350, 354
Alleyn, Edward, 93, 110, 115, 118, 121
Allgood, Sara, 373
alliteration, 29, 379
anachronism, 28–9, 100, 185, 356

Anne, Queen, 281
Anne of Denmark (Queen), 188, 189
anticlimax, 346
antihero, 388, 397
Appius and Virginia, 80
apron (stage), 239, 240, 269, 275, 276, 277, 300, 307, 308
aquatic (theatre), 275, 307
Archer, William, 327, 338–9
Arden, John, 397, 401ff, *Serjeant Musgrave's Dance*, 401ff
Arden of Faversham, 211–12
Aristotle, 27, 84, 250, 292, 379, 400
Arsinoe, 287
Artaud, Antonin, 220, 392, 403
artificial comedy, 326
Arts Theatre, 386
Ashcroft, Dame Peggy, 227
aside, 95, 102, 127–8, 152ff, 175, 182, 209, 210, 220, 222, 228, 230, 234, 235, 236, 240, 241, 247, 261, 269, 290, 294, 295, 300, 308, 317, 328, 336
Auden, W. H., *The Ascent of F6*, 382
audience, xiii, xiv, 1, 187, 237ff, 255ff, 274ff, 280ff, 302ff, 313, 347, 352, 361, 400, 405, 406, 414
Avenue Theatre, 344

backcloth, 190, 193
Bacon, Francis, 187

Bagnold, Enid, 407
balcony, 96, 99, 119, 228, 234, 240, 314
Bale, John, 67, 72
ballad (singers), 3, 61, 211, 401
ballad opera, 285, 286
ballet, 187, 198, 248, 277, 310
Bancroft, Squire, 308, 311, 329
banqueting hall, 192
Barker, Harley Granville, 147, 346, 349, 354, 362ff, 404, *The Madras House*, 363, *The Voysey Inheritance*, 362, *Waste*, 362, 404
Barnes, Peter, 185, *The Bewitched*, 393, *Laughter*, 393, *Leonardo's Last Supper*, 393, *The Ruling Class*, 392–3
Barry, Elizabeth, 241, 256, 260, 264
Bartholomew Faire, 180
bear-baiting, 179
Beaumont, Francis, 202ff, 242, *The Knight of the Burning Pestle*, 203ff, *Philaster, or, Love Lies a-Bleeding*, 206, 260, *The Woman Hater*, 203
Becket, Thomas à, 378
Beckett, Samuel, 220, 383ff, 385, 389, 396, *Act Without Words, I*, 387, *Come and Go*, 387, *Endgame*, 385ff, *Happy Days*, 387, *Krapp's Last Tape*, 387, *Not I*, 387, *Play*, 387, *That Time*, 387, *Waiting for Godot*, 177, 384ff, 394
Behn, Aphra, 263ff, *The Town-Fopp*, 263, *The Rover*, 263ff
Bell, (Bishop) George, 378
Berlin Volksbühne, 399
Berliner Ensemble, 398
Betterton, Mary, 264
Betteton, Thomas, 242, 247, 256, 261, 263
Bevington, David, 87

Birmingham Repertory Theatre, 77
black comedy, 125ff, 133, 220, 355, 371, 389, 391, 392
Blackfriars, 91, 96, 122, 148, 176, 193, 199, 203, 204, 206, 216, 224
blank verse, 84, 151, 179, 201, 252, 282
blocking, 201, 307, 326
blood tubs, 313
Bogdanov, Michael, 28, 112, 185
Boland, Bridget, 407
Bond, Edward, 403ff, *Bingo*, 404, *Early Morning*, 404, *Lear*, 404, *Saved*, 404
Booth, Barton, 274
Booth, Edwin, 310
booth stage, 52, 96
Bosch, Hieronymus, 34
Boswell, James, 292
Bottom the Weaver, 237
Boucicault, Dion, 372, *Arrah-Na-Pogue*, 321, *The Colleen Bawn*, 321ff, *The Shaughraun*, 321
Boutell, Elizabeth, 261, 266
box, pit and gallery, 279, 305
box set, 308, 328, 329, 360
boy actors, 106–7, 134, 164ff, 169, 184, 192, 206, 216, 237
boy companies (*see also* child companies), 88ff
Bracegirdle, Anne, 266, 268
Braynes, John, 92
Brecht, Bertolt, 129, 151, 155, 331, 341, 347, 360, 376, 380, 383, 398ff, 400, 403, 407, 409, 413
breeches scene (breeches part), 164, 245, 260, 264
Brent, Nathaniel, 197
Brenton, Howard, 405
Bridges Street Theatre, 238
Britannia Theatre, 314

Britten, Benjamin, 382
Brome, Richard, 33
Brook, Peter, 361
Brown, John Russell, 121
Browne, E. Martin, 22, 380
Brueghel, Pieter, 34
Buckingham, George Villiers, Duke of, *The Rehearsal*, 253-4
Buckstone, J. B., *Luke the Labourer*, 317
Bunyan, John, *The Pilgrim's Progress*, 48
Burbage, James, 54, 89, 91
Burbage, Richard, 91, 93, 216, 217
burlesque, 64-5, 91, 137, 169, 203, 205, 215, 216, 220, 253, 269, 271, 284ff, 296, 318, 324, 344-6, 349, 394
burletta, 285, 310, 322
Bury St Edmunds, 20, 277
Busino, Orazio, 196
Byford, Roy, 184
Byron, H. J., 314

cabaret, 61, 400, 408
Cambridge, 54, 77, 89, 104, 107, 120
Camilla, 287
Campbell, Mrs Patrick, 335, 337
Campion, Thomas, *Lords' Masque*, 196
candles, 240, 278, 305
Canterbury Festival, 378, 407
Capell, Edward, 143
Carpenter, J. E., *Love and Honour*, 216
Carrington, Charles, 339
Carte, D'Oyly, 307
Castelvetro, Lodovico, 84
Castle of Perseverance, The, 42ff, 56
catharsis, 400
Catherine of Aragon, 5

censorship (*see also* Lord Chamberlain), 404, 407
Centlivre, Susannah, *A Bold Stroke for a Wife*, 263
Chamberlain, John, 196
Chambers, E. K., 12
changeable scenery: *see* scenery
Chapman, George, 90
character (characterization, *see also* type), 10, 21, 41, 55, 61, 81, 102, 152, 155, 166, 168ff, 171ff, 181, 186, 207, 219, 268, 301, 312, 314, 348, 351, 367, 368, 375, 377, 383, 388-9, 409
Charles I, 188, 237
Charles II, 164, 193, 237ff, 245, 255, 274
Chekhov, Anton, 255, 259, 331, 337, 361, 362, 372, 376, 389
Chester, 20, 28ff, *Breviarye*, 21
Children of the Chapel Royal, 88, 90, 91, 122
Children of the Queen's Revels, 203, 216
Children of St Paul's, 90
chorus (choric), 63, 77, 81, 84, 86, 111, 130, 154, 156, 166, 220, 221, 374, 379-80, 381
Christmas, 5, 6, 8, 9, 35, 84
Church, the, 1-2, 7ff, 19, 40, 60
Churchill, Caryl, 409ff, 414, *Cloud Nine*, 410ff, *Serious Money*, 413, *The Skriker*, 413, *Top Girls*, 413
Churchill, Sir Winston, 364, 405
Cibber, Colley, 266, 270, 274, 277, 285, *The Careless Husband*, 282, *Love's Last Shift*, 245, 270, 282
cinema: *see* film
city comedy, 180, 199ff
Civil War, the, 187, 249
Clement V, Pope, 17
clown (clowning), 3, 7, 37, 47, 67, 79, 80, 154, 174, 384-5

Cockpit Theatre, the (Drury Lane), 91, 237
Collier, Jeremy, 266, 270, 281, 282
Colman, George (the Elder), 286, 290
comedy, 35–7, 41, 47, 52, 67, 74, 104ff, 125, 133, 160ff, 168ff, 199ff, 232, 234, 242ff, 248, 255ff, 282ff, 290ff, 337, 343, 356, 389
comic opera, 285, 324, 343, 350
comic relief, 161
commedia dell'arte, 154, 174, 209, 285, 323, 324, 385
Congreve, William, 265ff, 269, *The Double Dealer*, 265, *Love for Love*, 266, *The Old Bachelor*, 265, *The Way of the World*, 244, 246, 264, 266ff, 297
continuity, 147, 186
conventions, xiii–xiv, 1, 377ff, 412
Cooke, T. P., 318
Cooper, Gladys, 337
Cornish, William, 90
Cornwall, 23, 27
Corpus Christi cycle, 2, 8, 9, 16ff, 40, 121
costume (costume design), 27, 49, 61, 73, 87, 100, 104, 123, 142ff, 166, 175, 179, 186, 187ff, 200, 218, 242, 244, 279, 310, 313, 314, 361, 366, 368, 378
coup de théâtre, 293, 334, 403
couplets (rhyming), 6, 69, 73, 82, 156, 205, 250, 251
Court, the, 41, 61, 67, 68, 73, 88–90, 101, 106, 185, 187ff, 200, 241, 255
Coventry, 21ff
Coward, Sir Noël, 255
Craig, Edward Gordon, 350, 368

Cranmer, (Archbishop) Thomas, 72
Cromwell, Oliver, 129, 237
Cromwell, Thomas, 72
cross-casting, 409ff
Crowne, John, *Sir Courtly Nice*, 259
cruelty, theatre of, 220, 403
Cumberland, Richard, 289, *The West Indian*, 291
Curll, Edmund, 247
curtain, 95, 119, 190, 196, 239, 307, 413
Curtain Theatre, 93, 212
cutting (text), 312

Dada, 395
dance, dancing, 61, 65, 73, 90, 92, 145ff, 187ff, 201, 204, 213, 218, 226, 229, 232, 235, 252, 254, 265, 288, 302, 317, 324, 369, 409, 413
Daniel, Samuel, 188, *Tethys' Festival*, 195
danse macabre, 220, 231, 403
Davenant, Sir William, 237–8, *The Siege of Rhodes*, 237, 238
Davies, H. Walford, 59
daylight convention, 96, 101, 113
Dekker, Thomas, 4, 200ff, *The Roaring Girl*, 207, *The Shoemaker's Holiday*, 199ff, 204
Delaney, Shelagh, *A Taste of Honey*, 407
Dench, Dame Judi, 227
design, scene, 190, 193ff, 278ff
deus ex machina, 70, 202
Deuteronomy, 2
Dexter, John, 212
Devine, George, 185, 396, 399
dialectical drama, 347
dialogue, 102, 388–9, 409–10
Dibdin, Charles, 318

Dibdin, T. J., 322
Dickens, Charles, 4, 291, 303–4, 318, 331, 352
diorama, 307
director, 310, 361, 400, 403
discovery (scene, space), 96, 119, 126, 127, 130, 134, 135, 174, 215, 226, 235, 298
discussion drama, 346ff, 357ff
disguise, disguising, 72, 86ff, 186, 207, 208, 210, 221, 264
Disher, Maurice Willson, 318, 321
Dobrée, Bonamy, 259
documentary (drama), 364, 413
Doggett, Thomas, 274
Dorset Garden Theatre, 238, 256, 274
domestic drama, 211ff, 236
doors, 95, 98, 119, 130, 134, 138, 153, 239, 240, 259, 269, 275, 277, 299, 306, 307, 308
Downer, Alan, 81
double entendre, 213, 269
doubling, 61, 69, 70, 72, 86ff, 109, 205, 312, 351, 405
drawing-room comedy, 380–1, 413
Drayton, Michael, 121
drolls, 237
Drury Lane, Theatre Royal, 238–9, 242, 252, 262, 274ff, 285, 287, 290, 291, 297, 300, 303, 305, 309, 310
Dryden, John, 252ff, 259, *All for Love*, 250, 252, *The Conquest of Granada*, 252–3, *A Defence of an Essay of Dramatic Poesy*, 184, *An Essay of Dramatic Poesy*, 250, 251, 252, *An Essay of Heroic Plays*, 250, 252, *Marriage à la Mode*, 248, *Secret Love*, 260, *Sir Martin Mar-All*, 238; *Troilus and Cressida*, 250, 252

Dublin, 13, 263, 270, 321, 360, 365ff, 372
Duke of York's Theatre, 344, 363
Dukes, Ashley, 382
Duke's Men (James, Duke of York' company), 238, 242
Dulac, Edmund, 370
Dumas, Alexandre (fils), 408
dumb show, 85, 101, 103, 111, 116, 117, 119, 159, 169, 210, 215, 221, 222, 224, 225, 227, 231, 232, 235, 236, 285
Dunlop, Frank, 224
Duse, Eleonora, 357
Dyer, Chris, 111

Easter, 5, 8, 9, 10
eavesdropping, 149ff, 240
Edinburgh Festival, 74, 393, 403
Edward I, 5
Edwards, Richard, 90, *Damon and Pithias*, 269
eidophusikon, 279
Eliot, T. S., 8, 102, 376, *The Cocktail Party*, 380–1, *The Family Reunion*, 380–1, *Murder in the Cathedral*, 378ff, 382, *Poetry and Drama*, 381, 382, *The Three Voices of Poetry*, 377
electricity, 307
Elizabeth I, 39, 51, 54, 80, 84, 88, 90, 100, 188, 200
Elizabethan revival, 361
Elizabethan playhouse (stage), 42, 60, 64, 91ff, 93ff, 101, 377
Elliston, Robert, 309–10, 318
empathy, 400
Encore, 398, 399
English Stage Company, 396ff
ensemble (acting), 312, 329, 346, 361
epic theatre, 360, 382, 399, 401, 409

epilogue, 95, 158, 241, 351, 356
Ervine, St John, 375
Ethelwold, Saint, 3, 11–12
Etherege, Sir George, 256ff, *The Man of Mode*, 241, 247, 248–9, 256ff, *She Would If She Could*, 245, 259
Eucharist, 16, 17
Euripides, *Alcestis*, 381
Evans, Dame Edith, 246
Evelyn, John, 253
Evelyn, Mary, 253
Everyman, 40, 41, 56ff, 69, 129
exposition, 289, 319, 332, 336, 399
extravaganza, 285, 310, 322, 324
expressionism, 354, 358, 360, 375, 382, 392
Eyre, Richard, 14

fan, 246–7
farce, 65, 78, 102, 109, 126, 133, 135, 161, 172, 229, 232, 285, 292, 324, 325, 343, 375, 383, 391, 403, 409, 413
Farquhar, George, 263, 270, The Beaux' Stratagem, 248, 270–2, 295, *The Constant Couple*, 281, *The Recruiting Officer*, 270, *Sir Harry Wildair*, 270
Farrant, Richard, 90
feminism, 265, 341
Feydeau, Georges, 324
Fielding, Henry 275, *Joseph Andrews* 283, *Tom Jones*, 297
film (cinema), 99, 317, 360, 399, 406, 413
Finney, Albert, 125
Fitzgerald, Barry, 373, 374
Fitzgiggo riots, 276
flats, 307
Fletcher, John, 202, 206ff, 242, *The Faithful Shepherdess* 206, *Philaster or Loves Lies a-Bleeding*, 206

floats (*see also* footlights), 278
flying ballet, 308
flying machinery, 92, 96
folk drama (folk tale), 1, 5, 61, 98, 107, 109
Foote, Samuel, 290
footlights, 315
fop, 244, 259
Ford, John, 232ff, *The Broken Heart*, 233, *Love's Sacrifice*, 233, *Perkin Warbeck*, 233, *'Tis Pity She's a Whore*, 233
Fortune Theatre, 93, 94, 95, 110, 118
'fourth wall', 308
fourteeners, 82
France (*see also* Paris), 242, 250, 258, 277, 280, 285, 303, 360, 376
French farce, 61, 369
Friel, Brian, *Dancing in Lughnasa*, 376, *Faith Healer*, 376, *Philadelphia, Here I Come!*, 376
fringe theatre (alternative theatre), 403, 407
Fry, Christopher, 8, *A Sleep of Prisoners*, 382–3

Gager, William, 89–90
gallery, 94, 96, 238, 275
Galsworthy, John, 346, 363ff, *Justice*, 364, 365, *Loyalties*, 364, *The Silver Box*, 364, *Strife*, 364–5
Gammer Gurton's Needle, 61, 77ff
Garrick Club, 299
Garrick, David, 172, 178, 210, 242, 247, 278, 279, 280, 290, 298, 301, *Catherine and Petruchio*, 285, *A Christmas Tale*, 279, *The Country Girl*, 262, *The Lying Valet*, 285, *Miss in Her Teens*, 285

gaslight, 306
gauze, 194, 240, 307, 321
Gay, John, *The Beggar's Opera*, 285ff, *Polly*, 286, *The What D'Ye Call It*, 285
Gems, Pam, 408ff, *The Blue Angel*, 408, *Camille*, 408, *Queen Christina*, 408, *Piaf*, 408
Genet, Jean, *Le Balcon*, 179
George I, 274
Georgian theatre, 274ff
German drama, 360, 375, 385, 399, 400
Gestalten, 48
gestic poetry, 151
gesture, 138ff, 151, 166, 239, 247–8, 280, 308, 309, 315, 326, 328, 379
ghosts, 111, 159, 215, 232, 351
Gibbon's tennis court, 238
Gielgud, Sir John, 325, 391
Gifford, Henry, 275
Gilbert, W. S., and Sir Arthur Sullivan, *HMS Pinafore*, 324, *Patience*, 307
Gismonde de Salerne, 81
gleemen, 3
Globe Theatre, 93, 94, 100, 118, 119, 173, 176, 203, 206, 216, 217, 222, 224
Goldsmith, Oliver, 255, 282, 291ff, *An Essay on the Theatre*, 292, *The Good-Natured Man*, 291–2, *She Stoops to Conquer*, 149, 292ff
Goldman's Fields, 275
Gordon, Ruth, 262
Granville-Barker, Harley, *see* Barker, Harley Granville
Gray's Inn, 81
Greek tragedy, 81, 85, 103, 232, 379, 381
Greene, Robert, 107ff, 116, *The Comical History of*

Alphonsus, King of Aragon, 107, *Friar Bacon and Friar Bungay* 108–9, 118, *The Scottish History of James the Fourth*, 108
Greg, W. W., 20
Gregory, Lady, 366, 367, 371, 407
Gregory (Pope), *Antiphonarium*, 9
Grien, J. T., 339
Griffin, Hayden, 406
Griffiths, Trevor, *Comedians*, 393
Grindal, (Archbishop) Edmund, 39
groove and shutter, 193, 194, 196, 238, 239, 274
Grosseteste, (Bishop) Robert, 17
guilds, 23–4
Guthrie, Sir Tyrone, 74, 174, 176, 361
Gwyn, Nell, 252, 260

Hair, 404
Hall, Sir Peter, 125, 386
Hall, Edward, 188
Hall, Joseph, 121
Hallam, Lewis, 242
Handke, Peter, 392
Hands, Terry, 185, 229
Hankin, St John, 347
Hardison, O. B., 8, 9
Hardy, Thomas, 76
Hare, David, 403ff, 414, *Absence of War*, 407, *Brassneck*, 405, *Fanshen*, 405, *Knuckle*, 405, *A Map of the World*, 405ff, *Murmuring Judges*, 407, *Plenty*, 405, *Racing Demon*, 407, *Teeth n' Smiles*, 405
harlequinade, 129, 278, 322
Harlequin Dr Faustus, 285
Harlequin Sorcerer, 285
Hart, Charles, 252, 260

Hauptmann, Gerhart, 337
hautboys, 100, 145, 235
Haymarket Theatre, 270, 275, 287, 290, 308, 311, 332
Hazlewood, C. H., 314
Hazlitt, William, 255, 309
Heaven, 15, 21, 22, 27
Hegge, Robert, 20
Hell, 14–15, 21, 22, 27, 28
Henrietta Maria (Queen), 188
Henry VIII, 39, 68, 72, 90, 187–8
Henslowe, Philip, 93, 94, 95, 99, 100, 110, 118–19, 123, 179
heroic drama (heroic tragedy), 249ff, 272, 288
Heywood, John, 67, *The Four Ps*, 68, *John John the Husband*, 54, 61, 68, 73, *The Pardoner and the Friar*, 61, 67, *The Play of Love*, 67, *The Play of the Weather*, 67, 79–80
Heywood, Thomas, *The Four Prentices of London*, 203, *A Woman Killed with Kindness*, 211ff
high comedy, 324, 328
Hill, Aaron, 280
history (play), 71ff, 108, 128, 160, 179, 356
Hobbes, Thomas, 250
Hobson, Harold, 358
Hofmannsthal, Hugo von, 59
Hogarth, William, 271
Holcroft, Thomas, *A Tale of Mystery*, 303
Holinshed, Raphael, *Chronicles*, 128
Holland, Henry, 275
Hope Theatre, 179
Hordern, Sir Michael, 394
Horniman, Annie, 367
'houses', 116, 190
Howard, Alan, 256
Howard, James, *The English Monsieur*, 259

humour, 35–7, 129, 135, 214, 244, 259, 269, 371
humours, comedy of, 102, 171ff, 179, 186, 206, 291, 296
Hunnis, William, 90
Hunt, Leigh, 322
Hutton, Matthew, 39

Ibsen, Henrik (Ibsenism), 255, 309, 336, 337, 339–40, 343, 361, 362, 366, 397, *A Doll's House*, 314, 339, 340, 342, *Ghosts*, 339, 340, *The Pillars of Society*, 339
illusion, 3, 56, 74, 94, 97, 99, 151ff, 157, 160, 182, 186, 193, 204, 210, 226, 239, 241, 251, 308, 361, 394, 400, 405, 407, 413
improvisation, 62ff, 65ff
Inchbald, Elizabeth, *Every One Has His Faults*, 263
Independent Theatre Society, 329
induction, 102, 107, 109, 154
Inner Temple, 81, 84, 87
Innes, Christopher, 405
Inns of Court, 81, 88, 91
innuendo, 261, 294
interlude, 60ff, 204
intimacy, 52, 61, 67, 100, 238, 239, 241, 255, 308
Irish drama, 249, 365ff
Irish dramatic movement, 365ff
Irish Literary Society (National Theatre Society), 365–6
Irving, Sir Henry, 129, 210, 274, 306, 311
Isherwood, Christopher, *The Ascent of F6*, 382
Italy, Italian, 169, 173, 210, 212, 218, 221, 228, 233, 237–8, 277, 285, 287

Jacobean drama, 168ff, 199ff

James I, 91, 168, 188, 197, 229
Jeans, Isobel, 262
Jellicoe, Ann, *The Knack*, 407
Jerold, Douglas, *Black-Eyed Susan*, 318ff
Jocasta, 81
Johnson, Samuel, 292
joint stock company, 409
Jones, Inigo, 101, 119, 148, 188ff, 237, *The Hue and Cry after Cupid*, 193, *The Temple of Jove*, 196
jongleurs, 3
Jonson, Ben, 90, 102, 120, 168ff, 188ff, 207, 237, 242, 291, 296, 301, *The Alchemist*, 176ff, 186, 280, *Bartholomew Fair*, 3, 172, 179ff, 186, 200, *Cataline*, 179, *Chloridia*, 198, *The Devil's an Ass*, 185, *Everyman in His Humour*, 144, 169ff, *Hymenaei*, 193, 197, *Lord Haddington's Masque*, 192, *Love's Triumphs through Calipoli*, 198, *The Magnetic Lady*, 185, *The Masque of Augurs*, 198, *The Masque of Blackness*, 188ff, *The Masque of Queens*, 193, *The New Inn*, 155, *Oberon*, 148, 193ff, *Pleasure Reconciled to Virtue*, 188, 196ff, *Sejanus*, 179, *The Staple of News*, 89, 170, 185, *The Tale of a Tub*, 185, *Timber*, 121, *Volpone*, 169, 173ff, 186
Joyce, James, 395, 413

Kafka, Franz, 387, 390
Kean, Charles, 306, 310
Kean, Edmund, 172, 210, 303, 310
Kelly, Hugh, *False Delicacy*, 291
Kemble, John Philip, 309, 313
Kemp, Robert, 74

Kemp, William, 80
Kendle, Madge, 337
Killigrew, Thomas, 238, *The Parson's Wedding*, 260
King Darius, 86
King's Men (Company), 91, 100, 173, 176, 179, 185, 206, 216, 224, 229, 238, 252
kitchen-sink (drama), 397
Kitely, Timothy, 204
Kolve, V. A., 29
Krause, David, 373
Kyd, Thomas, 110ff, 116, 214, *The Spanish Tragedy*, 103, 110–16, 118, 119, 120

La Branche, Linda, 265
Lacy, John, 253
Lady Elizabeth's Men, 179, 230
Lahr, John, 392
Lamb, Charles, 233
Langhans, Edward A., 239
Langley, Francis, 93
Latin, 8ff, 17, 28, 29, 30, 61, 115
Lee, Nathaniel, *The Rival Queens*, 243, 352
Leicester, Earl of (Men), 27, 89, 92
Leigh, Elinor, 266
Lessing, Doris, 407
Lewis, 'Monk', *The Castle Spectre*, 303
lighting (design), 92, 148, 149, 166, 195, 218, 240, 278ff, 300, 305ff, 359, 361, 399, 413
Lincoln's Inn Fields, 238, 259, 266, 274, 285, 287
Lindsay, Sir David, *A Satire of the Three Estates*, 73ff
Lisle's tennis court, 238
Littlewood, Joan, 129, 407
Little Theatre, Haymarket, 275
liturgical drama, 7ff
localizing, 25–6, 50ff, 98, 147ff, 166, 168, 173, 240, 259, 411

Lord Chamberlain, 281, 286, 322, 341, 404

Lord Chamberlain's Men, 91, 93, 169

Loutherbourg, Philip de, 278–9

Ludus Coventriae, 20

Lyceum Theatre, 129, 311

Lyly, John, 90, 105ff, 116, *Campaspe*, 106, *Endymion*, 106, *Euphues*, 105, *Gallathea*, 106–7, *Midas*, 105, *Sappho and Phao*, 105–6

MacCarthy, Desmond, 345, 356, 358

Machiavelli, 112, 126, 128, 169

machinery, stage, 170, 185, 190, 191, 193, 197, 251, 304, 307

MacOwan, Michael, 383

Macready, William Charles, 172, 306

Maeterlinck, Maurice, 367

make-up, 175, 315

Malone, Edmund, 147

Mankind, 40, 42, 51ff, 56

Manley, Mary de la Riviere, 263

manners, comedy of, 210, 248, 272, 324, 325, 343, 350

mansion (staging), 20, 21–2, 50, 116, 190

Marlowe, Christopher, 117, 118ff, *Dido Queen of Carthage*, 122, *Doctor Faustus*, 48, 56, 60, 94, 98, 99, 103, 119, 120, 121, 128ff, 135, *Edward II*, 121, 128–9, *The Jew of Malta*, 99, 102, 118, 119, 121, 122, 125ff, 135, *The Massacre at Paris*, 128, *Tamberlaine*, 98, 104, 110, 118, 119, 121, 122ff, 135

Marston, John, 90, 101, 210, 214ff, 222, 236, 378, *Antonio and Mellida*, 101, 214–15, *Antonio's Revenge*, 214ff, *The*

Fawn, 216, *The Malcontent*, 159, 216ff

Martyn, Edward, 365

Masefield, John, 347

mask, 174, 246, 368, 399

masque, masquing, 50, 61, 85, 92, 101, 116, 117, 146, 148, 157, 159, 185, 187ff, 210, 217, 220, 221, 224, 227, 229, 234, 236, 237, 265

Mass, the, 8–9, 13

Massinger, Philip, 209–10, *The City Madam*, 210, *A New Way to Pay Old Debts*, 210

Matthews, Charles, 308, 310

Matins, 9

Maturin, Charles, *Bertram, or, The Castle of St Aldobrand*, 302

McCarthy, Lillah, 349

McCormick, F. J., 373

McKellen, Sir Ian, 225

McKenna, Siobhan, 357, 358

McKern, Leo, 177

McLuhan, Marshall, 48

Medwall, Henry, *Fulgens and Lucrece*, 53, 61, 62ff, *Nature*, 54, 87

Mellon, John, 135

melodrama, 155, 201, 203, 214, 217, 302, 310ff, 313ff, 328, 337, 341, 342, 343, 356, 364, 365, 372, 373

Merchant Taylors Hall, 71

Mercury Theatre, 382, 407

metadrama, metatheatre, 56, 64, 148, 149, 154, 160, 161, 165, 215

Middleton, Thomas, 90, 207ff, 210, 218, 228ff, 236, *The Changeling*, 228, 230ff, *A Chaste Maid in Cheapside*, 207, 210, *A Game at Chess*, 229, *A Mad World My Masters*, 207, 208, *Michaelmas*

Term, 207–8, *The Roaring Girl*, 207, *A Trick to Catch the Old One*, 207, 208ff, 210, *Women Beware Women*, 228–9, *Your Five Gallants*, 207
minstrels, 2–3, 154
mirroring, 328
Misogonus, 50
'modern dress', 244
Molière, *L'Avare*, 209, *L'Ecole des femmes*, 260, 297, 299, *Tartuffe*, 297
Moncrieff, W. T., *The Lear of Private Life*, 316
Monmouth, Duke of, 249
monologue, 117, 378
Monstrous Regiment, 408
Moore, George, 366
morality play, 40ff, 69, 102, 121, 129, 219, 229, 353
More, Thomas, 62
morris dancing, 3, 8
Morton, John, 62
movement, 138ff, 151, 166, 227, 246, 248, 280, 308, 328, 368
Mrs Worthington's Daughters, 408
Mucedorus, 203
Mulryne, J. R., 115
multiple (simultaneous) staging, 51, 98, 106, 109, 116, 150
mummers, mumming, 2ff, 61
Mundus et Infans, 40, 87
Murdoch, Iris, 407
Murphy, Tom, 376
music, 28, 29, 46, 61, 65, 78, 85–6, 88, 90, 92, 99, 101, 123, 133, 145ff, 159, 160, 169, 187ff, 213, 214, 215, 216, 217, 226, 227, 229, 241, 251, 252, 254, 285, 287, 302, 317, 320, 368, 382, 399, 409
musical comedy, 'musicals', 198, 317, 365, 413

music hall, 61, 314, 384, 400, 401
mystery play, *see* Corpus Christi cycle
Mystère d'Adam, Le, 13–15
mystères, 13ff

Naipaul, V. S., 406
Nash, Beau, 297
Nashe, Thomas, 121, 122
Nathan, George Jean, 382
National Theatre (*also* Royal N. T.), 111, 125, 201, 393, 394, 404, 405, 407, 408, 409
naturalism, 255, 308, 361, 366, 391, 393, 401
Nelligan, Kate, 405
neoclassicism (neoclassical tragedy), 250, 252, 280, 332
Neuss, Paula, 71
Newcastle, Duchess of, 263
New Haven, 341
New York, 310, 321, 341, 355
Nichols, John, 54
Nicoll, Allardyce, 187
night scenes, 149
Noh drama, 367
North, Lord, 289
Norton, Thomas and T. Sackville, *Gorboduc*, 61, 111
North, Sir Thomas (Plutarch's *Lives*), 138, 143
Novelty Theatre, 339
N-Town cycle, 20, 22, 28, 37, 43
Nunn, Trevor, 218

O'Brien, Timothy, 229
O'Casey, Sean, 367, 372ff, *Cock-a-Doodle Dandy*, 376, *Juno and the Paycock*, 372–3, *The Plough and the Stars*, 372, 373ff, *Purple Dust*, 376, *The Shadow of a Gunman*, 372, *The Silver Tassie*, 375
Odell, Thomas, 275
Oldfield, Anne, 270

Old Vic Theatre, 174, 177, 185, 212

Olivier, Laurence (Lord), 162, 401

Olympic Revels, 322

Olympic Theatre, 310, 322, 329

on-stage audience, 154, 157, 158, 159, 174

open stage, open staging, 98, 361, 382, 413

opera, 86, 187, 189, 198, 237, 248, 251, 252, 277, 287, 288, 317, 318, 324, 354

opéra comique, 279

operetta, 285, 345

O. P. riots, 313

Orton, Joe, 391ff, *Entertaining Mr Sloane*, 392, *Loot*, 292, *What the Butler Saw*, 392

Osborne, John, 397ff, *The Entertainer*, 400, *Look Back in Anger*, 397

Otway, Thomas, *The Orphan*, 281, *Venice Preserved*, 281

Oxford, 54, 89, 104, 109

Oxford, Earl of, 105

pace, 141, 147, 186, 209, 227, 228, 233, 268, 287, 294, 299, 300, 324, 328, 334, 383

pageant, pageantry, 2, 4, 100, 123, 137, 157, 216

pageant wagon, 18, 20, 120

Palladio, Andrea, 192

pantomime, 3, 129, 285, 322

parable, 55, 401

Paradise, 14–15, 21, 28

parataxis, 166

Paris, 273, 303, 331, 383

parody, 112, 131, 158, 205, 253, 254, 269, 271, 272, 284, 294, 371, 393, 402, 409

pastoral (play), 99, 104ff, 107, 206

Pavilion Theatre, 314

Payne, Ben Iden, 367

Pearse, Padraig, 374

Pearson, Hesketh, 325

Peele, George, 109ff, 116, *The Old Wives' Tale*, 109–11, 203

Peers, Edward, 90

penny gaff, 313

Pepys, Samuel, 129, 184, 233, 241

Pepusch, J. C., 287

perspective scenery, 277–8

Phelps, Samuel, 310

Philip IV of Spain, 229

Philip, Katherine, 263, *Pompey*, 263

Phillips, John, *Patient and Meek Grissell*, 86

Phoenix Theatre, 91, 230, 233

Pickering, John, *Horestes*, 86

picture-frame (stage), 301, 306, 308

pièce bien faite (*see* the well-made play)

Pimlott, Steven, 380

Pinero, Sir Arthur Wing, *Dandy Dick*, 334, *The Gay Lord Quex*, 324, *Lady Bountiful*, 335, *The Magistrate* (*Little Lies*), 334, *The Money-Spinner*, 335, *The Profligate*, 335, *The Schoolmistress*, 334, *The Second Mrs Tanqueray*, 335ff, 338, *Trelawney of the Wells*, 334–5

Pinter, Harold, 387ff, *Betrayal*, 391, *The Birthday Party*, 388, 389ff, *The Dumb Waiter*, 388–9, *The Homecoming*, 388, *Landscape*, 391, *Mountain Language*, 391, *The New World Order*, 391, *No Man's Land*, 391, *Old Times*, 389, 391, *One for the Road*, 391, *The Room*, 388–9, *Silence*, 391, *A Slight Ache*, 389

Pirandello, Luigi, 215, 394, 406,
    *Six Characters in Search of an
    Author*, 204
Piscator, Erwin, 360, 399
Pix, Mary, 265
Pixérécourt, Guilbert de,
    Coelina, 302
place (*see also* unities), 147ff, 203
Planché, J. R., 310, 322
platea [place], 3, 15, 22, 23, 26,
    42, 70, 384
platform (Elizabethan stage), 95,
    168, 176, 180, 185, 186
Plautus, 61, 75, *Aulularia*, 54,
    Miles Gloriosus, 75
Playfair, Sir Nigel, 289
play-within-the-play, 103, 112,
    116, 117, 119, 150, 154, 156ff,
    169, 170, 175, 182, 202, 210,
    253, 289, 351, 394, 401
plot (plotting), 41, 102, 169, 293,
    294, 348, 379, 383, 388, 399
Plowright, Joan, 262
Poel, William, 59, 147, 316, 350,
    361, 362
poetic drama, 367
politics, 68ff, 71ff, 187, 229, 356,
    375, 403, 405–6, 414
Pollard, A., 10, 30, 33
portable theatre, 403
Potter, John, 275
presenter, 56, 63, 153, 154, 155,
    159, 217, 220
Preston, Thomas, *Cambises*, 61,
    80ff, 86
Prince of Wales Theatre, 311, 329
Princess's Theatre, 310
problem comedy, 161
problem play, 302, 331, 332,
    335, 336, 337, 343, 362, 365
processional staging, 21
processions (progresses), 2, 4,
    100, 101, 169, 188, 200, 216
prologue, 56, 95, 102, 154, 241,
    351

properties, 57, 61, 98, 99, 123,
    144ff, 147, 166, 219, 235, 244,
    333, 399, 413
proscenium arch (stage), 193,
    196, 198, 239, 240, 272, 277,
    278, 305, 306, 361, 388, 397,
    400, 405, 413
prose, 102, 143, 256, 369
Prowse, Philip, 224
Prudentius, *Psychomachia*, 40
Purvis, J. S., 33, 35, 36

Queen's Men, 212, 222, 233
Queen's Theatre, Haymarket,
    275
Quem quaeritis?, 3, 10–13

Rabelais, François, 173
radio, 360, 409, 410, 412
raked stage, 193
Rastel, John, *The Four
    Elements*, 56
realism, 32, 51, 61, 67, 91, 109,
    110, 168, 171, 199, 207, 210,
    234, 248, 255, 259, 302, 308,
    328ff, 334, 338ff, 360, 362,
    375, 378, 409, 413
Red Bull Theatre, 212, 222
Redford, John, 90
Red Lion Inn, 92
Regularis Concordia, 3, 11
Regulation Act, 304
'rehearsal' play, 254
Reinhardt, Max, 59
religious drama, 3, 16
Renaissance, 89, 99, 120, 129,
    210, 218, 221, 226
repartee, 256
Respublica, 87
Restoration, 164, 184, 206, 233,
    237ff, 278, 301
Return from Parnassus, The, 104
Revels Office, 51, 92, 100, 188,
    190
revenge tragedy, 110, 169, 214,
    231, 233

revolve, 193, 406
rhetoric, 90, 121
rhyme, 153
rhyme-royal, 66, 71
Rich, Christopher, 274
Rich, John, 274, 278, 285
Richardson, Sir Ralph, 391
Ridler, Anne, *The Shadow Factory*, 407
rime couée, 65
ritual, 4, 42, 121, 123, 130, 133, 134, 135, 137, 140, 159, 227, 334, 368, 379, 380, 403, 413
Robertson, Agnes, 321
Robertson, Tom, 309, 329, 334, 364, *Caste*, 329ff, *M.P.*, 329, *Ours*, 329, *Play*, 329, *School*, 329, *Society*, 329
Robin Hood plays, 7
Robins, Elizabeth, *Votes for Women!*, 407
Rochester, Earl of, 248, 256, 264
role-playing, 151ff, 166, 179, 186, 210, 220, 221, 226, 295
Roman (New) comedy, 74–5, 154, 172
romance, 99, 104ff, 108, 200, 251
Romantic poets, 304
Rome, Roman, 1, 8, 16, 35, 39, 61, 66, 89, 179
Roper, William, 62
Rose Theatre, 93, 94, 110, 118ff, 135, 200
Rossiter, A. P., 48
Round House, The, 185
round, theatre (staging) in the, 23, 41ff, 94, 361
Rowe, Nicholas, 147, *Jane Shore*, 282
Rowley, William, 228, *see also* Middleton, *The Changeling*
Royal Court Theatre, 346, 350, 362, 364, 396ff, 404, 408, 409, 412, 414

Royal National Theatre, *see* National Theatre
Royal Shakespeare Company, 128, 185, 204, 218, 229, 231, 256, 380, 408
royalties, 318
Royalty Theatre, 275
Royal Victoria Theatre, 314
Rutland House, 237

Sadler's Wells Theatre, 275, 307, 310
Salisbury Court Theatre, 230
Samhain, 366ff, 368
Sardou, Victorien, 303, 331
satire, 104, 122, 161, 173, 179, 186, 199, 200, 207, 216, 221, 255, 284, 285, 289, 291, 296, 297, 325, 337, 343, 349, 393
Savoy Theatre, 307
Sayers, Dorothy, *The Zeal of Thy House*, 407
Scala Theatre, 311
scène à faire, 332, 333, 336, 340, 362
scenery, 92, 98, 99, 147, 184, 193, 237–8, 241, 251, 277ff, 293, 297, 307, 310, 317, 328, 366, 398, 404, 405
Scott, Sir Walter, 303–4
Scribe, Eugène, 303, 324, 331, 340
Second Shepherds' Play, 37–9
Seinte Resureccion, La, 13
semiotics, 138
Seneca, 61, 81, 111ff
sentimental comedy, 280ff, 290ff, 296ff, 372
Serlio, Sebastiano, 192–3
sermon, 40, 55
Servandoni, Giovanni, 278
set, setting (*see also* scenery), 191, 201, 251, 297, 308, 316, 320, 361, 363, 368, 385, 398
sexuality, 245, 255ff, 260, 271, 314, 341, 404

'shadow' ('heavens'), 96, 119
Shadwell, Thomas, *Bury Fair*, 266, *The Humourists*, 184, *The Squire of Alsatia*, 266, *A True Widow*, 246
Shaffer, Peter, *Equus*, 404
Shakespeare, William, 27, 35, 84, 91, 93, 136ff, 168, 169, 185, 278, 293, 301, 310, 312, 404, *All's Well That Ends Well*, 142, 146, 148, 149, 154, 156, 165, *Antony and Cleopatra*, 90, 100, 145, 155, 161, 166, *As You Like It*, 12, 90, 107, 137, 148, 154, 155, 158, 163, 164, 165–6, 295, *Coriolanus*, 138, 140, 143, 157, 309, *Cymbeline*, 148, 159, 164, *Hamlet*, 85, 105, 112, 121, 137, 142, 144, 146, 149, 150, 152, 153, 154, 155, 158–9, 163, 214, 219, 309, 347, 351, 393, 400, *1 Henry IV*, 79, 88, 98, 102, 152, 154, 156, 160, 162–3, 166, *2 Henry IV*, 144, 163, 165, *Henry V*, 143, *Henry VI*, 118, 153, 156, *Henry VIII*, 100, 148, *Julius Caesar*, 100, 159, *King Lear*, 48, 56, 98, 99, 102, 136, 140, 142, 143, 145, 147, 148, 154, 156, 160–1, 166, 227, 280, 306, 385, *Love's Labour's Lost*, 104, 143, 149, 157, 159, 165, *Macbeth*, 90, 137, 144, 148, 149, 152–3, 157, 159, 161, 280, *Measure for Measure*, 148, 155, 162, 165, *The Merchant of Venice*, 90, 98, 103, 107, 137, 145, 154, 162, 164, 165, 310, *A Midsummer Night's Dream*, 101, 107, 138, 145, 147, 149, 154, 155, 157, 159, 160, 161–2, 163, 203, *Much Ado about Nothing*, 145–6, 147, 149, 162, 284, *Othello*, 80, 139, 146, 149, 150, 155, 157, 161, 310, 311, *Pericles*, 159, *Richard II*, 144–5, *Richard III*, 79, 98, 150, 156, 159, 280, *Romeo and Juliet*, 5, 141, 146, 148, 149, 150–1, 161, 166–7, 233, 235, *The Taming of the Shrew*, 110, 155, 158, 285, *The Tempest*, 56, 138–9, 148, 155, 156, 159, 162, 200, *Titus Andronicus*, 118, 119, 120, *Troilus and Cressida*, 142, 153, 155, 156, 166, *Twelfth Night*, 143, 144, 149, 154, 162, 163, 164, *The Two Gentlemen of Verona*, 154, 164, *The Winter's Tale*, 80, 94, 145, 151, 159–60, 165
Shaw, George Bernard, 221, 255, 259, 303, 309, 338ff, 360, 362, 404, *Arms and the Man*, 343ff, 348, *Back to Methuselah*, 354, *Caesar and Cleopatra*, 354, *Candida*, 343, 348, *Fanny's First Play*, 351, *Getting Married*, 347, *Heartbreak House*, 354–5, *John Bull's Other Island*, 347, *Major Barbara*, 347, 349, 351ff, 354, *Man and Superman*, 347, 348, 349ff, 354, *The Man of Destiny*, 344, *Our Theatres in the Nineties*, 338, *The Philanderer*, 340, *Plays Pleasant*, 343, *Plays Unpleasant*, 339, 341, 347, *Pygmalion*, 348, *The Quintessence of Ibsenism*, 340, 343, 347, 348, *Saint Joan*, 355ff, *Mrs Warren's Profession*, 340ff, 343, 404, 409, *Widowers' Houses*, 339–40, 343, 348, *You Never Can Tell*, 344

Sher, Anthony, 412
Sherburne, Edward, 197
Sheridan, Richard Brinsley, 255, 296ff, *The Critic*, 148, 289, *The Rivals*, 296–7, *The School for Scandal*, 297ff
Shirley, James, 164, 169, 188, *The Triumph of Love*, 188
shutters (*see also* grooves and shutters), 278, 293, 299, 307
Siddons, Henry, 315
Siddons, Sarah, 301, 305
Sidney, Sir Philip, 84, 102–3, *An Apology for Poetry*, 26–7, 81, 105
Simonson, Lee, 355
simultaneous staging, *see* multiple staging
Skelton, John, *Magnificence*, 61, 68ff, 87
Skeltonics, 71
slapstick, 324
Smirke, Robert, 305
Smith, Dodie, 407
Smith, Maggie, 262
Smith, William, 243
soliloquy, 95, 102, 112, 125, 137, 148, 152ff, 156, 157, 182, 201, 217, 220, 236, 241, 290, 317, 330, 333, 336, 361, 379
song, singing, 28, 29, 61, 73, 78, 90, 99, 101, 106, 145ff, 169, 189ff, 201, 204, 205, 213, 217, 226, 229, 251, 285, 287, 317, 324, 409, 413
sonnet, 153, 156
Southerne, Thomas, *Oroonoko*, 281
space, 150, 166, 185, 383
Spark, Muriel, 407
Speaight, Robert, 316
spectacle, 101, 115, 135, 169, 170, 185, 187ff, 193, 196, 200, 236, 251, 252, 272, 277, 302, 307, 313, 320, 413

Spectator, The, 242, 250
speech, *see* voice
Spielberg, Steven, 413
Spillane, Mickey, 408
spotlight, 359
Spring Gardens, 279
Stafford-Clark, Max, 409
stage-posts, 119, 179
Stage Society, The, 341, 346, 362
Stanislavsky, Konstantin, 56
Star Chamber, 39
star system, 309ff, 346
'station' (*see also* mansion), 20, 21
Stations of the Cross, 50
Steele, Sir Richard, 256, 266, *The Conscious Lovers*, 283
St Gall, 10
St George's Play, 5–6
St James's Park, 258
St James's Theatre, 311, 325ff, 332ff
St Mark, 10
St Paul's Boys, 101, 105, 199, 214
stock company, 312
Stoppard, Tom, 393ff, *Arcadia*, 396, *Indian Ink*, 396, *Jumpers*, 394, *The Real Inspector Hound*, 394, *Rosencrantz and Guildenstern Are Dead*, 393–4, *Travesties*, 394ff
Strange's Men, Lord, 118
Street, Peter, 94
Streeter, Robert, 252
street theatre, 2ff, 403
Strindberg, August, 255, 337
strolling players, 2, 4, 88
sub-plot, 103, 154, 212, 230, 296
stylization, 105, 199, 207, 208, 218, 326
Summers, Montague, 184, 262
surrealism, 382, 383ff, 389, 391, 395
Surrey Theatre, 309–10, 314, 318

Swan Theatre, 93, 95, 96
Swan Theatre (Stratford upon Avon), 380
Swift, Jonathan, 286
sword dancers, 3
Sword Dance Play, 6
symbolism, 6, 61, 99, 103, 135, 177, 190, 213, 218, 235, 353, 354, 360, 367ff, 375, 381, 397, 400, 401
symbolist poetry, 376
Synge, J. M., 367, 369ff, *The Playboy of the Western World*, 369ff, 373, *The Shadow of the Glen*, 369

tableau, 5, 101, 103, 111, 154, 224, 232, 234, 235, 300, 316, 320, 330, 334, 342, 364
tableau vivant, 18, 123, 135
Tarlton, Richard, 80
Tate, Nahum, *King Lear*, 250
Taylor, John Russell, 394
Taylor, Tom, *The Ticket-of-Leave Man*, 329
television, 360, 388, 412
tennis courts, 238
Tennyson, William, 391
Terence, 61, 75, *Eunuchus*, 75, 260
Terry, Ellen, 311
Theatre, The, 92–3
Théâtre Alfred Jarry, 221
Theatre Guild, 346, 355
Theatre Workshop, 129, 407
'thesis' play, 347
Thomas, Brandon, *Charley's Aunt*, 324
Thorndike, Dame Sybil, 354, 357, 358
Three Marys, The, 10–13, 30
thunder, 100, 131
time, 98, 148ff, 166, 168, 174, 203, 384, 411
tiring house (room), 95

tournaments, 2
Tourneur, Cyril, 210, 218, 222, 236, *The Revenger's Tragedy*, 218
Towneley Plays, 19
Townshend, Charles (Lord), 286
tragedy, 81, 102, 110, 168, 179, 207, 210ff, 242ff, 247, 248, 282, 304, 332, 356, 358, 372, 375, 383
tragi-comedy, 81, 104, 200, 202, 206, 207, 216, 221, 249
transformation scene, 193, 194, 198, 324
transparent scenery (*see also* gauze), 278, 307, 321
trap (door), 95, 119, 120, 127, 215
traverse curtain, 99, 226
trial scene, 320, 356, 362
Triumph of Isabella, The, 18
tropes, 9
Trotter, Catherine, 263
Tudor hall, 52, 53ff, 66, 99
Tudor staging, 14, 27
types ('flat' characters), 172, 297, 312, 373
Tzara, Tristan, 395

Udall, Nicholas, *Ralph Roister Doister*, 74ff
United Company, 238
unities (of time and place), 27, 75, 77, 84, 130, 169, 170, 174, 176, 180–1, 186, 201, 212, 241, 251, 282
university drama, 89
University Wits, 89, 104ff, 120
Urban IV (Pope), 17

Valenciennes Passion Play, 22
Vanbrugh, Sir John, 275, *The Mistake*, 242, *The Provoked Wife*, 266, 280, *The Relapse*, 244, 259, 266, 270

Vedrenne, J. E., 346, 362
Venetian Vespers, 10
Verdi, Giuseppe, 409
verse drama, 366, 376ff
Vestris, Madame, 308, 310, 322, 324
Vice, the, 67, 76, 79ff, 102, 109, 128
vices, 47ff, 87
Victoria, Queen, 309, 311, 337
Victorian theatre, 198, 201, 302ff, 360
Vienna, Council of, 17
Visitatio Sepulchri, 10–12
voice (speech), 10, 137, 179, 186, 216, 239, 247, 268, 280, 299, 308, 316, 328, 379, 412

Wakefield cycle, 19, 27ff
Walkley, A. B., 349
Walpole, Horace, 272
Walpole, Sir Robert, 286
Warning for Fair Women, A, 211
Webb, John, 237
Webber, Sir Andrew Lloyd, 413
Webster, John, 210, 221ff, 236, *The Devil's Law-Case*, 221, *The Duchess of Malfi*, 159, 221, 224ff, 232, *The White Devil*, 221–4
well-made play (*la pièce bien faite*), 201, 303, 331ff, 337, 388, 398, 399
Wesker, Arnold, 391
Westcott, Sebastian, 90
Westminster Hall, 187
Whitefriars, 91
Whitehall, 148, 190, 195
Wickham, Glynne, 61, 180
Wilde, Oscar, 255, 309, 311, 335, 353, *An Ideal Husband*, 332, *The Importance of Being Earnest*, 324ff, 395–6, *Lady Windermere's Fan*, 332ff, *A Woman of No Importance*, 332

Wilder, Thornton, *The Skin of Our Teeth*, 28
Wilks, Robert, 270, 274, 280
Willett, John, 399
Williams, Clifford, 128
Wilson, J. H., 248, 253
Wilton, Marie, 311
Winchester Cathedral, 3, 10, 11
wings, wing-pieces, 193, 239, 274, 293, 307
Winter Garden Theatre, 310–11
Wisdom, 40
Wit and Wisdom, 50
Witt, John de, 93, 95
Wolfitt, Sir Donald, 210
Wolsey, Thomas (Cardinal), 68
women, *see* actress
Women's Theatre Company, The, 408
Women's Theatre Group, The, 408
women playwrights, 263ff, 407ff
Wood, John, 259
Wordsworth, William, 256
Wycherley, William, 269, *The Country Wife*, 248, 260, 266, 297, 299, *The Gentleman Dancing-Master*, 259

Yeats, W. B., 347, 365ff, 373, 376, 382, *At the Hawk's Well*, 367, 368–70, *The Countess Cathleen*, 367, *Four Plays for Dancers*, 367, 368, *The Hour-Glass*, 368, *On Baile's Strand*, 367
York cycle, 19, 21ff
Yorkshire Tragedy, A, 211
Young Vic Theatre, the, 185